BRIEF MICROSOFT®
OFFICE 97
PROFESSIONAL

Robert T. Grauer / Maryann Barber

University of Miami

Prentice Hall, Upper Saddle River, New Jersey 07458

Acquisitions Editor: Carolyn Henderson
Assistant Editor: Audrey Regan
Editorial Assistant: Lori Cardillo
Executive Marketing Manager: Nancy Evans
Editorial/Production Supervisor: Greg Hubit
Project Manager: Lynne Breitfeller
Senior Manufacturing Supervisor: Paul Smolenski
Manufacturing Coordinator: Lisa DiMaulo
Manufacturing Manager: Vincent Scelta
Senior Designer/Interior and Cover Design: Suzanne Behnke
Design Director: Patricia Wosczyk
Composition: GTS Graphics

ISBN 0-13-754185-6

Prentice-Hall International (UK) Limited, London
Prentice-Hall of Australia Pty. Limited, Sydney
Prentice-Hall Canada Inc., Toronto
Prentice-Hall Hispanoamericana, S.A., Mexico
Prentice-Hall of India Private Limited, New Delhi
Prentice-Hall of Japan, Inc., Tokyo
Simon & Schuster Asia Pte. Ltd., Singapore
Editora Prentice-Hall do Brasil, Ltda., Rio de Janeiro

Printed in the United States of America

10 9 8 7 6 5 4 3 2 1

Contents

Exploring Microsoft® Word 97

1

Microsoft® Word 97: What Will Word Processing Do for Me?   1

2

Gaining Proficiency: Editing and Formatting   47

3

Enhancing a Document: The Web and Other Resources   97

1

Introduction to Microsoft® Excel: What Is a Spreadsheet?   1

2

Gaining Proficiency: Copying, Formatting, and Isolating Assumptions   37

3

Graphs and Charts: Delivering a Message 69

Exploring Microsoft® Access 97

1

Introduction to Microsoft® Access: What Is a Database? 1

2

Tables and Forms: Design, Properties, Views, and Wizards   31

3

Information from the Database: Reports and Queries   77

EXPLORING MICROSOFT® POWERPOINT 97

1

Introduction to PowerPoint: Presentations Made Easy   1

2

Creating a Presentation: Content, Formatting, and Animation   35

To Marion, Benjy, Jessica, and Ellie

—Robert Grauer

To Frank, Jessica, and My Parents

—Maryann Barber

PREFACE

We are proud to announce the third edition of the *Exploring Windows* series in conjunction with the release of Microsoft Office 97. The Internet and World Wide Web are thoroughly incorporated throughout the new edition. Students learn Office applications as before, and are sent to the Web as appropriate for supplementary assignments. The *Exploring Windows* home page (www.prenhall.com/grauer) contains additional material, which can be downloaded to enhance the text. The icon at the left appears throughout the series whenever there is a Web reference.

Brief Microsoft Office 97 Professional is comprised of selected (and abbreviated) chapters from individual books in the series. It was developed for the instructor who seeks to cover "all" of Microsoft Office, but who has only limited time for each application. Instructors seeking additional material should consider *Exploring Microsoft Office 97, Volume I,* which is approximately 250 pages longer than *Brief Office Professional.* Instructors requiring even more extensive coverage should consider the standalone texts: *Exploring Microsoft Word 97, Exploring Microsoft Excel 97, Exploring Microsoft Access 97,* and *Exploring Microsoft PowerPoint 97.* Other books in the series include *Exploring the Internet, Second Edition,* and *Exploring Microsoft Office 97, Volume II.* The latter contains the advanced chapters and appendices from the individual books that were not included in Volume I.

The *Exploring Windows* series will appeal to students in a variety of disciplines, including business, liberal arts, and the sciences. Each book has a consistent presentation that stresses the benefits of the Windows environment, especially the common user interface, multitasking, and the extensive online help facility. Students are taught concepts, not just keystrokes or mouse clicks, with hands-on exercises in every chapter providing the necessary practice to master the material.

The *Exploring Windows* series is different from other books, both in its scope and in the way in which material is presented. Students learn by doing. Concepts are stressed and memorization is minimized. Shortcuts and other important information are consistently highlighted in the many tips that appear throughout the series. Every chapter contains an average of three guided exercises to be completed at the computer. Equally important are the end-of-chapter exercises that not only review the material, but extend it as well. The end-of-chapter problems are a distinguishing feature of the entire series, an integral part of the learning process, and a powerful motivational tool for students to learn and explore. Instructors may also assign the hands-on exercises within each chapter to ensure further practice on the part of their students.

Each book in the *Exploring Windows* series is accompanied by a comprehensive Instructor's Resource Manual with tests, PowerPoint lectures, and student/ instructor resource disks. (The Instructor's Resource Manual for the entire series is also available on a single CD-ROM.) Instructors can also use the Prentice Hall Computerized Online Testing System to prepare customized tests for their courses and may obtain Interactive Multimedia courseware as a further supplement. The *Exploring Windows* series is part of the Prentice Hall custom binding program.

FEATURES AND BENEFITS

Brief Microsoft Office 97 Professional begins with an introductory section, which emphasizes the common user interface. Although no previous knowledge is assumed on the part of the reader, students who already know one Office application are encouraged to apply that information to learn another.

MICROSOFT OFFICE 97: SIX APPLICATIONS IN ONE

OVERVIEW

Word processing, spreadsheets, and data management have always been significant microcomputer applications. The early days of the PC saw these applications emerge from different vendors with radically different user interfaces. WordPerfect, Lotus, and dBASE, for example, were dominant applications in their respective areas, and each was developed by a different company. The applications were totally dissimilar, and knowledge of one did not help in learning another.

The widespread acceptance of Windows 3.1 promoted the concept of a common user interface, which required all applications to follow a consistent set of conventions. This meant that all applications worked essentially the same way, and it provided a sense of familiarity when you learned a new application, since every application presented the same user interface. The development of a suite of applications from a single vendor extended this concept by imposing additional similarities on all applications within the suite.

This introduction will acquaint you with *Microsoft Office 97* and its four major applications—*Word, Excel, PowerPoint,* and *Access.* The single biggest difference between Office 97 and its predecessor, Office 95, is that the Internet has become an integral part of the Office suite. Thus, we also discuss *Internet Explorer,* the Web browser included in Office 97, and *Microsoft Outlook,* the e-mail and scheduling program that is built into Office 97. The icon at the left of this paragraph appears throughout the text to highlight references to the Internet and enhance your use of Microsoft Office. Our introduction also includes the Clip Gallery, WordArt, and Office Art, three tools built into Microsoft Office that help you to add interest to your documents. And finally, we discuss Object Linking and Embedding, which enables you to combine data from multiple applications into a single document.

Our primary purpose in this introduction is to emphasize the similarities between the applications in Office 97 and to help you transfer your knowledge from one application to the next. You will find the same commands in the same menus. You will also recognize familiar

xvii

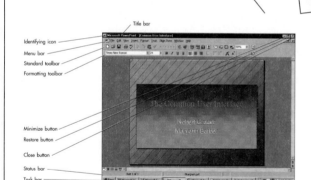

(c) Microsoft PowerPoint

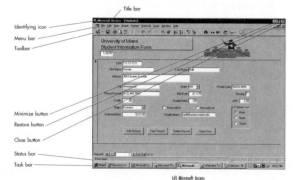

(d) Microsoft Access

FIGURE 1   The Common User Interface (continued)

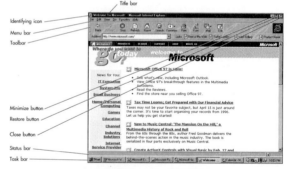

(e) Internet Explorer

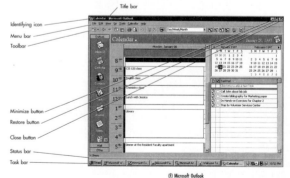

(f) Microsoft Outlook

FIGURE 1   The Common User Interface (continued)

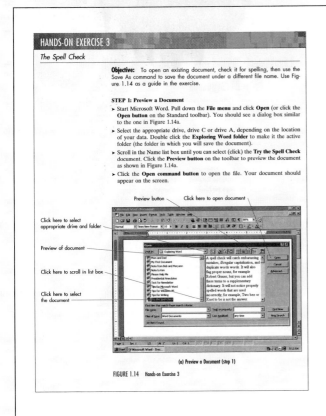

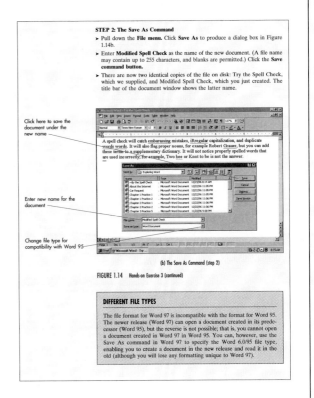

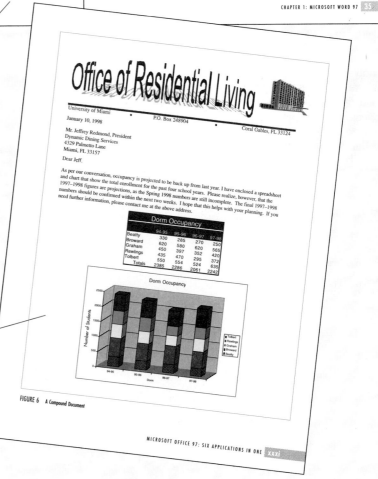

A total of 27 in-depth tutorials (hands-on exercises) guide the reader at the computer. Each tutorial is accompanied by numerous tips that present different ways to accomplish a given task, but in a logical and relaxed fashion.

Object Linking and Embedding is stressed throughout the text, beginning in the introductory section on Microsoft Office. The reader is shown the power of this all-important technology, which is present in all Office applications.

2. Use the Employee database in the Exploring Access folder to create the reports listed below. (This is the same database that was used earlier in Chapters 1 and 2.)

   a. A report containing all employees in sequence by location and alphabetically within location. Show the employee's last name, first name, location, title, and salary. Include summary statistics to display the total salaries in each location as well as for the company as a whole.

   b. A report containing all employees in sequence by title and alphabetically within title. Show the employee's last name, first name, location, title, and salary. Include summary statistics to show the average salary for each title as well as the average salary in the company.

   c. Add your name to the report header in the report so that your instructor will know the reports came from you. Print both reports and submit them to your instructor.

3. Use the United States database in the Exploring Access folder to create the report shown in Figure 3.11. (This is the same database that was used in Chapters 1 and 2.) The report lists states by geographic region, and alphabetically within region. It includes a calculated field, Population Density, which is computed by dividing a state's population by its area. Summary statistics are also required as shown in the report.

   Note that the report header contains a map of the United States that was taken from the Microsoft Clip Gallery. The instructions for inserting an object can be found on page 81 in conjunction with an earlier problem. Be sure to include your name in the report footer so that your instructor will know that the report comes from you.

4. Use the Bookstore database in the Exploring Access folder to create the report shown in Figure 3.12. (This is the same database that was used in the hands-on exercises in Chapter 1.)

   The report header in Figure 3.12 contains a graphic object that was taken from the Microsoft Clip Gallery. You are not required to use this specific image, but you are required to insert a graphic. The instructions for inserting an object can be found on page 81 in conjunction with an earlier problem. Be sure to include your name in the report header so that your instructor will know that the report comes from you.

5. Use the Super Bowl database in the Exploring Access folder to create the report in Figure 3.13, which lists the participants and scores in every game played to date. It also displays the Super Bowl logo, which we downloaded from the home page of the NFL (www.nfl.com). Be sure to include your name in the report footer so that your instructor will know that the report comes from you. (See the Super Bowl case study for suggestions on additional reports or queries that you can create from this database.)

6. There are many sources of help for Access as well as every Office application. You can use the regular Help facility or you can go to the Microsoft web site to obtain the latest information. Start Access, pull down the Help menu, click Microsoft on the Web, then click online support to go to the home page for Microsoft Access. Explore the various options that are available, then write a short summary of your findings and submit it to your instructor as proof you did this exercise. Figure 3.14 displays the feature articles that were available when this book went to press and provides an indication of what you can expect to find.

United States By Region

Region	Name	Capital	Population	Area	Population Density
Middle Atlantic					
	Delaware	Dover	666,168	2,057	323.85
	Maryland	Annapolis	4,781,468	10,577	452.06
	New Jersey	Trenton	7,730,188	7,836	986.50
	New York	Albany	17,990,455	49,576	362.89
	Pennsylvania	Harrisburg	11,881,643	45,333	262.10
	Total for Region:		43,049,922	115,379	
	Average for Region:		8,609,984.40	23,075.80	477.48
Mountain					
	Arizona	Phoenix	3,665,228	113,909	32.18
	Colorado	Denver	3,294,394	104,247	31.60
	Idaho	Boise	1,006,749	83,557	12.05
	Montana	Helena	799,065	147,138	5.43
	Nevada	Carson City	1,201,833	110,540	10.87
	New Mexico	Santa Fe	1,515,069	121,666	12.45
	Utah	Salt Lake City	1,722,850	84,916	20.29
	Wyoming	Cheyenne	453,588	97,914	4.63
	Total for Region:		13,658,776	863,887	
	Average for Region:		1,707,347.00	107,985.88	16.19
New England					
	Connecticut	Hartford	3,287,116	5,009	656.24
	Maine	Augusta	1,227,928	33,215	36.97
	Massachusetts	Boston	6,016,425	8,257	728.65
	New	Concord	1,109,252	9,304	119.22
	Rhode Island	Providence	1,003,464	1,214	826.58
	Vermont	Montpellier	562,758	9,609	58.57
	Total for Region:		13,206,943	66,608	
	Average for Region:		2,201,157.17	11,101.33	404.37

Saturday, January 11, 1997   Page 1 of 3

FIGURE 3.11   Screen for Practice Exercise 3

Every chapter ends with several practice problems that are ideal for class assignments. An OLE icon appears whenever a solution requires data from multiple applications. The Web icon appears when a student is sent to the Internet.

This exercise from Word asks the student to create a flyer but does not provide specific instructions. Note, too, the use of embedded objects to reinforce the discussion on OLE.

FIGURE 3.9   Document for Practice Exercise 1

Brief Office 97 Professional is written for the novice and assumes no previous knowledge of application software. Each program (Word, Excel, Access, and PowerPoint) starts with an introductory chapter that defines basic terminology.

Brief Office 97 Professional emphasizes concepts as well as keystrokes and mouse clicks. Students are provided with the rationale for what they are doing and are able to extend the information to additional learning on their own.

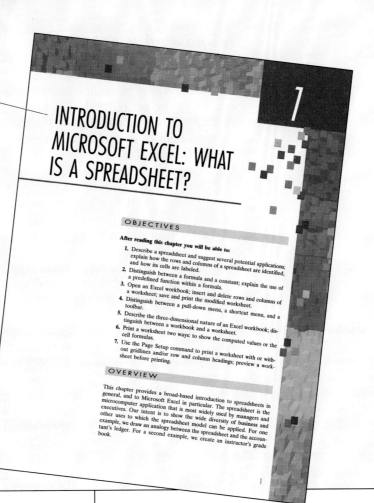

INTRODUCTION TO MICROSOFT EXCEL: WHAT IS A SPREADSHEET?

OBJECTIVES

After reading this chapter you will be able to:

1. Describe a spreadsheet and suggest several potential applications; explain how the rows and columns of a spreadsheet are identified, and how its cells are labeled.
2. Distinguish between a formula and a constant; explain the use of a predefined function within a formula.
3. Open an Excel workbook; insert and delete rows and columns of a worksheet; save and print the modified worksheet.
4. Distinguish between a pull-down menu, a shortcut menu, and a toolbar.
5. Describe the three-dimensional nature of an Excel workbook; distinguish between a workbook and a worksheet.
6. Print a worksheet two ways: to show the computed values or the cell formulas.
7. Use the Page Setup command to print a worksheet with or without gridlines and/or row and column headings; preview a worksheet before printing.

OVERVIEW

This chapter provides a broad-based introduction to spreadsheets in general, and to Microsoft Excel in particular. The spreadsheet is the microcomputer application that is most widely used by managers and executives. Our intent is to show the wide diversity of business and other uses to which the spreadsheet model can be applied. For one example, we draw an analogy between the spreadsheet and the accountant's ledger. For a second example, we create an instructor's grade book.

CREATING A PRESENTATION

The text of a presentation can be developed in the Slide view or the Outline view or a combination of the two. You can begin in the Outline view, switch to the Slide view to see how a particular slide will look, return to the Outline view to enter the text for additional slides, and so on. We prefer the Outline view because it displays the text for many slides at once. It also enables you to change the order of slides and to move and copy text from one slide to another.

> **CRYSTALLIZE YOUR MESSAGE**
>
> Every presentation exists to deliver a message, whether it's to sell a product, present an idea, or provide instruction. Decide on the message you want to deliver, then write the text for the presentation. Edit the text to be sure it is consistent with your objective. Then, and only then, should you think about formatting, but always keep the message foremost in your mind.

The Outline View

Figure 2.1 displays the outline of the presentation we will develop in this chapter. The outline shows the title of each slide, followed by the text on that slide. (Graphic elements such as clip art and charts are not visible in the Outline.) Each slide is numbered, and the numbers adjust automatically for the insertion or deletion of slides as you edit the presentation.

A *slide icon* appears between the number and title of the slide. The icon is subtly different, depending on the slide layout. In Figure 2.1, for example, the same icon appears next to slides 1 through 6 and indicates the slides contain only text. A different icon appears next to slide 7 and indicates the presence of a graphic element, such as clip art.

Each slide begins with a title, followed by bulleted items, which are indented one to five levels corresponding to the importance of the item. The main points appear on level one. Subsidiary items are indented below the main point to which they apply. Any item can be *promoted* to a higher level or *demoted* to a lower level, either before or after the text is entered.

Consider, for example, slide 4 in Figure 2.1a. The title of the slide, *Develop the Content*, appears immediately after the slide number and icon. The first bullet, *Use the Outline view*, is indented one level under the title, and it in turn has two subsidiary bullets. The next main bullet, *Review the flow of ideas*, is moved back to level one, and it, too, has two subsidiary bullets.

The outline is (to us) the ideal way to create and edit the presentation. The *insertion point* marks the place where new text is entered; this is established by clicking anywhere in the outline. (The insertion point is automatically placed at the title of the first slide in a new presentation.) To enter text, click in the outline to establish the insertion point, then start typing. Press enter after typing the title of a slide or after entering the text of a bulleted item, which starts a new slide or bullet, respectively. The new item may then be promoted (by pressing **Shift+Tab**) or demoted (by pressing **Tab**) as necessary.

Editing is accomplished through the same techniques used in other Windows applications. For example, you can use the Cut, Copy, and Paste commands in the Edit menu (or the corresponding buttons on the Standard toolbar) to move and copy selected text, or you can simply drag and drop text from one place to another.

1	A Guide to Successful Presentations
	Robert Grauer and Maryann Barber
2	Define the Audience
	• Who is in the audience
	– Managers
	– Coworkers
	– Clients
	• What are their expectations
3	Create the Presentation
	• Develop the content
	• Format the presentation
	• Animate the slide show
4	Develop the Content
	• Use the Outline view
	– Demote items (Tab)
	– Promote items (Shift+Tab)
	• Review the flow of ideas
	– Cut, copy, and paste text
	– Drag and drop
5	Format the Presentation
	• Choose a design template
	• Customize the design
	– Change the color scheme
	– Change background shading
	• Modify slide masters
6	Animate the Slide Show
	• Transitions
	• Builds
	• Hidden slides
7	Tips for Delivery
	• Rehearse Timings
	• Arrive early
	• Maintain eye contact
	• Know your audience

(a) The Expanded Outline

1	A Guide to Successful Presentations
2	Define the Audience
3	Create the Presentation
4	Develop the Content
5	Format the Presentation
6	Animate the Slide Show
7	Tips for Delivery

(b) The Collapsed Outline

FIGURE 2.1   The Outline View

Figure 2.1b displays a collapsed view of the outline, which displays only the title of each slide. The advantage to this view is that you can see more slides on the screen at the same time, making it easier to move slides within the presentation. The slides are expanded or collapsed by using the appropriate tool on the Outline toolbar as described in a hands-on exercise. (The *Outline toolbar* appears automatically when you switch to the Outline view. As with the Standard and Formatting toolbars in Chapter 1, a ScreenTip will appear when you point to a button to describe its function.)

Text is formatted by using the select-then-do approach common to Word and Excel; that is, you select the text, then you execute the appropriate command or click the appropriate button. The selected text remains highlighted and is affected by all subsequent commands until you click elsewhere in the outline.

Acknowledgments

We want to thank the many individuals who helped bring this project to fruition. We are especially grateful to our editor at Prentice Hall, Carolyn Henderson, without whom the series would not have been possible. Cecil Yarbrough and Susan Hoffman did an outstanding job in checking the manuscript for technical accuracy. Suzanne Behnke developed the innovative and attractive design. John DeLara and David Nusspickel were responsible for our Web site. Carlotta Eaton of Radford University and Karen Vignare of Alfred University wrote the instructor manuals and Dave Moles produced the CD. Paul Smolenski was the manufacturing supervisor. Lynne Breitfeller was project manager. Greg Hubit was in charge of production and kept the project on target from beginning to end. Nancy Evans, our marketing manager at Prentice Hall, developed the innovative campaigns, which made the series a success. Lori Cardillo, editorial assistant at Prentice Hall, helped in ways too numerous to mention. We also want to acknowledge our reviewers who, through their comments and constructive criticism, greatly improved the *Exploring Windows* series.

Lynne Band, Middlesex Community College
Stuart P. Brian, Holy Family College
Carl M. Briggs, Indiana University School of Business
Kimberly Chambers, Scottsdale Community College
Alok Charturvedi, Purdue University
Jerry Chin, Southwest Missouri State University
Dean Combellick, Scottsdale Community College
Cody Copeland, Johnson County Community College
Larry S. Corman, Fort Lewis College
Janis Cox, Tri-County Technical College
Martin Crossland, Southwest Missouri State University
Paul E. Daurelle, Western Piedmont Community College
David Douglas, University of Arkansas
Carlotta Eaton, Radford University
Raymond Frost, Central Connecticut State University
James Gips, Boston College
Vernon Griffin, Austin Community College
Michael Hassett, Fort Hays State University
Wanda D. Heller, Seminole Community College
Bonnie Homan, San Francisco State University
Ernie Ivey, Polk Community College
Mike Kelly, Community College of Rhode Island
Jane King, Everett Community College
John Lesson, University of Central Florida

David B. Meinert, Southwest Missouri State University
Bill Morse, DeVry Institute of Technology
Alan Moltz, Naugatuck Valley Technical Community College
Kim Montney, Kellogg Community College
Kevin Pauli, University of Nebraska
Mary McKenry Percival, University of Miami
Delores Pusins, Hillsborough Community College
Gale E. Rand, College Misericordia
Judith Rice, Santa Fe Community College
David Rinehard, Lansing Community College
Marilyn Salas, Scottsdale Community College
John Shepherd, Duquesne University
Helen Stoloff, Hudson Valley Community College
Margaret Thomas, Ohio University
Mike Thomas, Indiana University School of Business
Suzanne Tomlinson, Iowa State University
Karen Tracey, Central Connecticut State University
Sally Visci, Lorain County Community College
David Weiner, University of San Francisco
Connie Wells, Georgia State University
Wallace John Whistance-Smith, Ryerson Polytechnic University
Jack Zeller, Kirkwood Community College

A final word of thanks to the unnamed students at the University of Miami, who make it all worthwhile. And most of all, thanks to you, our readers, for choosing this book. Please feel free to contact us with any comments and suggestions.

Robert T. Grauer
rgrauer@umiami.miami.edu
www.bus.miami.edu/~rgrauer
www.prenhall.com/grauer

Maryann Barber
mbarber@homer.bus.miami.edu
www.bus.miami.edu/~mbarber

MICROSOFT OFFICE 97: SIX APPLICATIONS IN ONE

Word processing, spreadsheets, and data management have always been significant microcomputer applications. The early days of the PC saw these applications emerge from different vendors with radically different user interfaces. WordPerfect, Lotus, and dBASE, for example, were dominant applications in their respective areas, and each was developed by a different company. The applications were totally dissimilar, and knowledge of one did not help in learning another.

The widespread acceptance of Windows 3.1 promoted the concept of a common user interface, which required all applications to follow a consistent set of conventions. This meant that all applications worked essentially the same way, and it provided a sense of familiarity when you learned a new application, since every application presented the same user interface. The development of a suite of applications from a single vendor extended this concept by imposing additional similarities on all applications within the suite.

This introduction will acquaint you with *Microsoft Office 97* and its four major applications—*Word, Excel, PowerPoint,* and *Access.* The single biggest difference between Office 97 and its predecessor, Office 95, is that the Internet has become an integral part of the Office suite. Thus, we also discuss *Internet Explorer,* the Web browser included in Office 97, and *Microsoft Outlook,* the e-mail and scheduling program that is built into Office 97. The icon at the left of this paragraph appears throughout the text to highlight references to the Internet and enhance your use of Microsoft Office. Our introduction also includes the Clip Gallery, WordArt, and Office Art, three tools built into Microsoft Office that help you to add interest to your documents. And finally, we discuss Object Linking and Embedding, which enables you to combine data from multiple applications into a single document.

Our primary purpose in this introduction is to emphasize the similarities between the applications in Office 97 and to help you transfer your knowledge from one application to the next. You will find the same commands in the same menus. You will also recognize familiar toolbars and will be able to take advantage of similar keyboard shortcuts. You will learn that help can be obtained in a variety of ways, and that it is consistent in every application. Our goal is to show you how much you already know and to get you up and running as quickly as possible.

TRY THE COLLEGE BOOKSTORE

Any machine you buy will come with Windows 95 (or Windows 97), but that is only the beginning since you must also obtain the application software you intend to run. Some hardware vendors will bundle (at no additional cost) Microsoft Office as an inducement to buy from them. If you have already purchased your system and you need software, the best place to buy Microsoft Office is the college bookstore, where it can be obtained at a substantial educational discount.

MICROSOFT OFFICE 97

All Office applications share the ***common Windows interface*** with which you may already be familiar. (If you are new to Windows 95, then read the appendix on the "Essentials of Windows.") Microsoft Office 97 runs equally well under Windows 95, Windows 97, or Windows NT.

Figure 1 displays a screen from each major application in Microsoft Office— Word, Excel, PowerPoint, and Access. Our figure also includes screens from Internet Explorer and Mircosoft Outlook, both of which are part of Office 97. Look closely at Figure 1, and realize that each screen contains both an application window and a document window, and that each document window has been maximized within the application window. The title bars of the application and document windows have been merged into a single title bar that appears at the top of the application window. The title bar displays the application (e.g., Microsoft Word in Figure 1a) as well as the name of the document (Web Enabled in Figure 1a) on which you are working.

All six screens in Figure 1 are similar in appearance even though the applications accomplish very different tasks. Each application window has an identifying icon, a menu bar, a title bar, and a minimize, maximize or restore, and a close button. Each document window has its own identifying icon, and its own minimize, maximize or restore, and close button. The Windows taskbar appears at the bottom of each application window and shows the open applications. The status bar appears above the taskbar and displays information relevant to the window or selected object.

Each major application in Microsoft Office uses a consistent command structure in which the same basic menus are found in all applications. The File, Edit, View, Insert, Tools, Window, and Help menus are present in all six applications. The same commands are found in the same menus. The Save, Open, Print, and Exit commands, for example, are contained in the File menu. The Cut, Copy, Paste, and Undo commands are found in the Edit menu.

The means for accessing the pull-down menus are consistent from one application to the next. Click the menu name on the menu bar, or press the Alt key plus the underlined letter of the menu name; for example, press Alt+F to pull down the File menu. If you already know some keyboard shortcuts in one application, there is a good chance that the shortcuts will work in another application. Ctrl+Home and Ctrl+End, for example, move to the beginning and end of a document, respectively. Ctrl+B, Ctrl+I, and Ctrl+U boldface, italicize, and underline text. Ctrl+X (the "X" is supposed to remind you of a pair of scissors), Ctrl+C, and Ctrl+V will cut, copy, and paste, respectively.

Title bar

Identifying icon

Menu bar

Standard toolbar

Formatting toolbar

Minimize button

Restore button

Close button

Status bar

Task bar

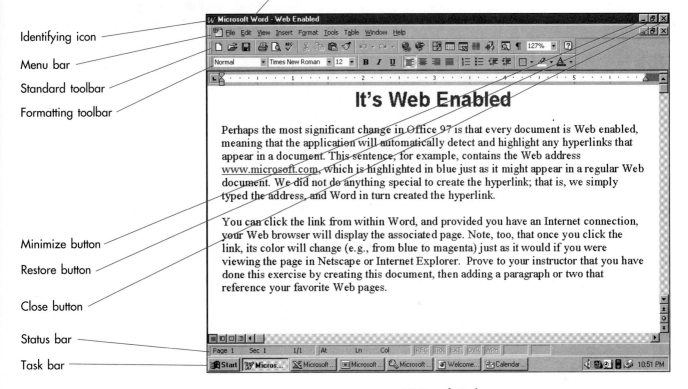

(a) Microsoft Word

Title bar

Identifying icon

Menu bar

Standard toolbar

Formatting toolbar

Minimize button

Restore button

Close button

Status bar

Task bar

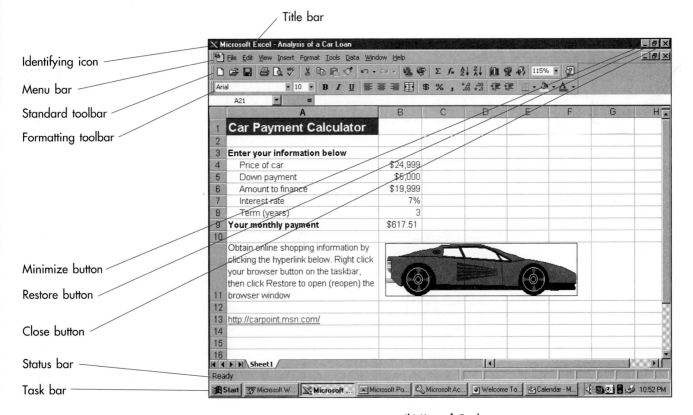

(b) Microsoft Excel

FIGURE 1   The Common User Interface

Title bar

Identifying icon

Menu bar

Standard toolbar

Formatting toolbar

Minimize button

Restore button

Close button

Status bar

Task bar

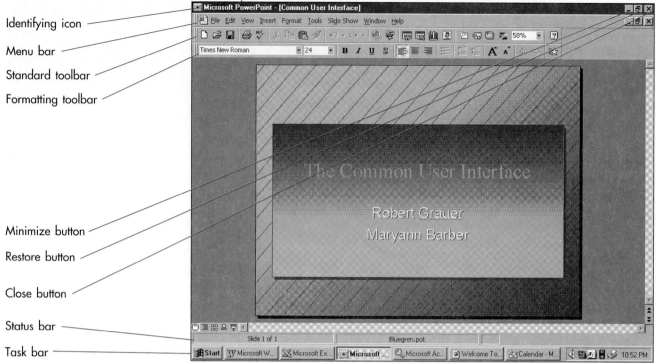

(c) Microsoft PowerPoint

Title bar

Identifying icon

Menu bar

Toolbar

Minimize button

Restore button

Close button

Status bar

Task bar

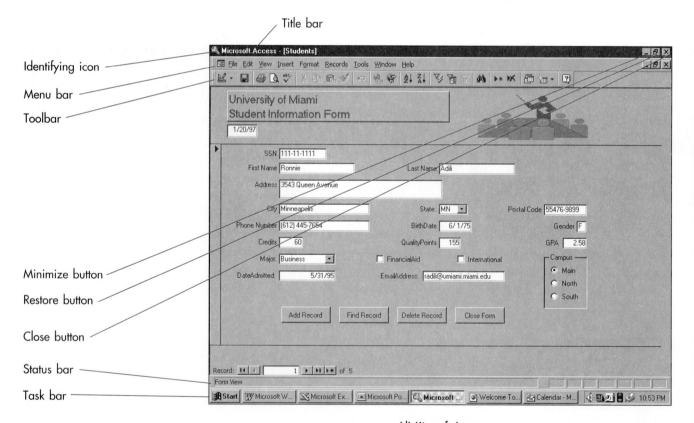

(d) Microsoft Access

FIGURE 1   The Common User Interface (continued)

Title bar

Identifying icon

Menu bar

Toolbar

Minimize button

Restore button

Close button

Status bar

Task bar

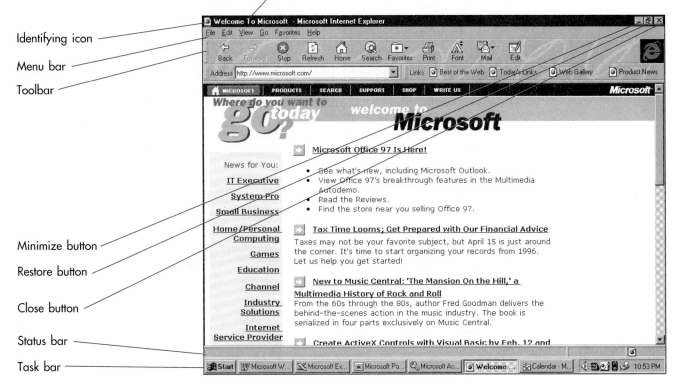

(e) Internet Explorer

Title bar

Identifying icon

Menu bar

Toolbar

Minimize button

Restore button

Close button

Status bar

Task bar

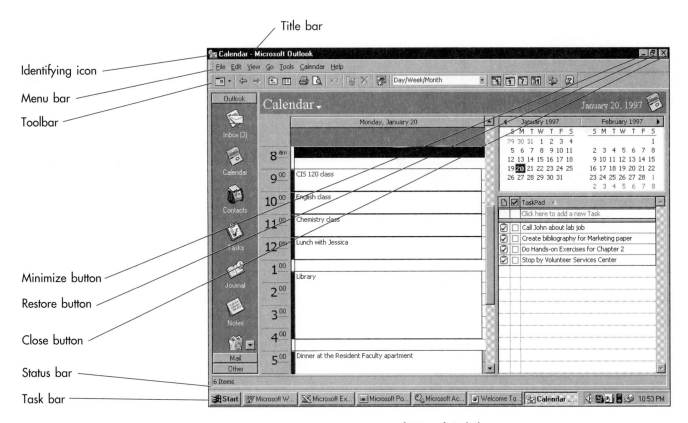

(f) Microsoft Outlook

FIGURE 1   The Common User Interface (continued)

The four major applications use consistent (and often identical) dialog boxes. The dialog boxes to open and close a file, for example, are identical in every application. All four applications also share a common dictionary. The AutoCorrect feature (to correct common spelling mistakes) works identically in all four applications. The help feature also functions identically.

There are, of course, differences between the applications. Each application has unique menus and toolbars. Nevertheless, the Standard and Formatting toolbars in the major applications contain many of the same tools (especially the first several tools on the left of each toolbar). The **Standard toolbar** contains buttons for basic commands such as Open, Save, or Print. It also contains buttons to cut, copy, and paste, and these buttons are identical in all four applications. The **Formatting toolbar** provides access to common operations such as boldface or italics, or changing the font or point size; again, these buttons are identical in all four applications. ScreenTips are present in all applications.

STANDARD OFFICE VERSUS OFFICE PROFESSIONAL

Microsoft distributes both a Standard and a Professional edition of Office 97. Both versions include Word, Excel, PowerPoint, Internet Explorer, and Outlook. Office Professional also has Microsoft Access. The difference is important when you are shopping and you are comparing prices from different sources. Be sure to purchase the version that is appropriate for your needs.

Help for Office 97

Several types of help are available in Office 97. The most basic is accessed by pulling down the Help menu and clicking the Contents and Index command to display the Help Contents window as shown in Figures 2a and 2b. (The Help screens are from Microsoft Word, but similar screens are available for each of the other applications.) The **Contents tab** in Figure 2a is analogous to the table of contents in an ordinary book. It displays the major topics in the application as a series of books that are open or closed. You can click any closed book to open it, which in turn displays additional books and/or help topics. Conversely, you can click any open book to close it and gain additional space on the screen.

The **Index tab** in Figure 2b is similar to the index of an ordinary book. Enter the first several letters of the topic to look up, such as "we" in Figure 2b. Help then returns all of the topics beginning with the letters you entered. Select the topic you want, then display the topic for immediate viewing, or print it for later reference. (The Find tab, not shown in Figure 2, contains a more extensive listing of entries than does the Index tab. It lets you enter a specific word, then it returns every topic that contains that word.)

The **Office Assistant** in Figure 2c is new to Office 97 and is activated by clicking the Office Assistant button on the Standard toolbar or by pressing the F1 function key. The Assistant enables you to ask a question in English, then it returns a series of topics that attempt to answer your question.

Additional help can be obtained from the Microsoft Web site as shown in Figure 2d, provided you have access to the Internet. The easiest way to access the site is to pull down the Help menu from any Office application, click Microsoft on the Web, then click Online Support. This, in turn, will start the Internet Explorer and take you to the appropriate page on the Web, where you will find the most current information available as well as the most detailed support. You can, for example, access the same knowledge base as that used by Microsoft support engineers when you call for technical assistance.

Topic may be viewed or
printed by clicking
appropriate command button

Double click closed book to
open it and display additional
help topics

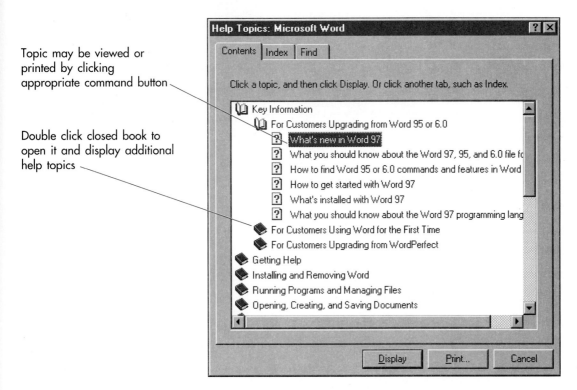

(a) Contents Tab

Type the first few letters in
the topic to look up

Select the desired topic

Click Display button to
view the information

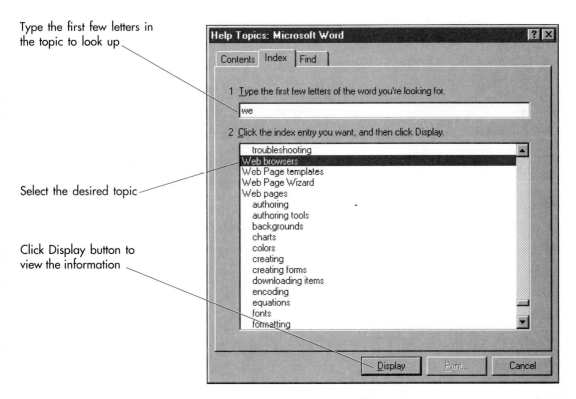

(b) Index Tab

FIGURE 2   Help with Microsoft Office

Help screen contains links
to additional information

Click any topic to display
the help screen

Enter your question, then
click the Search button

Office Assistant (other images
are available)

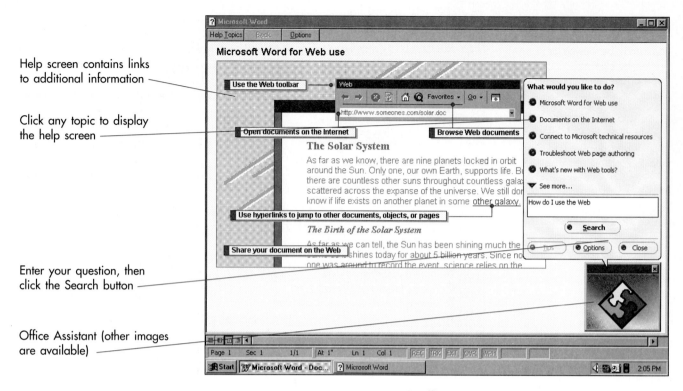

(c) The Office Assistant

Internet Explorer
opens automatically

Web address

Link to Frequently
Asked Questions

Click the link to
desired information

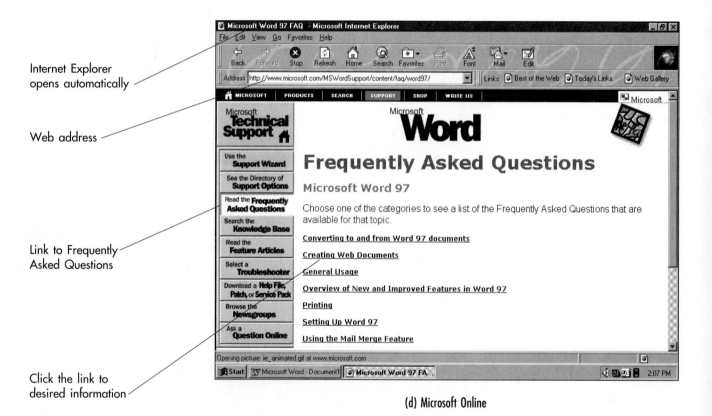

(d) Microsoft Online

FIGURE 2   Help with Microsoft Office (continued)

Office Shortcut Bar

The **_Microsoft Office Shortcut Bar_** provides immediate access to each application within Microsoft Office. It consists of a row of buttons and can be placed anywhere on the screen. The Shortcut Bar is anchored by default on the right side of the desktop, but you can position it along any edge, or have it "float" in the middle of the desktop. You can even hide it from view when it is not in use.

Figure 3a displays the Shortcut Bar as it appears on our desktop. The buttons that are displayed (and the order in which they appear) are established through the Customize dialog box in Figure 3b. Our Shortcut Bar contains a button for each Office application, a button for the Windows Explorer, and a button for Bookshelf Basics.

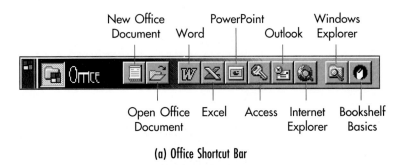

(a) Office Shortcut Bar

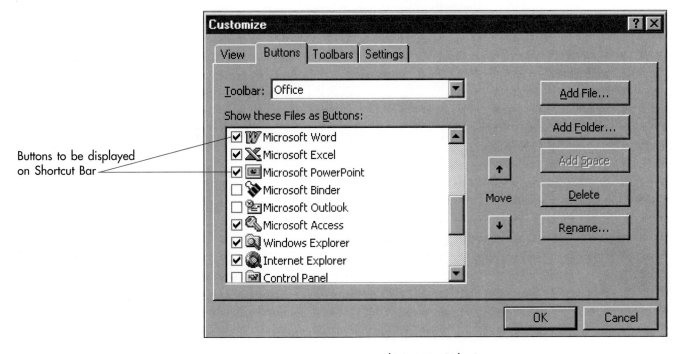

(b) Customize Dialog Box

FIGURE 3   Microsoft Office Shortcut Bar

Docucentric Orientation

Our Shortcut Bar contains two additional buttons: to open an existing document and to start a new document. These buttons are very useful and take advantage of the "docucentric" orientation of Microsoft Office, which lets you think in terms

Selected folder

Double click document
name to open it

List of files in the folder

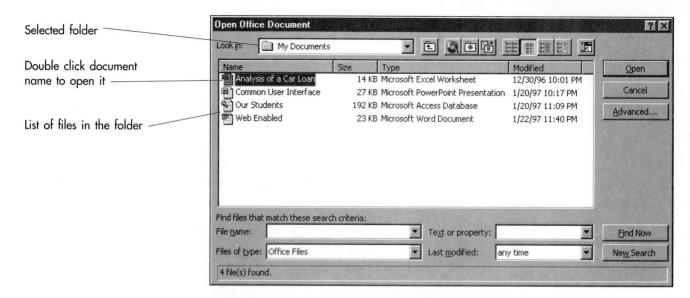

(a) Open an Existing Document

Letters & Faxes tab

Double click template
name to open it

Details button

Preview of template

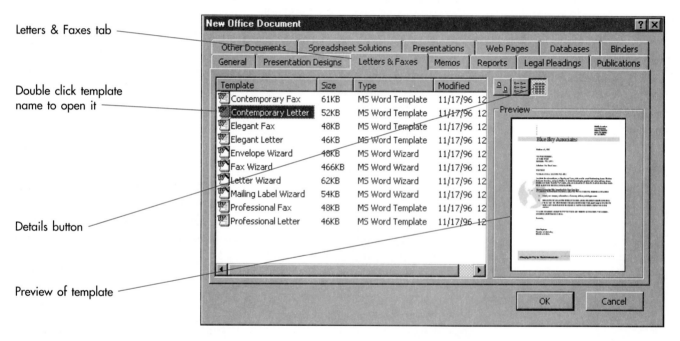

(b) Start a New Document

FIGURE 4   Document Orientation

of a document rather than the associated application. You can still open a document in traditional fashion, by starting the application (e.g., clicking its button on the Shortcut Bar), then using the File Open command to open the document. It's easier, however, to locate the document, then double click its icon, which automatically loads the associated program.

Consider, for example, the Open dialog box in Figure 4a, which is displayed by clicking the Open a Document button on the Shortcut Bar. The Open dialog box is common to the major Office applications, and it works identically in each application. The My Documents folder is selected in Figure 4a, and it contains four documents of various file types. The documents are displayed in the Details view, which shows the document name, size, file type, and date and time the document was last modified. To open any document—for example, "Analysis of a Car Loan"—just double click its name or icon. The associated application (Microsoft Excel in this example) will be started automatically; and it, in turn, will open the selected workbook.

The "docucentric" orientation also applies to new documents. Click the Start a New Document button on the Office Shortcut Bar, and you display the New dialog box in Figure 4b. Click the tab corresponding to the type of document you want to create, such as Letters & Faxes in Figure 4b. Change to the Details view, then click (select) various templates so that you can choose the one most appropriate for your purpose. Double click the desired template to start the application, which opens the template and enables you to create the document.

CHANGE THE VIEW

The toolbar in the Open dialog box contains buttons to display the documents within the selected folder in one of several views. Click the Details button to switch to the Details view and see the date and time the file was last modified, as well as its size and type. Click the List button to display an icon representing the associated application, enabling you to see many more files than in the Details view. The Preview button lets you see a document before you open it. The Properties button displays information about the document, including the number of revisions.

SHARED APPLICATIONS AND UTILITIES

Microsoft Office includes additional applications and shared utilities, several of which are illustrated in Figure 5. The *Microsoft Clip Gallery* in Figure 5a has more than 3,000 clip art images and almost 150 photographs, each in a variety of categories. It also contains a lesser number of sound files and video clips. The Clip Gallery can be accessed from every Office application, most easily through the Insert Picture command, which displays the Clip Gallery dialog box.

The *Microsoft WordArt* utility adds decorative text to a document, and is accessed through the Insert Picture command from Word, Excel, or PowerPoint. WordArt is intuitive and easy to use. In essence, you choose a style for the text from among the selections in the dialog box of Figure 5b, then you enter the specific text in a second dialog box (which is not shown in Figure 5). It's fun, it's easy, and you can create some truly dynamite documents that will add interest to a document.

Office Art consists of a set of drawing tools that is found on the Drawing toolbar in Word, Excel, or PowerPoint. You don't have to be an artist—all it takes is a little imagination and an appreciation for what the individual tools can do. In Figure 5c, for example, we began with a single clip art image, copied it several times within the PowerPoint slide, then rotated and colored the students as shown. We also used the AutoShapes tool to add a callout for our student.

Microsoft Bookshelf Basics contains three of the nine books available in the complete version of Microsoft Bookshelf (which is an additional cost item). The *American Heritage Dictionary,* the *Original Roget's Thesaurus,* and the *Columbia Dictionary of Quotations* are provided at no charge. An excerpt from the *American Heritage Dictionary* is illustrated in Figure 5d. Enter the word you are looking for in the text box on the left, then read the definition on the right. You can click the sound icon and hear the pronunciation of the word.

Choose the type of object

Choose the category

Choose the image

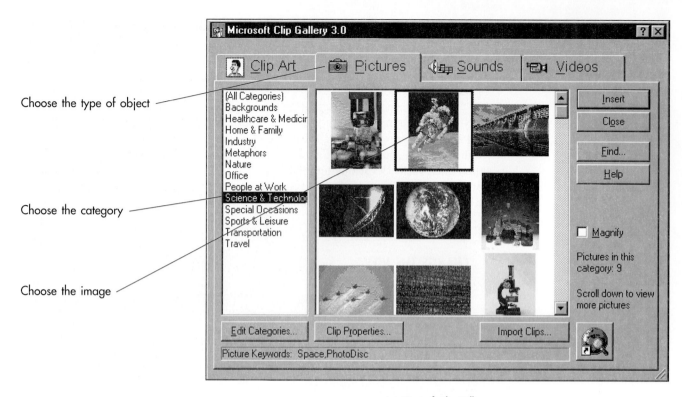

(a) Microsoft Clip Gallery

Select the style to display a second dialog box in which you enter your text

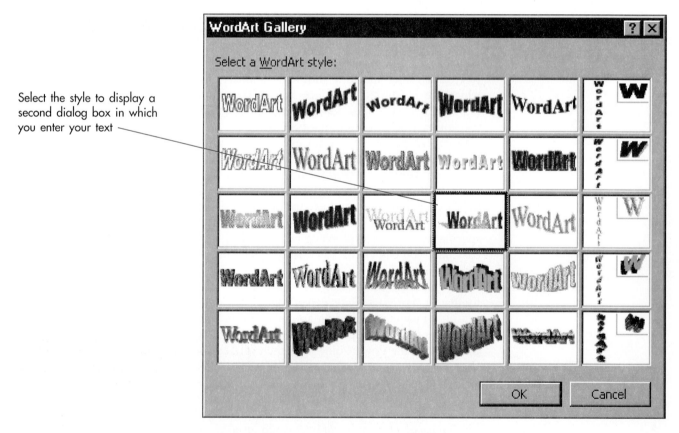

(b) WordArt

FIGURE 5   Shared Applications

Color objects in clip art

Create callout

Callout tool

Drawing toolbar

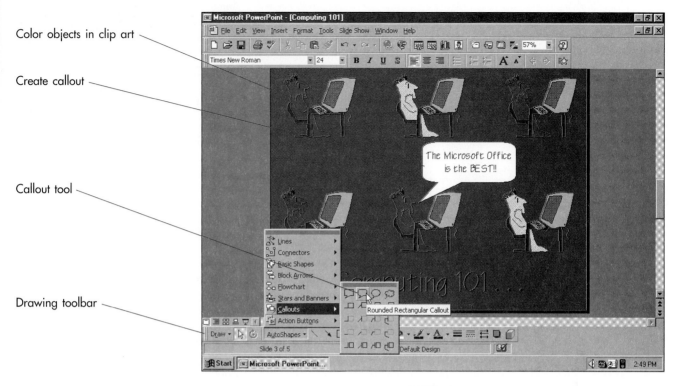

(c) Office Art

Enter word

Click to
hear pronunciation

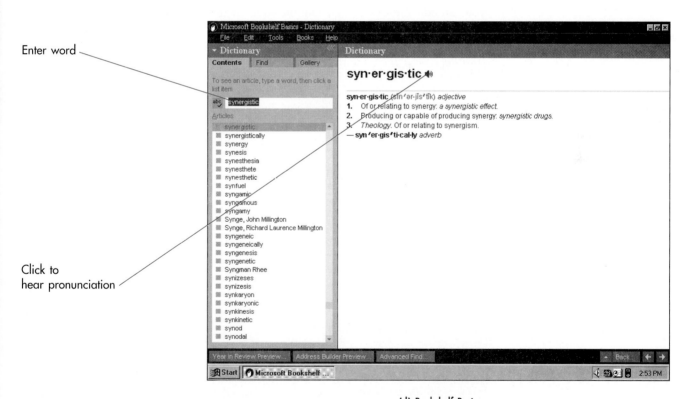

(d) Bookshelf Basics

FIGURE 5   Shared Applications (continued)

OBJECT LINKING AND EMBEDDING

The applications in Microsoft Office are thoroughly integrated with one another. They look alike and they work in consistent fashion. Equally important, they share information through a technology known as *Object Linking and Embedding (OLE)*, which enables you to create a *compound document* containing data (objects) from multiple applications.

The compound document in Figure 6 was created in Word, and it contains objects (a worksheet and a chart) that were created in Excel. The letterhead uses a logo that was taken from the Clip Gallery, while the name and address of the recipient were drawn from an Access database. The various objects were inserted into the compound document through linking or embedding, which are actually two very different techniques. Both operations, however, are much more sophisticated than simply pasting an object, because with either linking or embedding, you can edit the object by using the tools of the original application.

The difference between linking and embedding depends on whether the object is stored within the compound document (*embedding*) or in its own file (*linking*). An *embedded object* is stored in the compound document, which in turn becomes the only user (client) of that object. A *linked object* is stored in its own file, and the compound document is one of many potential clients of that object. The compound document does not contain the linked object per se, but only a representation of the object as well as a pointer (link) to the file containing the object. The advantage of linking is that the document is updated automatically if the object changes.

The choice between linking and embedding depends on how the object will be used. Linking is preferable if the object is likely to change and the compound document requires the latest version. Linking should also be used when the same object is placed in many documents so that any change to the object has to be made in only one place. Embedding should be used if you need to take the object with you (to a different computer) and/or if there is only a single destination document for the object.

Office of Residential Living

| University of Miami | • | P.O. Box 248904 | • | Coral Gables, FL 33124 |

January 10, 1998

Mr. Jeffrey Redmond, President
Dynamic Dining Services
4329 Palmetto Lane
Miami, FL 33157

Dear Jeff,

As per our conversation, occupancy is projected to be back up from last year. I have enclosed a spreadsheet and chart that show the total enrollment for the past four school years. Please realize, however, that the 1997–1998 figures are projections, as the Spring 1998 numbers are still incomplete. The final 1997–1998 numbers should be confirmed within the next two weeks. I hope that this helps with your planning. If you need further information, please contact me at the above address.

Dorm Occupancy				
	94-95	95-96	96-97	97-98
Beatty	330	285	270	250
Broward	620	580	620	565
Graham	450	397	352	420
Rawlings	435	470	295	372
Tolbert	550	554	524	635
Totals	2385	2286	2061	2242

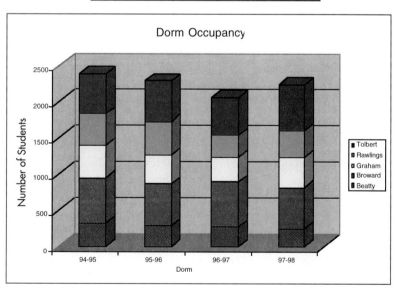

FIGURE 6   A Compound Document

The common user interface requires every Windows application to follow a consistent set of conventions and ensures that all applications work basically the same way. The development of a suite of applications from a single vendor extends this concept by imposing additional similarities on all applications within the suite.

Microsoft distributes both a Standard and a Professional edition of Office 97. Both versions include Word, Excel, PowerPoint, Internet Explorer, and Outlook. Office Professional also has Microsoft Access. The single biggest difference between Office 97 and its predecessor, Office 95, is that the Internet has become an integral part of the Office suite.

Help for all Office applications is available in a variety of formats. The Help Contents window provides access to a Contents and Index tab in which you look up specific topics. The Office Assistant enables you to ask a question in English. Still additional help is available from the Microsoft Web site, provided you have access to the Internet.

Microsoft Office includes several additional applications and shared utilities that can be used to add interest to a document. The Clip Gallery has more than 3,000 clip art images, 150 photographs, and a lesser number of sound files and video clips. WordArt enables you to create decorative text, while Office Art consists of a powerful set of drawing tools.

The Microsoft Office Shortcut Bar provides immediate access to each application in Microsoft Office. The Shortcut Bar is fully customizable with respect to the buttons it displays, its appearance, and its position on the desktop. The Open a Document and Start a New Document buttons enable you to think in terms of a document rather than the associated application.

Object Linking and Embedding (OLE) enables you to create a compound document containing data (objects) from multiple applications. Linking and embedding are different operations. The difference between the two depends on whether the object is stored within the compound document (embedding) or in its own file (linking).

KEY WORDS AND CONCEPTS

Common Windows
    interface
Compound document
Contents tab
Docucentric orientation
Embedding
Formatting toolbar
Index tab
Internet Explorer
Linking
Microsoft Access

Microsoft Bookshelf
    Basics
Microsoft Clip Gallery
Microsoft Excel
Microsoft Office
    Professional
Microsoft Office
    Shortcut Bar
Microsoft Outlook
Microsoft PowerPoint
Microsoft Standard
    Office

Microsoft Word
Microsoft WordArt
Object Linking and
    Embedding (OLE)
Office Art
Office Assistant
Online help
Shared applications
Standard toolbar

MICROSOFT® WORD 97: WHAT WILL WORD PROCESSING DO FOR ME?

After reading this chapter you will be able to:

1. Define word wrap; differentiate between a hard and a soft return.
2. Distinguish between the insert and overtype modes.
3. Describe the elements on the Microsoft Word screen.
4. Create, save, retrieve, edit, and print a simple document.
5. Check a document for spelling; describe the function of the custom dictionary.
6. Describe the AutoCorrect feature; explain how it can be used to create your own shorthand.
7. Use the thesaurus to look up synonyms and antonyms.
8. Explain the objectives and limitations of the grammar check; customize the grammar check for business or casual writing.
9. Differentiate between the Save and Save As commands; describe various backup options that can be selected.

OVERVIEW

Have you ever produced what you thought was the perfect term paper only to discover that you omitted a sentence or misspelled a word, or that the paper was three pages too short or one page too long? Wouldn't it be nice to make the necessary changes, and then be able to reprint the entire paper with the touch of a key? Welcome to the world of word processing, where you are no longer stuck with having to retype anything. Instead, you retrieve your work from disk, display it on the monitor and revise it as necessary, then print it at any time, in draft or final form.

This chapter provides a broad-based introduction to word processing in general and Microsoft Word in particular. We begin by presenting (or perhaps reviewing) the essential concepts of a word processor, then show you how these concepts are implemented in Word. We show you how to create a document, how to save it on disk, then retrieve the document you just created. We introduce you to the spell check and thesaurus, two essential tools in any word processor. We also present the grammar check as a convenient way of finding a variety of errors but remind you there is no substitute for carefully proofreading the final document.

THE BASICS OF WORD PROCESSING

All word processors adhere to certain basic concepts that must be understood if you are to use the programs effectively. The next several pages introduce ideas that are applicable to any word processor (and which you may already know). We follow the conceptual material with a hands-on exercise that enables you to apply what you have learned.

The Insertion Point

The *insertion point* is a flashing vertical line that marks the place where text will be entered. The insertion point is always at the beginning of a new document, but it can be moved anywhere within an existing document. If, for example, you wanted to add text to the end of a document, you would move the insertion point to the end of the document, then begin typing.

Word Wrap

A newcomer to word processing has one major transition to make from a typewriter, and it is an absolutely critical adjustment. Whereas a typist returns the carriage at the end of every line, just the opposite is true of a word processor. One types continually *without* pressing the enter key at the end of a line because the word processor automatically wraps text from one line to the next. This concept is known as *word wrap* and is illustrated in Figure 1.1.

The word *primitive* does not fit on the current line in Figure 1.1a, and is automatically shifted to the next line, *without* the user having to press the enter key. The user continues to enter the document, with additional words being wrapped to subsequent lines as necessary. The only time you use the enter key is at the end of a paragraph, or when you want the insertion point to move to the next line and the end of the current line doesn't reach the right margin.

Word wrap is closely associated with another concept, that of hard and soft returns. A *hard return* is created by the user when he or she presses the enter key at the end of a paragraph; a *soft return* is created by the word processor as it wraps text from one line to the next. The locations of the soft returns change automatically as a document is edited (e.g., as text is inserted or deleted, or as margins or fonts are changed). The locations of the hard returns can be changed only by the user, who must intentionally insert or delete each hard return.

There are two hard returns in Figure 1.1b, one at the end of each paragraph. There are also six soft returns in the first paragraph (one at the end of every line except the last) and three soft returns in the second paragraph. Now suppose the margins in the document are made smaller (that is, the line is made longer) as shown in Figure 1.1c. The number of soft returns drops to four and two (in the first and second paragraphs, respectively) as more text fits on a line and fewer lines are needed. The revised document still contains the two original hard returns, one at the end of each paragraph.

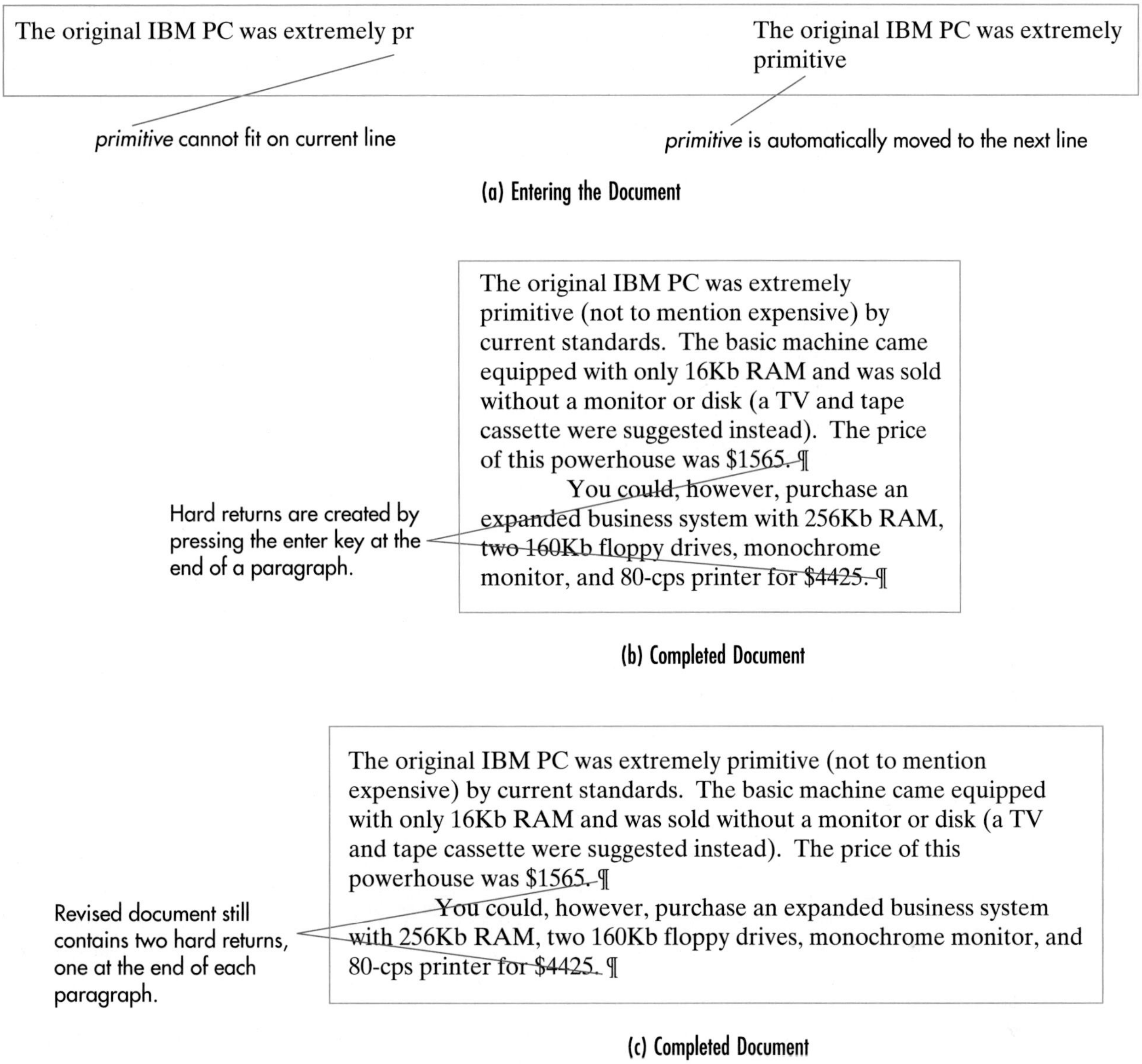

The original IBM PC was extremely pr

The original IBM PC was extremely
primitive

primitive cannot fit on current line

primitive is automatically moved to the next line

(a) Entering the Document

The original IBM PC was extremely
primitive (not to mention expensive) by
current standards. The basic machine came
equipped with only 16Kb RAM and was sold
without a monitor or disk (a TV and tape
cassette were suggested instead). The price
of this powerhouse was $1565. ¶
        You could, however, purchase an
expanded business system with 256Kb RAM,
two 160Kb floppy drives, monochrome
monitor, and 80-cps printer for $4425. ¶

Hard returns are created by
pressing the enter key at the
end of a paragraph.

(b) Completed Document

The original IBM PC was extremely primitive (not to mention
expensive) by current standards. The basic machine came equipped
with only 16Kb RAM and was sold without a monitor or disk (a TV
and tape cassette were suggested instead). The price of this
powerhouse was $1565. ¶
        You could, however, purchase an expanded business system
with 256Kb RAM, two 160Kb floppy drives, monochrome monitor, and
80-cps printer for $4425. ¶

Revised document still
contains two hard returns,
one at the end of each
paragraph.

(c) Completed Document

FIGURE 1.1   **Word Wrap**

Toggle Switches

Suppose you sat down at the keyboard and typed an entire sentence without pressing the Shift key; the sentence would be in all lowercase letters. Then you pressed
the Caps Lock key and retyped the sentence, again without pressing the Shift key.
This time the sentence would be in all uppercase letters. You could repeat the
process as often as you like. Each time you pressed the Caps Lock key, the sentence would switch from lowercase to uppercase and vice versa.

The point of this exercise is to introduce the concept of a ***toggle switch,*** a
device that causes the computer to alternate between two states. The Caps Lock
key is an example of a toggle switch. Each time you press it, newly typed text will
change from uppercase to lowercase and back again. We will see several other
examples of toggle switches as we proceed in our discussion of word processing.

Insert versus Overtype

Microsoft Word is always in one of two modes, *insert* or *overtype.* (The insert mode is the default and the one you will be in most of the time.) Text that is entered into a document during the insert mode moves existing text to the right to accommodate the characters being added. Text entered from the overtype mode replaces (overtypes) existing text. Regardless of which mode you are in, text is always entered or replaced immediately to the right of the insertion point.

The insert mode is best when you enter text for the first time, but either mode can be used to make corrections. The insert mode is the better choice when the correction requires you to add new text; the overtype mode is easier when you are substituting one or more character(s) for another. The difference is illustrated in Figure 1.2.

Figure 1.2a displays the text as it was originally entered, with two misspellings. The letters *se* have been omitted from the word *insert,* and an *x* has been erroneously typed instead of an *r* in the word *overtype.* The insert mode is used in Figure 1.2b to add the missing letters, which in turn moves the rest of the line to the right. The overtype mode is used in Figure 1.2c to replace the *x* with an *r.*

Misspelled words

> The inrt mode is better when adding text that has been omitted; the ovextype mode is easier when you are substituting one (or more) characters for another.

(a) Text to Be Corrected

se has been inserted and existing text moved to the right

> The insert mode is better when adding text that has been omitted; the ovextype mode is easier when you are substituting one (or more) characters for another.

(b) Insert Mode

r replaces the *x*

> The insert mode is better when adding text that has been omitted; the overtype mode is easier when you are substituting one (or more) characters for another.

(c) Overtype Mode

FIGURE 1.2   Insert and Overtype Modes

Deleting Text

The backspace and Del keys delete one character immediately to the left or right of the insertion point, respectively. The choice between them depends on when you need to erase a character(s). The backspace key is easier if you want to delete a character immediately after typing it. The Del key is preferable during subsequent editing.

You can delete several characters at one time by selecting (dragging the mouse over) the characters to be deleted, then pressing the Del key. And finally, you can delete and replace text in one operation by selecting the text to be replaced and then typing the new text in its place.

LEARN TO TYPE

The ultimate limitation of any word processor is the speed at which you enter data; hence the ability to type quickly is invaluable. Learning how to type is easy, especially with the availability of computer-based typing programs. As little as a half hour a day for a couple of weeks will have you up to speed, and if you do any significant amount of writing at all, the investment will pay off many times.

INTRODUCTION TO MICROSOFT WORD

We used Microsoft Word to write this book, as can be inferred from the screen in Figure 1.3. Your screen will be different from ours in many ways. You will not have the same document nor is it likely that you will customize Word in exactly the same way. You should, however, be able to recognize the basic elements that are found in the Microsoft Word window that is open on the desktop.

There are actually two open windows in Figure 1.3—an application window for Microsoft Word and a document window for the specific document on which you are working. Each window has its own Minimize, Maximize (or Restore), and Close buttons. Both windows have been maximized, and thus the title bars have been merged into a single title bar that appears at the top of the application window and reflects the application (Microsoft Word) as well as the document name (Word Chapter 1). A menu bar appears immediately below the title bar. Vertical and horizontal scroll bars appear at the right and bottom of the document window. The Windows taskbar appears at the bottom of the screen and shows the open applications.

Microsoft Word is also part of the Microsoft Office suite of applications, and thus shares additional features with Excel, Access, and PowerPoint, that are also part of the Office suite. *Toolbars* provide immediate access to common commands and appear immediately below the menu bar. The toolbars can be displayed or hidden using the Toolbars command in the View menu.

The *Standard toolbar* contains buttons corresponding to the most basic commands in Word—for example, opening a file or printing a document. The icon on the button is intended to be indicative of its function (e.g., a printer to indicate the Print command). You can also point to the button to display a *ScreenTip* showing the name of the button. The *Formatting toolbar* appears under the Standard toolbar and provides access to common formatting operations such as boldface, italics, or underlining.

The toolbars may appear overwhelming at first, but there is absolutely no need to memorize what the individual buttons do. That will come with time. We

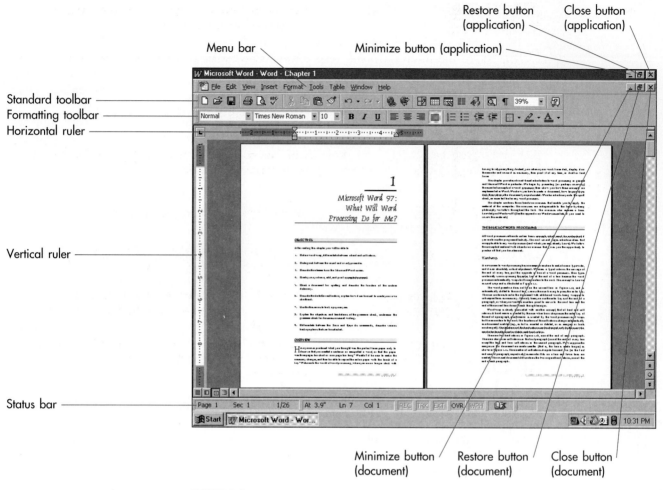

Menu bar

Restore button (application)

Close button (application)

Minimize button (application)

Standard toolbar

Formatting toolbar

Horizontal ruler

Vertical ruler

Status bar

Minimize button (document)

Restore button (document)

Close button (document)

FIGURE 1.3 Microsoft Word

suggest, however, that you will have a better appreciation for the various buttons if you consider them in groups, according to their general function, as shown in Figure 1.4a.

The *horizontal ruler* is displayed underneath the toolbars and enables you to change margins, tabs, and/or indents for all or part of a document. A *vertical ruler* shows the vertical position of text on the page and can be used to change the top or bottom margins.

The *status bar* at the bottom of the document window displays the location of the insertion point (or information about the command being executed.) The status bar also shows the status (settings) of various indicators—for example, OVR to show that Word is in the overtype, as opposed to the insert, mode.

HELP FOR MICROSOFT WORD

Office 97 offers help from a variety of sources. You can pull down the Help menu as you can with any Windows application and/or you can click the Office Assistant button on the Standard toolbar. You can also go to the Microsoft Web site to obtain more recent, and often more detailed, information. You will find the answer to frequently asked questions, and you can access the same Knowledge Base used by Microsoft support engineers.

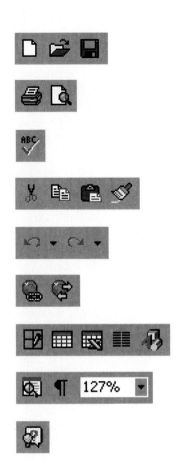

Starts a new document, opens an existing document, or saves the document in memory

Prints the document or previews the document prior to printing

Checks the spelling and grammar of the document

Cuts, copies, or pastes the selected text; copies the formatting of the selected text

Undoes or redoes a previously executed command

Inserts a hyperlink or toggles the display of the Web toolbar on and off

Draws a table, inserts a table, inserts an Excel worksheet, creates columns, or toggles the display of the Drawing toolbar on and off

Toggles the Document map feature on and off, toggles the nonprinting characters on and off, or changes the zoom percentage

Displays the Office Assistant. (The lightbulb indicates the Assistant has a suggestion)

(a) Standard Toolbar

Applies a specific style to the selected text

Changes the typeface, or changes the type size

Toggles boldface, italics, and underline on and off

Aligns left, center, right, or full

Creates a numbered or bulleted list; decreases or increases the indent

Creates a border, applies highlighting to the selected text, or applies color to the selected text

(b) Formatting Toolbar

FIGURE 1.4   Toolbars

The ***File menu*** is a critically important menu in virtually every Windows application. It contains the Save and Open commands to save a document on disk, then subsequently retrieve (open) that document at a later time. The File menu also contains the Print command to print a document, the Close command to close the current document but continue working in the application, and the Exit command to quit the application altogether.

The ***Save command*** copies the document that is being edited (the document in memory) to disk. The Save As dialog box appears the first time that the document is saved so that you can specify the file name and other required information. All subsequent executions of the Save command save the document under the assigned name, replacing the previously saved version with the new version.

The Save As dialog box requires a file name (e.g., My First Document in Figure 1.5a), which can be up to 255 characters in length. The file name may contain spaces and commas. (Periods are permitted, but discouraged, since they are too easily confused with DOS extensions.)

The dialog box also requires the specification of the drive and folder in which the file is to be saved as well as the file type that determines which application the file is associated with. (Long-time DOS users will remember the three-character extension at the end of a file name—for example, DOC—to indicate the associated application. The extension may be hidden in Windows 95 according to options set through the View menu in My Computer or the Windows Explorer.

The ***Open command*** brings a copy of a previously saved document into memory enabling you to work with that document. The Open command displays the Open dialog box in which you specify the file to retrieve. You indicate the drive (and optionally the folder) that contains the file, as well as the type of file you want to retrieve. Word will then list all files of that type on the designated drive (and folder), enabling you to open the file you want.

The Save and Open commands work in conjunction with one another. The Save As dialog box in Figure 1.5a, for example, saves the file *My First Document* onto the disk in drive A. The Open dialog box in Figure 1.5b brings that file back into memory so that you can work with the file, after which you can save the revised file for use at a later time.

The toolbars in the Save As dialog and Open dialog boxes have several buttons in common that enable you to list the files in different ways. The Details view is selected in both dialog boxes and shows the file size as well as the date and time a file was last modified. The List button displays only the file names, and hence more files are visible at one time. The Preview button lets you see a document before you open it. The Properties button displays information about the document including the number of revisions.

SEARCH THE WEB

Microsoft Office 97 enables you to open and/or search for a Web document without having to exit from the application. Pull down the File menu and click the Open command to display the Open dialog box, from where you can click the Search the Web button. Your Web browser will open automatically and connect you to a search page in which you enter keywords, provided you have an Internet connection.

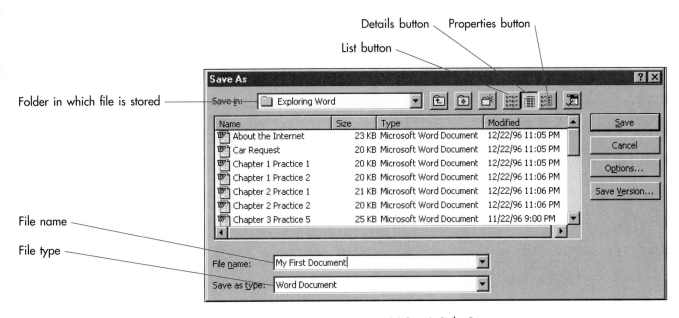

Details button Properties button

List button

Folder in which file is stored

File name

File type

(a) Save As Dialog Box

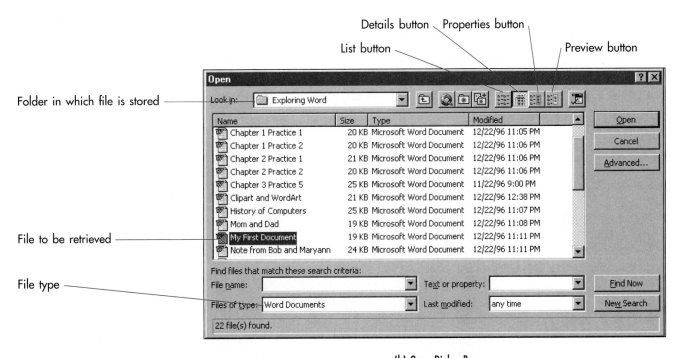

Details button Properties button

List button

Preview button

Folder in which file is stored

File to be retrieved

File type

(b) Open Dialog Box

FIGURE 1.5 The Save and Open Commands

LEARNING BY DOING

Every chapter contains a series of hands-on exercises that enable you to apply what you learn at the computer. The exercises in this chapter are linked to one another in that you create a simple document in exercise one, then open and edit that document in exercise two. The ability to save and open a document is critical, and you do not want to spend an inordinate amount of time entering text unless you are confident in your ability to retrieve it later.

My First Document

Objective: To start Microsoft Word in order to create, save, and print a simple document. To execute commands via the toolbar or from pull-down menus. Use Figure 1.6 as a guide in doing the exercise.

STEP 1: Welcome to Windows

➤ Turn on the computer and all of its peripherals. The floppy drive should be empty prior to starting your machine. This ensures that the system starts from the hard disk, which contains the Windows files, as opposed to a floppy disk, which does not.

➤ Your system will take a minute or so to get started, after which you should see the Windows desktop in Figure 1.6a. Do not be concerned if the appearance of your desktop is different from ours.

➤ You may see additional objects on the desktop in Windows 95 and/or the active desktop content in Windows 97. It doesn't matter which operating system you are using because Office 97 runs equally well under both Windows 95 and Windows 97 (as well as Windows NT).

➤ You may see a Welcome to Windows 95/Windows 97 dialog box with command buttons to take a tour of the operating system. If so, click the appropriate button(s) or close the dialog box.

(a) The Windows Desktop (step 1)

FIGURE 1.6   Hands-on Exercise 1

TAKE THE WINDOWS TOUR

Windows 95 greets you with a Welcome window that contains a command button to take you on a 10-minute tour. Click the command button and enjoy the show. If you do not see the Welcome window when you start Windows 95, click the Start button, click Run, type C:\WELCOME in the Open *text box,* and press the enter key. Windows 97 was not available when we went to press, but we expect it to have a similar option.

STEP 2: Obtain the Practice Files

➤ We have created a series of practice files (commonly called a "data disk") for you to use throughout the text. Your instructor will make these files available to you in a variety of ways:
  - You can download the files from our Web site if you have access to the Internet and World Wide Web (see boxed tip).
  - The files may be on a network drive, in which case you can use the Windows Explorer to copy the files from the network to a floppy disk.
  - There may be an actual "data disk" that you are to check out from the lab in order to use the Copy Disk command to duplicate the disk.
➤ Check with your instructor for additional information.

DOWNLOAD THE PRACTICE FILES

You can download the practice files for any book in the *Exploring Windows* series from Bob Grauer's home page (www.bus.miami.edu/~rgrauer). Use any Web browser to get to Bob's page, then click the link to the *Exploring Windows* series, where you choose the appropriate book and download the file. Be sure to read the associated "read me" file, which provides additional information about downloading the file.

STEP 3: Start Microsoft Word

➤ Click the **Start button** to display the Start menu. Click (or point to) the **Programs menu,** then click **Microsoft Word** to start the program.
➤ Close the Office Assistant if it appears. (The Office Assistant is illustrated in step 6 of this exercise.)
➤ If necessary, click the **Maximize button** in the application window so that Word takes the entire desktop as shown in Figure 1.6b. Click the **Maximize button** in the document window (if necessary) so that the document window is as large as possible.
➤ Do not be concerned if your screen is different from ours as we include a troubleshooting section immediately following this exercise.

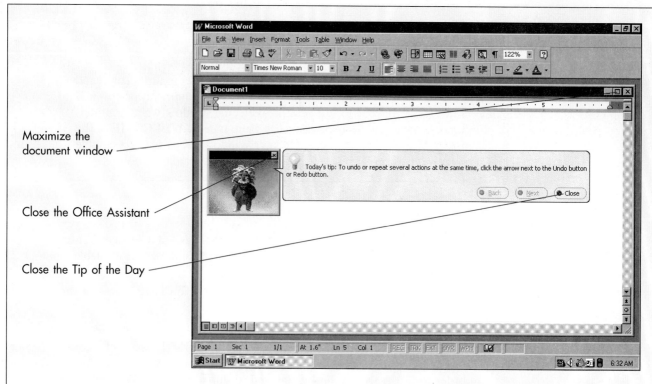

Maximize the document window

Close the Office Assistant

Close the Tip of the Day

(b) Start Word (step 3)

FIGURE 1.6   Hands-on Exercise 1 (continued)

CHOOSE YOUR OWN ASSISTANT

You can choose your own personal assistant from one of several available images. Click the Office Assistant button on the Standard toolbar to display the Assistant, click the Options button to display the Office Assistant dialog box, click the Gallery tab, then click the Next button repeatedly to cycle through the available images. Click OK to select the image and close the dialog box. (The Office 97 CD is required for certain characters.)

STEP 4: Create the Document

➤ Create the document in Figure 1.6c. Type just as you would on a typewriter with one exception; do *not* press the enter key at the end of a line because Word will automatically wrap text from one line to the next.

➤ Press the **enter key** at the end of the paragraph.

➤ You may see a red or green wavy line to indicate spelling or grammatical errors respectively. Both features are discussed later in the chapter.

➤ Point to the red wavy line (if any), click the **right mouse button** to display a list of suggested corrections, then click (select) the appropriate substitution.

➤ Ignore the green wavy line (if any).

Show/Hide ¶ button (displays/
hides nonprinting characters)

Press the enter key at the end
of the paragraph

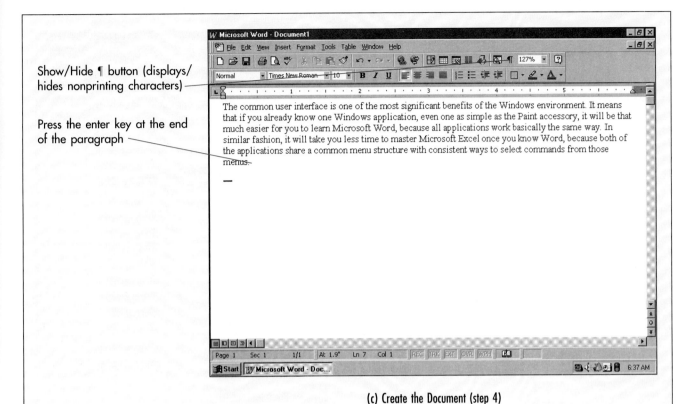

(c) Create the Document (step 4)

FIGURE 1.6   Hands-on Exercise 1 (continued)

WHAT HAPPENED TO THE INS KEY?

Every previous version of Word has used the Ins key to toggle between
the Insert and Overtype modes. Unfortunately this simple technique no
longer works in Word 97, as the key has been disabled. Instead, Microsoft
directs you to pull down the Tools menu, click the Options command,
select the Edit tab, then check (clear) the box for Overtype (Insert) mode.
Fortunately, we found our own toggle switch—double click the OVR indicator on the status bar to switch back and forth between the two modes.

STEP 5: Save the Document

➤ Pull down the **File menu** and click **Save** (or click the **Save button** on the Standard toolbar). You should see the Save As dialog box in Figure 1.6d. If necessary, click the **Details button** so that the display on your monitor more
closely matches our figure.

➤ To save the file:

• Click the **drop-down arrow** on the Save In list box.

• Click the appropriate drive, drive C or drive A, depending on whether or
not you installed the data disk on your hard drive.

• Double click the **Exploring Word folder,** to make it the active folder (the
folder in which you will save the document).

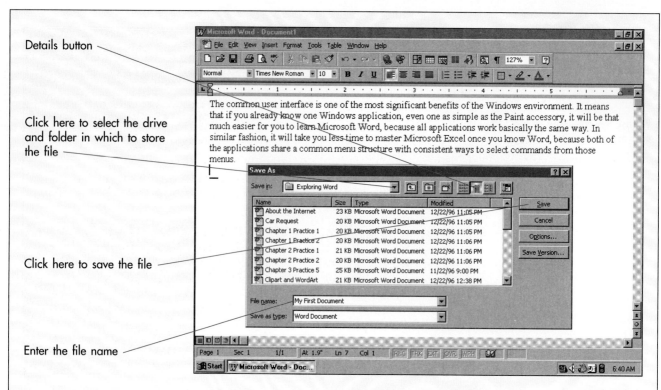

Details button

Click here to select the drive and folder in which to store the file

Click here to save the file

Enter the file name

(d) Save the Document (step 5)

FIGURE 1.6   Hands-on Exercise 1 (continued)

- Click and drag over the default entry in the File name text box. Type **My First Document** as the name of your document. (A DOC extension will be added automatically when the file is saved to indicate that this is a Word document.)

- Click **Save** or press the **enter key.** The title bar changes to reflect the document name.

➤ Add your name at the end of the document, then click the **Save button** on the Standard toolbar to save the document with the revision. This time the Save As dialog box does not appear, since Word already knows the name of the document.

CHANGE THE DEFAULT FOLDER

The default folder is the folder where Word opens (saves) documents unless it is otherwise instructed. To change the default folder, pull down the Tools menu, click Options, click the File Locations tab, click Documents, and click the Modify command button. Enter the name of the new folder (for example, C:\Exploring Word), click OK, then click the Close button. The next time you access the File menu, the default folder will reflect these changes.

STEP 6: The Office Assistant

➤ Click the **Office Assistant button** on the Standard toolbar to display the Office Assistant. (You may see a different character than the one we have selected.)

➤ Enter your question—for example, **How do I print a document?**—as shown in Figure 1.6e, then click the **Search button** to look for the answer.

➤ The size of the dialog box expands as the Assistant suggests several topics that may be appropriate to answer your question.

➤ Click the first topic, **Print a document,** which in turn displays a help screen with detailed information. Read the help screen, then close the Help window.

Click Office Assistant button

Close the Assistant when finished

Enter question and click search

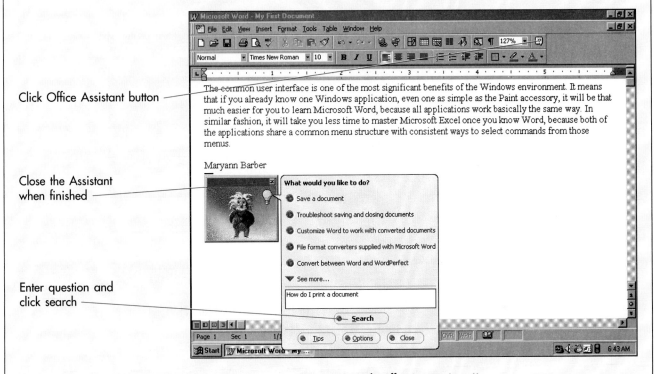

(e) The Office Assistant (step 6)

FIGURE 1.6   Hands-on Exercise 1 (continued)

TIP OF THE DAY

You can set the Office Assistant to greet you with a "Tip of the Day" whenever you start Word. If the Office Assistant is not visible, click the Office Assistant button on the Standard toolbar to start the Assistant, then click the Options button to display the Office Assistant dialog box. Check the Show the Tip of the Day at the startup box, then click OK. The next time you start Word, you will be greeted by the Assistant, who will offer you a tip of the day.

STEP 7: Print the Document

➤ You can print the document in one of two ways:

- Pull down the **File menu.** Click **Print** to display the dialog box of Figure 1.6f. Click the **OK command button** to print the document.
- Click the **Print button** on the Standard toolbar to print the document immediately without displaying the Print dialog box.

Print button

Click here to print the file

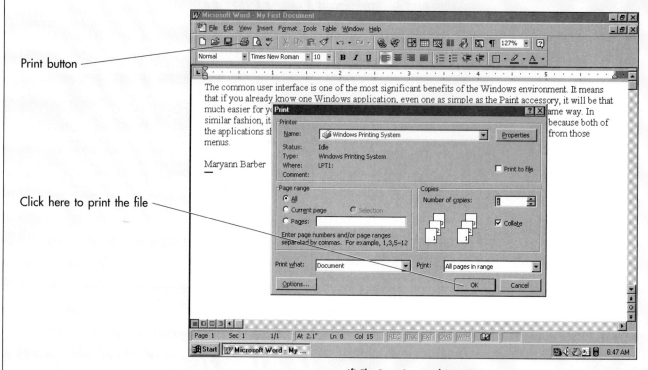

(f) The Print Command (step 7)

FIGURE 1.6   Hands-on Exercise 1 (continued)

ABOUT MICROSOFT WORD

Pull down the Help menu and click About Microsoft Word to display the specific release number and other licensing information, including the product serial number. This help screen also contains two very useful command buttons, System Information and Technical Support. The first button displays information about the hardware installed on your system, including the amount of memory and available space on the hard drive. The Technical Support button provides telephone numbers for technical assistance.

STEP 8: Close the Document

➤ Pull down the **File menu.** Click **Close** to close this document but remain in Word. (Click **Yes** if prompted to save the document.) The document disappears from the screen, but Word is still open.

➤ Pull down the **File menu** a second time. Click **Exit** to close Word if you do not want to continue with the next exercise at this time.

TROUBLESHOOTING

We trust that you completed the hands-on exercise without difficulty, and that you were able to create, save, and print the document in Figure 1.6. There is, however, one area of potential confusion in that Word offers different views of the same document, depending on the preferences of the individual user. It also gives you the option to display (hide) its various toolbars. Thus your screen will not match ours exactly, and, indeed, there is no requirement that it should. The *contents* of the document, however, should be identical to ours.

Figure 1.6 displayed the document in the ***Normal view.*** Figure 1.7 displays an entirely different view called the ***Page Layout view.*** Each view has its advantages. The Normal view is generally faster, but the Page Layout view more closely resembles the printed page as it displays top and bottom margins, headers and footers, graphic elements in their exact position, a vertical ruler, and other elements not seen in the Normal view. The Normal view is preferable only when entering text and editing. The Page Layout view is used to apply the finishing touches and check a document prior to printing. Note, too, that each view can be displayed at different magnifications.

Your screen may or may not match either figure, and you will undoubtedly develop preferences of your own. The following suggestions will help you match the screens of Figure 1.6:

■ If the application window for Word does not take the entire screen, and/or the document does not take the entire window within Word, click the Maximize button in the application and/or the document window.

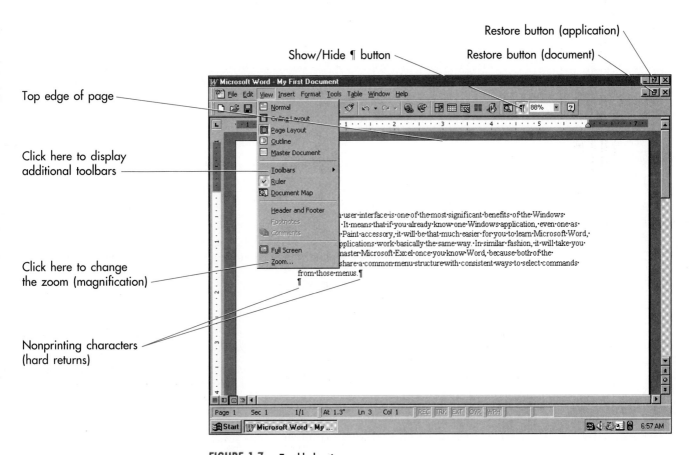

FIGURE 1.7   Troubleshooting

- If the text does not come up to the top of the screen—that is, you see the top edge of the page (as in Figure 1.7)—it means that you are in the Page Layout view instead of the Normal view. Pull down the View menu and click Normal to match the document in Figure 1.6c.

- If the text seems unusually large or small, it means that you or a previous user elected to zoom in or out to get a different perspective on the document. Pull down the View menu, click Zoom, then click Page Width so that the text takes the entire line.

- If you see the ¶ and other nonprinting symbols, it means that you or a previous user elected to display these characters. Click the Show/Hide ¶ button on the Standard toolbar to make the symbols disappear.

- If the Standard or Formatting toolbar is missing and/or a different toolbar is displayed, pull down the View menu, click Toolbars, then click the appropriate toolbars on or off. If the ruler is missing, pull down the View menu and click Ruler.

- The automatic spell check may (or may not) be implemented as indicated by the appearance (absence) of the open book icon on the status bar. If you do not see the icon, pull down the Tools menu, click Options, click the Spelling and Grammar tab, then check the box for Check Spelling as you type.

THE WRONG KEYBOARD

Microsoft Word facilitates conversion from WordPerfect by providing an alternative (software-controlled) keyboard that implements WordPerfect conventions. If you are sharing your machine with others, and if various keyboard shortcuts do not work as expected, it could be because someone else has implemented the WordPerfect keyboard. Pull down the Tools menu, click Options, then click the General tab in the dialog box. Clear the check box next to Navigation keys for WordPerfect users to return to the normal Word keyboard.

HANDS-ON EXERCISE 2

Modifying an Existing Document

Objective: To open an existing document, revise it, and save the revision. To demonstrate the Undo command and online help. Use Figure 1.8 as a guide in doing the exercise.

STEP 1: Open an Existing Document

➤ Click the **Start menu.** Click (or point to) the **Program menu,** then click **Microsoft Word** to start the program. Close the Office Assistant if it appears.

➤ Maximize the application window (if necessary). Maximize the document window as well.

➤ Pull down the **File menu** and click **Open** (or click the **Open button** on the Standard toolbar). You should see a dialog box similar to the one in Figure 1.8a. (The Exploring Word folder is not yet selected.)

➤ To open a file:

- Click the **Details button** to change to the Details view. Click and drag the vertical border between columns to increase (or decrease) the size of a column.
- Click the **drop-down arrow** on the Look In list box.
- Click the appropriate drive, drive C or drive A, depending on the location of your data.
- Double click the **Exploring Word folder** to make it the active folder (the folder in which you will save the document).
- Click the **down arrow** in the Name list box, then scroll until you can select **My First Document** from the first exercise. Click the **Open command button** to open the file.

➤ Your document should appear on the screen.

Details button

Click here to select the drive and folder in which the file is stored

Click and drag here to change column width

Click the file to be retrieved

Click here to open the file

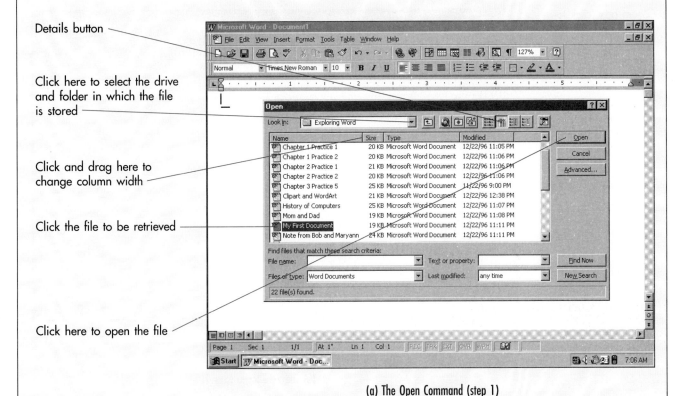

(a) The Open Command (step 1)

FIGURE 1.8   Hands-on Exercise 2

THE MOST RECENTLY OPENED FILE LIST

The easiest way to open a recently used document is to select the document directly from the File menu. Pull down the File menu, but instead of clicking the Open command, check to see if the document appears on the list of the most recently opened documents at the bottom of the menu. If so, you can click the document name rather than having to make the appropriate selections through the Open dialog box.

STEP 2: The View Menu (Troubleshooting)

➤ Modify the settings within Word so that the appearance of your document matches Figure 1.8b.

- To change to the Normal view, pull down the **View menu** and click **Normal** (or click the **Normal View** button at the bottom of the window).
- To change the amount of text that is visible on the screen, click the **drop-down arrow** on the Zoom Control box on the Standard toolbar and select **Page Width.**
- To display (hide) the ruler, pull down the **View menu** and toggle the **Ruler command** on or off. End with the ruler on.

➤ There may still be subtle differences between your screen and ours, depending on the resolution of your monitor. These variations, if any, need not concern you at all as long as you are able to complete the exercise.

Zoom box (click to change magnification)

Horizontal ruler

Page Layout button

Normal View button

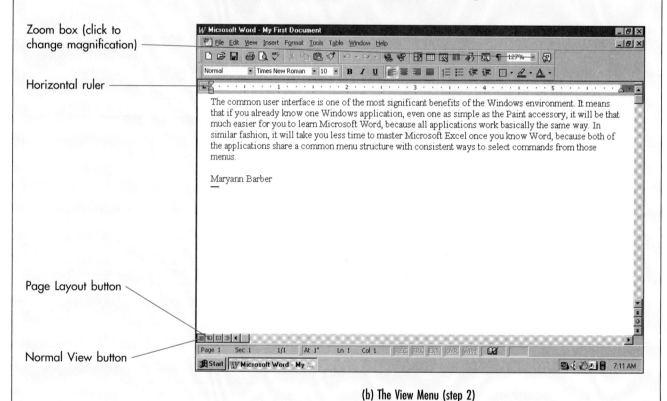

(b) The View Menu (step 2)

FIGURE 1.8   Hands-on Exercise 2 (continued)

DISPLAY (HIDE) TOOLBARS WITH THE RIGHT MOUSE BUTTON

Point to any visible toolbar, then click the right mouse button to display a shortcut menu listing the available toolbars. Click the individual toolbars on or off as appropriate. If no toolbars are visible, pull down the View menu, click Toolbars, then display or hide the desired toolbars.

STEP 3: Display the Hard Returns

➤ The **Show/Hide ¶** button on the Standard toolbar functions as a toggle switch to display (hide) the hard returns (and other nonprinting characters) in a document.

➤ Click the **Show/Hide ¶ button** to display the hard returns as in Figure 1.8c. Click the **Show/Hide ¶ button** a second time to hide the nonprinting characters. Display or hide the paragraph markers as you see fit.

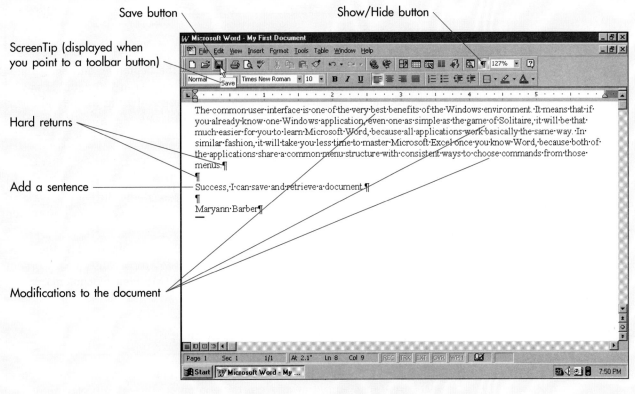

(c) Modify the Document (steps 3 and 4)

FIGURE 1.8   Hands-on Exercise 2 (continued)

SCREENTIPS

Point to any button on any toolbar and Word displays a ScreenTip containing the name of the button to indicate its function. If pointing to a button has no effect, pull down the View menu, click Toolbars, then click Customize to display the Customize dialog box. Click the Options tab, check the box to Show ScreenTips on Toolbars, then close the dialog box.

STEP 4: Modify the Document

➤ Press **Ctrl+End** to move to the end of the document. Press the **up arrow key** once or twice until the insertion point is on a blank line above your name. If necessary, press the **enter key** once (or twice) to add blank line(s).

➤ Add the sentence, **Success, I can save and retrieve a document!,** as shown in Figure 1.8c.

➤ Make the following additional modifications to practice editing:
 • Change the phrase *most significant* to **very best.**
 • Change *Paint accessory* to **game of Solitaire.**
 • Change the word *select* to **choose.**
➤ Switch between the insert and overtype modes as necessary. Double click the **OVR indicator** on the status bar to toggle between the insert and overtype modes.

MOVING WITHIN A DOCUMENT

Press Ctrl+Home and Ctrl+End to move to the beginning and end of a document, respectively. These shortcuts work not just in Word, but in any other Windows application, and are worth remembering as they allow your hands to remain on the keyboard as you type.

STEP 5: Save the Changes

➤ It is very, very important to save your work repeatedly during a session so that you do not lose it all in the event of a power failure or other unforeseen event.
➤ Pull down the **File menu** and click **Save,** or click the **Save button** on the Standard toolbar. You will not see the Save As dialog box because the document is saved automatically under the existing name (My First Document).

KEEP DUPLICATE COPIES OF IMPORTANT FILES

It is absolutely critical to maintain duplicate copies of important files on a separate disk stored away from the computer. In addition, you should print each new document at the end of every session, saving it before printing (power failures happen when least expected—for example, during the print operation). Hard copy is not as good as a duplicate disk, but it is better than nothing.

STEP 6: Selecting Text

➤ Point to the first letter in the first sentence. Press and hold the left mouse button as you drag the mouse over the first sentence. Release the mouse.
➤ The sentence should remain selected as shown in Figure 1.8d. The selected text is the text that will be affected by the next command. Click anywhere else in the document to deselect the text.
➤ Point to any word in the first sentence, then press and hold the **Ctrl key** as you click the mouse, to select the entire sentence. Press the **Del key** to delete the selected text (the first sentence) from the document.

Click and drag over the
first sentence to select it ——

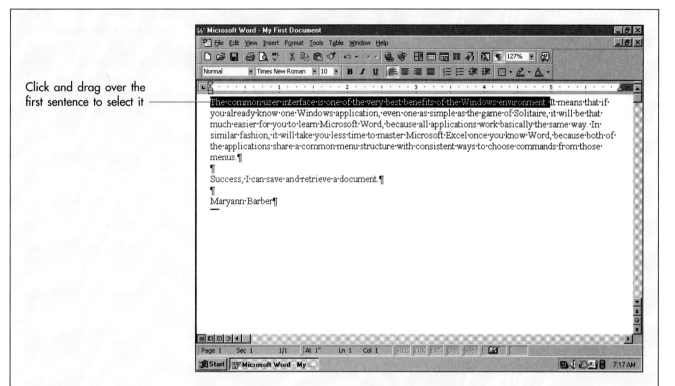

(d) Selecting Text (step 6)

FIGURE 1.8   Hands-on Exercise 2 (continued)

PICK UP THE MOUSE

It seems that you always run out of room on your real desk, just when you need to move the mouse a little further. The solution is to pick up the mouse and move it closer to you—the pointer will stay in its present position on the screen, but when you put the mouse down, you will have more room on your desk in which to work.

STEP 7: The Undo Command

➤ Pull down the **Edit menu** as shown in Figure 1.8e. Click **Undo** to reverse (undo) the last command.

100 LEVELS OF UNDO

The ***Undo command*** is present in Word as it is in every Windows application. Incredible as it sounds, however, Word enables you to undo the last 100 changes to a document. Click the drop-down arrow next to the Undo button to produce a list of your previous actions. (The most recent command is listed first.) Click the action you want to undo, which also undoes all of the preceding commands. Undoing the fifth command in the list, for example, will also undo the preceding four commands.

Click here to
undo the deletion ————

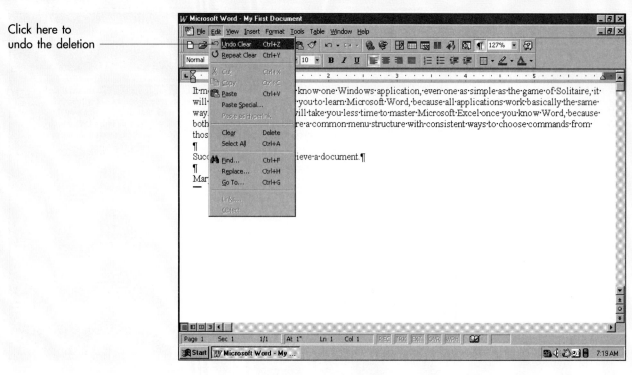

(e) The Undo Command (step 7)

FIGURE 1.8   Hands-on Exercise 2 (continued)

➤ The deleted text should be returned to your document. The Undo command
is a tremendous safety net and can be used at almost any time.
➤ Click anywhere outside the selected text to deselect the sentence.

STEP 8: The Help Menu
➤ Pull down the **Help menu.** Click **Contents and Index** to display the Help top-
ics window in Figure 1.8f.
➤ Click the **Index tab.** Type **Undo** (the topic you wish to look up). The Undo
topic is automatically selected.
➤ Click **Display** to show a second help screen with detailed information.
➤ Click the **Close button** to close the Help window.

TIPS FROM THE OFFICE ASSISTANT

The Office Assistant indicates it has a suggestion by displaying a lightbulb.
Click the lightbulb to display the tip, then click the Back or Next button
as appropriate to view additional tips. The Assistant will not, however,
repeat a tip from an earlier session unless you reset it at the start of a new
session. This is especially important to remember in a laboratory situation
where you are sharing a computer with other students. To reset the tips,
click the Assistant to display a balloon asking what you want to do, click
the Options button in the balloon, click Options, then click the button to
Reset My Tips.

Print button

Save button

Click the Index tab

Type undo

Click Display button to display help text

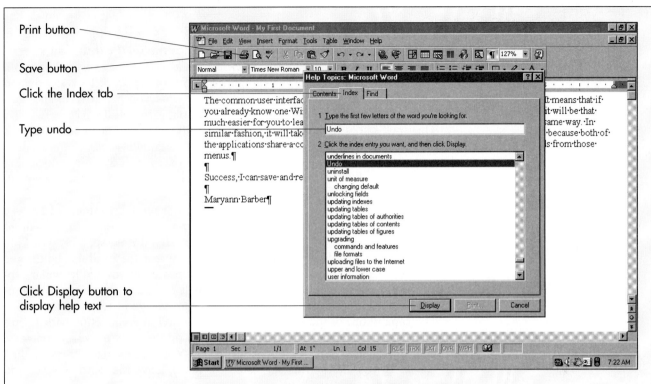

(f) The Help Menu (step 8)

FIGURE 1.8   Hands-on Exercise 2 (continued)

STEP 9: Print the Revised Document

➤ Click the **Save button** on the Standard toolbar to save the revised document a final time.

➤ Click the **Print button** to print the document. Submit the printed document to your instructor as proof you did Hands-on Exercises 1 and 2.

➤ Pull down the **File menu.** Click **Close** to close the document and remain in Word. Click **Exit** if you do not want to continue with the next exercise at this time.

DOCUMENT PROPERTIES

Prove to your instructor how hard you've worked by printing various statistics about your document, including the number of revisions and the total editing time. Pull down the File menu, click the Print command to display the Print dialog box, click the drop down arrow in the Print What list box, select Document properties, then click OK. You can view the information (without printing) by pulling down the File menu, clicking the Properties command, then selecting the Statistics tab from the resulting dialog box.

There is simply no excuse to misspell a word, since the ***spell check*** is an integral part of Microsoft Word. (The spell check is also available for every other application in the Microsoft Office.) Spelling errors make your work look sloppy and discourage the reader before he or she has read what you had to say. They can cost you a job, a grade, a lucrative contract, or an award you deserve.

The spell check can be set to automatically check a document as text is entered, or it can be called explicitly by clicking the Spelling and Grammar button on the Standard toolbar. The spell check compares each word in a document to the entries in a built-in dictionary, then flags any word that is in the document, but not in the built-in dictionary, as an error.

The dictionary included with Microsoft Office is limited to standard English and does not include many proper names, acronyms, abbreviations, or specialized terms, and hence, the use of any such item is considered a misspelling. You can, however, add such words to a ***custom dictionary*** so that they will not be flagged in the future. The spell check will inform you of repeated words and irregular capitalization. It cannot, however, flag properly spelled words that are used improperly, and thus cannot tell you that *Two bee or knot too be* is not the answer.

The capabilities of the spell check are illustrated in conjunction with Figure 1.9a. The spell check goes through the document and returns the errors one at a time, offering several options for each mistake. You can change the misspelled word to one of the alternatives suggested by Word, leave the word as is, or add the word to a custom dictionary.

The first error is the word *embarassing,* with Word's suggestion(s) for correction displayed in the list box in Figure 1.9b. To accept the highlighted suggestion, click the Change command button and the substitution will be made automatically in the document. To accept an alternative suggestion, click the desired word, then click the Change command button. Alternatively, you can click the AutoCorrect button to correct the mistake in the current document, and, in addition, automatically correct the same mistake in any future document.

The spell check detects both irregular capitalization and duplicated words, as shown in Figures 1.9c and 1.9d, respectively. The error in Figure 1.9e, *Grauer,* is not a misspelling per se, but a proper noun not found in the standard dictionary. No correction is required and the appropriate action is to ignore the word (taking no further action)—or better yet, add it to the custom dictionary so that it will not be flagged in future sessions. And finally, we could not resist including the example in Figure 1.9f, which shows another use of the spell check. (It's included for devotees of crossword puzzles who need a five-letter word beginning with *s* and ending with *n.*)

Flagged errors

A spelling checker will catch embarassing mistakes, iRregular capitalization, and duplicate words words. It will also flag proper nouns, for example, Robert Grauer, but you can add these terms to an auxiliary dictionary so that they will not be flagged in the future. It will not, however, notice properly spelled words that are used incorrectly; for example, Two bee or knot too be is not the answer.

(a) The Text

FIGURE 1.9   The Spell Check

Word not found in the dictionary ———

Selected suggestion ———

Click here to substitute
selected suggestion ———

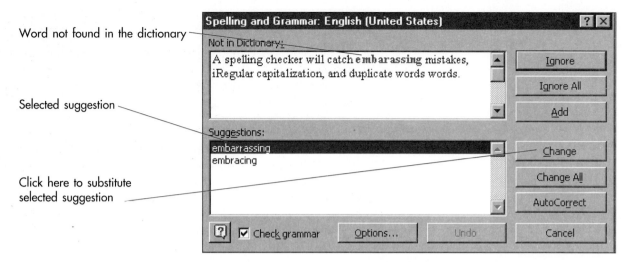

(b) Ordinary Misspelling

Irregular capitalization
is flagged as an error ———

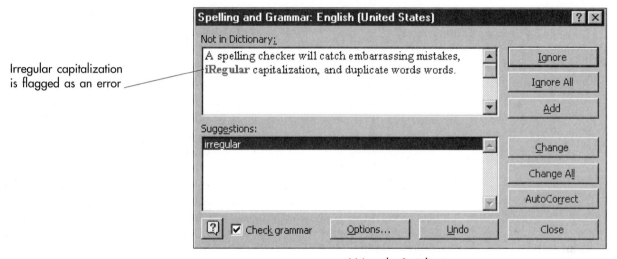

(c) Irregular Capitalization

Click here to delete
duplicated word ———

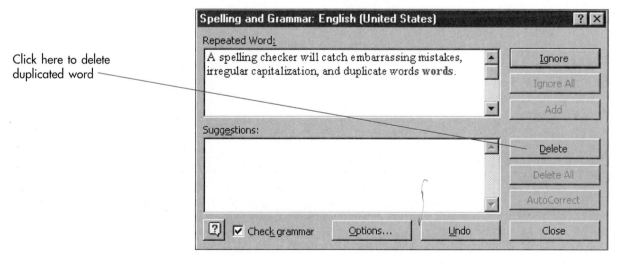

(d) Duplicated Word

FIGURE 1.9   The Spell Check (continued)

Click here to ignore word
as no correction is necessary

Click here to add word to
the custom dictionary

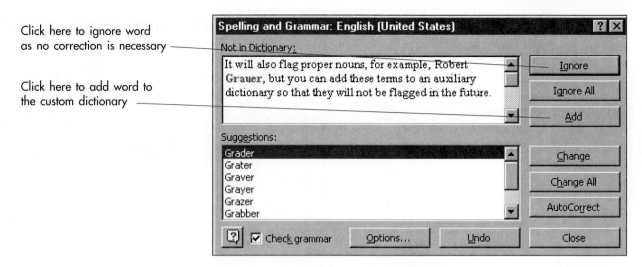

(e) Proper Noun

? represents unknown character

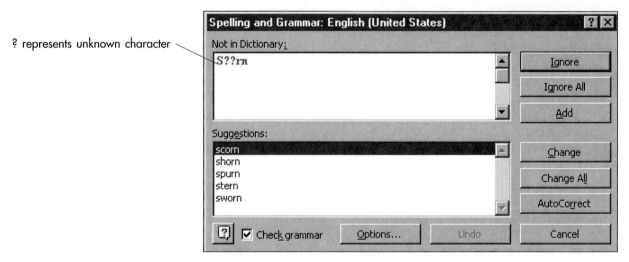

(f) Help with Crosswords

FIGURE 1.9   The Spell Check (continued)

AutoCorrect

The *AutoCorrect* feature corrects mistakes as they are made without any effort on your part. It makes you a better typist. If, for example, you typed *teh* instead of *the*, Word would change the spelling without even telling you. Word will also change *adn* to *and, i* to *I,* and *occurence* to *occurrence.*

Microsoft Word includes a predefined table of common mistakes and uses that table to make substitutions whenever it encounters an error it recognizes. You can add additional items to the table to include the frequent errors you make. You can also use the feature to define your own shorthand—for example, cis for Computer Information Systems as shown in Figure 1.10.

The AutoCorrect will also correct mistakes in capitalization; for example, it will capitalize the first letter in a sentence, recognize that MIami should be Miami, and capitalize the days of the week. It's even smart enough to correct the accidental use of the Caps Lock key, and it will toggle the key off!

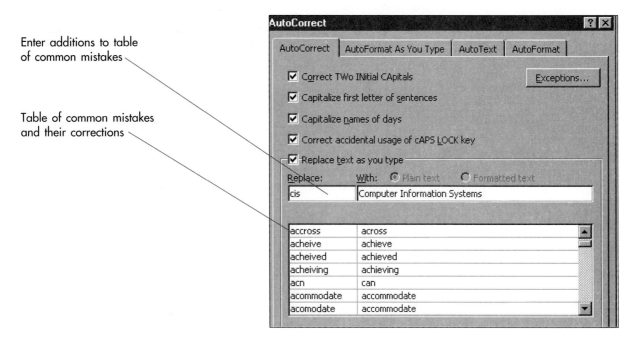

Enter additions to table of common mistakes

Table of common mistakes and their corrections

FIGURE 1.10   AutoCorrect

THESAURUS

Mark Twain said the difference between the right word and almost the right word is the difference between a lightning bug and lightning. The ***thesaurus*** is an important tool in any word processor and is both fun and educational. It helps you to avoid repetition, and it will polish your writing.

The thesaurus is called from the Language command in the Tools menu. You position the cursor at the appropriate word within the document, then invoke the thesaurus and follow your instincts. The thesaurus recognizes multiple meanings and forms of a word (for example, adjective, noun, and verb) as in Figure 1.11a, and (by double clicking) allows you to look up any listed meaning to produce additional choices as in Figure 1.11b. You can explore further alternatives by selecting a synonym and clicking the Look Up button. The thesaurus also provides a list of antonyms for most entries, as in Figure 1.11c.

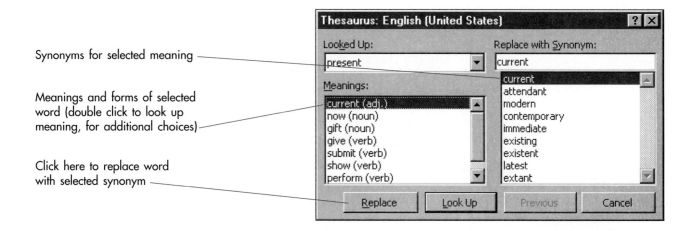

Synonyms for selected meaning

Meanings and forms of selected word (double click to look up meaning, for additional choices)

Click here to replace word with selected synonym

(a) Initial Word

FIGURE 1.11   The Thesaurus

Additional choices produced by
double clicking selected meaning

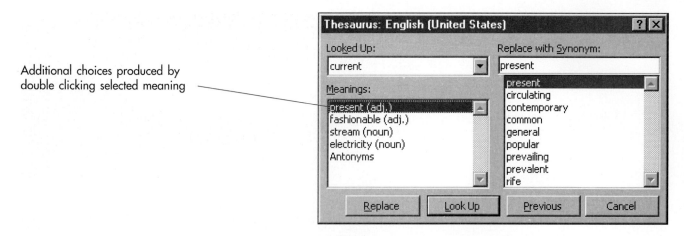

(b) Additional Choices

Antonyms for current word

Click here to see antonyms

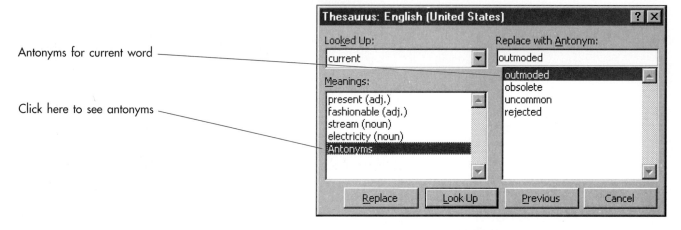

(c) Antonyms

FIGURE 1.11   The Thesaurus (continued)

GRAMMAR CHECK

The **grammar check** attempts to catch mistakes in punctuation, writing style, and word usage by comparing strings of text within a document to a series of predefined rules. As with the spell check, errors are brought to the screen where you can accept the suggested correction and make the replacement automatically, or more often, edit the selected text and make your own changes.

You can also ask the grammar check to explain the rule it is attempting to enforce. Unlike the spell check, the grammar check is subjective, and what seems appropriate to you may be objectionable to someone else. Indeed, the grammar check is quite flexible, and can be set to check for different writing styles; that is, you can implement one set of rules to check a business letter and a different set of rules for casual writing. Many times, however, you will find that the English language is just too complex for the grammar check to detect every error, although it will find many errors.

The grammar check caught the inconsistency between subject and verb in Figure 1.12a and suggested the appropriate correction (am instead of are). In Figure 1.12b, it suggested the elimination of the superfluous comma. These examples show the grammar check at its best, but it is often more subjective and less capable. It detected the error in Figure 1.12c, for example, but suggested an inappropriate correction, "to complicate" as opposed to "too complicated". Suffice it to say, that there is no substitute for carefully proofreading every document.

Suggested correction is appropriate

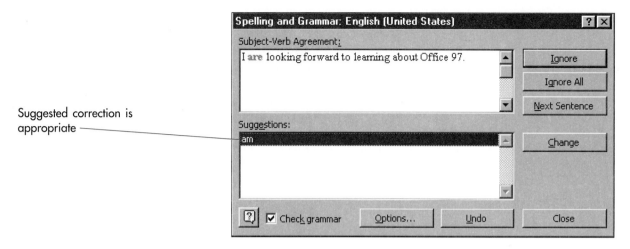

(a) Inconsistent Verb

Double punctuation is deleted

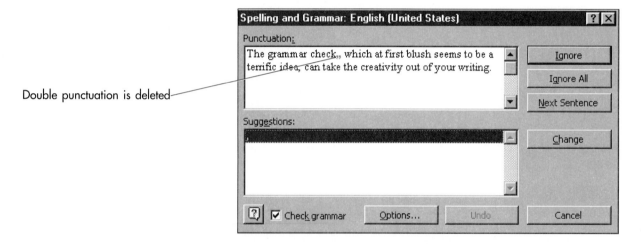

(b) Doubled Punctuation

Suggested correction is not appropriate

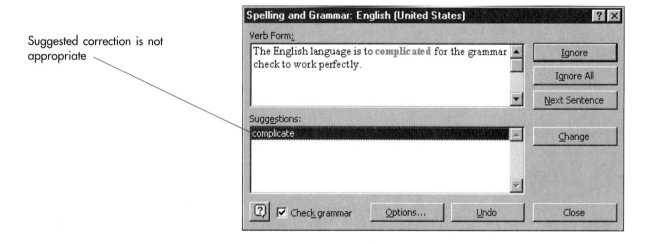

(c) Limitations

FIGURE 1.12   The Grammar Check

The Save command was used in the first two exercises. The Save As command will be introduced in the next exercise as a very useful alternative. We also introduce you to different backup options. We believe that now, when you are first starting to learn about word processing, is the time to develop good working habits.

You already know that the Save command copies the document currently being edited (the document in memory) to disk. The initial execution of the command requires you to assign a file name and to specify the drive and folder in which the file is to be stored. All subsequent executions of the Save command save the document under the original name, replacing the previously saved version with the new one.

The **Save As command** saves another copy of a document under a different name (and/or a different file type), and is useful when you want to retain a copy of the original document. The Save As command provides you with two copies of a document. The original document is kept on disk under its original name. A copy of the document is saved on disk under a new name and remains in memory. All subsequent editing is done on the new document.

We cannot overemphasize the importance of periodically saving a document, so that if something does go wrong, you won't lose all of your work. Nothing is more frustrating than to lose two hours of effort, due to an unexpected program crash or to a temporary loss of power. Save your work frequently, at least once every 15 minutes. Pull down the File menu and click Save, or click the Save button on the Standard toolbar. Do it!

QUIT WITHOUT SAVING

There will be times when you do not want to save the changes to a document, such as when you have edited it beyond recognition and wish you had never started. Pull down the File menu and click the Close command, then click No in response to the message asking whether you want to save the changes to the document. Pull down the File menu and reopen the file (it should be the first file in the list of most recently edited documents), then start over from the beginning.

Backup Options

Microsoft Word offers several different **backup** options. We believe the two most important options are to create a backup copy in conjunction with every save command, and to periodically (and automatically) save a document. Both options are implemented in step 3 in the next hands-on exercise.

Figure 1.13 illustrates the option to create a backup copy of the document every time a Save command is executed. Assume, for example, that you have created the simple document, *The fox jumped over the fence* and saved it under the name "Fox". Assume further that you edit the document to read, *The quick brown fox jumped over the fence,* and that you saved it a second time. The second save command changes the name of the original document from "Fox" to "Backup of Fox", then saves the current contents of memory as "Fox". In other words, the disk now contains two versions of the document: the current version "Fox" and the most recent previous version "Backup of Fox".

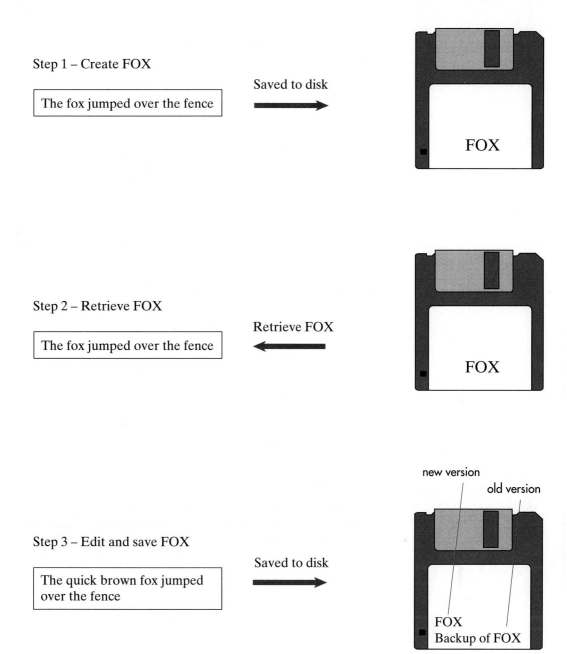

Step 1 – Create FOX

The fox jumped over the fence

Saved to disk

FOX

Step 2 – Retrieve FOX

The fox jumped over the fence

Retrieve FOX

FOX

Step 3 – Edit and save FOX

The quick brown fox jumped over the fence

Saved to disk

new version

old version

FOX
Backup of FOX

FIGURE 1.13   Backup Procedures

The cycle goes on indefinitely, with "Fox" always containing the current version, and "Backup of Fox" the most recent previous version. Thus if you revise and save the document a third time, "Fox" will contain the latest revision while "Backup of Fox" would contain the previous version alluding to the quick brown fox. The original (first) version of the document disappears entirely since only two versions are kept.

The contents of "Fox" and "Backup of Fox" are different, but the existence of the latter enables you to retrieve the previous version if you inadvertently edit beyond repair or accidentally erase the current "Fox" version. Should this occur (and it will), you can always retrieve its predecessor and at least salvage your work prior to the last save operation.

Objective: To open an existing document, check it for spelling, then use the Save As command to save the document under a different file name. Use Figure 1.14 as a guide in the exercise.

STEP 1: Preview a Document

➤ Start Microsoft Word. Pull down the **File menu** and click **Open** (or click the **Open button** on the Standard toolbar). You should see a dialog box similar to the one in Figure 1.14a.

➤ Select the appropriate drive, drive C or drive A, depending on the location of your data. Double click the **Exploring Word folder** to make it the active folder (the folder in which you will save the document).

➤ Scroll in the Name list box until you can select (click) the **Try the Spell Check** document. Click the **Preview button** on the toolbar to preview the document as shown in Figure 1.14a.

➤ Click the **Open command button** to open the file. Your document should appear on the screen.

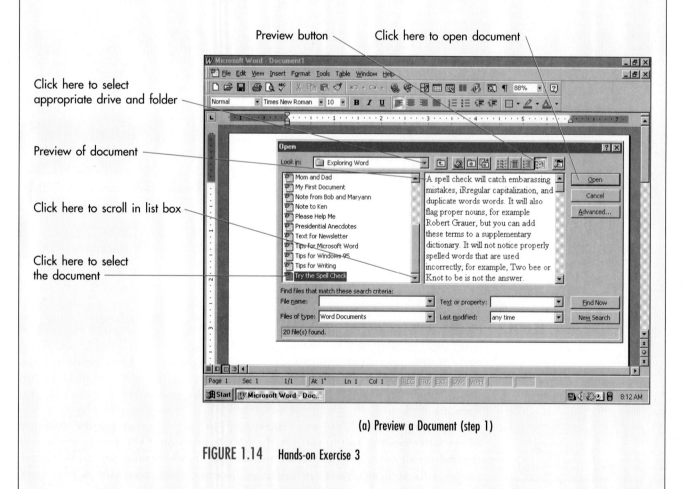

(a) Preview a Document (step 1)

FIGURE 1.14   Hands-on Exercise 3

STEP 2: The Save As Command

➤ Pull down the **File menu.** Click **Save As** to produce a dialog box in Figure 1.14b.

➤ Enter **Modified Spell Check** as the name of the new document. (A file name may contain up to 255 characters, and blanks are permitted.) Click the **Save command button.**

➤ There are now two identical copies of the file on disk: Try the Spell Check, which we supplied, and Modified Spell Check, which you just created. The title bar of the document window shows the latter name.

Click here to save the document under the new name

Enter new name for the document

Change file type for compatibility with Word 95

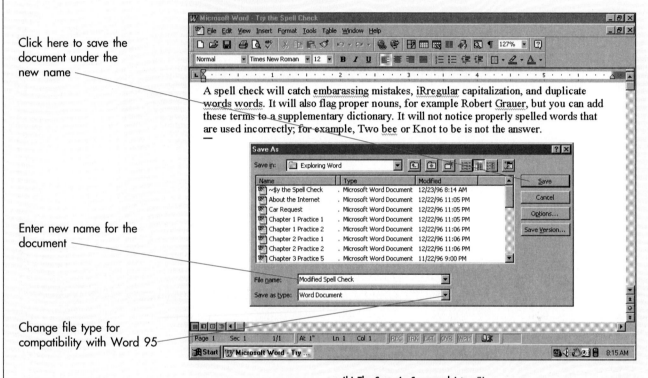

(b) The Save As Command (step 2)

FIGURE 1.14   Hands-on Exercise 3 (continued)

DIFFERENT FILE TYPES

The file format for Word 97 is incompatible with the format for Word 95. The newer release (Word 97) can open a document created in its predecessor (Word 95), but the reverse is not possible; that is, you cannot open a document created in Word 97 in Word 95. You can, however, use the Save As command in Word 97 to specify the Word 6.0/95 file type, enabling you to create a document in the new release and read it in the old (although you will lose any formatting unique to Word 97).

STEP 3: Establish Automatic Backup

➤ Pull down the **Tools menu.** Click **Options.** Click the **Save tab** to display the dialog box of Figure 1.14c.

➤ Click the first check box to choose **Always Create Backup Copy.**

➤ Set the other options as you see fit; for example, you can specify that the document be saved automatically every 10–15 minutes. Click **OK.**

Title bar reflects the new document

Click the Save tab

Click desired options

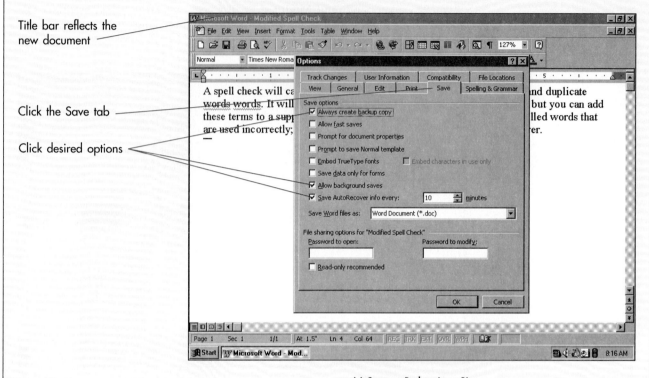

(c) Create a Backup (step 3)

FIGURE 1.14   Hands-on Exercise 3 (continued)

STEP 4: The Spell Check

➤ If necessary, press **Ctrl+Home** to move to the beginning of the document. Click the **Spelling and Grammar button** on the Standard toolbar to check the document.

➤ "Embarassing" is flagged as the first misspelling as shown in Figure 1.14d. Click the **Change button** to accept the suggested spelling.

➤ "iRregular" is flagged as an example of irregular capitalization. Click the **Change button** to accept the suggested correction.

➤ Continue checking the document, which displays misspellings and other irregularities one at a time. Click the appropriate command button as each mistake is found.

• Click the **Delete button** to remove the duplicated word.

• Click the **Ignore button** to accept Grauer (or click the **Add button** to add Grauer to the custom dictionary).

➤ The grammar check is illustrated in step 5.

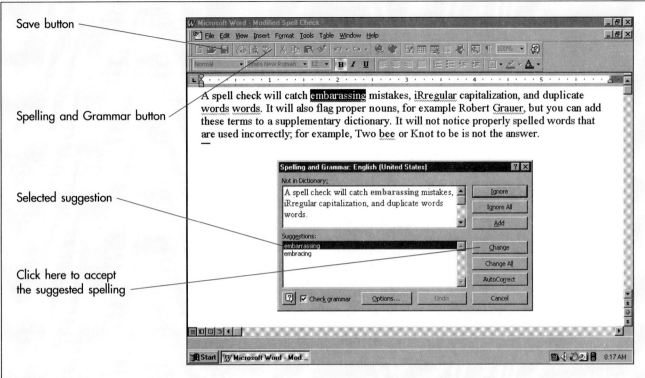

Save button

Spelling and Grammar button

Selected suggestion

Click here to accept
the suggested spelling

(d) The Spell Check (step 4)

FIGURE 1.14   Hands-on Exercise 3 (continued)

AUTOMATIC SPELLING AND GRAMMAR CHECKING

Red and green wavy lines may appear throughout a document to indicate spelling and grammatical errors, respectively. Point to any underlined word, then click the right mouse button to display a context-sensitive help menu with suggested corrections. To enable (disable) these options, pull down the Tools menu, click the Options command, click the Spelling and Grammar tab, and check (clear) the options to check spelling (or grammar) as you type.

STEP 5: The Grammar Check

➤ The last sentence, "Two bee or knot to be is not the answer", should be flagged as an error, as shown in Figure 1.14e. If this is not the case:

- Pull down the **Tools menu,** click **Options,** then click the **Spelling and Grammar tab.**

- Check the box to **Check Grammar with Spelling,** then click the button to **Recheck document.** Click **Yes** when told that the spelling and grammar check will be reset, then click **OK** to close the Options dialog box.

- Press **Ctrl+Home** to return to the beginning of the document, then click the **Spelling and Grammar button** to recheck the document.

➤ Click the **Assistant button** in the Spelling and Grammar dialog box for an explanation of the error. The Office Assistant will appear, indicating that

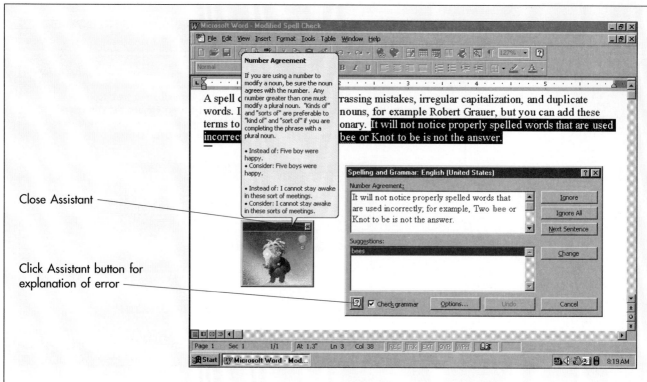

Close Assistant

Click Assistant button for explanation of error

(e) The Grammar Check (step 5)

FIGURE 1.14   Hands-on Exercise 3 (continued)

there needs to be number agreement between subject and verb. Close the Office Assistant after you have read the explanation.

➤ Click **Ignore** to reject the suggestion. Click **OK** when you see the dialog box, indicating the spelling and grammar check is complete.

CHECK SPELLING ONLY

The grammar check is invoked by default in conjunction with the spell check. You can, however, check the spelling of a document without checking its grammar. Pull down the Tools menu, click Options to display the Options dialog box, then click the Spelling and Grammar tab. Clear the box to check grammar with spelling, then click OK to accept the change and close the dialog box.

STEP 6: The Thesaurus

➤ Select (click) the word *incorrectly,* which appears on the last line of your document as shown in Figure 1.14f.

➤ Pull down the **Tools menu,** click **Language,** then click **Thesaurus** to display synonyms for the word you selected.

➤ Select (click) *inaccurately,* the synonym you will use in place of the original word. Click the **Replace button** to make the change automatically.

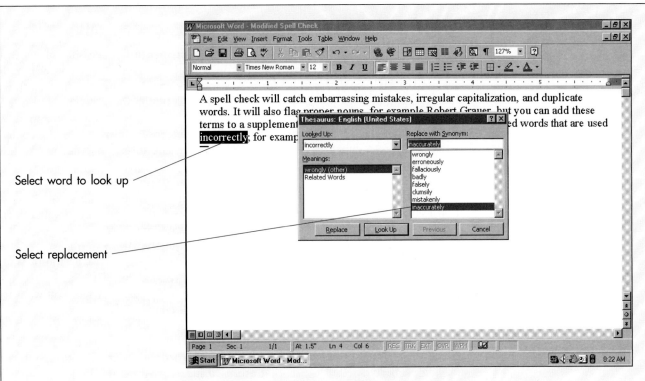

Select word to look up

Select replacement

(f) The Thesaurus (step 6)

FIGURE 1.14   Hands-on Exercise 3 (continued)

STEP 7: AutoCorrect

➤ Press **Ctrl+Home** to move to the beginning of the document.

➤ Type the *misspelled* phrase **Teh Spell Check was used to check this document.** Try to look at the monitor as you type to see the AutoCorrect feature in action; Word will correct the misspelling and change *Teh* to *The*.

➤ If you did not see the correction being made, click the arrow next to the Undo command on the Standard toolbar and undo the last several actions. Click the arrow next to the Redo command and redo the corrections.

➤ Save the document.

CREATE YOUR OWN SHORTHAND

Use AutoCorrect to expand abbreviations such as "usa" for United States of America. Pull down the Tools menu, click AutoCorrect, type the abbreviation in the Replace text box and the expanded entry in the With text box. Click the Add command button, then click OK to exit the dialog box and return to the document. The next time you type usa in a document, it will automatically be expanded to United States of America.

STEP 8: Exit Word

➤ Pull down the **File menu.** Click **Exit** to exit Word.

The chapter provided a broad-based introduction to word processing in general and to Microsoft Word in particular. Help is available from many sources. You can use the Help menu or the Office Assistant as you can in any Office application. You can also go to the Microsoft Web site to obtain more recent, and often more detailed, information.

Microsoft Word is always in one of two modes, insert or overtype; the choice between the two depends on the desired editing. The insertion point marks the place within a document where text is added or replaced.

The enter key is pressed at the end of a paragraph, but not at the end of a line because Word automatically wraps text from one line to the next. A hard return is created by the user when he or she presses the enter key; a soft return is created by Word as it wraps text and begins a new line.

The Save and Open commands work in conjunction with one another. The Save command copies the document in memory to disk under its existing name. The Open command retrieves a previously saved document. The Save As command saves the document under a different name and is useful when you want to retain a copy of the current document prior to all changes.

A spell check compares the words in a document to those in a standard and/or custom dictionary and offers suggestions to correct the mistakes it finds. It will detect misspellings, duplicated phrases, and/or irregular capitalization, but will not flag properly spelled words that are used incorrectly.

The AutoCorrect feature corrects predefined spelling errors and/or mistakes in capitalization, automatically, as the words are entered. The feature can also be used to create a personal shorthand as it will expand abbreviations as they are typed.

The thesaurus suggests synonyms and/or antonyms. It can also recognize multiple forms of a word (noun, verb, and adjective) and offer suggestions for each. The grammar check searches for mistakes in punctuation, writing style, and word usage by comparing strings of text within a document to a series of predefined rules.

KEY WORDS AND CONCEPTS

AutoCorrect	Office Assistant	Status bar
Backup	Open command	Text box
Custom dictionary	Overtype mode	Thesaurus
File menu	Page Layout view	Toggle switch
Formatting toolbar	Save As command	Toolbar
Grammar check	Save command	Undo command
Hard return	ScreenTip	Vertical ruler
Horizontal ruler	Show/Hide ¶ button	View menu
Insert mode	Soft return	Word wrap
Insertion point	Spell check	
Normal view	Standard toolbar	

Practice with Word 97

1. Retrieve the *Chapter1 Practice 1* document shown in Figure 1.15 from the Exploring Word folder, then make the following changes:

   a. Select the text *Your name* and replace it with your name.

   b. Replace *May 31, 1997* with the current date.

   c. Insert the phrase *one or* in line 2 so that the text reads ... *one or more characters than currently exist.*

   d. Delete the word *And* from sentence four in line 5, then change the w in *when* to a capital letter to begin the sentence.

   e. Change the phrase *most efficient* to *best.*

   f. Place the insertion point at the end of sentence 2, make sure you are in the insert mode, then add the following sentence: *The insert mode adds characters at the insertion point while moving existing text to the right in order to make room for the new text.*

   g. Press Ctrl+End to position the insertion point at the end of the last sentence, press the enter key twice in a row, then enter the following text: *There are several keys that function as toggle switches of which you should be aware. The Caps Lock key toggles between upper- and lowercase letters, and the Num Lock key alternates between typing numbers and using the arrow keys.*

   h. Save the revised document, then print it and submit it to your instructor as proof you did the exercise.

To: Your Name

From: Robert Grauer and Maryann Barber

Subject: Microsoft Word for Windows

Date: May 31, 1997

This is just a short note to help you get acquainted with the insertion and replacement modes in Word for Windows. When the editing to be done results in more characters than currently exist, you want to be in the insertion mode when making the change. On the other hand, when the editing to be done contains the same or fewer characters, the replacement mode is best. And when replacing characters, it is most efficient to use the mouse to select the characters to be deleted and then just type the new characters; the selected characters are automatically deleted and the new characters typed take their place.

FIGURE 1.15   Document for Practice Exercise 1

2. Select-then-do: Formatting is not covered until Chapter 2, but we think you are ready to try your hand at basic formatting now. Most formatting operations are done in the context of select-then-do as described in the document in Figure 1.16. You select the text you want to format, then you execute the appropriate formatting command, most easily by clicking the appropriate button on the Formatting toolbar. The function of each button should be apparent from its icon, but you can simply point to a button to display a ScreenTip that is indicative of the button's function.

An unformatted version of the document in Figure 1.16 exists on the data disk as *Chapter1 Practice 2*. Open the document, then format it to match the completed version in Figure 1.16. Just select the text to format, then click the appropriate button. We changed type size in the original document to 24 points for the title and 12 points for text in the document itself. Be sure to add your name and date as shown in the figure.

Select-Then-Do

Many operations in Word are executed as select-then-do operations. You first select a block of text, then you issue a command that will affect the selected text. You may select the text in many different ways, the most basic of which is to click and drag over the desired characters. You may also take one of many shortcuts, which include double clicking on a word, pressing Ctrl as you click a sentence, and triple clicking on a paragraph.

Once text is selected, you may then delete it, **boldface** or *italicize* it, or even change its color. You may move it or copy it to another location, in the same or a different document. You can highlight it, underline, or even check its spelling. Then, depending on whether or not you like what you have done, you may undo it, redo it, and/or repeat it on subsequently selected text.

Jessica Kinzer
September 1, 1997

FIGURE 1.16   Document for Practice Exercise 2

3. Your background: Write a short description of your computer background similar to the document in Figure 1.17. Indicate whether you own a PC, whether you have access to one at work, and/or whether you are considering purchase. Include any other information you wish about yourself and/or your computer-related background.

Place your name somewhere in the document in boldface italics. We would also like you to use boldface and italics to emphasize the components of any computer system you describe. Use any font or point size you like. Note, too, the last paragraph, which asks you to print the summary statistics for the document when you submit the assignment to your instructor. (Use the tip on Document Properties on page 25 to print the total editing time and other information about your document.)

The Computer and Me

My name is Jessica Kinzer and I am a complete novice when it comes to computers. I did not take a computer course in high school and this is my first semester at the University of Miami. My family does not own a computer, nor have I had the opportunity to use one at work. So when it comes to beginners, I am a beginner's beginner. I am looking forward to taking this course, as I have heard that it will truly make me computer literate. I know that I desperately need computer skills not only when I enter the job market, but to survive my four years here as well. I am looking forward to learning Word, Excel, and PowerPoint and I hope that I can pick up some Internet skills as well.

I did not buy a computer before I came to school as I wanted to see what type of system I would be using for my classes. After my first few weeks in class, I think that I would like to buy a *200 Mz Pentium* machine with *32Mb RAM* and a *3 Gb hard drive.* I would like a *12X speed CD-ROM* and a *sound card* (with *speakers,* of course). I also would like to get a *laser printer.* Now, if only I had the money.

This document did not take long at all to create as you can see by the summary statistics that are printed on the next page. I think I will really enjoy this class.

Jessica Kinzer
March 2, 1997

FIGURE 1.17   Document for Practice Exercise 3

4. The cover page: Create a cover page that you can use for your assignments this semester. Your cover page should be similar to the one in Figure 1.18 with respect to content and should include the title of the assignment, your name, course information, and date. The formatting is up to you.

    Print the completed cover page and submit it to your instructor for inclusion in a class contest to judge the most innovative design. If you are ambitious, read ahead to Chapter 3 to learn how to insert clip art into a document. You can create some very attractive pages.

5. Figure 1.19 contains the draft version of the *Chapter 1 Practice 5* document contained on the data disk.
    a. Proofread the document and circle any mistakes in spelling, grammar, capitalization, or punctuation.
    b. Open the document in Word and run the spell check. Did Word catch any mistakes you missed? Did you find any errors that were missed by the program?
    c. Use the thesaurus to come up with alternative words for *document,* which appears entirely too often within the paragraph.
    d. Run the grammar check on the revised document. Did the program catch any grammatical errors you missed? Did you find any mistakes that were missed by the program?
    e. Add your name to the revised document, save it, print it, and submit the completed document to your instructor.

Exploring Word Assignment

Jessica Kinzer
CIS 120
September 1, 1997

FIGURE 1.18 Document for Practice Exercise 4

The Grammar Check

All documents should be thoroughly proofed before they be printed and distributed. This means that documents, at a minimum should be spell cheked,, grammar cheked, and proof read by the author. A documents that has spelling errors and/or grammatical errors makes the Author look unprofessional and illiterate and their is nothing worse than allowing a first impression too be won that makes you appear slopy and disinterested, and a document full or of misteakes will do exactly that. Alot of people do not not realize how damaging a bad first impression could be, and documents full of misteakes has cost people oppurtunities that they trained and prepared many years for.

Microsoft Word includes an automated grammar check that will detect many, but certainly not all, errors as the previous paragraph demonstrates. Unlike the spell check, the grammar check is subjective, and what seems appropriate to you may be objectionable to someone else. The English language is just to complicated for the grammar check to detect every error, or even most errors. Hence there is no substitute for carefully proof reading a document your self. Hence there is no substitute for carefully proof reading a document your self.

FIGURE 1.19 Document for Practice Exercise 5

6. The document in Figure 1.20 illustrates a new feature in Office 97 in which all applications automatically detect any hyperlinks that are embedded in a document. All you need to do is enter the link, and the application automatically converts it to a hyperlink. You can then click on the link to open Internet Explorer and display the associated Web page, provided you have an Internet connection. See for yourself by creating the document in Figure 1.20 and submitting it to your instructor.

As indicated, Word will, by default, convert any Internet path (e.g., any text beginning with http:// or www) to a hyperlink. If this is not the case, pull down the Tools menu, click AutoCorrect, then click the AutoFormat-as-you-Type tab. Check the box in the Replace-as-you-Type area for Internet and Network paths. Click OK. The next time you enter a Web or e-mail address, it will be converted automatically to a hyperlink.

It's Web-Enabled

Perhaps the most significant change in Office 97 is that every document is Web-enabled, meaning that the application will automatically detect and highlight any hyperlinks that appear in a document. This sentence, for example, contains the Web address, www.microsoft.com, which is highlighted in blue just as it might appear in a regular Web document. We did not do anything special to create the hyperlink; that is, we simply typed the address, and Word in turn created the hyperlink.

You can click the link from within Word, and provided you have an Internet connection, your Web browser will display the associated page. Note, too, that once you click the link, its color will change (e.g., from blue to magenta) just as it would if you were viewing the page in Netscape or the Internet Explorer. Prove to your instructor that you have done this exercise by creating this document, then adding a paragraph or two that reference your favorite Web pages.

FIGURE 1.20 Document for Practice Exercise 6

7. Webster Online: Figure 1.21 shows our favorite online dictionary, which is accessed most easily by clicking the Search button in Internet Explorer, then clicking the link to Definitions and Quotes. Enter the word you want to look up (*oxymoron,* for example), then press the Look Up Word button to display the definition in Figure 1.21. This is truly an interactive dictionary because most words in it are created as hyperlinks, which in turn will lead you to other definitions. Use the dictionary to look up the meaning of the word *palindrome.* How many examples of oxymorons and palindromes can you think of?

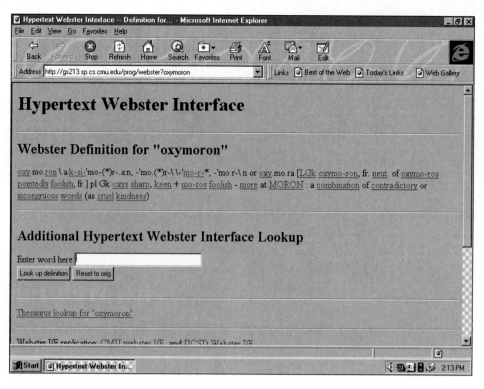

FIGURE 1.21 Screen for Practice Exercise 7

GAINING PROFICIENCY: EDITING AND FORMATTING

OBJECTIVES

After reading this chapter you will be able to:

1. Define the select-then-do methodology; describe several shortcuts with the mouse and/or the keyboard to select text.
2. Use the clipboard and/or the drag-and-drop capability to move and copy text within a document.
3. Use the Find, Replace, and Go To commands to substitute one character string for another.
4. Define scrolling; scroll to the beginning and end of a document.
5. Distinguish between the Normal and Page Layout views; state how to change the view and/or magnification of a document.
6. Define typography; distinguish between a serif and a sans serif typeface; use the Format Font command to change the font and/or type size.
7. Use the Format Paragraph command to change line spacing, alignment, tabs, and indents, and to control pagination.
8. Use the Borders and Shading command to box and shade text.
9. Describe the Undo and Redo commands and how they are related to one another.
10. Use the Page Setup command to change the margins and/or orientation; differentiate between a soft and a hard page break.

OVERVIEW

The previous chapter taught you the basics of Microsoft Word and enabled you to create and print a simple document. The present chapter significantly extends your capabilities, by presenting a variety of commands to change the contents and appearance of a document. These operations are known as editing and formatting, respectively.

You will learn how to move and copy text within a document and how to find and replace one character string with another. You will also learn the basics of typography and be able to switch between the different fonts included within Windows. You will be able to change alignment, indentation, line spacing, margins, and page orientation. All of these commands are used in three hands-on exercises, which require your participation at the computer, and which are the very essence of the chapter.

As you read the chapter, realize that there are many different ways to accomplish the same task and that it would be impossible to cover them all. Our approach is to present the overall concepts and suggest the ways we think are most appropriate at the time we introduce the material. We also offer numerous shortcuts in the form of boxed tips that appear throughout the chapter and urge you to explore further on your own. It is not necessary for you to memorize anything as online help is always available. Be flexible and willing to experiment.

WRITE NOW, EDIT LATER

You write a sentence, then change it, and change it again, and one hour later you've produced a single paragraph. It happens to every writer—you stare at a blank screen and flashing cursor and are unable to write. The best solution is to brainstorm and write down anything that pops into your head, and to keep on writing. Don't worry about typos or spelling errors because you can fix them later. Above all, resist the temptation to continually edit the few words you've written because overediting will drain the life out of what you are writing. The important thing is to get your ideas on paper.

SELECT-THEN-DO

Many operations in Word take place within the context of a *select-then-do* methodology; that is, you select a block of text, then you execute the command to operate on that text. The most basic way to select text is by dragging the mouse; that is, click at the beginning of the selection, press and hold the left mouse button as you move to the end of the selection, then release the mouse.

There are, however, a variety of shortcuts to facilitate the process; for example, double click anywhere within a word to select the word, or press the Ctrl key and click the mouse anywhere within a sentence to select the sentence. Additional shortcuts are presented in each of the hands-on exercises, at which point you will have many opportunities to practice selecting text.

Selected text is affected by any subsequent operation; for example, clicking the Bold or Italic button changes the selected text to boldface or italics, respectively. You can also drag the selected text to a new location, press the Del key to erase the selected text, or execute any other editing or formatting command. The text continues to be selected until you click elsewhere in the document.

THE RIGHT MOUSE BUTTON

Point anywhere within a document, then click the right mouse button to display a shortcut menu. Shortcut menus contain commands appropriate to the item you have selected. Click in the menu to execute a command, or click outside the menu to close the menu without executing a command.

MOVING AND COPYING TEXT

The ability to move and/or copy text is essential in order to develop any degree of proficiency in editing. A move operation removes the text from its current location and places it elsewhere in the same (or even a different) document; a copy operation retains the text in its present location and places a duplicate elsewhere. Either operation can be accomplished using the Windows clipboard and a combination of the **Cut, Copy,** and **Paste commands.** (A shortcut, using the mouse to **drag-and-drop** text from one location to another, is described in step 8 in the first hands-on exercise.)

The **clipboard** is a temporary storage area available to any Windows application. Selected text is cut or copied from a document and placed onto the clipboard from where it can be pasted to a new location(s). A move requires that you select the text and execute a Cut command to remove the text from the document and place it on the clipboard. You then move the insertion point to the new location and paste the text from the clipboard into that location. A copy operation necessitates the same steps except that a Copy command is executed rather than a cut, leaving the selected text in its original location as well as placing a copy on the clipboard.

The Cut, Copy, and Paste commands are found in the Edit menu, or alternatively, can be executed by clicking the appropriate buttons on the Standard toolbar. The contents of the clipboard are replaced by each subsequent Cut or Copy command, but are unaffected by the Paste command; that is, the contents of the clipboard can be pasted into multiple locations in the same or different documents.

DELETE WITH CAUTION

You work too hard developing your thoughts to see them disappear in a flash. Hence, instead of deleting large blocks of text, try moving them to the end of your document (or even a new document) from where they can be recalled later if you change your mind. A related practice is to remain in the insert mode (as opposed to overtype) to prevent the inadvertent deletion of existing text as new ideas are added.

UNDO AND REDO COMMANDS

The **Undo command** was introduced in Chapter 1, but it is repeated here because it is so valuable. The command is executed from the Edit menu or by clicking the Undo button on the Standard toolbar. Word enables you to undo up to the last 100 changes to a document. You just click the arrow next to the Undo button on the Standard toolbar to display a reverse-order list of your previous commands, then you click the command you want to undo, which also undoes all of the preceding commands. Undoing the fifth command in the list, for example, will also undo the preceding four commands.

The **Redo command** redoes (reverses) the last command that was undone. As with the Undo command, the Redo command redoes all of the previous commands prior to the command you select. Redoing the fifth command in the list, for example, will also redo the preceding four commands. The Undo and Redo commands work in conjunction with one another; that is, every time a command is undone it can be redone at a later time.

FIND, REPLACE, AND GO TO COMMANDS

The Find, Replace, and Go To commands share a common dialog box with different tabs for each command as shown in Figure 2.1. The **Find command** locates one or more occurrences of specific text (e.g., a word or phrase). The **Replace command** goes one step further in that it locates the text, and then enables you to optionally replace (one or more occurrences of) that text with different text. The **Go To command** goes directly to a specific place (e.g., a specific page) in the document.

Search text ———

Search will be case-sensitive (will not find *There* or *THERE*) ———

Search will find whole words only (will not find *therefore* or *thereby*) ———

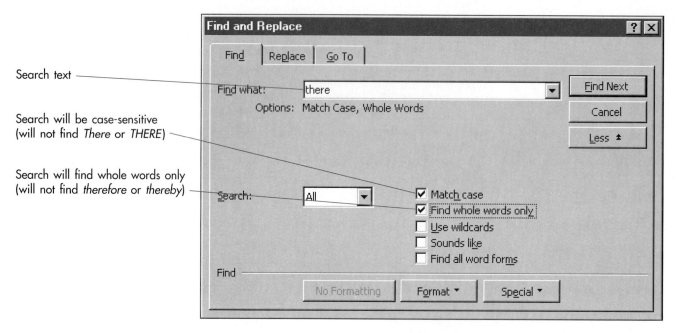

(a) Find Command

Search text ———

Replacement text ———

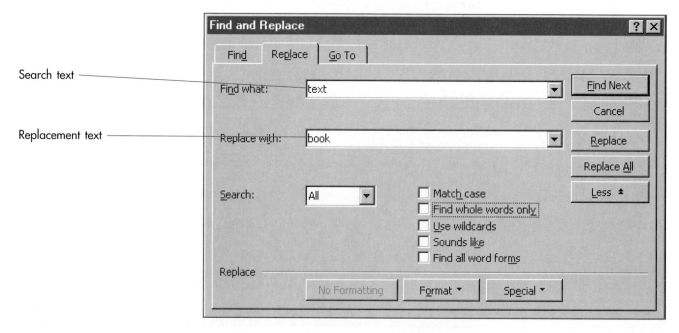

(b) Replace Command

FIGURE 2.1   The Find, Replace, and Go To Commands

Page to go to

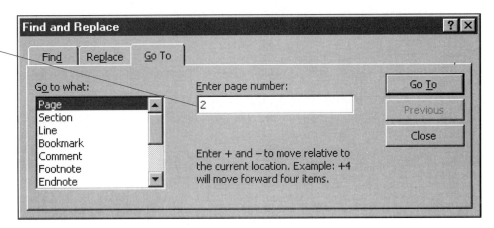

(c) Go To Command

FIGURE 2.1   The Find, Replace, and Go To Commands (continued)

The search in both the Find and Replace commands is case-sensitive or case-insensitive. A ***case-sensitive search*** (where Match Case is selected as in Figure 2.1a) matches not only the text, but also the use of upper- and lowercase letters. Thus, *There* is different from *there,* and a search on one will not identify the other. A ***case-sensitive search*** (where Match Case is *not* as selected in Figure 2.1b) is just the opposite and finds both *There* and *there.* A search may also specify ***whole words only*** to identify *there,* but not *therefore* or *thereby.* And finally, the search and replacement text can also specify different numbers of characters; for example, you could replace *16* with *sixteen.*

The Replace command in Figure 2.1b implements either ***selective replacement,*** which lets you examine each occurrence of the character string in context and decide whether to replace it, or ***automatic replacement,*** where the substitution is made automatically. Selective replacement is implemented by clicking the Find Next command button, then clicking (or not clicking) the Replace button to make the substitution. Automatic replacement (through the entire document) is implemented by clicking the Replace All button. This often produces unintended consequences and is not recommended; for example, if you substitute the word *text* for *book,* the phrase *text book* would become *text text,* which is not what you had in mind.

The Find and Replace commands can include formatting and/or special characters. You can, for example, change all italicized text to boldface, or you can change five consecutive spaces to a tab character. You can also use ***wild cards*** in the character string. For example, to find all four-letter words that begin with "f" and end with "l" (such as *fall, fill,* or *fail*), search for f??l. (The question mark stands for any character, just like a wild card in a card game.) You can also search for all forms of a word; for example, if you specify *am,* it will also find *is* and *are.* You can even search for a word based on how it sounds. When searching for *Marion,* for example, check the Sounds Like check box, and the search will find both *Marion* and *Marian.*

SCROLLING

Scrolling occurs when a document is too large to be seen in its entirety. Figure 2.2a displays a large printed document, only part of which is visible on the screen as illustrated in Figure 2.2b. In order to see a different portion of the document, you need to scroll, whereby new lines will be brought into view as the old lines disappear.

To: Our Students
From: Robert Grauer and Maryann Barber

Welcome to the wonderful world of word processing. Over the next several chapters we will build a foundation in the basics of Microsoft Word, then teach you to format specialized documents, create professional looking tables and charts, and produce well-designed newsletters. Before you know it, you will be a word processing and desktop publishing wizard!

The first chapter presented the basics of word processing and showed you how to create a simple document. You learned how to insert, replace, and/or delete text. This chapter will teach you about fonts and special effects (such as boldfacing and italicizing) and how to use them effectively — how too little is better than too much.

You will go on to experiment with margins, tab stops, line spacing, and justification, learning first to format simple documents and then going on to longer, more complex ones. It is with the latter that we explore headers and footers, page numbering, widows and orphans (yes, we really did mean widows and orphans). It is here that we bring in graphics, working with newspaper-type columns, and the elements of a good page design. And without question, we will introduce the tools that make life so much easier (and your writing so much more impressive) — the Speller, Grammar Checker, Thesaurus, Glossaries, and Styles.

If you are wondering what all these things are, read on in the text and proceed with the hands-on exercises. Create a simple newsletter, then really knock their socks off by adding graphics, fonts, and WordArt. Create a simple calendar and then create more intricate forms that no one will believe were done by little old you. Create a resume with your beginner's skills, and then make it look like so much more with your intermediate (even advanced) skills. Last, but not least, run a mail merge to produce the cover letters that will accompany your resume as it is mailed to companies across the United States (and even the world).

It is up to you to practice, for it is only through working at the computer that you will learn what you need to know. Experiment and don't be afraid to make mistakes. Practice and practice some more.

Our goal is for you to learn and to enjoy what you are learning. We have great confidence in you, and in our ability to help you discover what you can do. You can visit the home page for the *Exploring Windows* series at www.prenhall.com/grauer. You can also send us e-mail. Bob's address is rgrauer@umiami.miami.edu. Maryann's address is mbarber@homer.bus.miami.edu. As you read the last sentence, notice that Word 97 is Web-enabled and that the Internet and e-mail references appear as hyperlinks in this document. You can click the address of our home page from within Word and your browser will display the page, provided you have an Internet connection. You can also click the e-mail address to open your mail program, provided it has been configured correctly.

We look forward to hearing from you and hope that you will like our textbook. You are about to embark on a wonderful journey toward computer literacy. Be patient and inquisitive.

(a) Printed Document

FIGURE 2.2   Scrolling

Scroll box is midway within the vertical scroll bar

Hyperlink is underlined and in color

Click e-mail address to send a message

Horizontal scroll bar

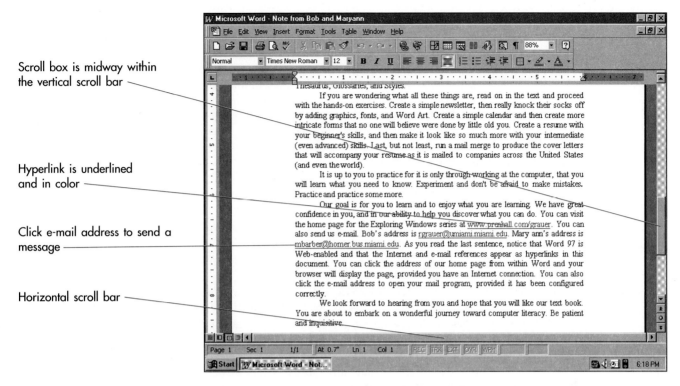

(b) Screen Display

FIGURE 2.2 Scrolling (continued)

Scrolling comes about automatically as you reach the bottom of the screen. Entering a new line of text, clicking on the down arrow within the scroll bar, or pressing the down arrow key brings a new line into view at the bottom of the screen and simultaneously removes a line at the top. (The process is reversed at the top of the screen.)

Scrolling can be done with either the mouse or the keyboard. Scrolling with the mouse (e.g., clicking the down arrow in the scroll bar) changes what is displayed on the screen, but does not move the insertion point, so that you must click the mouse after scrolling prior to entering the text at the new location. Scrolling with the keyboard, however (e.g., pressing Ctrl+Home or Ctrl+End to move to the beginning or end of a document, respectively), changes what is displayed on the screen as well as the location of the insertion point, and you can begin typing immediately.

Scrolling occurs most often in a vertical direction as shown in Figure 2.2. It can also occur horizontally, when the length of a line in a document exceeds the number of characters that can be displayed horizontally on the screen.

IT'S WEB ENABLED

Every document in Office 97 is Web-enabled, which means that Internet and e-mail references appear as hyperlinks within a document. Thus you can click the address of any Web page from within Word and your browser will display the page, provided you have an Internet connection. You can also click the e-mail address to open your mail program, provided it has been configured correctly.

The **View menu** provides different views of a document. Each view can be displayed at different magnifications, which in turn determine the amount of scrolling necessary to see remote parts of a document.

The **Normal view** is the default view and it provides the fastest way to enter text. The **Page Layout** view more closely resembles the printed document and displays the top and bottom margins, headers and footers, page numbers, graphics, and other features that do not appear in the Normal view. The Normal view tends to be faster because Word spends less time formatting the display.

The **Zoom command** displays the document on the screen at different magnifications; for example, 75%, 100%, or 200%. (The Zoom command does not affect the size of the text on the printed page.) A Zoom percentage (magnification) of 100% displays the document in the approximate size of the text on the printed page. You can increase the percentage to 200% to make the characters appear larger. You can also decrease the magnification to 75% to see more of the document at one time.

Word will automatically determine the magnification if you select one of three additional Zoom options—Page Width, Whole Page, or Many Pages (Whole Page and Many Pages are available only in the Page Layout view). Figure 2.3a, for example, displays a two-page document in Page Layout view. Figure 2.3b shows the corresponding settings in the Zoom command. (The 37% magnification is determined automatically once you specify the number of pages as shown in the figure.)

Click to change Zoom percentage

Top and bottom margins are displayed

Click here to change to Page Layout view

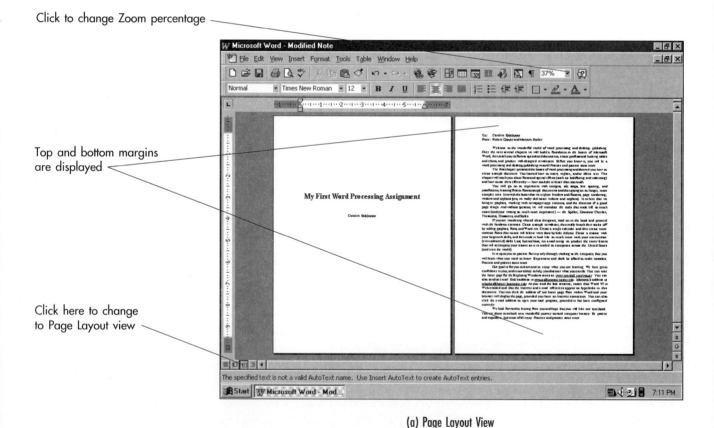

(a) Page Layout View

FIGURE 2.3   View Menu and Zoom Command

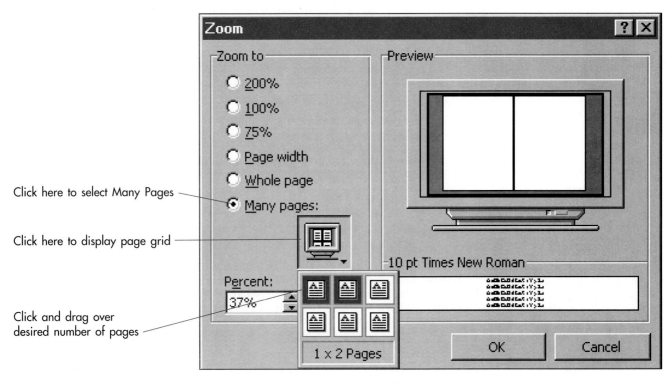

Click here to select Many Pages

Click here to display page grid

Click and drag over
desired number of pages

(b) Zoom Command

FIGURE 2.3   View Menu and Zoom Command (continued)

HANDS-ON EXERCISE 1

Editing a Document

Objective: To edit an existing document; to change the view and magnification of a document; to scroll through a document. To use the Find and Replace commands; to move and copy text using the clipboard and the drag-and-drop facility. Use Figure 2.4 as a guide in the exercise.

STEP 1: View Menu and Zoom Command

➤ Start Word as described in the hands-on exercises from Chapter 1. Pull down the **File menu** and click **Open** (or click the **Open button** on the toolbar).

  • Click the **drop-down arrow** on the Look In list box. Click the appropriate drive, drive C or drive A, depending on the location of your data.

  • Double click the **Exploring Word folder** to make it the active folder (the folder in which you will save the document).

  • Scroll in the Name list box (if necessary) until you can click the **Note from Bob and Maryann** to select this document. Double click the **document icon** or click the **Open command button** to open the file.

➤ The document should appear on the screen as shown in Figure 2.4a.

➤ Change to the Page Layout view at Page Width magnification:

  • Pull down the **View menu** and click **Page Layout** (or click the **Page Layout button** above the status bar) as shown in Figure 2.4a.

  • Click the **down arrow** in the Zoom box to change to **Page Width.**

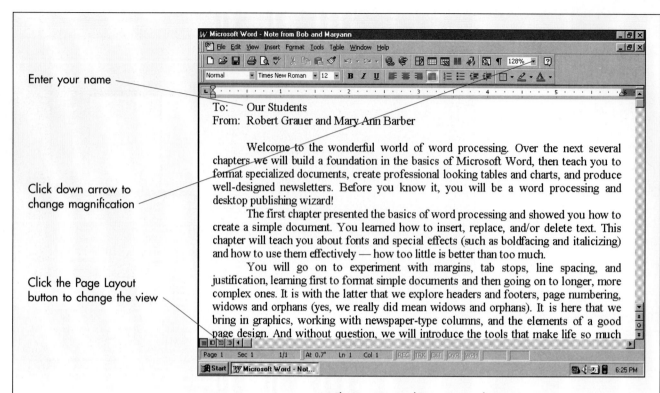

Enter your name

Click down arrow to change magnification

Click the Page Layout button to change the view

(a) The View Menu and Zoom Command (step 1)

FIGURE 2.4 Hands-on Exercise 1

➤ Click and drag the mouse to select the phrase **Our Students,** which appears at the beginning of the document. Type your name to replace the selected text.

➤ Pull down the **File menu,** click the **Save As** command, then save the document as **Modified Note.** (This creates a second copy of the document and leaves the original unchanged.)

CREATE A BACKUP COPY

The Options button in the Save As dialog box enables you to specify the backup options in effect. Click the Options command button, then check the box to Always Create Backup Copy. The next time you save the document, the previous version on disk becomes a backup copy while the document in memory becomes the current version on disk.

STEP 2: Scrolling

➤ Click and drag the **scroll box** within the vertical scroll bar to scroll to the end of the document as shown in Figure 2.4b. Click immediately before the period at the end of the last sentence.

➤ Type a **comma,** then insert the phrase **but most of all, enjoy.**

➤ Drag the **scroll box** to the top of the scroll bar to get back to the beginning of the document. Click immediately before the period ending the first sentence, press the **space bar,** then add the phrase **and desktop publishing.**

➤ Save the document.

Drag scroll box to
scroll more quickly

Insert this phrase at
the end of the document

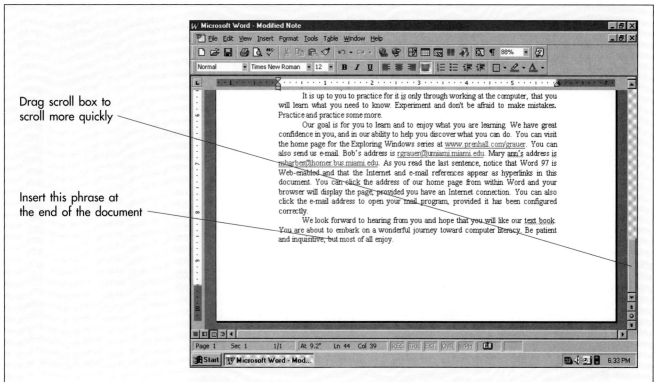

(b) Scrolling (step 2)

FIGURE 2.4   Hands-on Exercise 1 (continued)

THE MOUSE AND THE SCROLL BAR

Scroll quickly through a document by clicking above or below the scroll box to scroll up or down an entire screen. Move to the top, bottom, or an approximate position within a document by dragging the scroll box to the corresponding position in the scroll bar; for example, dragging the scroll box to the middle of the bar moves the mouse pointer to the middle of the document. Scrolling with the mouse does not change the location of the insertion point, however, and thus you must click the mouse at the new location prior to entering text at that location.

STEP 3: The Replace Command

➤ Press **Ctrl+Home** to move to the beginning of the document. Pull down the **Edit menu.** Click **Replace** to produce the dialog box of Figure 2.4c. Click the **More button** to display the available options.

• Type **text** in the Find what text box.

• Press the **Tab key.** Type **book** in the Replace with text box.

➤ Click the **Find Next button** to find the first occurrence of the word *text*. The dialog box remains on the screen and the first occurrence of *text* is selected. This is *not* an appropriate substitution; that is, you should not substitute *book* for *text* at this point.

➤ Click the **Find Next button** to move to the next occurrence without making the replacement. This time the substitution is appropriate.

Save button

First occurrence of Find string is selected (not an appropriate substitution)

Click here to find next occurrence of Find string

Find string

Replacement string

Click here to make a replacement (when appropriate)

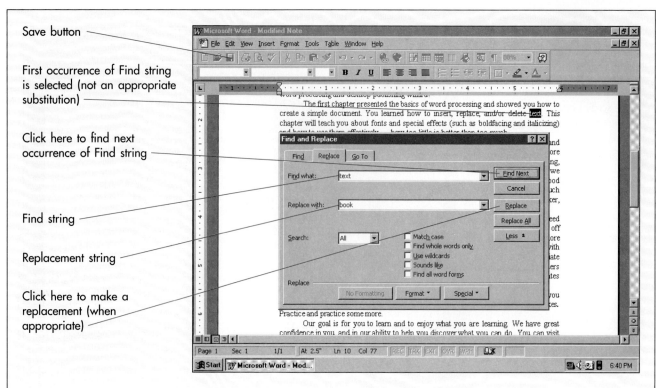

(c) Replace Command (step 3)

FIGURE 2.4   Hands-on Exercise 1 (continued)

➤ Click **Replace** to make the change and automatically move to the next occurrence where the substitution is again inappropriate. Click **Find Next** a final time. Word will indicate that it has finished searching the document. Click **OK.**

➤ Change the Find and Replace strings to **Mary Ann** and **Maryann,** respectively. Click the **Replace All** button to make the substitution globally without confirmation. Word will indicate that it has finished searching and that two replacements were made. Click **OK.**

➤ Click the **Close command button** to close the dialog box. Click the **Save button** to save the document. Scroll through the document to review your changes.

SCROLLING WITH THE KEYBOARD

Press Ctrl+Home and Ctrl+End to move to the beginning and end of a document, respectively. Press Home and End to move to the beginning and end of a line. Press PgUp or PgDn to scroll one screen in the indicated direction. The advantage of scrolling via the keyboard (instead of the mouse) is that the location of the insertion point changes automatically and you can begin typing immediately.

STEP 4: The Clipboard

➤ Press **PgDn** to scroll toward the end of the document until you come to the paragraph beginning **It is up to you.** Select the sentence **Practice and practice some more** by dragging the mouse over the sentence. (Be sure to include the period.) The sentence will be selected as shown in Figure 2.4d.

➤ Pull down the **Edit menu** and click the **Copy command** or click the **Copy button** on the Standard toolbar.

➤ Press **Ctrl+End** to scroll to the end of the document. Press the **space bar.** Pull down the **Edit menu** and click the **Paste command** (or click the **Paste button** on the Standard toolbar).

➤ Move the insertion point to the end of the first paragraph (following the exclamation point after the word *Wizard*). Press the **space bar.** Click the **Paste button** on the Standard toolbar to paste the sentence a second time.

Click here to copy the selected sentence to the clipboard

Click and drag to select the sentence

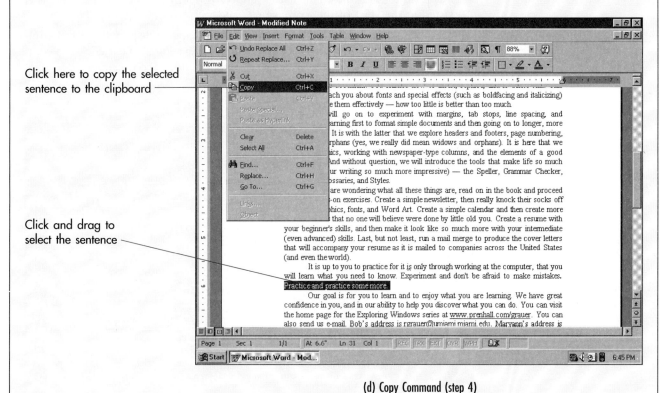

(d) Copy Command (step 4)

FIGURE 2.4   Hands-on Exercise 1 (continued)

CUT, COPY, AND PASTE

Ctrl+X, Ctrl+C, and **Ctrl+V** are keyboard shortcuts to cut, copy, and paste, respectively. (The shortcuts are easier to remember when you realize that the operative letters X, C, and V are next to each other at the bottom left side of the keyboard.) You can also use the Cut, Copy, and Paste buttons on the Standard toolbar.

STEP 5: Undo and Redo Commands

➤ Click the **drop-down arrow** next to the Undo button to display the previously executed actions as in Figure 2.4e. The list of actions corresponds to the editing commands you have issued since the start of the exercise. (Your list will be different from ours if you deviated from any instructions in the hands-on exercise.)

➤ Click **Paste** (the first command on the list) to undo the last editing command; the sentence, Practice and practice some more, disappears from the end of the first paragraph.

➤ Click the remaining steps on the undo list to retrace your steps through the exercise one command at a time. Alternatively, you can scroll to the bottom of the list and click the last command, which automatically undoes all of the preceding commands.

➤ Either way, when the undo list is empty, you will have the document as it existed at the start of the exercise.

➤ Click the **drop-down arrow** for the Redo command to display the list of commands you have undone; click each command in sequence (or click the command at the bottom of the list) and you will restore the document.

➤ Save the document.

Down arrow for Undo tool

Down arrow for Redo tool

List of actions

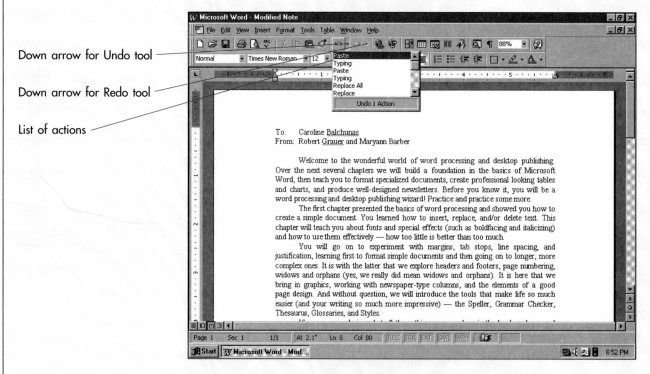

(e) Undo and Redo Commands (step 5)

FIGURE 2.4   Hands-on Exercise 1 (continued)

STEP 6: Drag and Drop

➤ Click and drag to select the phrase **format specialized documents** (including the comma and space) as shown in Figure 2.4f, then drag the phrase to its new location immediately before the word *and*. (A dotted vertical bar appears as you drag the text, to indicate its new location.)

➤ Release the mouse button to complete the move.

➤ Click the **drop-down arrow** for the Undo command; click **Move** to undo the move.

➤ To copy the selected text to the same location (instead of moving it), press and hold the **Ctrl key** as you drag the text to its new location. (A plus sign appears as you drag the text, to indicate it is being copied rather than moved.)

➤ Practice the drag-and-drop procedure several times until you are confident you can move and copy with precision.

➤ Click anywhere in the document to deselect the text. Save the document.

Click and drag phrase to new location

Dotted vertical bar shows where phrase will be placed

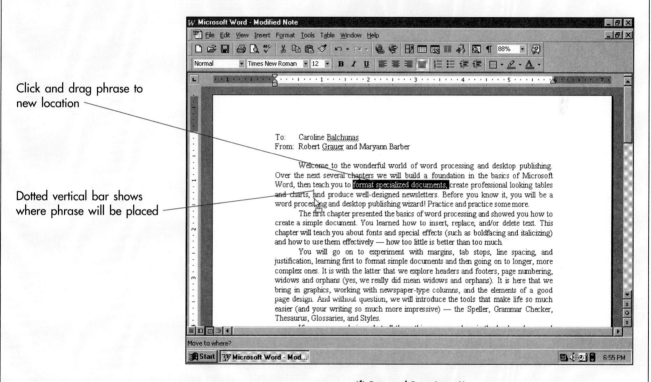

(f) Drag and Drop (step 6)

FIGURE 2.4   Hands-on Exercise 1 (continued)

STEP 7: The Print Preview Command

➤ Pull down the **File menu** and click **Print Preview** (or clock the **Print Preview button** on the Standard toolbar). You should see your entire document as shown in Figure 2.4g.

➤ Check that the entire document fits on one page—that is, check that you can see all three lines in the last paragraph. If not, click the **Shrink to Fit button** on the toolbar to automatically change the font sizes in the document to force it on one page.

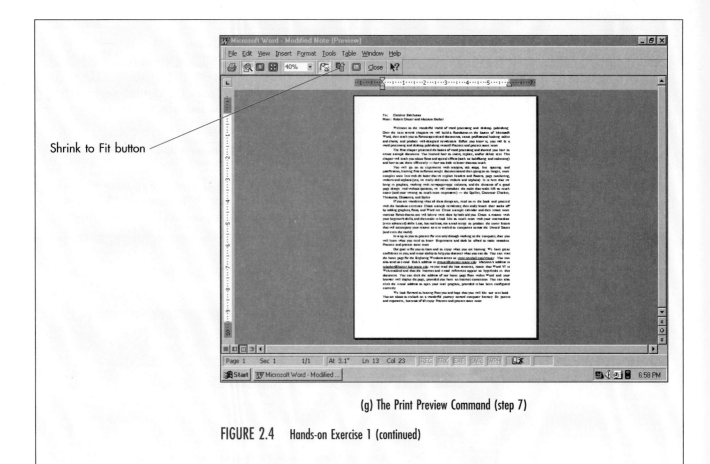

Shrink to Fit button

(g) The Print Preview Command (step 7)

FIGURE 2.4   Hands-on Exercise 1 (continued)

➤ Click the **Print button** to print the document so that you can submit it to your instructor. Click the **Close button** to exit Print Preview and return to your document.
➤ Close the document. Exit Word if you do not want to continue with the next exercise at this time.

TYPOGRAPHY

Typography is the process of selecting typefaces, type styles, and type sizes. The importance of these decisions is obvious, for the ultimate success of any document depends greatly on its appearance. Type should reinforce the message without calling attention to itself and should be consistent with the information you want to convey.

Typeface

A ***typeface*** is a complete set of characters (upper- and lowercase letters, numbers, punctuation marks, and special symbols). Figure 2.5 illustrates three typefaces— ***Times New Roman, Arial,*** and ***Courier New***—that are supplied with Windows, and which in turn are accessible from any Windows application.

One definitive characteristic of any typeface is the presence or absence of tiny cross lines that end the main strokes of each letter. A ***serif*** typeface has these lines. A ***sans serif*** typeface (*sans* from the French for *without*) does not. Times New Roman and Courier New are examples of a serif typeface. Arial is a sans serif typeface.

Typography is the process of selecting typefaces, type styles, and type sizes. A serif typeface has tiny cross strokes that end the main strokes of each letter. A sans serif typeface does not have these strokes. Serif typefaces are typically used with large amounts of text. Sans serif typefaces are used for headings and limited amounts of text. A proportional typeface allocates space in accordance with the width of each character and is what you are used to seeing. A monospaced typeface uses the same amount of space for every character. A well-designed document will limit the number of typefaces so as not to overwhelm the reader.

(a) Times New Roman (serif and proportional)

Typography is the process of selecting typefaces, type styles, and type sizes. A serif typeface has tiny cross strokes that end the main strokes of each letter. A sans serif typeface does not have these strokes. Serif typefaces are typically used with large amounts of text. Sans serif typefaces are used for headings and limited amounts of text. A proportional typeface allocates space in accordance with the width of each character and is what you are used to seeing. A monospaced typeface uses the same amount of space for every character. A well-designed document will limit the number of typefaces so as not to overwhelm the reader.

(b) Arial (sans serif and proportional)

```
Typography is the process of selecting typefaces, type styles,
and type sizes. A serif typeface has tiny cross strokes that end
the main strokes of each letter. A sans serif typeface does not
have these strokes. Serif typefaces are typically used with large
amounts of text. Sans serif typefaces are used for headings and
limited amounts of text. A proportional typeface allocates space
in accordance with the width of each character and is what you
are used to seeing. A monospaced typeface uses the same amount of
space for every character. A well-designed document will limit
the number of typefaces so as not to overwhelm the reader.
```

(c) Courier New (serif and monospaced)

FIGURE 2.5   Typefaces

Serifs help the eye to connect one letter with the next and are generally used with large amounts of text. This book, for example, is set in a serif typeface. A sans serif typeface is more effective with smaller amounts of text and appears in headlines, corporate logos, airport signs, and so on.

A second characteristic of a typeface is whether it is monospaced or proportional. A **monospaced typeface** (e.g., Courier New) uses the same amount of space for every character regardless of its width. A **proportional typeface** (e.g., Times New Roman or Arial) allocates space according to the width of the character. Monospaced fonts are used in tables and financial projections where text must be precisely lined up, one character underneath the other. Proportional typefaces create a more professional appearance and are appropriate for most documents.

Any typeface can be set in different **type styles** (e.g., regular, **bold,** or *italic*). A **font** (as the term is used in Windows) is a specific typeface in a specific style; for example, *Times New Roman Italic,* Arial Bold**,** or **`Courier New Bold Italic.`**

TYPOGRAPHY TIP—USE RESTRAINT

More is not better, especially in the case of too many typefaces and styles, which produce cluttered documents that impress no one. Try to limit yourself to a maximum of two typefaces per document, but choose multiple sizes and/or styles within those typefaces. Use boldface or italics for emphasis; but do so in moderation, because if you emphasize too many elements, the effect is lost.

Type Size

Type size is a vertical measurement and is specified in points, where one **point** is equal to $\frac{1}{72}$ of an inch; that is, there are 72 points to the inch. The measurement is made from the top of the tallest letter in a character set (for example, an uppercase T) to the bottom of the lowest letter (for example, a lowercase y). Most documents are set in 10 or 12 point type. Newspaper columns may be set as small as 8 point type. Type sizes of 14 points or higher are ineffective for large amounts of text. Figure 2.6 shows the same phrase set in varying type sizes.

Some typefaces appear larger (smaller) than others even though they may be set in the same point size. The type in Figure 2.6a, for example, looks smaller than the corresponding type in Figure 2.6b even though both are set in the same point size.

Format Font Command

The **Format Font command** gives you complete control over the typeface, size, and style of the text in a document. Executing the command before entering text will set the format of the text you type from that point on. You can also use the command to change the font of existing text by selecting the text, then executing the command. Either way, you will see the dialog box in Figure 2.7, in which you specify the font (typeface), style, and point size.

You can choose any of the special effects (e.g., ~~strikethrough~~ or SMALL CAPS) and/or change the underline options (whether or not spaces are to be underlined). You can even change the color of the text on the monitor, but you need a color printer for the printed document. (The Character Spacing and Animation tabs produce different sets of options in which you control the spacing and appearance of the characters and are beyond the scope of our discussion.)

This is Arial 8 point type

This is Arial 10 point type

This is Arial 12 point type

This is Arial 18 point type

This is Arial 24 point type

This is Arial 30 point type

(a) Sans Serif Typeface

This is Times New Roman 8 point type

This is Times New Roman 10 point type

This is Times New Roman 12 point type

This is Times New Roman 18 point type

This is Times New Roman 24 point type

This is Times New Roman 30 point

(b) Serif Typeface

FIGURE 2.6   Type Size

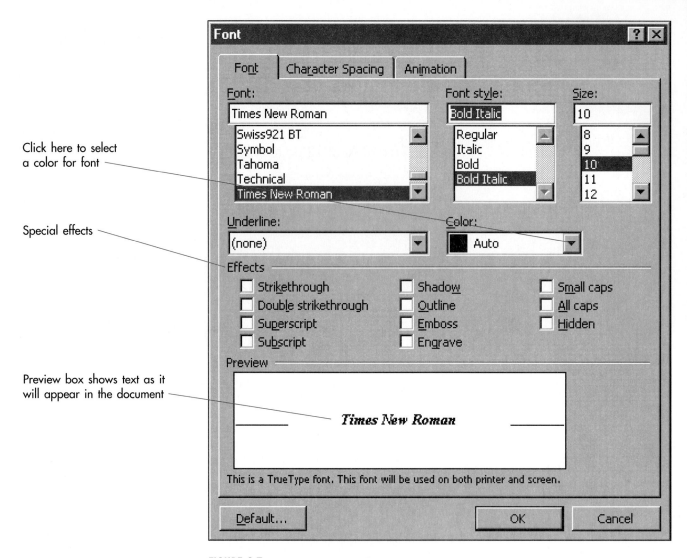

Click here to select
a color for font

Special effects

Preview box shows text as it
will appear in the document

FIGURE 2.7   Format Font Command

The Preview box shows the text as it will appear in the document. The message at the bottom of the dialog box indicates that Times New Roman is a TrueType font and that the same font will be used on both the screen and the monitor. TrueType fonts ensure that your document is truly WYSIWYG (What You See Is What You Get) because the fonts you see on the monitor will be identical to those in the printed document.

PAGE SETUP COMMAND

The **Page Setup command** in the File menu lets you change margins, paper size, orientation, paper source, and/or layout. All parameters are accessed from the dialog box in Figure 2.8 by clicking the appropriate tab within the dialog box.

The default margins are indicated in Figure 2.8a and are one inch on the top and bottom of the page, and one and a quarter inches on the left and right. You can change any (or all) of these settings by entering a new value in the appropriate text box, either by typing it explicitly or clicking the up/down arrow. All of the settings in the Page Setup command apply to the whole document regardless of the position of the insertion point. (Different settings can be established for different parts of a document by creating sections, which is beyond the scope of our present discussion.)

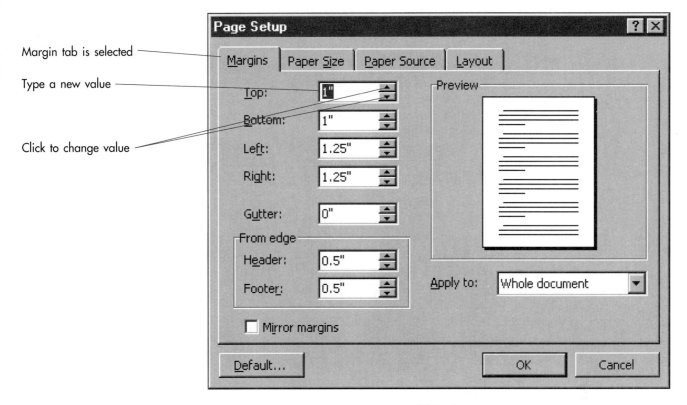

Margin tab is selected

Type a new value

Click to change value

(a) Margins

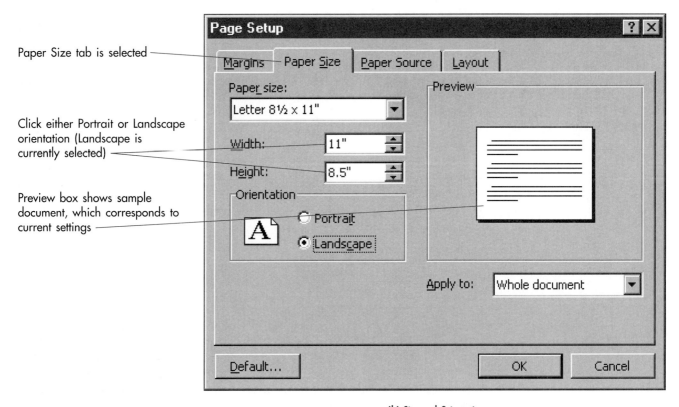

Paper Size tab is selected

Click either Portrait or Landscape orientation (Landscape is currently selected)

Preview box shows sample document, which corresponds to current settings

(b) Size and Orientation

FIGURE 2.8   Page Setup Command

The Paper Size tab within the Page Setup command enables you to change the orientation of a page as shown in Figure 2.8b. ***Portrait orientation*** is the default. ***Landscape orientation*** flips the page 90 degrees so that its dimensions are 11 × 8½ rather than the other way around. Note, too, the Preview area in both Figures 2.8a and 2.8b, which shows how the document will appear with the selected parameters.

The Paper Source tab is used to specify which tray should be used on printers with multiple trays, and is helpful when you want to load different types of paper simultaneously. The Layout tab is used to specify options for headers and footers (text that appears at the top or bottom of each page in a document).

Page Breaks

One of the first concepts you learned was that of word wrap, whereby Word inserts a soft return at the end of a line in order to begin a new line. The number and/or location of the soft returns change automatically as you add or delete text within a document. Soft returns are very different from the hard returns inserted by the user, whose number and location remain constant.

In much the same way, Word creates a ***soft page break*** to go to the top of a new page when text no longer fits on the current page. And just as you can insert a hard return to start a new paragraph, you can insert a ***hard page break*** to force any part of a document to begin on a new page. A hard page break is inserted into a document using the Break command in the Insert menu or through the Ctrl+enter keyboard shortcut. (You can prevent the occurrence of awkward page breaks through the Format Paragraph command as described later in the chapter.

AN EXERCISE IN DESIGN

The following exercise has you retrieve an existing document from the set of practice files, then experiment with various typefaces, type styles, and point sizes. The original document uses a monospaced (typewriter style) font, without boldface or italics, and you are asked to improve its appearance. The first step directs you to save the document under a new name so that you can always return to the original if necessary.

There is no right and wrong with respect to design, and you are free to choose any combination of fonts that appeals to you. The exercise takes you through various formatting options but lets you make the final decision. It does, however, ask you to print the final document and submit it to your instructor.

IMPOSE A TIME LIMIT

A word processor is supposed to save time and make you more productive. It will do exactly that, provided you use the word processor for its primary purpose—writing and editing. It is all too easy, however, to lose sight of that objective and spend too much time formatting the document. Concentrate on the content of your document rather than its appearance. Impose a time limit on the amount of time you will spend on formatting. End the session when the limit is reached.

Objective: To experiment with character formatting; to change fonts and to use boldface and italics; to copy formatting with the format painter; to insert a page break and see different views of a document. Use Figure 2.9 as a guide in the exercise.

STEP 1: Open the Existing Document

➤ Start Word. Pull down the **File menu** and click **Open** (or click the **Open button** on the toolbar). To open a file:
  • Click the **drop-down arrow** on the Look In list box. Click the appropriate drive, drive C or drive A, depending on the location of your data.
  • Double click the **Exploring Word folder** to make it the active folder (the folder in which you will open and save the document).
  • Scroll in the **Open list box** (if necessary) until you can click **Tips for Writing** to select this document. Double click the **document icon** or click the **Open command button** to open the file.
➤ Pull down the **File menu.** Click the **Save As command** to save the document as **Modified Tips.**
➤ Pull down the **View menu** and click **Normal** (or click the **Normal View button** above the status bar).
➤ Set the magnification (zoom) to **Page Width.**

SELECTING TEXT

The *selection bar,* a blank column at the far left of the document window, makes it easy to select a line, paragraph, or the entire document. To select a line, move the mouse pointer to the selection bar, point to the line and click the left mouse button. To select a paragraph, move the mouse pointer to the selection bar, point to any line in the paragraph, and double click the mouse. To select the entire document, move the mouse pointer to the selection bar and press the Ctrl key while you click the mouse.

STEP 2: The Right Mouse Button

➤ Select the first tip as shown in Figure 2.9a. Point to the selected text and click the **right mouse button** to display the shortcut menu.
➤ Click outside the menu to close the menu without executing a command.
➤ Press the **Ctrl key** as you click the selection bar to select the entire document, then click the **right mouse button** to display the shortcut menu.
➤ Click **Font** to execute the Format Font command.

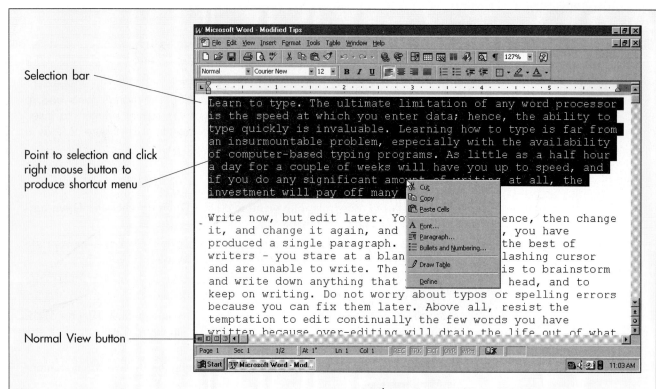

Selection bar

Point to selection and click right mouse button to produce shortcut menu

Normal View button

(a) Shortcut Menu (step 2)

FIGURE 2.9   Hands-on Exercise 2

STEP 3: Changing Fonts

➤ Click the **down arrow** on the Font list box of Figure 2.9b to scroll through the available fonts. Select a different font, such as Times New Roman.

➤ Click the **down arrow** in the Font Size list box to choose a point size.

➤ Click **OK** to change the font and point size for the selected text.

➤ Pull down the **Edit menu** and click **Undo** (or click the **Undo button** on the Standard toolbar) to return to the original font.

➤ Experiment with different fonts and/or different point sizes until you are satisfied with the selection. We chose 12 point Times New Roman.

FIND AND REPLACE FORMATTING

The Replace command enables you to replace formatting as well as text. To replace any text set in bold with the same text in italics, pull down the Edit menu, and click the Replace command. Click the Find what text box, but do *not* enter any text. Click the More button to expand the dialog box. Click the Format command button, click Font, click Bold in the Font Style list, and click OK. Click the Replace with text box and again do *not* enter any text. Click the Format command button, click Font, click Italic in the Font Style list, and click OK. Click the Find Next or Replace All command button to do selective or automatic replacement. Use a similar technique to replace one font with another.

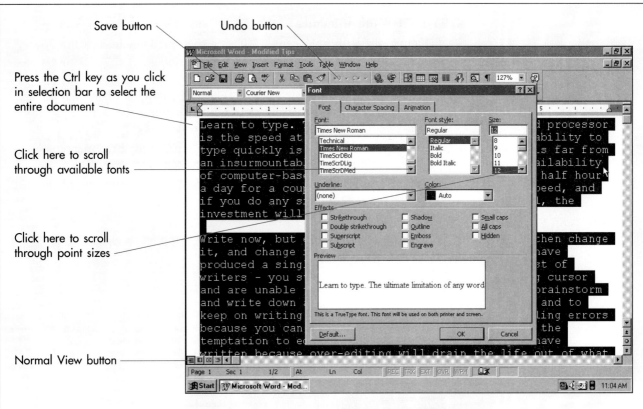

Save button

Undo button

Press the Ctrl key as you click in selection bar to select the entire document

Click here to scroll through available fonts

Click here to scroll through point sizes

Normal View button

(b) Format Font Command (step 3)

FIGURE 2.9   Hands-on Exercise 2 (continued)

STEP 4: Boldface and Italics

➤ Drag the mouse over the sentence **Learn to type** at the beginning of the document.

➤ Click the **Italic button** on the Formatting toolbar to italicize the selected phrase, which will remain selected after the italics take effect.

➤ Click the **Bold button** to boldface the selected text. The text is now in bold italic.

➤ Experiment with different styles (bold, italics, underlining, or bold italic) until you are satisfied. The Italic, Bold, and Underline buttons function as toggle switches; that is, clicking the Italic button when text is already italicized returns the text to normal.

➤ Save the document

THE "WHAT'S THIS" BUTTON

Pull down the Help menu and click the What's This button command (or press Shift+F1). Point to any button on any toolbar (the mouse pointer changes to an arrow with a question mark), then click the button to display a Help balloon to explain the function of that button. Press the Esc key to close the balloon and return the mouse pointer to normal.

STEP 5: The Format Painter

➤ Click anywhere within the sentence Learn to Type. **Double click** the **Format Painter button** on the Standard toolbar. The mouse pointer changes to a paintbrush as shown in Figure 2.9c.

➤ Drag the mouse pointer over the next title, **Write now, edit later,** and release the mouse. The formatting from the original sentence (bold italic as shown in Figure 2.9c) has been applied to this sentence as well.

➤ Drag the mouse pointer (in the shape of a paintbrush) over the remaining titles (the first sentence in each paragraph) to copy the formatting.

➤ Click the **Format Painter button** after you have painted the title of the last tip to turn the feature off.

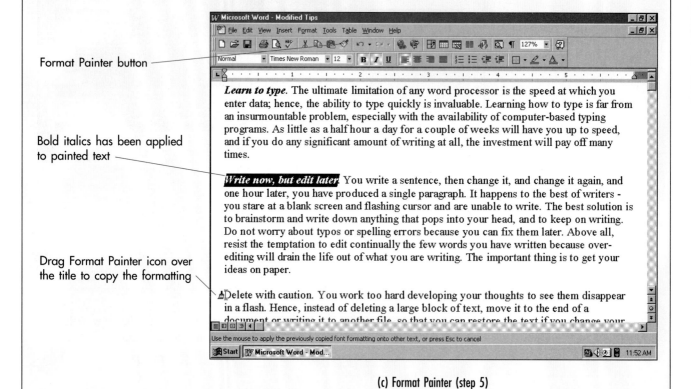

Format Painter button

Bold italics has been applied to painted text

Drag Format Painter icon over the title to copy the formatting

(c) Format Painter (step 5)

FIGURE 2.9   Hands-on Exercise 2 (continued)

THE FORMAT PAINTER

The *Format Painter* copies the formatting of the selected text to other places in a document. Select the text with the formatting you want to copy, then click or double click the Format Painter button on the Standard toolbar. Clicking the button will paint only one selection. Double clicking the button will paint multiple selections until the feature is turned off by again clicking the Format Painter button. Either way, the mouse pointer changes to a paintbrush, which you can drag over text to give it the identical formatting characteristics as the original selection.

STEP 6: Change Margins

➤ Press **Ctrl+End** to move to the end of the document as shown in Figure 2.9d. You will see a dotted line indicating a soft page break. (If you do not see the page break, it means that your document fits on one page because you used a different font and/or a smaller point size. We used 12 point Times New Roman.)

➤ Pull down the **File menu.** Click **Page Setup.** Click the **Margins tab** if necessary. Change the bottom margin to **.75** inch. Check that these settings apply to the **Whole Document.** Click **OK.** The page break disappears because more text fits on the page.

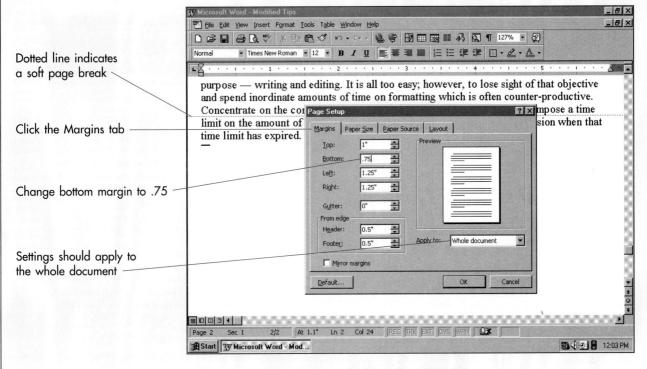

Dotted line indicates a soft page break

Click the Margins tab

Change bottom margin to .75

Settings should apply to the whole document

(d) Change Margins (step 6)

FIGURE 2.9 Hands-on Exercise 2 (continued)

DIALOG BOX SHORTCUTS

You can use keyboard shortcuts to select options in a dialog box. Press Tab (Shift+Tab) to move forward (backward) from one field or command button to the next. Press Alt plus the underlined letter to move directly to a field or command button. Press enter to activate the selected command button. Press Esc to exit the dialog box without taking action. Press the space bar to toggle check boxes on or off. Press the down arrow to open a drop-down list box once the list has been accessed, then press the up or down arrow to move between options in a list box.

STEP 7: Create a Title Page

➤ Press **Ctrl+Home** to move to the beginning of the document. Press **enter** three or four times to add a few blank lines.

➤ Press **Ctrl+enter** to insert a hard page break. You will see the words "Page Break" in the middle of a dotted line as shown in Figure 2.9e.

➤ Press the **up arrow key** three times. Enter the title **Tips for Writing.** Select the title, and format it in a larger point size, such as 24 points.

➤ Enter your name on the next line and format it in a different point size, such as 14 points. Select both the title and your name as shown in the figure. Click the **Center button** on the Formatting toolbar. Save the document.

Spelling and Grammar button

Center button

Click and drag to select both lines

Press Ctrl+enter to insert a hard page break

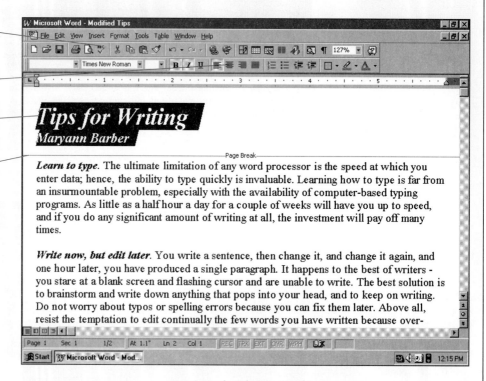

(e) Create the Title Page (step 7)

FIGURE 2.9 Hands-on Exercise 2 (continued)

THE SPELL CHECK

Use the spell check prior to saving a document for the last time, even if the document is just a sentence or two. Spelling errors make your work look sloppy and discourage the reader before he or she has read what you had to say. Spelling errors can cost you a job, a grade, or a lucrative contract. The spell check requires but a single click, so why not use it?

STEP 8: The Completed Document

➤ Pull down the **View menu** and click **Page Layout** (or click the **Page Layout button** above the status bar).

➤ Click the **Zoom Control arrow** on the Standard toolbar and select **Two Pages**. Release the mouse to view the completed document in Figure 2.9f. You may want to add additional blank lines at the top of the title page to move the title further down on the page.

➤ Save the document a final time. Exit Word if you do not want to continue with the next exercise at this time.

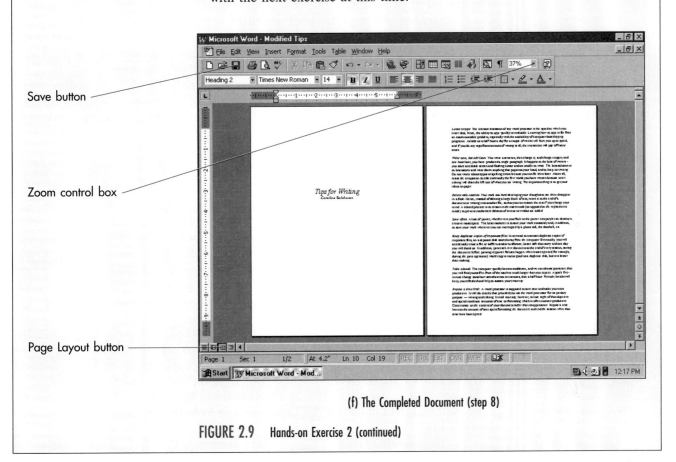

Save button

Zoom control box

Page Layout button

(f) The Completed Document (step 8)

FIGURE 2.9   Hands-on Exercise 2 (continued)

PARAGRAPH FORMATTING

A change in typography is only one way to alter the appearance of a document. You can also change the alignment, indentation, tab stops, or line spacing for any paragraph(s) within the document. You can control the pagination and prevent the occurrence of awkward page breaks by specifying that an entire paragraph has to appear on the same page, or that a one-line paragraph (e.g., a heading) should appear on the same page as the next paragraph. You can include borders or shading for added emphasis around selected paragraphs.

All of these features are implemented at the paragraph level and affect all selected paragraphs. If no paragraphs are selected, the commands affect the entire current paragraph (the paragraph containing the insertion point), regardless of the position of the insertion point when the command is executed.

Alignment

Text can be aligned in four different ways as shown in Figure 2.10. It may be justified (flush left/flush right), left aligned (flush left with a ragged right margin), right aligned (flush right with a ragged left margin), or centered within the margins (ragged left and right).

Left aligned text is perhaps the easiest to read. The first letters of each line align with each other, helping the eye to find the beginning of each line. The lines themselves are of irregular length. There is uniform spacing between words, and the ragged margin on the right adds white space to the text, giving it a lighter and more informal look.

Justified text produces lines of equal length, with the spacing between words adjusted to align at the margins. It may be more difficult to read than text that is left aligned because of the uneven (sometimes excessive) word spacing and/or the greater number of hyphenated words needed to justify the lines.

Type that is centered or right aligned is restricted to limited amounts of text where the effect is more important than the ease of reading. Centered text, for example, appears frequently on wedding invitations, poems, or formal announcements. Right aligned text is used with figure captions and short headlines.

Indents

Individual paragraphs can be indented so that they appear to have different margins from the rest of a document. Indentation is established at the paragraph level; thus different indentation can be in effect for different paragraphs. One paragraph may be indented from the left margin only, another from the right margin only, and a third from both the left and right margins. The first line of any paragraph may be indented differently from the rest of the paragraph. And finally, a paragraph may be set with no indentation at all, so that it aligns on the left and right margins.

The indentation of a paragraph is determined by three settings: the *left indent,* the *right indent,* and a *special indent* (if any). There are two types of special indentation, first line and hanging, as will be explained shortly. The left and right indents are set to zero by default, as is the special indent, and produce a paragraph with no indentation at all as shown in Figure 2.11a. Positive values for the left and right indents offset the paragraph from both margins as shown in Figure 2.11b.

The *first line indent* (Figure 2.11c) affects only the first line in the paragraph and is implemented by pressing the Tab key at the beginning of the paragraph. A *hanging indent* (Figure 2.11d) sets the first line of a paragraph at the left indent and indents the remaining lines according to the amount specified. Hanging indents are often used with bulleted or numbered lists.

INDENTS VERSUS MARGINS

Indents measure the distance between the text and the margins. *Margins* mark the distance from the text to the edge of the page. Indents are determined at the paragraph level, whereas margins are established at the section (document) level. The left and right margins are set (by default) to 1.25 inches each; the left and right indents default to zero. The first line indent is measured from the setting of the left indent.

We, the people of the United States, in order to form a more perfect Union, establish justice, insure domestic tranquillity, provide for the common defense, promote the general welfare, and secure the blessings of liberty to ourselves and our posterity, do ordain and establish this Constitution for the United States of America.

(a) Justified (flush left/flush right)

We, the people of the United States, in order to form a more perfect Union, establish justice, insure domestic tranquillity, provide for the common defense, promote the general welfare, and secure the blessings of liberty to ourselves and our posterity, do ordain and establish this Constitution for the United States of America.

(b) Left Aligned (flush left/ragged right)

We, the people of the United States, in order to form a more perfect Union, establish justice, insure domestic tranquillity, provide for the common defense, promote the general welfare, and secure the blessings of liberty to ourselves and our posterity, do ordain and establish this Constitution for the United States of America.

(c) Right Aligned (ragged left/flush right)

We, the people of the United States, in order to form a more perfect Union, establish justice, insure domestic tranquillity, provide for the common defense, promote the general welfare, and secure the blessings of liberty to ourselves and our posterity, do ordain and establish this Constitution for the United States of America.

(d) Centered (ragged left/ragged right)

FIGURE 2.10   Alignment

The left and right indents are defined as the distance between the text and the left and right margins, respectively. Both parameters are set to zero in this paragraph and so the text aligns on both margins. Different indentation can be applied to different paragraphs in the same document.

(a) No Indents

Positive values for the left and right indents offset a paragraph from the rest of a document and are often used for long quotations. This paragraph has left and right indents of one-half inch each. Different indentation can be applied to different paragraphs in the same document.

(b) Left and Right Indents

A first line indent affects only the first line in the paragraph and is implemented by pressing the Tab key at the beginning of the paragraph. The remainder of the paragraph is aligned at the left margin (or the left indent if it differs from the left margin) as can be seen from this example. Different indentation can be applied to different paragraphs in the same document.

(c) First Line Indent

A hanging indent sets the first line of a paragraph at the left indent and indents the remaining lines according to the amount specified. Hanging indents are often used with bulleted or numbered lists. Different indentation can be applied to different paragraphs in the same document.

(d) Hanging (Special) Indent

FIGURE 2.11   Indents

Tabs

Anyone who has used a typewriter is familiar with the function of the Tab key; that is, press Tab and the insertion point moves to the next *tab stop* (a measured position to align text at a specific place). The Tab key is much more powerful in Word as you can choose from four different types of tab stops (left, center, right, and decimal). You can also specify a *leader character,* typically dots or hyphens, to draw the reader's eye across the page. Tabs are often used to create tables within a document.

The default tab stops are set every ½ inch and are left aligned, but you can change the *alignment* and/or position with the Format Tabs command. Figure 2.12 illustrates a dot leader in combination with a right tab to produce a Table of Contents. The default tab stops have been cleared in Figure 2.12a, in favor of a single right tab at 5.5 inches. The option button for a dot leader has also been checked. The resulting document is shown in Figure 2.12b.

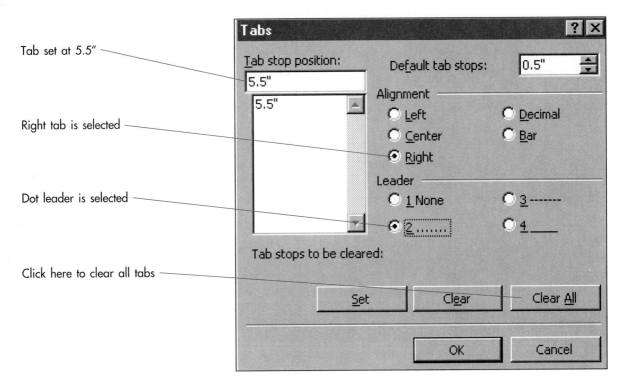

Tab set at 5.5″

Right tab is selected

Dot leader is selected

Click here to clear all tabs

(a) Tab Stops

Right tab with dot leader

(b) Table of Contents

FIGURE 2.12   Tabs

The Format Tabs command is quite powerful, so it is useful to repeat the different alignments:

- Left alignment, where the text *begins* at the tab stop, corresponds to the Tab key on a typewriter.
- Right alignment, where the text *ends* at the tab stop, is used to align page numbers in a table of contents or to align text at the right margin.
- Center alignment, where text centers over the tab stop, is used infrequently for special effect.
- Decimal alignment, which lines up numeric values in a column on the decimal point, is helpful with statistical text.

Line Spacing

Line spacing determines the space between the lines in a paragraph. Word provides complete flexibility and enables you to select any multiple of line spacing (single, double, line and a half, and so on). You can also specify line spacing in terms of points (there are 72 points per inch).

Line spacing is set at the paragraph level through the Format Paragraph command, which sets the spacing within a paragraph. The command also enables you to add extra spacing before the first line in a paragraph or after the last line. (Either technique is preferable to the common practice of single spacing the paragraphs within a document, then adding a blank line between paragraphs.)

FORMAT PARAGRAPH COMMAND

The **Format Paragraph command** is where you specify the alignment, indentation, line spacing, and pagination for the selected paragraph(s). As indicated, all of these features are implemented at the paragraph level and affect all selected paragraphs. If no paragraphs are selected, the command affects the entire current paragraph (the paragraph containing the insertion point), regardless of the position of the insertion point when the command is executed.

The Format Paragraph command is illustrated in Figure 2.13. The Indents and Spacing tab in Figure 2.13a calls for a hanging indent, line spacing of 1.5 lines, and justified alignment. The preview area within the dialog box enables you to see how the paragraph will appear within the document.

The Line and Page Breaks tab in Figure 2.13b illustrates an entirely different set of parameters in which you control the pagination within a document. You are already familiar with the concept of page breaks, and the distinction between soft page breaks (inserted by Word) versus hard page breaks (inserted by the user). The check boxes in Figure 2.13b enable you to prevent the occurrence of awkward soft page breaks that detract from the appearance of a document.

You might, for example, want to prevent widows and orphans, terms used to describe isolated lines that seem out of place. A *widow* refers to the last line of a paragraph appearing by itself at the top of a page. An *orphan* is the first line of a paragraph appearing by itself at the bottom of a page.

You can also impose additional controls by clicking one or more check boxes. Use the Keep Lines Together option to prevent a soft page break from occurring within a paragraph and ensure that the entire paragraph appears on the same page. (The paragraph is moved to the top of the next page if it doesn't fit on the bottom of the current page.) Use the Keep with Next option to prevent a soft page break between the two paragraphs. This option is typically used to keep a heading (a one-line paragraph) with its associated text in the next paragraph.

Full justification is selected

Hanging indent is selected

Line spacing is set at 1.5 lines

Preview box displays
a sample paragraph

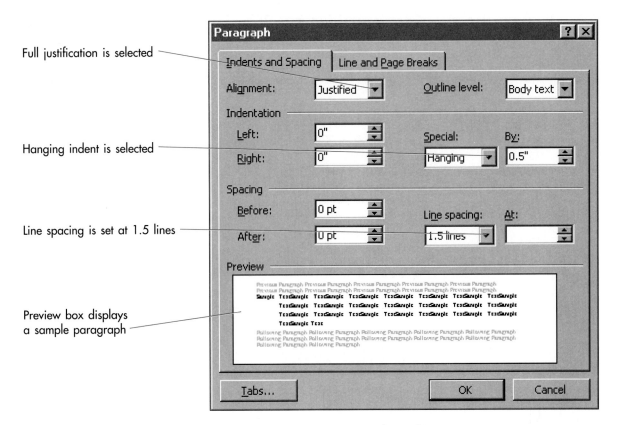

(a) Indents and Spacing

Line and Page Breaks tab
is selected

Pagination options prevent
awkward soft page breaks

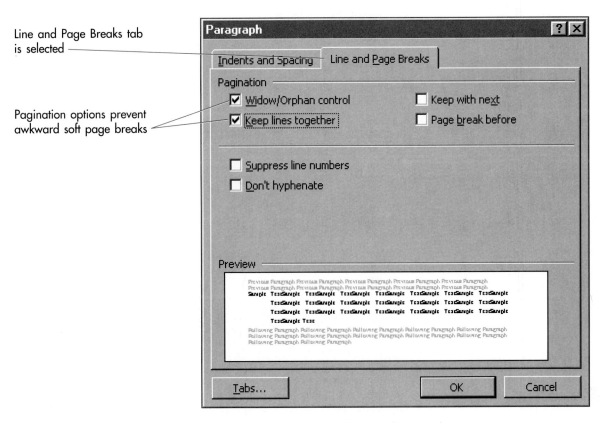

(b) Line and Page Breaks

FIGURE 2.13   Format Paragraph Command

Borders and Shading

The ***Borders and Shading command*** puts the finishing touches on a document and is illustrated in Figure 2.14. It lets you create boxed and/or shaded text as well as place horizontal or vertical lines around a paragraph. You can choose from several different line styles in any color (assuming you have a color printer). You can place a uniform border around a paragraph (choose Box), or you can choose a shadow effect with thicker lines at the right and bottom. You can also apply lines to selected sides of a paragraph(s) by selecting a line style, then clicking the desired sides as apprpriate.

Shading is implemented independently of the border. Clear (no shading) is the default. Solid (100%) shading creates a solid box where the text is turned white so you can read it. Shading of 10 or 20 percent is generally most effective to add emphasis to the selected paragraph. The Borders and Shading command is implemented on the paragraph level and affects the entire paragraph—either the current or selected paragraph(s).

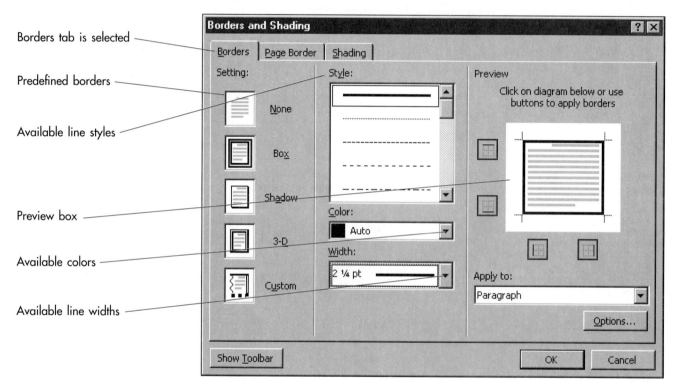

(a) Borders

FIGURE 2.14   Paragraph Borders and Shading

FORMATTING AND THE PARAGRAPH MARK

The paragraph mark ¶ at the end of a paragraph does more than just indicate the presence of a hard return. It also stores all of the formatting in effect for the paragraph. Hence in order to preserve the formatting when you move or copy a paragraph, you must include the paragraph mark in the selected text. Click the Show/Hide ¶ button on the toolbar to display the paragraph mark and make sure it has been selected.

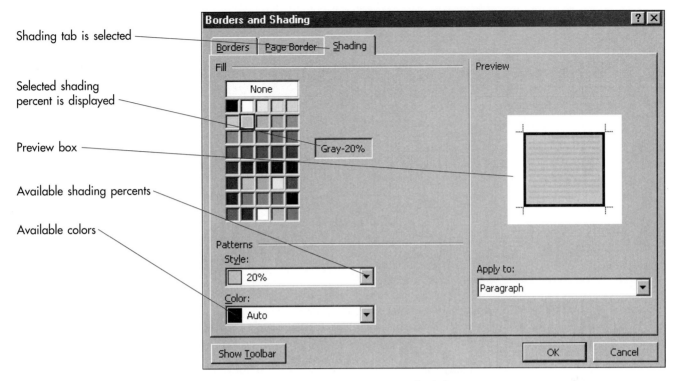

Shading tab is selected

Selected shading percent is displayed

Preview box

Available shading percents

Available colors

(b) Shading

FIGURE 2.14   Paragraph Borders and Shading (continued)

PARAGRAPH FORMATTING AND THE INSERTION POINT

Indents, tab stops, line spacing, alignment, pagination, borders, and shading are all set at the paragraph level and affect all selected paragraphs and/or the current paragraph (the paragraph containing the insertion point). The position of the insertion point within the paragraph does not matter as the insertion point can be anywhere within the paragraph when the Format Paragraph command is executed. Keep the concept of paragraph formatting in mind as you do the following hands-on exercise.

HANDS-ON EXERCISE 3

Paragraph Formatting

Objective: To implement line spacing, alignment, and indents; to implement widow and orphan protection; to box and shade a selected paragraph.

STEP 1: Load the Practice Document
➤ Open the **Modified Tips** document from the previous exercise. If necessary, change to the Page Layout view. Click the **Zoom drop-down arrow** and click **Two Pages** to match the view in Figure 2.15a.

➤ Select the entire second page as shown in the figure. Click the **right mouse button** to produce the shortcut menu. Click **Paragraph.**

Point to selected text and click right mouse button to produce shortcut menu

Click Page Layout button

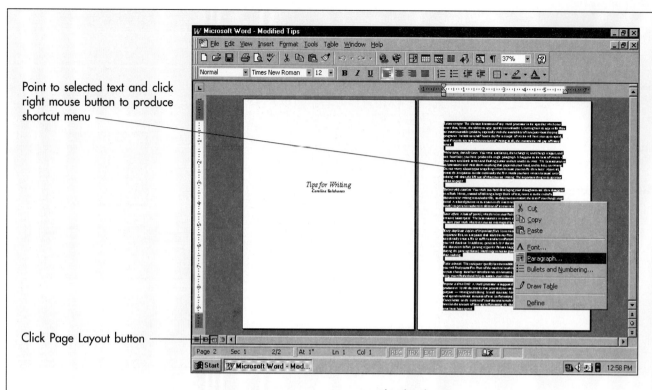

(a) Select-then-do (step 1)

FIGURE 2.15 Hands-on Exercise 3

SELECT TEXT WITH THE F8 EXTEND KEY

Move to the beginning of the text you want to select, then press the F8 (extend) key. The letters EXT will appear in the status bar. Use the arrow keys to extend the selection in the indicated direction; for example, press the down arrow key to select the line. You can also press any character—for example, a letter, space, or period—to extend the selection to the first occurrence of that character. Press Esc to cancel the selection mode.

STEP 2: Line Spacing, Justification, and Pagination

➤ If necessary, click the **Indents and Spacing tab** to view the options in Figure 2.15b.

• Click the **down arrow** on the list box for Line Spacing and select **1.5 Lines.**

• Click the **down arrow** on the Alignment list box and select **Justified** as shown in Figure 2.15b.

• The Preview area shows the effect of these settings.

➤ Click the tab for **Line and Page Breaks.**

• Check the box for **Keep Lines Together.** If necessary, check the box for **Widow/Orphan Control.**

➤ Click **OK** to accept all of the settings in the dialog box.

Click the Indents
and Spacing tab

Click the drop-down arrow
to select the alignment

Click the drop-down arrow
to select the line spacing

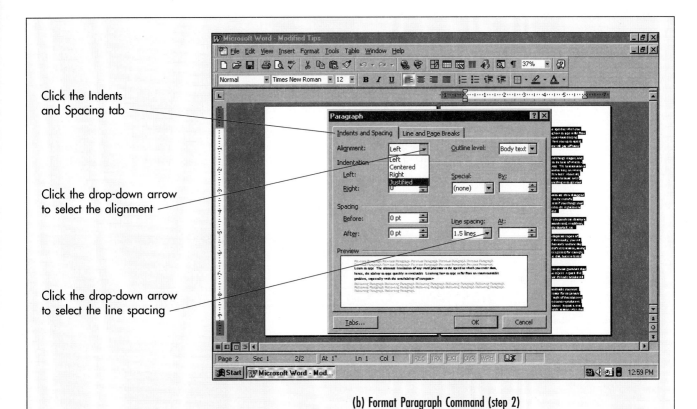

(b) Format Paragraph Command (step 2)

FIGURE 2.15   Hands-on Exercise 3 (continued)

➤ Click anywhere in the document to deselect the text and see the effects of the formatting changes:

- The document is fully justified and the line spacing has increased.
- The document now extends to three pages, with all of the fifth paragraph appearing on the last page.
- There is a large bottom margin on the second page as a consequence of keeping the lines together in paragraph five.

➤ Save the document.

CUSTOMIZE THE TOOLBAR

Customize the Formatting toolbar to display the buttons for line spacing. Point to any toolbar, click the right mouse button to display a shortcut menu, and click Customize to display the Customize dialog box. Click the Commands tab, select Format from the Categories list box, then scroll in the Commands list box until you click and drag the line spacing buttons to the end of the Formatting toolbar. You must drag the button within the Formatting toolbar (the mouse pointer will change to a + from an ×, indicating that you can copy the button). Close the Customize dialog box. The next time you want to change line spacing, just click the appropriate button on the Formatting toolbar.

STEP 3: Indents

➤ Select the second paragraph as shown in Figure 2.15c. (The second paragraph will not yet be indented.)

➤ Pull down the **Format menu** and click **Paragraph** (or press the **right mouse button** to produce the shortcut menu and click **Paragraph**).

➤ If necessary, click the **Indents and Spacing tab** in the Paragraph dialog box. Click the **up arrow** on the Left Indentation text box to set the **Left Indent** to **.5** inch. Set the **Right indent** to **.5** inch. Click **OK.** Your document should match Figure 2.15c.

➤ Save the document.

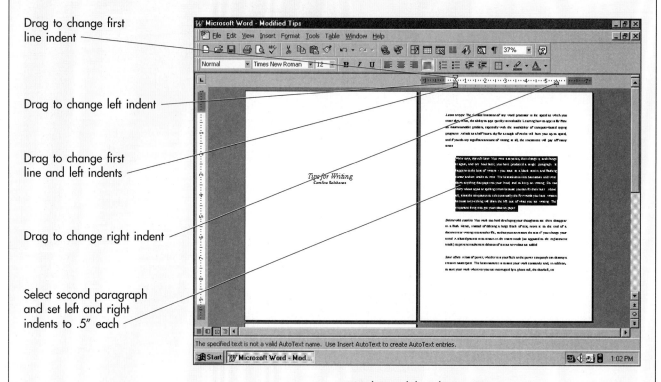

Drag to change first line indent

Drag to change left indent

Drag to change first line and left indents

Drag to change right indent

Select second paragraph and set left and right indents to .5" each

(c) Indents and the Ruler (step 3)

FIGURE 2.15   Hands-on Exercise 3 (continued)

INDENTS AND THE RULER

Use the ruler to change the special, left, and/or right indents. Select the paragraph (or paragraphs) in which you want to change indents, then drag the appropriate indent markers to the new location(s). If you get a hanging indent when you wanted to change the left indent, it means you dragged the bottom triangle instead of the box. Click the Undo button and try again. (You can always use the Format Paragraph command rather than the ruler if you continue to have difficulty.)

STEP 4: Borders and Shading

➤ Pull down the **Format menu.** Click **Borders and Shading** to produce the dialog box in Figure 2.15d.

➤ If necessary, click the **Borders tab.** Select a style and width for the line around the box. Click the rectangle labeled **Box** under Settings.

➤ Click the **Shading Tab.** Click the **down arrow** on the Style list box. Click **10%.**

➤ Click **OK** to accept the settings for both Borders and Shading.

➤ Save the document.

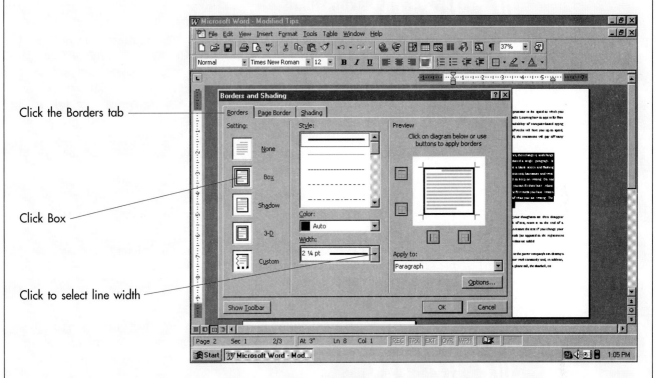

Click the Borders tab ────

Click Box ────

Click to select line width ────

(d) Borders and Shading Command (step 4)

FIGURE 2.15   Hands-on Exercise 3 (continued)

THE PAGE BORDER COMMAND

You can apply a border to the title page of your document, to every page except the title page, or to every page including the title page. Pull down the Format menu, click Borders and Shading, and click the Page Borders tab. First design the border by selecting a style, color, width, and art (if any). Then choose the page(s) to which you want to apply the border by clicking the drop-down arrow in the Apply to list box. Close the Borders and Shading dialog box. See practice exercise 5 at the end of the chapter.

STEP 5: Help with Formatting

➤ Pull down the **Help menu** and click the **What's This command** (or press **Shift+F1**). The mouse pointer changes to an arrow with a question mark.

➤ Click anywhere inside the boxed paragraph to display the formatting information shown in Figure 2.15e.

➤ Click in a different paragraph to see its formatting. Press the **Esc key** to return the pointer to normal.

DISPLAY THE HARD RETURNS

Many formattting commands are implemented at the paragraph level, and thus it helps to know where a paragraph ends. Click the Show/Hide ¶ button on the Standard toolbar to display the hard returns (paragraph marks) and other nonprinting characters (such as tab characters or blank spaces) contained within a document. The Show/Hide ¶ functions as a toggle switch; the first time you click it the hard returns are displayed, the second time you press it the returns are hidden, and so on.

STEP 6: The Zoom Command

➤ Pull down the **View menu.** Click **Zoom** to produce the dialog box in Figure 2.15f.

➤ Click the **Many Pages** option button. Click the **monitor icon** to display a sample selection box, then click and drag to display three pages across as shown in the figure. Release the mouse. Click **OK.**

STEP 7: Advice from the Office Assistant

➤ Click the **Office Assistant button** on the Standard toolbar or press the **F1 key** to display the Assistant. Click the lightbulb (assuming the Assistant has a suggestion) to display the tip. Click the **Back** or **Next** buttons as appropriate to view additional tips.

➤ The Assistant will not, however, repeat a tip from an earlier session unless you reset it at the start of a new session. To reset the tips, click the Assistant to display a balloon asking what you want to do, click the **Options button** in the balloon, click **Options,** then click the button to **Reset My Tips.**

HELP FOR MICROSOFT WORD

Microsoft Word offers help from a variety of sources. You can pull down the Help menu as you can with any Windows application and/or you can click the Office Assisant button on the Standard toolbar. You can also go to the Microsoft Web site to obtain more recent, and often more detailed, information. Pull down the Help menu, click Microsoft on the Web, then click Online Support to go to the Microsoft Web site, provided you have an Internet connection.

Formatting in effect for
selected paragraph

Click in paragraph

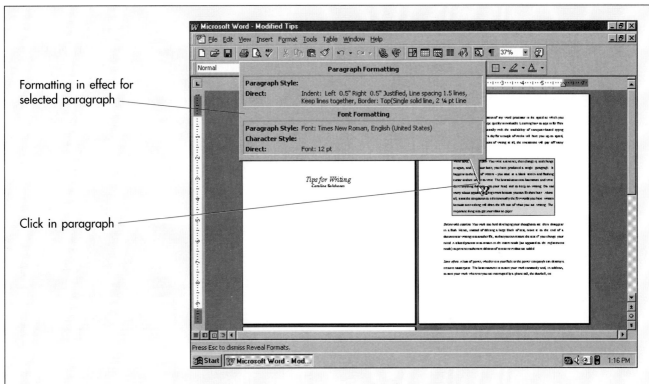

(e) Help with Formatting (step 5)

Decrease Indent button

Increase Indent button

Click Many Pages option

Click on monitor to
display page grid

Click and drag over desired
number of pages

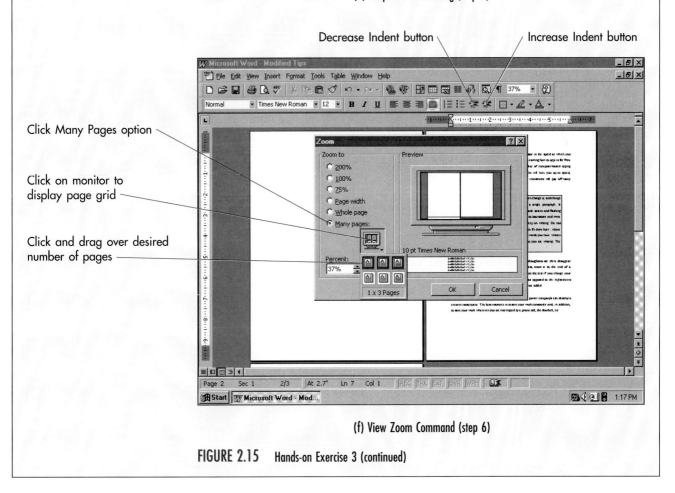

(f) View Zoom Command (step 6)

FIGURE 2.15   Hands-on Exercise 3 (continued)

STEP 8: The Completed Document

➤ Your screen should match the one in Figure 2.15g, which displays all three pages of the document.

➤ The Page Layout view displays both a vertical and a horizontal ruler. The boxed and indented paragraph is clearly shown in the second page.

➤ The soft page break between pages two and three occurs between tips rather than within a tip; that is, the text of each tip is kept together on the same page.

➤ Save the document a final time. Print the completed document and submit it to your instructor. Exit Word.

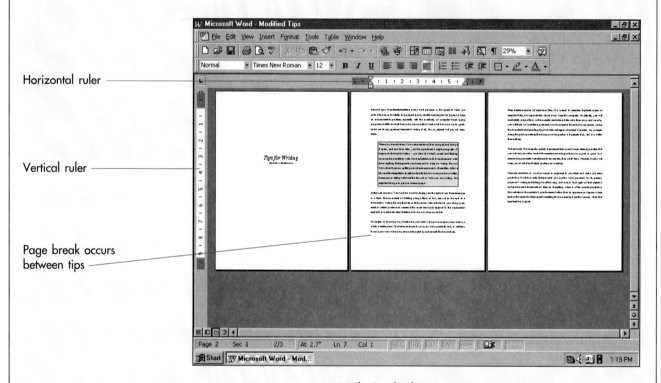

(g) The Completed Document (step 8)

FIGURE 2.15   Hands-on Exercise 3 (continued)

PRINT SELECTED PAGES

Why print an entire document if you want only a few pages? Pull down the File menu and click Print as you usually do to initiate the printing process. Click the Pages option button, then enter the page numbers and/or page ranges you want; for example, 3, 6–8 will print page three and pages six through eight.

Many operations in Word are done within the context of select-then-do; that is, select the text, then execute the necessary command. Text may be selected by dragging the mouse, by using the selection bar to the left of the document, or by using the keyboard. Text is deselected by clicking anywhere within the document.

The Find and Replace commands locate a designated character string and optionally replace one or more occurrences of that string with a different character string. The search may be case-sensitive and/or restricted to whole words as necessary.

Text is moved or copied through a combination of the Cut, Copy, and Paste commands and/or the drag-and-drop facility. The contents of the clipboard are replaced by any subsequent Cut or Copy command, but are unaffected by the Paste command; that is, the same text can be pasted into multiple locations.

The Undo command reverses the effect of previous commands. The Undo and Redo commands work in conjunction with one another; that is, every command that is undone can be redone at a later time.

Scrolling occurs when a document is too large to be seen in its entirety. Scrolling with the mouse changes what is displayed on the screen, but does not move the insertion point; that is, you must click the mouse to move the insertion point. Scrolling via the keyboard (for example, PgUp and PgDn) changes what is seen on the screen as well as the location of the insertion point.

The Page Layout view displays top and bottom margins, headers and footers, and other elements not seen in the Normal view. The Normal view is faster because Word spends less time formatting the display. Both views can be seen at different magnifications.

TrueType fonts are scaleable and accessible from any Windows application. The Format Font command enables you to choose the typeface (e.g., Times New Roman or Arial), style (e.g., bold or italic), point size, and color of text.

The Format Paragraph command determines the line spacing, alignment, indents, and text flow, all of which are set at the paragraph level. Borders and shading are also set at the paragraph level. Margins, page size, and orientation, are set in the Page Setup command and affect the entire document (or section).

KEY WORDS AND CONCEPTS

Alignment	First line indent	Monospaced typeface
Arial	Font	Normal view
Automatic replacement	Format Font command	Page break
Borders and Shading command	Format Painter	Page Layout view
Case-insensitive replacement	Format Paragraph command	Page Setup command
Case-sensitive replacement	Go To command	Paste command
Clipboard	Hanging indent	Point size
Copy command	Hard page break	Portrait orientation
Courier New	Indents	Proportional typeface
Cut command	Landscape orientation	Redo command
Drag and drop	Leader character	Replace command
Find command	Left indent	Right indent
	Line spacing	Sans serif typeface
	Margins	Scrolling
		Select-then-do

Selection bar   Times New Roman   Whole word
Selective replacement   Typeface   replacement
Serif typeface   Type size   Widows and orphans
Shortcut menu   Type style   Wild card
Soft page break   Typography   Zoom command
Special indent   Undo command
Tab stop   View menu

Practice with Word 97

1. Open the *Chapter 2 Practice 1* document that is displayed in Figure 2.16 and make the following changes.
   a. Copy the sentence *Discretion is the better part of valor* to the beginning of the first paragraph.
   b. Move the second paragraph to the end of the document.
   c. Change the typeface of the entire document to 12 point Arial.
   d. Change all whole word occurrences of *feel* to *think.*
   e. Change the spacing of the entire document from single spacing to 1.5. Change the alignment of the entire document to justified.
   f. Set the phrases *Format Font command* and *Format Paragraph command* in italics.
   g. Indent the second paragraph .25 inch on both the left and right.
   h. Box and shade the last paragraph.
   i. Create a title page that precedes the document. Set the title, *Discretion in Design,* in 24 point Arial bold and center it approximately two inches from the top of the page. Right align your name toward the bottom of the title page in 12 point Arial regular.
   j. Print the revised document and submit it to your instructor.

2. Figure 2.17 displays a completed version of the *Chapter 2 Practice 2* document that exists on the data disk. We want you to retrieve the original document from the data disk, then change the document so that it matches Figure 2.17. No editing is required as the text in the original document is identical to the finished document.

   The only changes are in formatting, but you will have to compare the documents in order to determine the nature of the changes. Color is a nice touch (which depends on the availability of a color printer) and is not required. Add your name somewhere in the document, then print the revised document and submit it to your instructor.

3. Create a simple document containing the text of the Preamble to the Constitution as shown in Figure 2.18.
   a. Set the Preamble in 12 point Times New Roman.
   b. Use single spacing and left alignment.
   c. Copy the Preamble to a new page, then change to a larger point size and more interesting typeface.
   d. Create a title page for your assignment, containing your name, course name, and appropriate title. Submit all three pages (the title page and both versions of the Preamble) to your instructor.

It is not difficult, especially with practice, to learn to format a document. It is not long before the mouse goes automatically to the Format Font command to change the selected text to a sans-serif font, to increase the font size, or to apply a boldface or italic style. Nor is it long before you go directly to the Format Paragraph command to change the alignment or line spacing for selected paragraphs.

What is not easy, however, is to teach discretion in applying formats. Too many different formats on one page can be distracting, and in almost all cases, less is better. Be conservative and never feel that you have to demonstrate everything you know how to do in each and every document that you create. Discretion is the better part of valor. No more than two different typefaces should be used in a single document, although each can be used in a variety of different styles and sizes.

It is always a good idea to stay on the lookout for what you feel are good designs and then determine exactly what you like and don't like about each. In that way, you are constantly building ideas for your own future designs.

FIGURE 2.16 Document for Practice Exercise 1

TYPOGRAPHY

The art of formatting a document is more than just knowing definitions, but knowing the definitions is definitely a starting point. A *typeface* is a complete set of characters with the same general appearance, and can be *serif* (cross lines at the end of the main strokes of each letter) or *sans serif* (without the cross lines). A *type size* is a vertical measurement, made from the top of the tallest letter in the character set to the bottom of the lowest letter in the character set. *Type style* refers to variations in the typeface, such as boldface and italics.

Several typefaces are shipped with Windows, including *Times New Roman,* a serif typeface, and *Arial*, a sans serif typeface. Times New Roman should be used for large amounts of text, whereas Arial is best used for titles and subtitles. It is best not to use too many different typefaces in the same document, but rather to use only one or two and then make the document interesting by varying their size and style.

FIGURE 2.17 Document for Practice Exercise 2

We, the people of the United States, in order to form a more perfect Union, establish justice, insure domestic tranquillity, provide for the common defense, promote the general welfare, and secure the blessings of liberty to ourselves and our posterity, do ordain and establish this Constitution for the United States of America.

FIGURE 2.18 Document for Practice Exercise 3

4. As indicated in the chapter, anyone who has used a typewriter is familiar with the function of the Tab key; that is, press Tab and the insertion point moves to the next tab stop (a measured position to align text at a specific place). The Tab key is more powerful in Word because you can choose from four different types of tab stops (left, center, right, and decimal). You can also specify a leader character, typically dots or hyphens, to draw the reader's eye across the page.

   Create the document in Figure 2.19 and add your name in the indicated position. (Use the Help facility to discover how to work with tab stops.) Submit the completed document to your instructor as proof that you have mastered the Tab key.

5. The Page Borders Command: Figure 2.20 illustrates a hypothetical title page for a paper describing the capabilities of borders and shading. The Borders and Shading command is applied at the paragraph level as indicated in the chapter. You can, however, select the Page Border tab within the Borders and Shading dialog box to create an unusual and attractive document. Experiment with the command to create a title page similar to Figure 2.20. Submit the document to your instructor as proof you did the exercise.

EXAMPLES OF TAB STOPS

Example 1 - Right tab at 6":

CIS 120   **Maryann Barber**
FALL 1997   **September 21, 1997**

Example 2 - Right tab with a dot leader at 6":

Chapter 1 1
Chapter 2 31
Chapter 3   56

Example 3 - Right tab at 1" and left tab at 1.25":

             To: Maryann Barber
           From: Joel Stutz
    Department: Computer Information Systems
        Subject: Exams

Example 4 - Left tab at 2" and a decimal tab at 3.5":

                        Rent $375.38
                        Utilities $125.59
                        Phone $56.92
                        Cable $42.45

FIGURE 2.19   Document for Practice Exercise 4

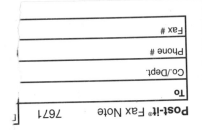

6. Exploring Fonts: The Fonts Folder within the Control Panel displays the names of the fonts available on a system and enables you to obtain a printed sample of any specific font. Click the Start button, click (or point to) the Settings command, click (or point to) Control Panel, then click the Fonts command to open the font folder and display the fonts on your system.

   a. Double click a font you want to view (e.g., Contemporary Brush in Figure 2.21), then click the Print button to print a sample of the selected font.

   b. Click the Fonts button on the Taskbar to return to the Fonts window and open a different font. Print a sample page of this font as well.

   c. Start Word. Create a title page containing your name, class, date, and the title of this assignment (My Favorite Fonts). Staple the three pages together (the title page and two font samples), then submit them to your instructor.

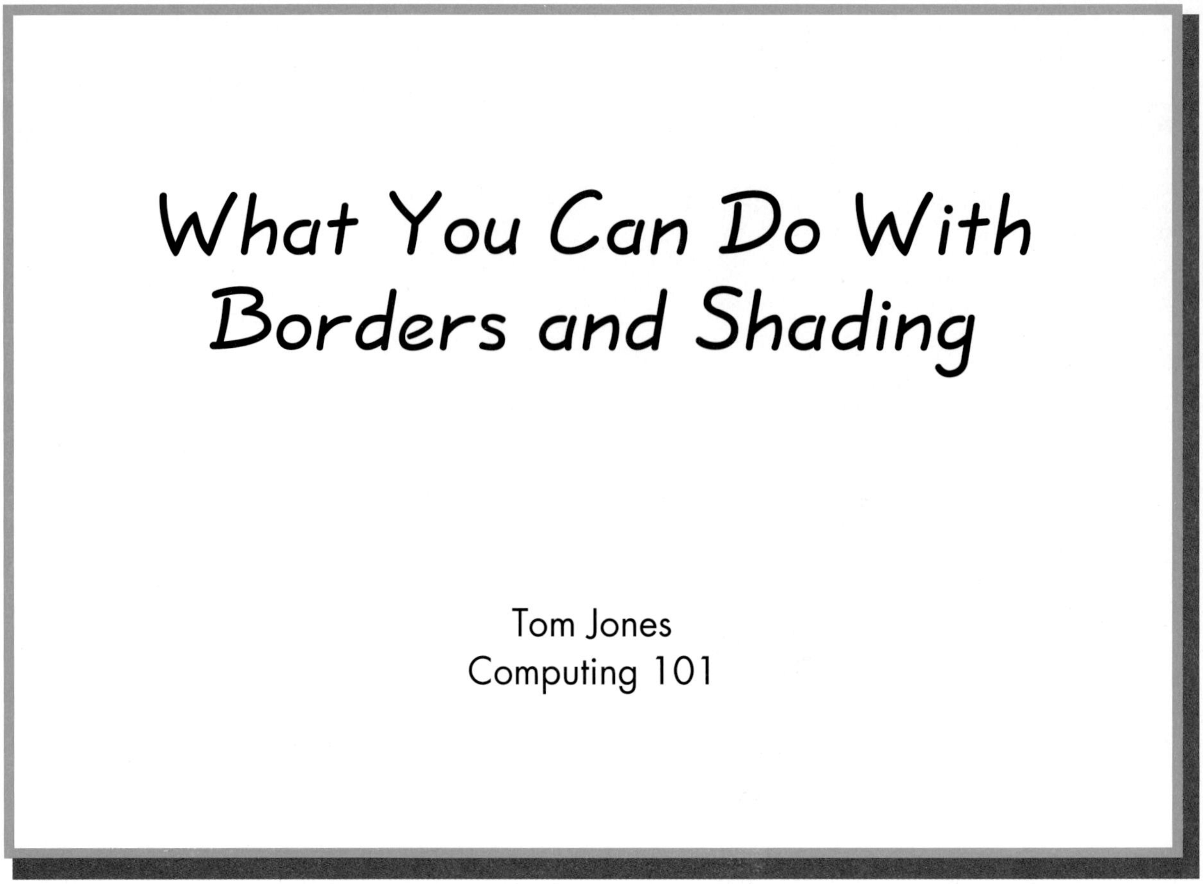

What You Can Do With Borders and Shading

Tom Jones
Computing 101

FIGURE 2.20 Document for Practice Exercise 5

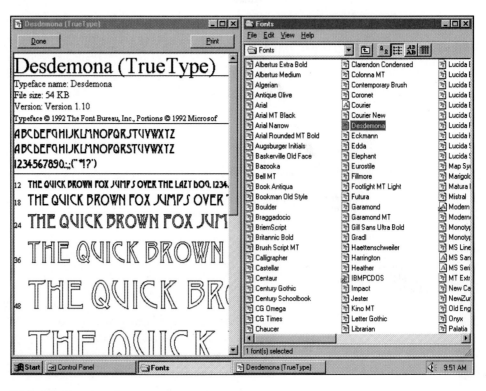

FIGURE 2.21 Screen for Practice Exercise 6

3

ENHANCING A DOCUMENT: THE WEB AND OTHER RESOURCES

OBJECTIVES

After reading this chapter you will be able to:

1. Describe object linking and embedding; explain how it is used to create a compound document.
2. Describe the resources in the Microsoft Clip Gallery; insert clip art and/or a photograph into a document.
3. Use the Format Picture command to wrap text around a clip art image; describe various tools on the Picture toolbar.
4. Use WordArt to insert decorative text into a document.
5. Describe the Internet and World Wide Web; explain how to display the Web toolbar within Microsoft Word.
6. Define a Web-enabled document; download resources from the Web for inclusion in a Word document.
7. Insert a footnote or endnote into a document to cite a reference.

OVERVIEW

This chapter describes how to enhance a document using resources within Microsoft Office as well as resources on the Internet and World Wide Web. We begin with the Microsoft Clip Gallery, a collection of clip art, photographs, sounds, and video clips that can be inserted into any Office document. We also introduce Microsoft WordArt to create special effects with text.

The clip art and photographs included within the Microsoft Clip Gallery pale in comparison to the resources on the Internet. Accordingly, we present a brief introduction to the Internet, then show you how to download a picture from the Web and insert it into a document. We also show you how to add footnotes to give appropriate credit to your sources.

We believe this to be a very enjoyable chapter that will add significantly to your capability in Microsoft Word. As always, learning is best accomplished by doing, and the hands-on exercises are essential to master the material.

The applications in Microsoft Office are thoroughly integrated with one another. Equally important, they share information through a technology known as *Object Linking and Embedding (OLE),* which enables you to create a *compound document* containing data (objects) from multiple applications.

Consider, for example, the compound document in Figure 3.1, which was created in Microsoft Word but contains objects (data) from other applications. The *clip art* (a graphic as opposed to a photograph) was taken from the Microsoft Clip Gallery. The title of the document was created using Microsoft WordArt. The document also illustrates the Insert Symbol command to insert special characters such as the Windows logo.

WordArt ————

Clip art ————

Clip art is available from a variety of sources including the Microsoft Clip Gallery, which is part of the Microsoft Office. One of our favorite images is that of the duck smashing a computer, which depicts the frustration that can affect anyone.

A computer does what you tell it to do, which is not necessarily what you want it to do. There can be a tremendous difference and hence the frustration felt by our duck. There is, however, a logical reason for everything the computer does or does not do, and sooner or later you will discover that reason, at which point everything will fall into place.

The complete Clip Gallery (on the Office 97 CD-ROM) contains more than 3,000 images in a variety of categories. It also has photographs, sound bites, and video clips, which enable you to create other types of documents. And even if you do not have access to the CD, you can use WordArt to create artistic effects to enhance any document.

WordArt enables you to create special effects with text. It lets you rotate and/or flip text, display it vertically on the page, shade it, slant it, arch it, or even print it upside down. Best of all, WordArt is intuitive and easy to use. In essence, you enter text into a dialog box, then you choose a shape for the text from a dialog box. You can create special effects by choosing one of several different shadows. You can vary the image even further by using any TrueType font on your system. It's fun, it's easy, and you can create some truly dynamite documents.

The Insert Symbol command enables you to insert special symbols into a document to give it a professional look. You can, for example, use ™ rather than TM, © rather than (C), or $\frac{1}{2}$ and $\frac{1}{4}$ rather than ¹/₂ and ¹/₄. It also enables you to insert accented characters as appropriate in English as in the word résumé, or in a foreign language to create properly accented words and phrases—for example, ¿Cómo está usted?

Windows logo added
through Insert Symbol
command ————

Natasha Colluci created this document using Microsoft Windows ®

FIGURE 3.1   A Compound Document

Microsoft Clip Gallery

The **Microsoft Clip Gallery** contains more than 3,000 clip art images and almost 150 photographs. It also contains sound files and video clips, although these objects are more common in PowerPoint presentations than in Word documents. The Clip Gallery can be accessed in a variety of ways, most easily through the **Insert Picture command,** which is available in every Office application.

To use the Clip Gallery, you choose the type of object by clicking the appropriate tab—for example, clip art in Figure 3.2a. Next you select the category, such as Science and Technology in Figure 3.2b, and an image within that category, such as the astronaut walking in space. And finally, you click the Insert button to insert the object (the clip art or photograph) into the document.

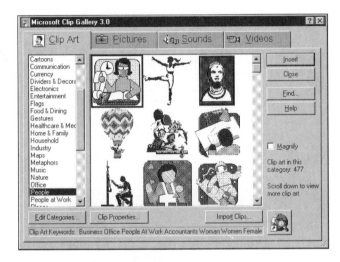

(a) Clip Art

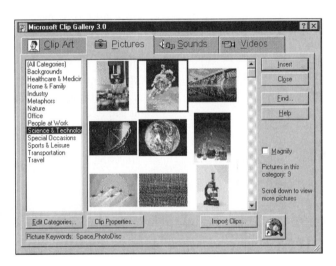

(b) Photographs

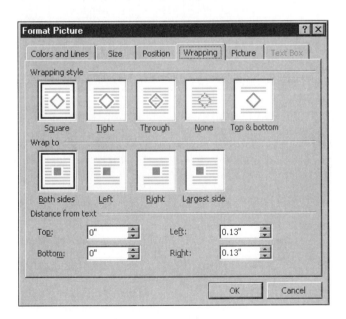

(c) Format Picture Command

(d) Compound Document

FIGURE 3.2   Microsoft Clip Gallery

Once the object has been inserted into a document, it can be moved and sized using various options within the **Format Picture command** shown in Figure 3.2c. You can, for example, wrap text around the picture, place a border around the picture, or even **crop** (cut out a part of) the picture if necessary. Figure 3.2d shows how the selected object appears in the completed document and is consistent with the selected options in the Format Picture dialog box. Note, too, the **sizing handles** on the graphic, which enable you to move and size the figure within the document.

The Insert Symbol Command

One characteristic of a professional document is the use of typographic symbols in place of ordinary typing—for example, ® rather than (R), © rather than (C), or ½ and ¼ rather than 1/2 and 1/4. Much of this formatting is implemented automatically by Word through substitutions built into the **AutoCorrect command.** Other characters, especially accented characters such as the "é" in résumé, or those in a foreign language (e.g., ¿Cómo está usted?), have to be inserted manually into a document.

Look carefully at the last line of Figure 3.1, and notice the Windows 95 logo at the end of the sentence. The latter was created through the **Insert Symbol command,** as shown in Figure 3.3. You select the font containing the desired character (e.g., Wingdings in Figure 3.3), then you select the character, and finally you click the Insert command button to place the character in the document.

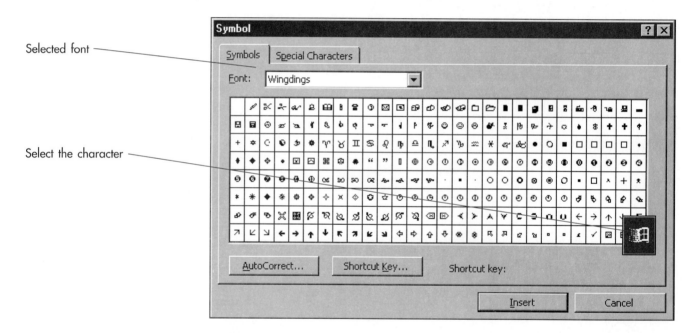

FIGURE 3.3 The Insert Symbol Command

THE WINGDINGS AND SYMBOLS FONTS

The Wingdings and Symbols fonts are two of the best-kept secrets in Windows 95. Both fonts contain a variety of special characters that can be inserted into a document through the Insert Symbol command. These fonts are scaleable to any point size, enabling you to create some truly unusual documents. (See practice exercise 3 at the end of the chapter.)

Microsoft WordArt

Microsoft WordArt is an application within Microsoft Office that creates decorative text to add interest to a document. You can use WordArt in addition to clip art, as was done in Figure 3.1, or in place of clip art if the right image is not available. You're limited only by your imagination, as you can rotate text in any direction, add three-dimensional effects, display the text vertically down the page, shade it, slant it, arch it, or even print it upside down.

WordArt is intuitive and easy to use. In essence, you choose a style for the text from among the selections in the dialog box of Figure 3.4a, then you enter your specific text as shown in Figure 3.4b. You can modify the style through various special effects, you can use any TrueType font on your system, and you can change the color or shading. Figure 3.4c shows the completed WordArt object. It's fun, it's easy, and you can create some truly dynamite documents.

Select WordArt style

Enter text

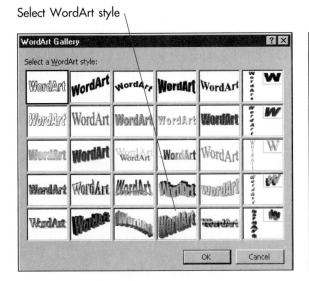

(a) Choose the Style

(b) Enter the Text

(c) Completed WordArt

FIGURE 3.4   Microsoft WordArt

Objective: To create a compound document containing clip art and WordArt. To illustrate the Insert Symbol command to place typographical symbols into a document. Use Figure 3.5 as a guide in the exercise.

STEP 1: The Microsoft Clip Gallery

➤ Start Word. Open the **Clipart and WordArt** document in the Exploring Word folder. Save the document as **Modified Clip Art and WordArt.**

➤ Check that the insertion point is at the beginning of the document. Pull down the **Insert menu,** click **Picture,** then click **ClipArt** to display the Microsoft Clip Gallery as shown in Figure 3.5a. Click **OK** if you see a dialog box reminding you that additional clip art is available on a CD-ROM.

➤ If necessary, click the **ClipArt tab** and select (click) the **Cartoons category.** Select the **Duck and Computer** (or a different image if you prefer), then click the **Insert button** to place the clip art into your document.

➤ The Microsoft Clip Gallery dialog box will close and the picture will be inserted into your document, where it can be moved and sized as described in the next several steps.

Select Duck and Computer

Select Cartoons

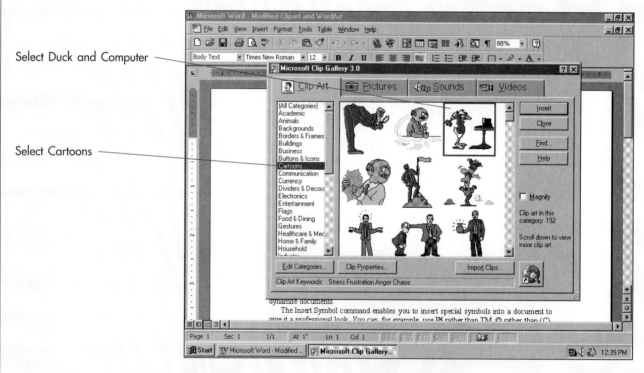

(a) The Clip Gallery (step 1)

FIGURE 3.5 Hands-on Exercise 1

ADDITIONAL CLIP IMAGES

The Microsoft Clip Gallery contains over 100MB of data consisting of more than 3,000 clip art images, 144 photographs, 28 sounds, and 20 video clips. Only a fraction of these are installed with Microsoft Office, but you can access the additional objects from the Office CD at any time. You can also install some or all of the objects on your hard disk, provided you have sufficient space. Start the Windows Explorer, then open the ClipArt folder on the Office CD. Double click the Setup icon to start the Setup Wizard, then follow the on-screen instructions to install the additional components you want.

STEP 2: Move and Size the Picture

➤ Word automatically selects the duck and changes to the Page Layout view in Figure 3.5b. Move and size the duck as described below.

➤ To move an object:

- Click the object (e.g., the duck) to display the sizing handles.
- Point to any part of the duck except a sizing handle (the mouse pointer changes to a four-sided arrow), then click and drag to move the duck elsewhere in the document. You can position the duck anywhere in the document, but you cannot wrap text around the duck until you execute the Format Picture command in step 3.

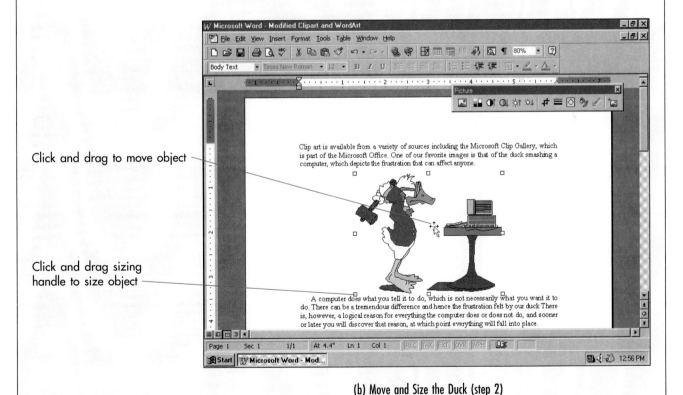

(b) Move and Size the Duck (step 2)

FIGURE 3.5   Hands-on Exercise 1 (continued)

➤ To size an object:

- Click the object (e.g., the duck) to display the sizing handles.
- Drag a corner handle (the mouse pointer changes to a double arrow) to change the length and width of the picture simultaneously; this keeps the graphic in proportion as it sizes it.
- Drag a handle on the horizontal or vertical border to change one dimension only; this distorts the picture.

➤ Save the document.

TO CLICK OR DOUBLE CLICK

Clicking an object selects the object and displays the sizing handles, allowing you to move and/or size the object. Double clicking an object starts the application that created it and enables you to modify the object using that application. Double click the duck, for example, and you display the Microsoft Clip Gallery dialog box, in which you can select a different picture and insert it into the document in place of the original.

STEP 3: Format the Picture

➤ Be sure the duck is still selected, then pull down the **Format menu** and select the **Picture command** to display the Format Picture dialog box in Figure 3.5c.

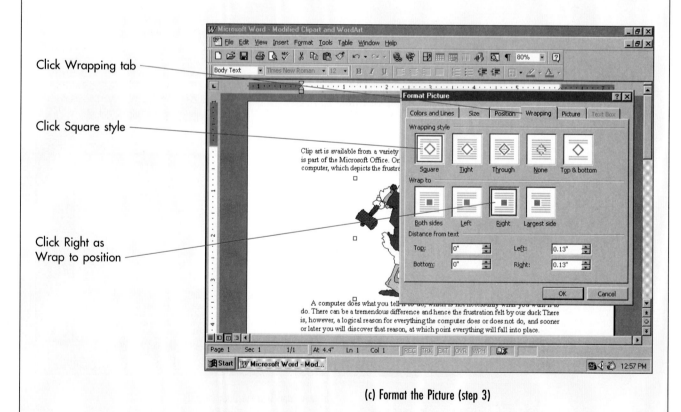

(c) Format the Picture (step 3)

FIGURE 3.5   Hands-on Exercise 1 (continued)

- ➤ Click the **Wrapping tab,** select **Square** as the Wrapping style, and click **right** as the Wrap to position. Click **OK** to close the Format Picture dialog box and implement these selections.
- ➤ The text should be wrapped to the right of the duck. Move and size the duck until you are satisfied with its position. Note, however, that the duck will always be positioned (wrapped) according to the settings in the Format Picture command.
- ➤ Save the document.

THE PICTURE TOOLBAR

The Picture toolbar offers the easiest way to execute various commands associated with a picture or clip art image. It is displayed automatically when a picture is selected; otherwise it is suppressed. As with any toolbar, you can point to a button to display a ScreenTip containing the name of the button, which indicates its function. You will find buttons for wrapping and formatting a picture, a Line Styles button to place a border around a picture, and a cropping button to crop (erase) part of a picture.

STEP 4: WordArt

- ➤ Press **Ctrl+Home** to move to the beginning of the document. Pull down the **Insert menu,** click **Picture,** then click **WordArt** to display the WordArt Gallery dialog box.
- ➤ Select the WordArt style you like (you can change it later). Click **OK.** You will see a second dialog box in which you enter the text. Enter **Enhancing a Document.** Click **OK.**
- ➤ The WordArt object appears in your document in the style you selected. Point to the WordArt object and click the **right mouse button** to display the shortcut menu in Figure 3.5d. Click **Format WordArt** to display the Format WordArt dialog box.
- ➤ Click the **Wrapping tab,** then select **Top & Bottom** as the Wrapping style. Click **OK.** It is important to select this wrapping option to facilitate placing the WordArt at the top of the document. Save the document.

FORMATTING WORDART

The WordArt toolbar offers the easiest way to execute various commands associated with a WordArt object. It is displayed automatically when a WordArt object is selected; otherwise it is suppressed. As with any toolbar, you can point to a button to display a ScreenTip containing the name of the button, which indicates its function. You will find buttons to display the text vertically, change the style or shape, and/or edit the text.

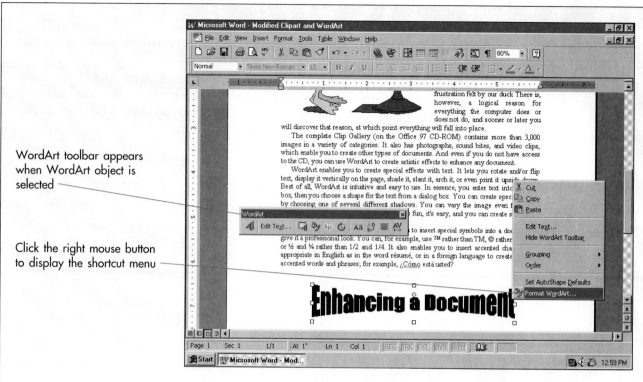

WordArt toolbar appears when WordArt object is selected

Click the right mouse button to display the shortcut menu

(d) WordArt (step 4)

FIGURE 3.5   Hands-on Exercise 1 (continued)

STEP 5: WordArt (continued)

➤ Click and drag the WordArt object to move it to the top of the document, as shown in Figure 3.5e. (The Format WordArt dialog box is not yet visible.)

➤ Point to the WordArt object, click the **right mouse button** to display a shortcut menu, then click **Format WordArt** to display the Format WordArt dialog box.

➤ Click the **Colors and Lines tab,** then click the **Fill Color drop-down arrow** to display the available colors. Select a different color (e.g., blue).

➤ Move and/or size the WordArt object as necessary. Save the document.

THE THIRD DIMENSION

You can make your WordArt images even more dramatic by adding 3-D effects. You can tilt the text up or down, right or left, increase or decrease the depth, and change the shading. Pull down the View menu, click Toolbars, click Customize to display the complete list of available toolbars, then check the box to display the 3-D Settings toolbar. Select the WordArt object, then experiment with various tools and special effects. The results are even better if you have a color printer.

Click Colors and Lines tab

Click Fill Color
drop-down arrow

Select a color

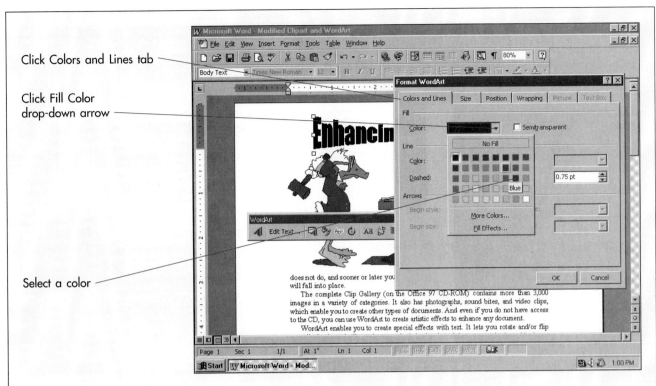

(e) WordArt Continued (step 5)

FIGURE 3.5   Hands-on Exercise 1 (continued)

STEP 6: The Insert Symbol Command

➤ Press **Ctrl+End** to move to the end of the document, as shown in Figure 3.5f. (The Symbol dialog box is not yet visible.) Press the **enter key** to insert a blank line at the end of the document.

➤ Type the sentence, **John Smith created this document using Microsoft Windows,** substituting your name for John Smith. Click the **Center button** on the Formatting toolbar to center the sentence.

➤ Pull down the **Insert menu,** click **Symbol,** then choose **Wingdings** from the Font list box. Click the **Windows logo** (the last character in the last line), click **Insert,** then close the Symbol dialog box.

➤ Click and drag to select the newly inserted symbol, click the **drop-down arrow** on the **Font Size box,** then change the font to **24** points. Press the **right arrow key** to deselect the symbol.

➤ Click the **drop-down arrow** on the **Font Size box** and change to **10 point type** so that subsequent text is entered in this size.

➤ Type **(r)** after the Windows logo and try to watch the monitor as you enter the text. The (r) will be converted automatically to ® because of the Auto-Format command, as described in the boxed tip on page 116.

➤ Save the document.

Font size box

Center button

Click Font drop-down arrow
to display available fonts

Select Windows logo

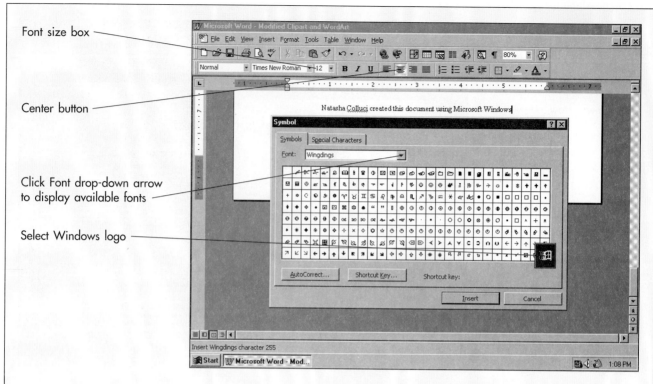

(f) Insert Symbol Command (step 6)

FIGURE 3.5   Hands-on Exercise 1 (continued)

AUTOCORRECT AND AUTOFORMAT

The AutoCorrect feature not only corrects mistakes as you type by substituting one character string for another (e.g., *the* for *teh*), but it will also substitute symbols for typewritten equivalents such as © for (c), provided the entries are included in the table of substitutions. The AutoFormat feature is similar in concept and replaces common fractions such as 1/2 or 1/4 with ½ or ¼. It also converts ordinal numbers such as 1st or 2nd to 1st or 2nd. See practice exercise 3 for additional examples. If either feature is not working, pull down the Tools menu, click the AutoCorrect command, then choose the appropriate settings within the AutoCorrect dialog box.

STEP 7: The Completed Document

➤ Click the **drop-down arrow** on the Zoom box and select **Whole Page** to preview the completed document as shown in Figure 3.5g.

➤ Print the document and submit it to your instructor as proof that you did the exercise. Close the document. Exit Word if you do not want to continue with the next exercise at this time.

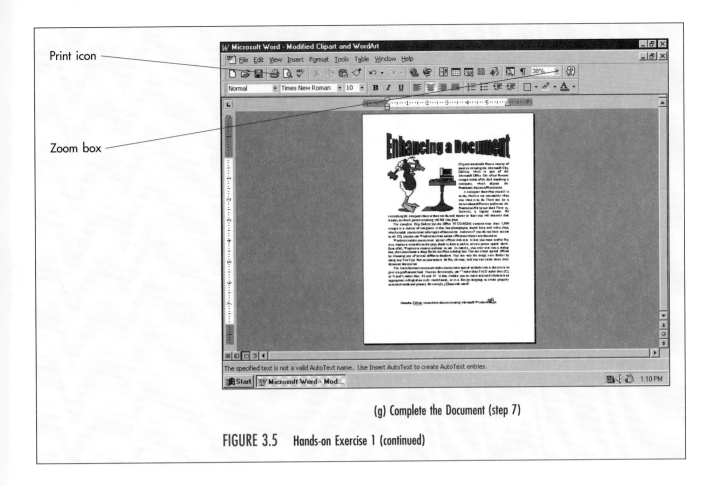

Print icon

Zoom box

(g) Complete the Document (step 7)

FIGURE 3.5   Hands-on Exercise 1 (continued)

RESOURCES FROM THE INTERNET AND WORLD WIDE WEB

The resources in the Microsoft Clip Gallery in Office 97 are impressive when compared to previous versions of Microsoft Office, but pale in comparison to what is available on the Internet and World Wide Web. Hence, any discussion of enhancing a document through clip art and/or photographs must also include the Internet. We begin with a brief description of the Internet and World Wide Web and then describe how to incorporate these resources into a Word document.

The *Internet* is a network of networks that connects computers across the country and around the world. It grew out of a U.S. Department of Defense (DOD) experimental project begun in 1969 to test the feasibility of a wide area (long distance) computer network over which scientists and military personnel could share messages and data.

The *World Wide Web* (*WWW,* or simply, the Web) is a very large subset of the Internet, consisting of those computers containing hypertext and/or hypermedia documents. A *hypertext document* is a document that contains a link (reference) to another document, which may be on the same computer, or even on a different computer, with the latter located anywhere in the world. *Hypermedia* is similar in concept, except that it provides links to graphic, sound, and video files in addition to text files.

Either type of document enables you to move effortlessly from one document (or computer) to another. And therein lies the fascination of the Web: By simply clicking link after link you move smoothly from one document to the next.

You can start your journey at your professor's home page in New York, for example, which may contain a reference to the Library of Congress, which in turn may take you to a different document, and on. So, off you go to Washington D.C., and from there to a different document on a computer across the country or perhaps around the world.

Every document in Office 97 is **_Web-enabled_,** meaning that the application (e.g., Microsoft Word) will automatically detect and highlight any **_hyperlinks_** that are entered into a document. The Word document in Figure 3.6, for example, displays the Web address www.microsoft.com in underlined blue text just as it would appear in a regular Web (hypertext) document. This is not merely a change in formatting, but an actual hyperlink to a document on the Web (or corporate intranet).

You can click the link from within Word and, provided you have an Internet connection, your Web browser will display the associated page. Note, too, that once you click the link, its color will change (e.g., from blue to magenta) just as it would if you were viewing the page in Netscape or the Internet Explorer. We did not do anything special to create the hyperlink; we simply typed the address as we were creating the document, and Word in turn created the hyperlink.

Look carefully at the screen in Figure 3.6, noting the presence of the **_Web toolbar_,** which appears immediately under the Formatting toolbar. (The Web toolbar is displayed by executing the Toolbars command from the View menu.) The Web toolbar contains buttons similar to those on the toolbar in Internet Explorer. You can, for example, enter the address (URL) of a Web page (or a local document) to activate your browser and access the page. You can use the Favorites button to add a page to your list of favorites and/or open a previously added page. You can click the Back and Forward buttons to move between previously displayed pages. And, as with any toolbar, ScreenTips are displayed when you point to a button whose name indicates its function.

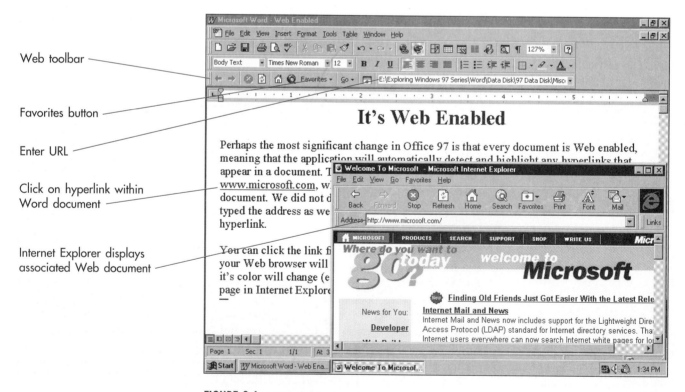

FIGURE 3.6   Internet Enhancements

Copyright Protection

A *copyright* provides legal protection for a written or artistic work, giving the author exclusive rights to its use and reproduction, except as governed under the fair use exclusion as explained below. Anything on the Internet or World Wide Web should be considered copyrighted unless the document specifically says it is in the *public domain,* in which case the author is giving everyone the right to freely reproduce and distribute the material.

Does copyright protection mean you cannot quote in your term papers statistics and other facts you find while browsing the Web? Does it mean you cannot download an image to include in your report? The answer to both questions depends on the amount of the material and on your intended use of the information. It is considered *fair use,* and thus not an infringement of copyright, to use a portion of the work for educational, nonprofit purposes, or for the purpose of critical review or commentary. In other words, you can use a quote, downloaded image, or other information from the Web *if* you cite the original work in your footnotes and/or bibliography. Facts themselves are not covered by copyright, so you can use statistical and other data without fear of infringement. You should, however, cite the original source in your document.

Footnotes and Endnotes

A *footnote* provides additional information about an item, such as its source, and appears at the bottom of the page where the reference occurs. An *endnote* is similar in concept but appears at the end of a document. A horizontal line separates the notes from the rest of the document.

The *Insert Footnote command* inserts a note into a document, and automatically assigns the next sequential number to that note. To create a note, position the insertion point where you want the reference, pull down the Insert menu, click Footnote to display the dialog box in Figure 3.7a, then choose either the

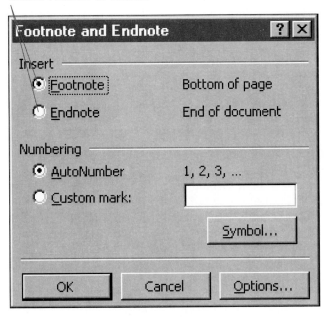

(a) Footnotes and Endnotes

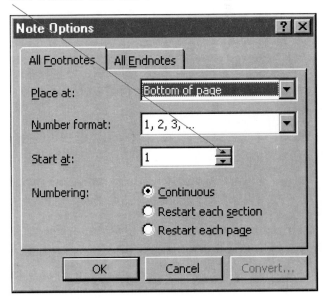

(b) Options

FIGURE 3.7 Footnotes and Endnotes

Footnote or Endnote option button. A superscript reference is inserted into the document, and you will be positioned at the bottom of the page (a footnote) or at the end of the document (an endnote) where you enter the text of the note.

The Options command button in the Footnote and Endnote dialog box enables you to modify the formatting of either type of note as shown in Figure 3.7b. You can change the numbering format (e.g., to Roman numerals) and/or start numbering from a number other than 1. You can also convert footnotes to endnotes or vice versa.

The Insert Footnote command adjusts for last-minute changes, either in your writing or in your professor's requirements. It will, for example, renumber all existing notes to accommodate the addition or deletion of a footnote or endnote. Existing notes are moved (or deleted) within a document by moving (deleting) the reference mark rather than the text of the footnote.

HANDS-ON EXERCISE 2

The Internet as a Resource

Objective: To download a picture from the Internet and use it in a Word document. Use Figure 3.8 as a guide in the exercise. The exercise requires that you have an Internet connection.

STEP 1: The Web Toolbar

➤ Start Word. Point to any toolbar, then click the **right mouse button** to display a context-sensitive menu, which lists the available toolbars in Word.

➤ Click **Web** to display the Web toolbar, as shown in Figure 3.8a. Do not be concerned if the position of your toolbars is different from ours.

➤ Click the **Address box.** Enter **www.whitehouse.gov** (the http:// is assumed), then press the **enter key** to connect to this site. Your Web browser (e.g., Internet Explorer) will open automatically and connect you to the White House home page.

➤ If the Internet Explorer window does not open on your desktop, point to its button on the Windows 95 taskbar, click the **right mouse button** to display a context-sensitive menu, then click the **Restore command** to display the window. Click the **Maximize button** so that your browser takes up the entire screen.

DOCKED VERSUS FLOATING TOOLBARS

A toolbar is either docked along an edge of a window or floating within the window. To move a docked toolbar, click and drag the move handle (the parallel lines that appear at the left of the toolbar) to a new position. To move a floating toolbar, click and drag its title bar—if you drag a floating toolbar to the edge of the window, it becomes a docked toolbar and vice versa. You can also change the shape of a floating toolbar by dragging any border in the direction you want to go. And finally, you can double click the background of any toolbar to toggle between a floating toolbar and a docked (fixed) toolbar.

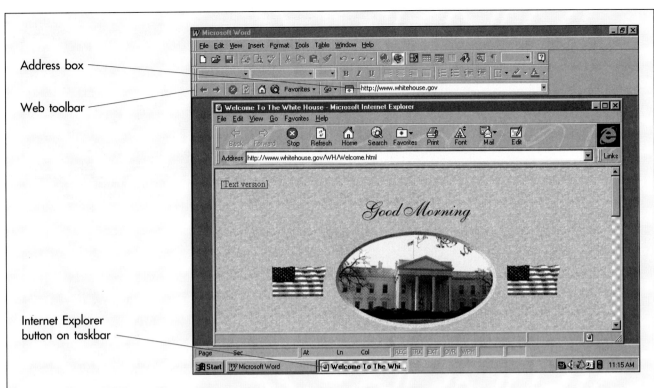

Address box

Web toolbar

Internet Explorer
button on taskbar

(a) The Web Toolbar (step 1)

FIGURE 3.8   Hands-on Exercise 2

STEP 2: Save the Picture

➤ You should be connected to the White House Web site. Click the **down arrow**
on the vertical scroll bar until you can click the link to **White House History
and Tours.**

➤ Click the link to **The Presidents of the United States** (or a similar link if the
site has changed since our last visit), then click the link to your favorite president, e.g., **John F. Kennedy.** You should see the screen in Figure 3.8b (the
Save As dialog box is not yet visible).

➤ Point to the picture of President Kennedy, click the **right mouse button** to
display a shortcut menu, then click the **Save Picture as command** to display
the Save As dialog box.

  • Click the **drop-down arrow** in the Save in list box to specify the drive and
    folder in which you want to save the graphic (e.g., the Exploring Word
    folder on drive C).

  • The file name and file type are entered automatically by Internet Explorer.
    (You may change the name, but don't change the file type.) Click the **Save
    button** to download the image. Remember the file name and location
    because you will need to access the file in the next step.

➤ The Save As dialog box will close automatically as soon as the picture has
been downloaded to your PC. Click the link to the **Inaugural Address** after
the dialog box closes.

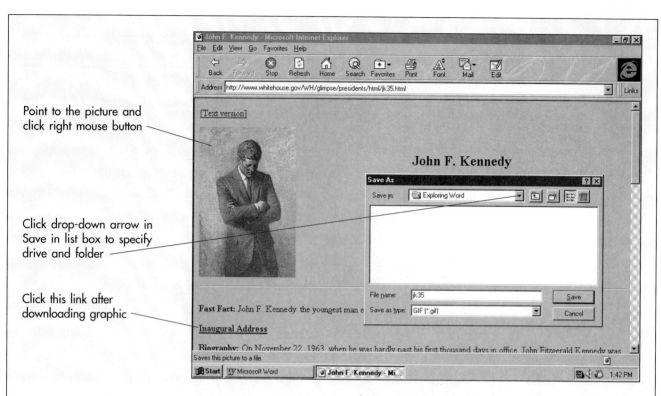

Point to the picture and click right mouse button

Click drop-down arrow in Save in list box to specify drive and folder

Click this link after downloading graphic

(b) Save the Picture (step 2)

FIGURE 3.8 Hands-on Exercise 2 (continued)

MULTITASKING

Multitasking—the ability to run multiple applications at the same time—is one of the primary advantages of the Windows environment. Minimizing an application is different from closing it, and you want to minimize, rather than close, an application to take advantage of multitasking. Closing an application removes it from memory so that you have to restart the application if you want to return to it later in the session. Minimizing, however, leaves the application open in memory, but shrinks its window to a button on the Windows 95 taskbar.

STEP 3: Copy the Quotation

➤ You should see the text of President Kennedy's address as shown in Figure 3.8c. Scroll down in the document until you can select the sentence beginning with **"And so, my fellow Americans..."**

➤ Point to the selected sentence, then click the **right mouse button** to display the shortcut menu. Click **Copy** to copy the selected text to the clipboard.

➤ Click the button for Microsoft Word on the taskbar, then open a new document. Pull down the **Edit menu** and click the **Paste command** (or click the **Paste button** on the Standard toolbar) to paste the contents of the clipboard (the quotation from President Kennedy) into the Word document.

➤ Save the document as **President Kennedy.** Close the Internet Explorer.

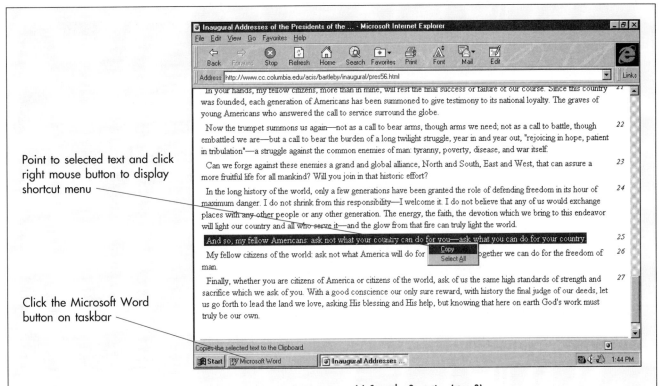

Point to selected text and click right mouse button to display shortcut menu

Click the Microsoft Word button on taskbar

(c) Copy the Quotation (step 3)

FIGURE 3.8   Hands-on Exercise 2 (continued)

THE CLIPBOARD

The clipboard is a temporary storage area that is available to all Windows applications. Selected text is cut or copied from a document and placed on the clipboard from where it can be pasted to a new location(s). You can use the clipboard (with the appropriate combination of Cut, Copy, and Paste commands) to move and copy text within a document. You can also use it to move and copy text from one document to another or from one application to another, e.g., from Internet Explorer to Microsoft Word.

STEP 4: Insert a Footnote

➤ Add quotation marks as shown in Figure 3.8d. Change the font to **28 point Times New Roman.** Click at the end of the quotation.

➤ Pull down the **Insert menu.** Click **Footnote** to display the Footnote and Endnote dialog box. Check that the option buttons for **Footnote** and **AutoNumber** are selected, then click **OK.**

➤ The insertion point moves to the bottom of the page, where you can add the text of the footnote. Enter **Inaugural Address, John F. Kennedy, January 20, 1961.** Click the **Close button** on the Footnote toolbar.

➤ Save the document.

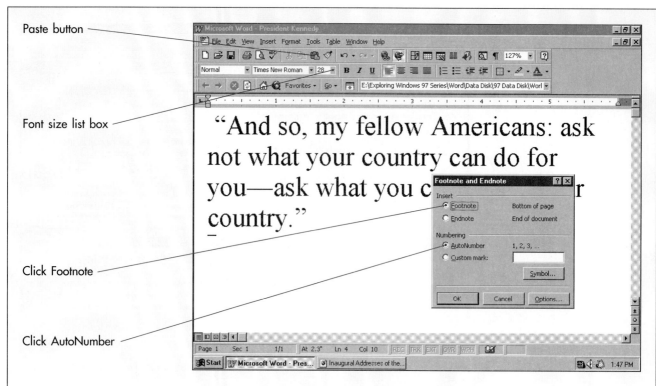

Paste button

Font size list box

Click Footnote

Click AutoNumber

"And so, my fellow Americans: ask not what your country can do for you—ask what you c[...]r country."

(d) Add a Footnote (step 4)

FIGURE 3.8 Hands-on Exercise 2 (continued)

STEP 5: Insert the Picture

➤ Press **Ctrl+Home** to move to the beginning of the document. Pull down the **Insert menu,** point to (or click) **Picture,** then click **From File** to display the Insert Picture dialog box shown in Figure 3.8e.

➤ Click the **drop-down arrow** on the Look in text box to select the drive and folder where you previously saved the picture (e.g., the Exploring Word folder on drive C).

➤ Select (click) **jk35,** which is the file containing the picture of President Kennedy. Click the **Preview button** (if necessary) to display the picture before inserting it into the document.

➤ Click **Insert,** and the picture of President Kennedy will appear in your document. Do not worry about its size or position at this time.

CROPPING A PICTURE

Select (click) a picture and Word automatically displays the Picture toolbar, which lets you modify the picture in subtle ways. The Crop tool is one of the most useful as it enables you to eliminate (crop) part of a picture. Select the picture to display the Picture toolbar and display the sizing handles. Click the Crop tool (the ScreenTip will display the name of the tool), then click and drag a sizing handle to crop the part of the picture you want to eliminate.

Preview button

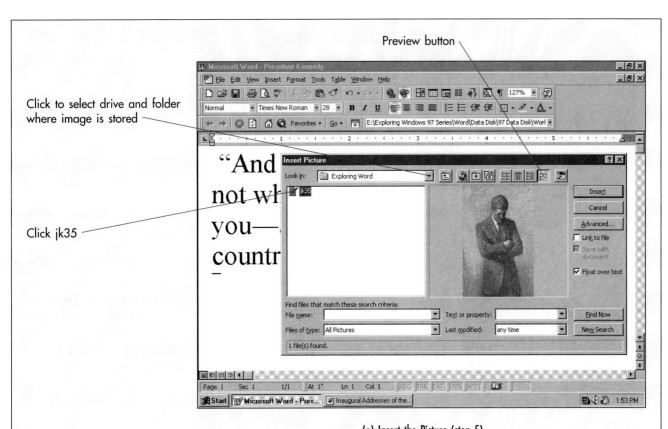

Click to select drive and folder where image is stored

Click jk35

(e) Insert the Picture (step 5)

FIGURE 3.8   Hands-on Exercise 2 (continued)

STEP 6: Move and Size the Picture
➤ Word automatically changes to the Page Layout View when you insert a picture. Zoom to **Whole Page** to view the document as shown in Figure 3.8f (the line styles are not yet visible).
➤ Move and size the picture until it is positioned as shown. Alternatively, you can experiment with a different layout for your document.
➤ Check that the picture is still selected. Click the **Line Styles button** on the Picture toolbar to display the styles in Figure 3.8f. Click the **1 pt line** to place a 1 point border around the picture.
➤ Center the quotation as a finishing touch. Save the document.

MISSING HYPERLINK

Word will, by default, convert any Internet path (e.g., any text beginning with http:// or www) to a hyperlink. If this is not the case, pull down the Tools menu, click AutoCorrect, then click the AutoFormat As You Type tab. Check the box in the Replace as you type area for Internet and Network paths. Click OK. The next time you enter a Web or e-mail address, it will be converted automatically to a hyperlink.

STEP 7: Insert a Second Footnote

➤ Click the **drop-down arrow** on the Zoom box to return to **Page Width.** Click below the picture. Press **enter** to add a blank line.

➤ Select the blank line and change the point size to 12, then add the text **Photograph is from the White House Web page** as shown in Figure 3.8g. Do not press the enter key.

➤ The insertion point should be immediately after the sentence you just entered. Pull down the **Insert menu,** click **Footnote** to display the Footnote and Endnote dialog box, then check that the option buttons for **Footnote** and **AutoNumber** are selected. Click **OK.**

➤ Word inserts a new footnote and simultaneously positions you at the bottom of the page to add the actual note. (If both footnotes do not fit on the bottom of the page, zoom back to the Whole Page and resize the picture.) The existing footnote has been changed to note number 2 (since it comes after the new footnote).

➤ Enter the complete reference **www.whitehouse.gov/WH/glimpse/presidents/html/jk35.html** as well as today's date. Word recognizes the Web address and automatically converts it to a hyperlink, enabling you to click on the link and return to the Web page from where you obtained the picture.

➤ Save the document, then print the document to submit to your instructor as proof you did the exercise.

➤ Exit Word if you do not want to continue with the next exercise at this time.

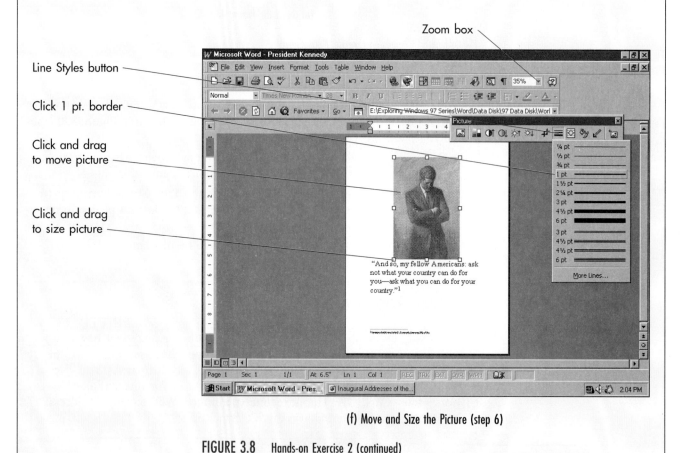

(f) Move and Size the Picture (step 6)

FIGURE 3.8   Hands-on Exercise 2 (continued)

Center button   Zoom box

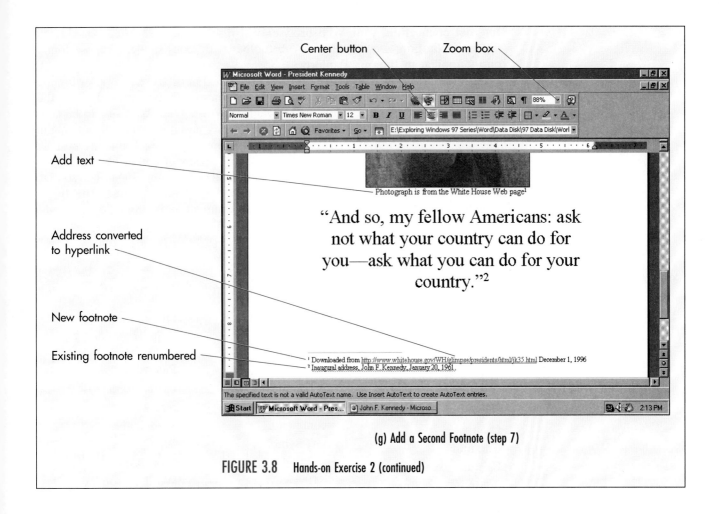

Add text

Address converted
to hyperlink

New footnote

Existing footnote renumbered

(g) Add a Second Footnote (step 7)

FIGURE 3.8   Hands-on Exercise 2 (continued)

SUMMARY

The applications in Microsoft Office are thoroughly integrated with one another. They look alike and work alike. Equally important, they share information through a technology known as Object Linking and Embedding (OLE), which enables you to create a compound document containing data (objects) from multiple applications.

The Microsoft Clip Gallery contains more than 3,000 clip art images and almost 150 photographs, each in a variety of categories. It also contains sound files and video clips, although these objects are more commonly used in PowerPoint presentations than in Word documents. Microsoft WordArt is an application within Microsoft Office that creates decorative text, which can be used to add interest to a document.

The Insert Symbol command provides access to special characters, making it easy to place typographic characters into a document. The symbols can be taken from any TrueType font and can be displayed in any point size.

The Internet is a network of networks. The World Wide Web (WWW, or simply the Web) is a very large subset of the Internet, consisting of those computers containing hypertext and/or hypermedia documents. Resources (e.g., clip art or photographs) can be downloaded from the Web for inclusion in a Word document.

Every document in Office 97 is Web-enabled, meaning that the application will automatically detect and highlight any hyperlinks that are entered in a document. You can click a hyperlink from within Word and, provided you have an

Internet connection, your Web browser will display the associated page. Each Office application also contains a Web toolbar with icons similar to those found on the toolbar in Internet Explorer.

A copyright provides legal protection to a written or artistic work, giving the author exclusive rights to its use and reproduction except as governed under the fair use exclusion. Anything on the Internet or World Wide Web should be considered copyrighted unless the document specifically says it is in the public domain. The fair use exclusion enables you to use a portion of the work for educational, nonprofit purposes, or for the purpose of critical review or commentary.

A footnote provides additional information about an item, such as its source, and appears at the bottom of the page where the reference occurs. The Insert Footnote command inserts a footnote into a document and automatically assigns the next sequential number to that note.

KEY WORDS AND CONCEPTS

AutoCorrect
AutoFormat
Clip art
Clipboard
Compound document
Copyright
Crop
Endnote
Fair use exclusion
Footnote
Format Picture
  command

Hyperlink
Hypermedia
Hypertext
Insert Footnote
  command
Insert Picture
  command
Insert Symbol
  command
Internet
Microsoft Clip Gallery
Microsoft WordArt

Object Linking
  and Embedding
  (OLE)
Picture toolbar
Public domain
Sizing handle
Web-enabled
Web toolbar
WordArt
WordArt toolbar
World Wide Web

PRACTICE WITH WORD 97

1. **Inserting Objects:** Figure 3.9 illustrates a flyer that we created for a hypothetical computer sale. We embedded clip art and WordArt and created what we believe is an attractive flyer. Try to duplicate our advertisement, or better yet, create your own. Include your name somewhere in the document as a sales associate. Be sure to spell check your ad, then print the completed flyer and submit it to your instructor.

2. **Exploring TrueType:** Installing Windows 95 also installs several TrueType fonts, which in turn are accessible from any application. Two of the fonts, Symbols and Wingdings, contain a variety of special characters that can be used to create some unusual documents. Use the Insert Symbol command, your imagination, and the fact that TrueType fonts are scaleable to any point size to re-create the documents in Figure 3.10. Better yet, use your imagination to create your own documents.

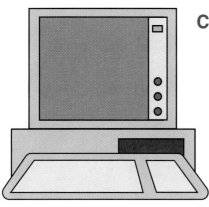

Computer World's Annual Pre-Inventory Sale

When: **Saturday, June 21, 1997**
             8:00AM - 10:00PM

Where: **13640 South Dixie Highway**

Computer World

Computers
Printers
Fax/Modems
CD-ROM drives
Sound Systems
Software
Etc.

Pre-Inventory Sale

Sales Associate: Bianca Costo

FIGURE 3.9   Document for Practice Exercise 1

Valentine's Day
We'll serenade your sweetheart
Call 284-LOVE

STUDENT COMPUTER LAB
Fall Semester Hours

FIGURE 3.10   Documents for Practice Exercise 2

3. It's Easier Than It Looks: The document in Figure 3.11 was created to illustrate the automatic formatting and correction facilities that are built into Microsoft Word. We want you to create the document, include your name at the bottom, then submit the completed document to your instructor as proof that you did the exercise. All you have to do is follow the instructions within the document and let Word do the formatting and correcting for you.

The only potential difficulty is that the options on your system may be set to negate some of the features to which we refer. Accordingly, you need to pull down the Tools menu, click the AutoCorrect command, and click the AutoFormat As You Type tab. Verify that the options referenced in the document are in effect. You also need to review the table of predefined substitutions on the AutoCorrect tab to learn the typewritten characters that will trigger the smiley faces, copyright, and registered trademark substitutions.

It's Easier Than It Looks

This document was created to demonstrate the AutoCorrect and AutoFormat features that are built into Microsoft Word. In essence, you type as you always did and enter traditional characters, then let Word perform its "magic" by substituting symbols and other formatting for you. Among the many features included in these powerful commands are the:

1. Automatic creation of numbered lists by typing a number followed by a period, tab, or right parenthesis. Just remember to press the return key twice to turn off this feature.
2. Symbols for common fractions such as $\frac{1}{2}$ or $\frac{1}{4}$.
3. Ordinal numbers with superscripts created automatically such as 1st, 2nd, or 3rd.
4. Copyright © and Registered trademark ® symbols.

AutoFormat will even add a border to a paragraph any time you type three or more hyphens, equal signs, or underscores on a line by itself.

===
_____

And finally, the AutoCorrect feature has built-in substitution for smiley faces that look best when set in a larger point size such as 72 points.

FIGURE 3.11   Document for Practice Exercise 3

4. What You Can Do with Clip Art: We are not artistic by nature, and there is no way that we could have created the original clip art image of the duck smashing the computer. We did, however, create the variation shown in Figure 3.12 by using various tools on the Drawing toolbar. All it took was a little imagination and a sense of what can be done.

Start by inserting the clip art image into a new document and displaying the Drawing toolbar. Select the clip art image, click the drop-down arrow on the Draw button on the Drawing toolbar, and click the Ungroup command. The duck and the computer are now separate objects, each of which can be selected and manipulated separately.

Click anywhere in the document to deselect both the duck and the computer, then select just the duck. Click the Copy button to copy the duck to the clipboard, then click the Paste button to duplicate the duck. Click and drag the second duck to the right side of the document. Click the drop-down arrow on the Draw button on the Drawing toolbar, click the Rotate or Flip command, then click Flip Horizontal to turn the duck around. To change the color and design of the duck's jacket, you need to ungroup the duck itself, then select the jacket and execute the appropriate command(s).

The rest is up to you. Use the ScreenTips and online help to learn about the different tools. Create one or more variations of the duck or any other clip art image and submit them to your instructor.

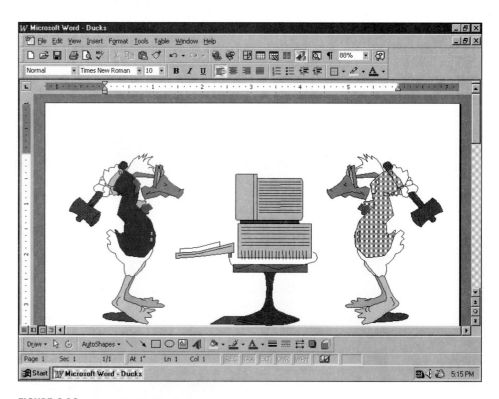

FIGURE 3.12   Screen for Practice Exercise 4

5. Presidential Anecdotes: Figure 3.13 displays the finished version of a document containing 10 presidential anecdotes. The anecdotes were taken from the book *Presidential Anecdotes,* by Paul F. Boller, Jr., published by Penguin Books (New York, NY, 1981). Open the *Chapter 3 Practice 5* document that is found on the data disk, then make the following changes:

a. Add a footnote after Mr. Boller's name, which appears at the end of the second sentence, citing the information about the book. This, in turn, renumbers all existing footnotes in the document.

b. Switch the order of the anecdotes for Lincoln and Jefferson so that the presidents appear in order. The footnotes for these references are changed automatically.

c. Convert all of the footnotes to endnotes, as shown in the figure.

d. Go to the White House Web site and download a picture of any of the 10 presidents, then incorporate that picture into a cover page. Remember to cite the reference with an appropriate footnote.

e. Submit the completed document to your instructor.

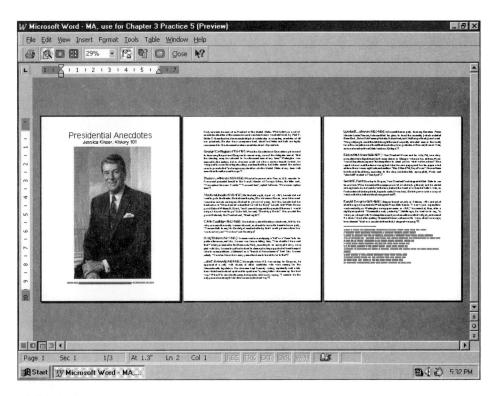

FIGURE 3.13 Screen for Practice Exercise 5

6. Photographs Online: The Smithsonian Institution is a priceless resource. Go to the home page of the Smithsonian (*www.si.edu*) and click the link to Resources, which takes you to the Photographs online page (*photo2.si.edu*) shown in Figure 3.14. Click the link to search the photo database. Use the technique described in the chapter to download two photographs. Then incorporate those pictures into a Word document describing those photographs. Be sure to include an appropriate footnote to cite the source.

7. Music on the Web: The World Wide Web is a source of infinite variety, including music from your favorite rock group. You can find biographical information and/or photographs such as the one in Figure 3.15. You can even find music, which you can download and play, provided you have the necessary hardware. Use any search engine to find documents about your favorite rock group, then incorporate the results of your research into a short paper to submit to your instructor.

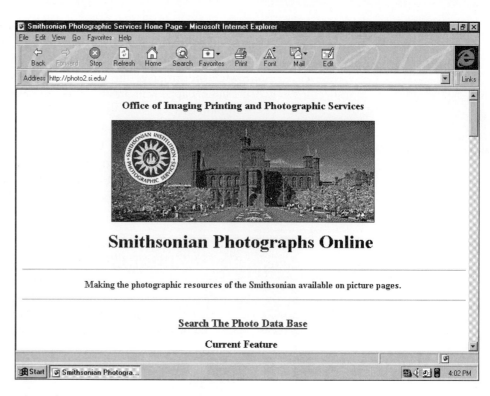

FIGURE 3.14   Screen for Practice Exercise 6

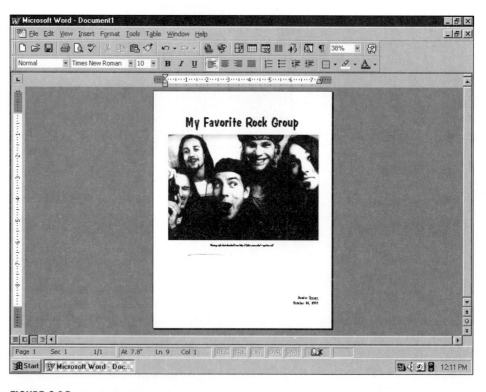

FIGURE 3.15   Screen for Practice Exercise 7

8. The iCOMP index was developed by Intel to compare the speeds of various microprocessors. We want you to search the Web and find a chart showing values in the current iCOMP index. (The chart you find need not be the same as the one in Figure 3.16.) Once you find the chart, download the graphic and incorporate it into a memo to your instructor. Add a paragraph or two describing the purpose of the index as shown in Figure 3.16.

A Comparison of Microcomputers

John Doe, CIS 120
(http://pentium.intel.com/procs/perf/icomp/index.htm)

The capability of a PC depends on the microprocessor on which it is based. Intel microprocessors are currently in their sixth generation, with each generation giving rise to increasingly powerful personal computers. All generations are upward compatible; that is, software written for one generation will automatically run on the next. This upward compatibility is crucial because it protects your investment in software when you upgrade to a faster computer.

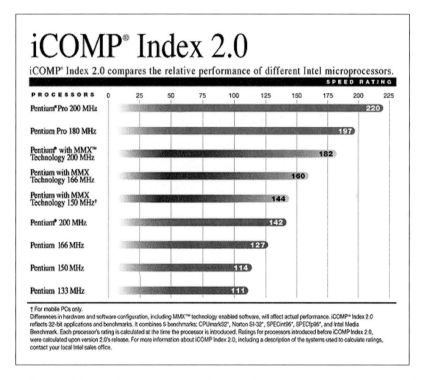

Each generation has multiple microprocessors that are differentiated by *clock speed*, an indication of how fast instructions are executed. Clock speed is measured in *megahertz* (MHz). The higher the clock speed, the faster the machine. Thus, all Pentiums are not created equal, because they operate at different clock speeds. The *Intel CPU Performance Index* (see chart) was created to compare the performance of one microprocessor to another. The index consists of a single number to indicate the relative performance of the microprocessor; the higher the number, the faster the processor.

FIGURE 3.16   Document for Practice Exercise 8

INTRODUCTION TO MICROSOFT EXCEL: WHAT IS A SPREADSHEET?

OBJECTIVES

After reading this chapter you will be able to:

1. Describe a spreadsheet and suggest several potential applications; explain how the rows and columns of a spreadsheet are identified, and how its cells are labeled.
2. Distinguish between a formula and a constant; explain the use of a predefined function within a formula.
3. Open an Excel workbook; insert and delete rows and columns of a worksheet; save and print the modified worksheet.
4. Distinguish between a pull-down menu, a shortcut menu, and a toolbar.
5. Describe the three-dimensional nature of an Excel workbook; distinguish between a workbook and a worksheet.
6. Print a worksheet two ways: to show the computed values or the cell formulas.
7. Use the Page Setup command to print a worksheet with or without gridlines and/or row and column headings; preview a worksheet before printing.

OVERVIEW

This chapter provides a broad-based introduction to spreadsheets in general, and to Microsoft Excel in particular. The spreadsheet is the microcomputer application that is most widely used by managers and executives. Our intent is to show the wide diversity of business and other uses to which the spreadsheet model can be applied. For one example, we draw an analogy between the spreadsheet and the accountant's ledger. For a second example, we create an instructor's grade book.

The chapter covers the fundamentals of spreadsheets as implemented in Excel, which uses the term worksheet rather than spreadsheet. It discusses how the rows and columns of an Excel worksheet are labeled, the difference between a formula and a constant, and the ability of a worksheet to recalculate itself after a change is made. We also distinguish between a worksheet and a workbook.

The hands-on exercises in the chapter enable you to apply all of the material at the computer, and are indispensable to the learn-by-doing philosophy we follow throughout the text. As you do the exercises, you may recognize many commands from other Windows applications, all of which share a common user interface and consistent command structure. Excel will be even easier to learn if you already know another application in Microsoft Office.

INTRODUCTION TO SPREADSHEETS

A *spreadsheet* is the computerized equivalent of an accountant's ledger. As with the ledger, it consists of a grid of rows and columns that enables you to organize data in a readily understandable format. Figures 1.1a and 1.1b show the same information displayed in ledger and spreadsheet format, respectively.

"What is the big deal?" you might ask. The big deal is that after you change an entry (or entries), the spreadsheet will, automatically and almost instantly, recompute all of the formulas. Consider, for example, the profit projection spreadsheet shown in Figure 1.1b. As the spreadsheet is presently constructed, the unit price is $20 and the projected sales are 1,200 units, producing gross sales of $24,000 ($20/unit × 1,200 units). The projected expenses are $19,200, which yields a profit of $4,800 ($24,000 − $19,200). If the unit price is increased to $22 per unit, the spreadsheet recomputes the formulas, adjusting the values of gross sales and net profit. The modified spreadsheet of Figure 1.1c appears automatically.

With a calculator and bottle of correction fluid or a good eraser, the same changes could also be made to the ledger. But imagine a ledger with hundreds of entries and the time that would be required to make the necessary changes to the ledger by hand. The same spreadsheet will be recomputed automatically by the computer. And the computer will not make mistakes. Herein lies the advantage of a spreadsheet—the ability to make changes, and to have the computer carry out the recalculation faster and more accurately than could be accomplished manually.

				1				2			3	4	5	6	
													Prepared by:		
													Approved by:		
1	UNIT PRICE						2	0							1
2	UNIT SALES				1	2	0	0							2
3	GROSS PROFIT				24	0	0	0							3
4															4
5	EXPENSES														5
6	PRODUCTION				10	0	0	0							6
7	DISTRIBUTION				1	2	0	0							7
8	MARKETING				5	0	0	0							8
9	OVERHEAD				3	0	0	0							9
10	TOTAL EXPENSES				19	2	0	0							10
11															11
12	NET PROFIT				4	8	0	0							12

(a) The Accountant's Ledger

FIGURE 1.1   The Accountant's Ledger

Unit price is
increased to $22

Formulas recompute
automatically

	A	B
1	Profit Projection	
2		
3	Unit Price	$20
4	Unit Sales	1,200
5	Gross Sales	$24,000
6		
7	Expenses	
8	Production	$10,000
9	Distribution	$1,200
10	Marketing	$5,000
11	Overhead	$3,000
12	Total Expenses	$19,200
13		
14	Net Profit	$4,800

	A	B
1	Profit Projection	
2		
3	Unit Price	$22
4	Unit Sales	1,200
5	Gross Sales	$26,400
6		
7	Expenses	
8	Production	$10,000
9	Distribution	$1,200
10	Marketing	$5,000
11	Overhead	$3,000
12	Total Expenses	$19,200
13		
14	Net Profit	$7,200

(b) Original Spreadsheet   (c) Modified Spreadsheet

FIGURE 1.1   The Accountant's Ledger (continued)

The Professor's Grade Book

A second example of a spreadsheet, one with which you can easily identify, is that of a professor's grade book. The grades are recorded by hand in a notebook, which is nothing more than a different kind of accountant's ledger. Figure 1.2 contains both manual and spreadsheet versions of a grade book.

Figure 1.2a shows a handwritten grade book as it has been done since the days of the little red schoolhouse. For the sake of simplicity, only five students are shown, each with three grades. The professor has computed class averages for each exam, as well as a semester average for every student, in which the final counts *twice* as much as either test; for example, Adams's average is equal to $(100+90+81+81)/4 = 88$.

Figure 1.2b shows the grade book as it might appear in a spreadsheet, and is essentially unchanged from Figure 1.2a. Walker's grade on the final exam in Figure 1.2b is 90, giving him a semester average of 85 and producing a class average on the final of 75.2 as well. Now consider Figure 1.2c, in which the grade on Walker's final has been changed to 100, causing Walker's semester average to change from 85 to 90, and the class average on the final to go from 75.2 to 77.2. As with the profit projection, a change to any entry within the grade book automatically recalculates all other dependent formulas as well. Hence, when Walker's final exam was regraded, all dependent formulas (the class average for the final as well as Walker's semester average) were recomputed.

As simple as the idea of a spreadsheet may seem, it provided the first major reason for managers to have a personal computer on their desks. Essentially, anything that can be done with a pencil, a pad of paper, and a calculator can be done faster and far more accurately with a spreadsheet. The spreadsheet, like the personal computer, has become an integral part of every type of business. Indeed, it is hard to imagine that these calculations were ever done by hand.

Final counts twice so average is
computed as (100 + 90 + 81 + 81)/4

	TEST 1	TEST 2	FINAL	AVERAGE
ADAMS	100	90	81	88
BAKER	90	76	87	85
GLASSMAN	90	78	78	81
MOLDOF	60	60	40	50
WALKER	80	80	90	85
CLASS AVERAGE	84.0	76.8	75.2	
NOTE: FINAL COUNTS DOUBLE				

(a) The Professor's Grade Book

	A	B	C	D	E
1	Student	Test 1	Test 2	Final	Average
2					
3	Adams	100	90	81	88.0
4	Baker	90	76	87	85.0
5	Glassman	90	78	78	81.0
6	Moldof	60	60	40	50.0
7	Walker	80	80	90	85.0
8					
9	Class Average	84.0	76.8	75.2	

Walker's original grade is 90

(b) Original Grades

	A	B	C	D	E
1	Student	Test 1	Test 2	Final	Average
2					
3	Adams	100	90	81	88.0
4	Baker	90	76	87	85.0
5	Glassman	90	78	78	81.0
6	Moldof	60	60	40	50.0
7	Walker	80	80	100	90.0
8					
9	Class Average	84.0	76.8	77.2	

Grade on Walker's
final is changed to 100

Formulas recompute automatically

(c) Modified Spreadsheet

FIGURE 1.2 The Professor's Grade Book

Row and Column Headings

A spreadsheet is divided into rows and columns, with each row and column assigned a heading. Rows are given numeric headings ranging from 1 to 16,384 (the maximum number of rows allowed). Columns are assigned alphabetic headings from column A to Z, then continue from AA to AZ and then from BA to BZ and so on, until the last of 256 columns (column IV) is reached.

The intersection of a row and column forms a *cell,* with the number of cells in a spreadsheet equal to the number of rows times the number of columns. The professor's grade book in Figure 1.2, for example, has 5 columns labeled A through E, 9 rows numbered from 1 to 9, and a total of 45 cells. Each cell has a unique *cell reference;* for example, the cell at the intersection of column A and row 9 is known as cell A9. The column heading always precedes the row heading in the cell reference.

Formulas and Constants

Figure 1.3 shows an alternate view of the spreadsheet for the professor's grade book that displays the *cell contents* rather than the computed *values.* This figure displays the actual entries (formulas and constants) that were entered into the individual cells, which enable the spreadsheet to recalculate formulas whenever any entry changes.

A *constant* is an entry that does not change. It may be a number, such as a student's grade on an exam, or it may be descriptive text (a label), such as a student's name. A *formula* is a combination of numeric constants, cell references, arithmetic operators, and/or functions (described below) that displays the result of a calculation. Every cell contains either a formula or a constant.

A formula always begins with an equal sign. Consider, for example, the formula in cell E3, =(B3+C3+2*D3)/4, which computes Adams's semester average. The formula is built in accordance with the professor's rules for computing a student's semester average, which counts the final twice as much as the other tests. Excel uses symbols +, −, *, /, and ^ to indicate addition, subtraction, multiplication, division, and exponentiation, respectively, and follows the normal rules of arithmetic precedence. Any expression in parentheses is evaluated first, then within an expression exponentiation is performed first, followed by multiplication or division in left to right order, then finally addition or subtraction, also in left-to-right order.

The formula in cell E3 takes the grade on the first exam (in cell B3), plus the grade on the second exam (in cell C3), plus two times the grade on the final (in cell D3), and divides the result by four. Thus, should any of the exam grades change, the semester average (a formula whose results depend on the individual exam grades) will also change. This, in essence, is the basic principle behind the spreadsheet and explains why, when one number changes, various other numbers throughout the spreadsheet change as well.

A formula may also include a *function,* or predefined computational task, such as the *AVERAGE function* in cells B9, C9, and D9. The function in cell B9, for example, =AVERAGE(B3:B7), is interpreted to mean the average of all cells starting at cell B3 and ending at cell B7 and is equivalent to the formula =(B3+B4+B5+B6+B7)/5. You can appreciate that functions are often easier to use than the corresponding formulas, especially with larger spreadsheets (and classes with many students).

Constant (entry that does not change)　　　Function (predefined computational task)　　　Formula (displays the result of a calculation)

	A	B	C	D	E
1	Student	Test 1	Test 2	Final	Average
2					
3	Adams	100	90	81	=(B3+C3+2*D3)/4
4	Baker	90	76	87	=(B4+C4+2*D4)/4
5	Glassman	90	78	78	=(B5+C5+2*D5)/4
6	Moldof	60	60	40	=(B6+C6+2*D6)/4
7	Walker	80	80	90	=(B7+C7+2*D7)/4
8					
9	Class Average	=AVERAGE(B3:B7)	=AVERAGE(C3:C7)	=AVERAGE(D3:D7)	

FIGURE 1.3　The Professor's Grade Book (cell formulas)

Figure 1.4 displays the professor's grade book as it is implemented in Microsoft Excel. Microsoft Excel is a Windows application, and thus shares the common user interface with which you are familiar. (It's even easier to learn Excel if you already know another Office application such as Microsoft Word.) You should recognize, therefore, that the desktop in Figure 1.4 has two open windows—an application window for Microsoft Excel and a document window for the workbook, which is currently open.

Each window has its own Minimize, Maximize (or Restore), and Close buttons. Both windows have been maximized and thus the title bars have been merged into a single title bar that appears at the top of the application window. The title bar reflects the application (Microsoft Excel) as well as the name of the workbook (Grade Book) on which you are working. A menu bar appears immediately below the title bar. Two toolbars, which are discussed in depth on page 8, appear below the menu bar. Vertical and horizontal scroll bars appear at the right and bottom of the document window. The Windows 95 taskbar appears at the bottom of the screen and shows the open applications.

The terminology is important, and we distinguish between spreadsheet, worksheet, and workbook. Excel refers to a spreadsheet as a **worksheet.** Spreadsheet is a generic term; *workbook* and *worksheet* are unique to Excel. An Excel **workbook** contains one or more worksheets. The professor's grades for this class are contained in the CIS120 worksheet within the Grade Book workbook. This workbook also contains additional worksheets (CIS223 and CIS316) as indicated by the worksheet tabs at the bottom of the window. These worksheets contain the professor's grades for other courses that he or she is teaching this semester. (See practice exercise 1 at the end of the chapter.)

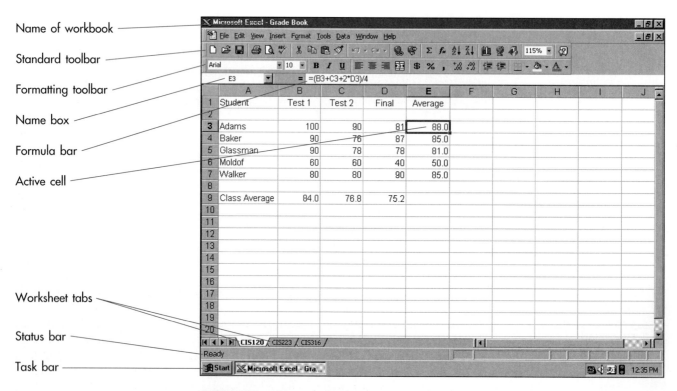

FIGURE 1.4   Professor's Grade Book

Figure 1.4 resembles the grade book shown earlier, but it includes several other elements that enable you to create and/or edit the worksheet. The heavy border around cell E3 indicates that it (cell E3) is the **active cell.** Any entry made at this time is made into the active cell, and any commands that are executed affect the contents of the active cell. The active cell can be changed by clicking a different cell, or by using the arrow keys to move to a different cell.

The displayed value in cell E3 is 88.0, but as indicated earlier, the cell contains a formula to compute the semester average rather than the number itself. The contents of the active cell, =(B3+C3+2*D3)/4, are displayed in the **formula bar** near the top of the worksheet. The cell reference for the active cell, cell E3 in Figure 1.4, appears in the **Name box** at the left of the formula bar.

The **status bar** at the bottom of the worksheet keeps you informed of what is happening as you work within Excel. It displays information about a selected command or an operation in progress.

THE EXCEL WORKBOOK

An Excel workbook is the electronic equivalent of the three-ring binder. A workbook contains one or more worksheets (or chart sheets), each of which is identified by a tab at the bottom of the workbook. The worksheets in a workbook are normally related to one another; for example, each worksheet may contain the sales for a specific division within a company. The advantage of a workbook is that all of its worksheets are stored in a single file, which is accessed as a unit.

Toolbars

Excel provides several different ways to accomplish the same task. Commands may be accessed from a pull-down menu, from a shortcut menu (which is displayed by pointing to an object and clicking the right mouse button), and/or through keyboard equivalents. Commands can also be executed from one of many **toolbars** that appear immediately below the menu bar. The Standard and Formatting toolbars are displayed by default. (All toolbars can be displayed or hidden by using the Tools command in the View menu.)

The **Standard toolbar** contains buttons corresponding to the most basic commands in Excel—for example, opening and closing a workbook, printing a workbook, and so on. The icon on the button is intended to be indicative of its function (e.g., a printer to indicate the Print command). You can also point to the button to display a **ScreenTip** showing the name of the button.

The **Formatting toolbar** appears under the Standard toolbar, and provides access to common formatting operations such as boldface, italics, or underlining. It also enables you to change the alignment of entries within a cell and/or change the font or color. The easiest way to master the toolbars is to view the buttons in groups according to their general function, as shown in Figure 1.5.

The toolbars may appear overwhelming at first, but there is absolutely no need to memorize what the individual buttons do. That will come with time. Indeed, if you use another office application such as Microsoft Word, you may already recognize many of the buttons on the Standard and Formatting toolbars. Most individuals start by using the pull-down menus, then look for shortcuts along the way.

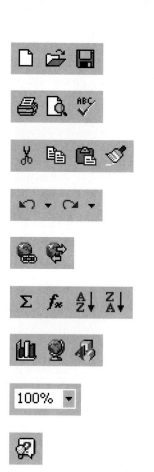

Opens a new workbook; opens an existing workbook; or saves the workbook to disk

Prints the workbook; previews the workbook prior to printing; checks spelling

Cuts or copies the selection to the clipboard; pastes the clipboard contents; copies the formatting of the selected cells

Undoes or redoes a previously executed command

Inserts a hyperlink or displays the Web toolbar

Sums the suggested range; displays the Paste Function dialog box; performs an ascending or descending sort

Starts the Chart Wizard; starts Microsoft Map; displays the Drawing toolbar

Changes the magnification

Displays the Office Assistant. The lightbulb indicates the Assistant has a suggestion.

(a) The Standard Toolbar

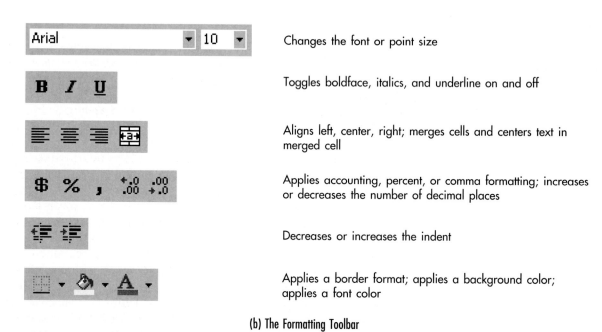

Changes the font or point size

Toggles boldface, italics, and underline on and off

Aligns left, center, right; merges cells and centers text in merged cell

Applies accounting, percent, or comma formatting; increases or decreases the number of decimal places

Decreases or increases the indent

Applies a border format; applies a background color; applies a font color

(b) The Formatting Toolbar

FIGURE 1.5   Toolbars

Entering Data

Data is entered into a worksheet by selecting a cell, then typing the constant or formula that is to go into that cell. The entry is displayed in the formula bar at the top of the window as it is being typed. The entry is completed by pressing the enter key, which moves the active cell to the cell immediately below the current cell, or by pressing any of the arrow keys to move to the next cell in the indicated direction. Pressing the right arrow key, for example, completes the entry and moves the active cell to the next cell in the same row. You can also complete the entry by clicking in a new cell, or by clicking the green check that appears to the left of the formula bar as data is entered.

To replace an existing entry, select the cell by clicking in the cell, or by using the keyboard to move to the cell. Type the corrected entry (as though you were entering it for the first time), then complete the entry as described above. To edit an entry, click in the formula bar, make the necessary changes, then press the enter key.

THE FILE MENU

The *File menu* is a critically important menu in virtually every Windows application. It contains the *Save command* to save a workbook to disk, and the *Open command* to subsequently retrieve (open) the workbook at a later time. The File Menu also contains the *Print command* to print a workbook, the *Close command* to close the current workbook but continue working in Excel, and the *Exit command* to quit Excel altogether.

The *Save command* copies the workbook that is currently being edited (the workbook in memory) to disk. The Save As dialog box appears the first time a workbook is saved so that you can specify the filename and other required information. All subsequent executions of the Save command save the workbook under the assigned name, replacing the previously saved version with the new version.

The Save As dialog box requires a filename (e.g., My First Spreadsheet in Figure 1.6a), which can be up to 255 characters in length. The filename may contain spaces and commas. The dialog box also requires the drive (and folder) in which the file is to be saved, as well as the file type that determines which application the file is associated with. (Long-time DOS users will remember the three-character extension at the end of a filename such as XLS to indicate an Excel workbook. The extension is generally hidden in Windows 95, according to options that are set through the View menu in My Computer or the Windows Explorer.)

The Open command brings a copy of a previously saved workbook into memory, enabling you to edit the workbook. The Open command displays the Open dialog box in which you specify the file to retrieve. You indicate the drive (and optionally the folder) that contains the file, as well as the type of file you want to retrieve. Excel will then list all files of that type on the designated drive (and folder), enabling you to open the file you want.

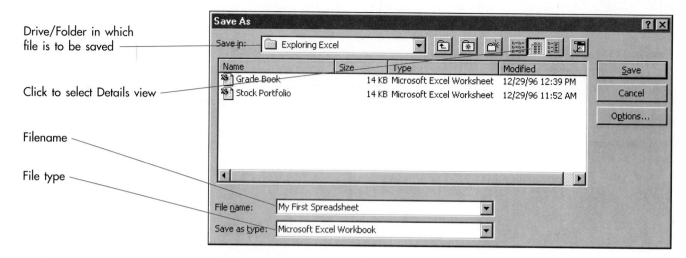

Drive/Folder in which file is to be saved

Click to select Details view

Filename

File type

(a) Save As Dialog Box

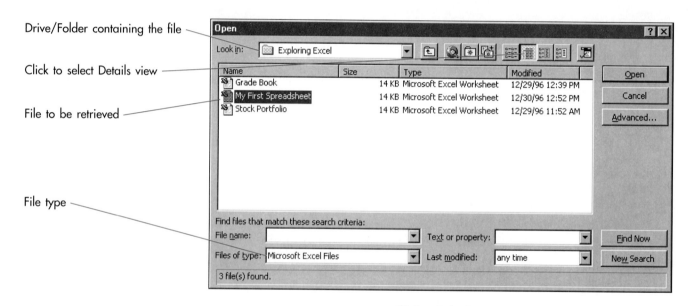

Drive/Folder containing the file

Click to select Details view

File to be retrieved

File type

(b) Open Dialog Box

FIGURE 1.6   The Save and Open Commands (continued)

The Save and Open commands work in conjunction with one another. The Save As dialog box in Figure 1.6a, for example, saves the file *My First Spreadsheet* in the Exploring Excel folder. (The drive is not visible in the figure.) The Open dialog box in Figure 1.6b brings that file back into memory so that you can work with the file, after which you can save the revised file for use at a later time.

The toolbars in the Save As dialog and Open dialog boxes have several buttons in common that enable you to list the files in different ways. The Details view is selected in both dialog boxes and shows the file size as well as the date and time a file was last modified. The List button displays only the file names and hence more files are visible at one time. The Preview button lets you see a workbook before you open it. The Properties button displays information about the workbook including the number of revisions.

We come now to the first of two hands-on exercises in this chapter that implement our learn-by-doing philosophy. The exercise shows you how to start Microsoft Excel and open the professor's grade book from the practice files that are referenced throughout the text. You can obtain a copy of the practice files from your instructor, or you can download the files as described in the exercise. The practice files contain a series of Excel workbooks that are used in various exercises throughout the text.

HANDS-ON EXERCISE 1

Introduction to Microsoft Excel

Objectives: To start Microsoft Excel; to open, modify, and print an existing worksheet. Use Figure 1.7 as a guide in the exercise.

STEP 1: Welcome to Windows

➤ Turn on the computer and all of its peripherals. The floppy drive should be empty prior to starting your machine. This ensures that the system starts by reading from the hard disk, which contains the Windows files, as opposed to a floppy disk, which does not.

➤ Your system will take a minute or so to get started, after which you should see the desktop in Figure 1.7a. Do not be concerned if the appearance of your desktop is different from ours.

➤ You may see additional objects on the desktop in Windows 95 and/or the active desktop content in Windows 97. It doesn't matter which operating system you are using because Office 97 runs equally well under both Windows 95 and Windows 97 (as well as Windows NT).

➤ You may see a Welcome to Windows 95 / Windows 97 dialog box with command buttons to take a tour of the operating system. If so, click the appropriate button(s) or close the dialog box.

TAKE THE WINDOWS TOUR

Windows 95 greets you with a Welcome window that contains a command button to take you on a 10-minute tour of Windows 95. Click the command button and enjoy the show. You might also try the What's New command button for a quick overview of changes from Windows 3.1. If you do not see the Welcome window when you start Windows 95, click the Start button, click Run, type WELCOME in the Open *text box,* and press enter. Windows 97 was not available when we went to press, but we expect it to have a similar feature.

Click the Start button

(a) Welcome to Windows (step 1)

FIGURE 1.7   Hands-on Exercise 1

STEP 2: Obtain the Practice Files

➤ We have created a series of practice files for you to use throughout the text. Your instructor will make these files available to you in a variety of ways:

• You can download the files from our Web site if you have access to the Internet and World Wide Web (see boxed tip).

• The files may be on a network drive, in which case you use the Windows Explorer to copy the files from the network to a floppy disk.

• There may be an actual "data disk" that you are to check out from the lab in order to use the Copy Disk command to duplicate the disk.

➤ Check with your instructor for additional information.

DOWNLOAD THE PRACTICE FILES

You can download the practice files for any book in the *Exploring Windows* series from Bob Grauer's home page (www.bus.miami.edu/~rgrauer). Use any Web browser to get to Bob's page, then click the link to the *Exploring Windows* series where you choose the appropriate book and download the file. Be sure to read the associated "read me" file, which provides additional information about downloading the file.

STEP 3: Start Microsoft Excel

➤ Click the **Start button** to display the Start menu. Click (or point to) the **Programs menu,** then click **Microsoft Excel** to start the program.

➤ Close the Office Assistant if it appears. (The Office Assistant is illustrated in step 7 of this exercise.)

➤ If necessary, click the **Maximize button** in the application window so that Excel takes the entire desktop as shown in Figure 1.7b. Click the **Maximize button** in the document window (if necessary) so that the document window is as large as possible.

Maximize the document window

Close the Office Assistant

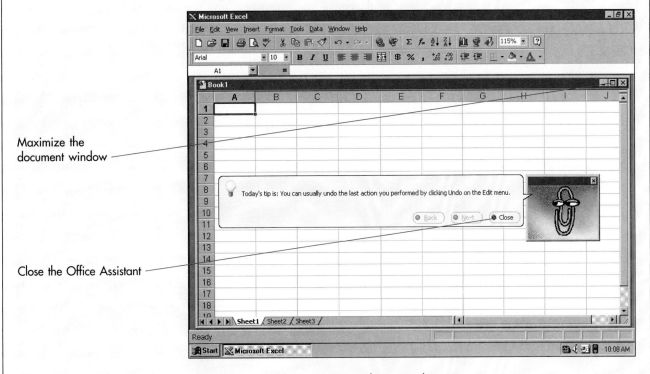

(b) Start Excel (step 3)

FIGURE 1.7   Hands-on Exercise 1 (continued)

CHOOSE YOUR OWN ASSISTANT

You can choose your own personal assistant from one of several available images. Click the Office Assistant button on the Standard toolbar to display the Assistant, click the options button to display the Office Assistant dialog box, click the Gallery tab, then click the Next button repeatedly to cycle through the available images. Click OK to select the image and close the dialog box. (The Office CD is required for some of the characters.)

STEP 4: Open the Workbook

➤ Pull down the **File menu** and click **Open** (or click the **Open button** on the Standard toolbar). You should see a dialog box similar to the one in Figure 1.7c.

➤ Click the **Details button** to change to the Details view. Click and drag the vertical border between two columns to increase (or decrease) the size of a column.

➤ Click the **drop-down arrow** on the Look In list box. Click the appropriate drive, drive C or drive A, depending on the location of your data. Double click the **Exploring Excel folder** to make it the active folder (the folder from which you will retrieve and into which you will save the workbook).

➤ Click the **down scroll arrow** if necessary in order to click **Grade Book** to select the professor's grade book. Click the **Open command button** to open the workbook and begin the exercise.

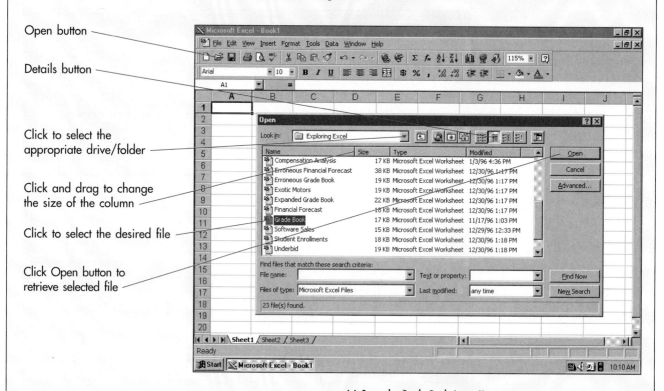

Open button

Details button

Click to select the appropriate drive/folder

Click and drag to change the size of the column

Click to select the desired file

Click Open button to retrieve selected file

(c) Open the Grade Book (step 4)

FIGURE 1.7   Hands-on Exercise 1 (continued)

MISSING TOOLBARS

The Standard and Formatting toolbars are displayed by default, but either or both can be hidden from view. To display (or hide) a toolbar, point to any toolbar, click the right mouse button to display the Toolbar shortcut menu, then click the individual toolbars on or off as appropriate. If you do not see any toolbars at all, pull down the View menu, click Toolbars to display a dialog box listing the available toolbars, check the toolbars you want displayed, and click OK.

STEP 5: The Active Cell, Formula Bar, and Worksheet Tabs

➤ You should see the workbook in Figure 1.7d. Click in **cell B3,** the cell containing Adams's grade on the first test. Cell B3 is now the active cell and is surrounded by a heavy border. The Name box indicates that cell B3 is the active cell, and its contents are displayed in the formula bar.

➤ Click in **cell B4** (or press the **down arrow key**) to make it the active cell. The Name box indicates cell B4 while the formula bar indicates a grade of 90.

➤ Click in **cell E3,** the cell containing the formula to compute Adams's semester average; the worksheet displays the computed average of 88.0, but the formula bar displays the formula, $=(B3+C3+2*D3)/4$, to compute that average based on the test grades.

➤ Click the **CIS223 tab** to view a different worksheet within the same workbook. This worksheet contains the grades for a different class.

➤ Click the **CIS316 tab** to view this worksheet. Click the **CIS120 tab** to return to this worksheet and continue with the exercise.

Formula bar displays cell contents (formula)

Name box indicates active cell (E3)

Cell displays the result of the formula entered in cell E3

Click to view CIS223 worksheet

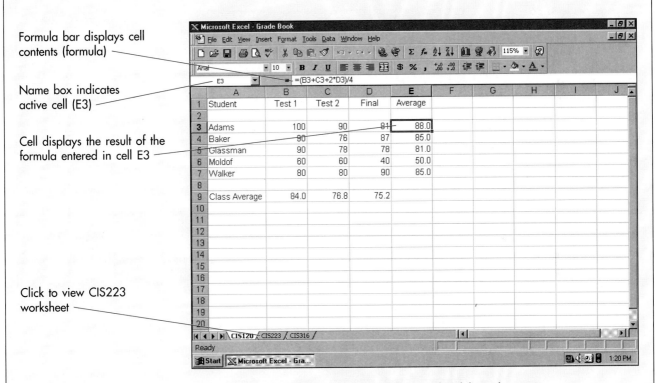

(d) The Active Cell, Formula Bar, and Worksheet Tabs (step 5)

FIGURE 1.7   Hands-on Exercise 1 (continued)

SCREENTIPS

Point to any button on any toolbar and Excel displays a ScreenTip containing the name of the button. If pointing to a button has no effect, pull down the View menu, click Toolbars, and then click Customize to display the Customize dialog box. Click the Options tab, check the box to Show ScreenTips on Toolbars, then close the dialog box.

STEP 6: Experiment (What If?)

➤ Click in **cell C4,** the cell containing Baker's grade on the second test. Enter a corrected value of **86** (instead of the previous entry of 76). Press **enter** (or click in another cell).

➤ The effects of this change ripple through the worksheet, automatically changing the computed value for Baker's average in cell E4 to 87.5. The class average on the second test in cell C9 changes to 78.8.

➤ Change Walker's grade on the final from 90 to **100.** Press **enter** (or click in another cell). Walker's average in cell E7 changes to 90.0, while the class average in cell D9 changes to 77.2.

➤ Your worksheet should match Figure 1.7e.

Undo button ———

Change grade to 86 ———

Change grade to 100 ———

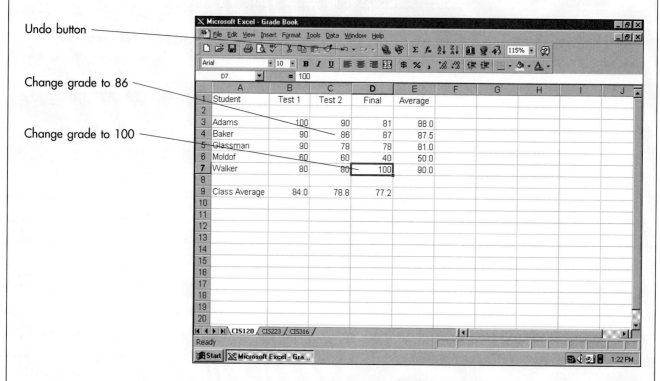

(e) What If (step 6)

FIGURE 1.7   Hands-on Exercise 1 (continued)

ABOUT MICROSOFT EXCEL

Pull down the Help menu and click About Microsoft Excel to display the specific release number as well as other licensing information, including the product serial number. This help screen also contains two very useful command buttons, System Info and Technical Support. The first button displays information about the hardware installed on your system, including the amount of memory and available space on the hard drive. The Technical Support button provides information on obtaining technical assistance.

STEP 7: The Office Assistant

➤ Click the **Office Assistant button** on the Standard toolbar to display the Office Assistant. (You may see a different character than the one we have selected.)

➤ Enter your question, for example, **How do I use the Office Assistant?** as shown in Figure 1.7f, then click the **Search button** to look for the answer.

➤ The size of the dialog box expands as the Assistant suggests several topics that may be appropriate to answer your question.

➤ Click any of the suggested topics, which in turn displays a help screen with detailed information. Read the help screen(s), close the Help Window, then close the Office Assistant.

Click the Office
Assistant button

Enter question and
click search

Close the Assistant
when finished

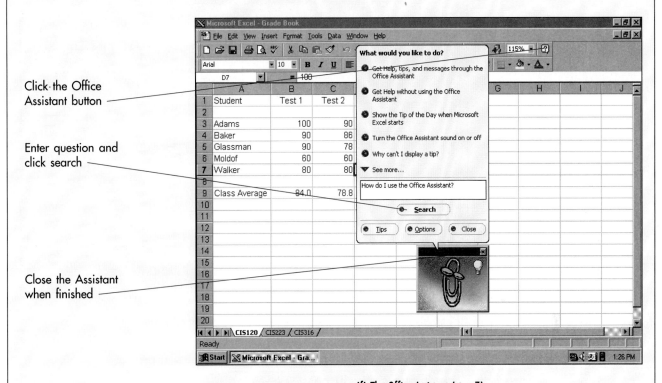

(f) The Office Assistant (step 7)

FIGURE 1.7   Hands-on Exercise 1 (continued)

TIP OF THE DAY

You can set the Office Assistant to greet you with a "Tip of the Day" whenever you start Word. If the Office Assistant is not visible, click the Office Assistant button on the Standard toolbar to start the Assistant, then click the options button to display the Office Assistant dialog box. Check the Show the Tip of the Day at the startup box, then click OK. The next time you start Excel, the Assistant will greet you and offer you a tip of the day.

STEP 8: Print the Worksheet

> ➤ Pull down the **File menu** and click **Save** (or click the **Save button** on the Standard toolbar).

> ➤ Pull down the **File menu.** Click **Print** to display a dialog box requesting information for the Print command as shown in Figure 1.7g. Click **OK** to accept the default options (you want to print only the selected worksheet).

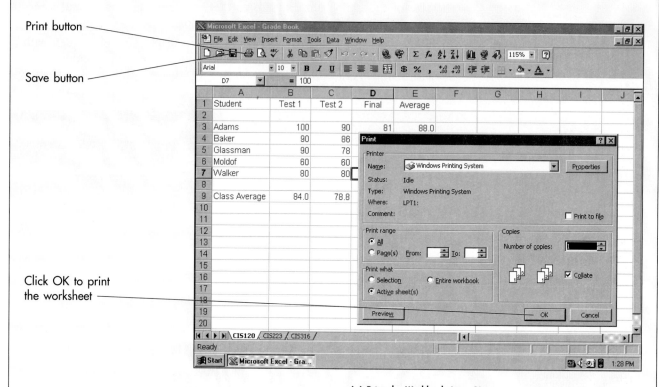

Print button

Save button

Click OK to print
the worksheet

(g) Print the Workbook (step 8)

FIGURE 1.7   Hands-on Exercise 1 (continued)

THE PRINT PREVIEW COMMAND

The *Print Preview command* displays the worksheet as it will appear when printed. The command is invaluable and will save you considerable time as you don't have to rely on trial and error to obtain the perfect printout. The Print Preview command can be executed from the File menu, via the Print Preview button on the Standard toolbar, or from the Print Preview command button within the Page Setup command.

STEP 9: Close the Workbook

> ➤ Pull down the **File menu.** Click **Close** to close the workbook but leave Excel open.

> ➤ Pull down the **File menu** a second time. Click **Exit** if you do not want to continue with the next exercise at this time.

We trust that you completed the hands-on exercise without difficulty and that you are more confident in your ability than when you first began. The exercise was not complicated, but it did accomplish several objectives and set the stage for a second exercise, which follows shortly.

Consider now Figure 1.8, which contains a modified version of the professor's grade book. Figure 1.8a shows the grade book at the end of the first hands-on exercise and reflects the changes made to the grades for Baker and Walker. Figure 1.8b shows the worksheet as it will appear at the end of the second exercise. Several changes bear mention:

1. One student has dropped the class and two other students have been added. Moldof appeared in the original worksheet in Figure 1.8a, but has somehow managed to withdraw; Coulter and Courier did not appear in the original grade book but have been added to the worksheet in Figure 1.8b.

2. A new column containing the students' majors has been added.

The implementation of these changes is accomplished through a combination of the Insert and Delete commands, which enable you to add or remove rows or columns as necessary.

Insert and Delete Commands

The *Insert command* adds row(s) or column(s) to an existing worksheet. The *Delete command* removes existing row(s) or column(s). Both commands auto-

Moldof will be dropped from class

	A	B	C	D	E
1	Student	Test 1	Test 2	Final	Average
2					
3	Adams	100	90	81	88.0
4	Baker	90	86	87	87.5
5	Glassman	90	78	78	81.0
6	Moldof	60	60	40	50.0
7	Walker	80	80	100	90.0
8					
9	Class Average	84.0	78.8	77.2	

(a) After Hands-on Exercise 1

A new column has been added (Major)

Two new students have been added

Moldof has been deleted

	A	B	C	D	E	F
1	Student	Major	Test 1	Test 2	Final	Average
2						
3	Adams	CIS	100	90	81	88.0
4	Baker	MKT	90	86	87	87.5
5	Coulter	ACC	85	95	100	95.0
6	Courier	FIN	75	75	85	80.0
7	Glassman	CIS	90	78	78	81.0
8	Walker	CIS	80	80	100	90.0
9						

(b) After Hands-on Exercise 2

FIGURE 1.8   The Modified Grade Book

matically adjust the cell references in existing formulas to account for the insertion or deletion of rows and columns within the worksheet.

Figure 1.9 displays the cell formulas in the professor's grade book and corresponds to the worksheets in Figure 1.8. The "before" and "after" worksheets reflect the insertion of a new column containing the students' majors, the addition of two new students, Coulter and Courier, and the deletion of an existing student, Moldof.

Let us consider the formula to compute Adams's semester average, which is contained in cell E3 of the original grade book, but in cell F3 in the modified grade book. The formula in Figure 1.9a referenced cells B3, C3, and D3 (the grades on test 1, test 2, and the final). The corresponding formula in Figure 1.9b reflects the fact that a new column has been inserted, and references cells C3, D3, and E3. The change in the formula is made automatically by Excel, without any action on the part of the user other than to insert the new column. The formulas for all other students have been adjusted in similar fashion.

Some students (all students below Baker) have had a further adjustment to reflect the addition of the new students through insertion of new rows in the worksheet. Glassman, for example, appeared in row 5 of the original worksheet, but appears in row 7 of the revised worksheet. Hence the formula to compute Glassman's semester average now references the grades in row 7, rather than in row 5 as in the original worksheet.

Finally, the formulas to compute the class averages have also been adjusted. These formulas appeared in row 9 of Figure 1.9a and averaged the grades in rows 3 through 7. The revised worksheet has a net increase of one student, which automatically moves these formulas to row 10, where the formulas are adjusted to average the grades in rows 3 through 8.

Formula references grades in B3, C3, and D3 →

Function references grades in rows 3–7 →

	A	B	C	D	E
1	Student	Test1	Test2	Final	Average
2					
3	Adams	100	90	81	=(B3+C3+2*D3)/4
4	Baker	90	86	87	=(B4+C4+2*D4)/4
5	Glassman	90	78	78	=(B5+C5+2*D5)/4
6	Moldof	60	60	40	=(B6+C6+2*D6)/4
7	Walker	80	80	100	=(B7+C7+2*D7)/4
8					
9	Class Average	=AVERAGE(B3:B7)	=AVERAGE(C3:C7)	=AVERAGE(D3:D7)	

(a) Before

	A	B	C	D	E	F
1	Student	Major	Test1	Test2	Final	Average
2						
3	Adams	CIS	100	90	81	=(C3+D3+2*E3)/4
4	Baker	MKT	90	86	87	=(C4+D4+2*E4)/4
5	Coulter	ACC	85	95	100	=(C5+D5+2*E5)/4
6	Courier	FIN	75	75	85	=(C6+D6+2*E6)/4
7	Glassman	CIS	90	78	78	=(C7+D7+2*E7)/4
8	Walker	CIS	80	80	100	=(C8+D8+2*E8)/4
9						
10	Class Average		=AVERAGE(C3:C8)	=AVERAGE(D3:D8)	=AVERAGE(E3:E8)	

Function changes to reference grades in rows 3–8 (due to addition of 2 new students and deletion of 1)

Formula changes to reference grades in C3, D3, and E3 due to addition of new column

(b) After

FIGURE 1.9   The Insert and Delete Commands

THE PAGE SETUP COMMAND

The Print command was used at the end of the first hands-on exercise to print the completed workbook. The *Page Setup command* gives you complete control of the printed worksheet as illustrated in Figure 1.10. Many of the options may not appear important now, but you will appreciate them as you develop larger and more complicated worksheets later in the text.

The Page tab in Figure 1.10a determines the orientation and scaling of the printed page. *Portrait orientation* ($8\frac{1}{2} \times 11$) prints vertically down the page. *Landscape orientation* ($11 \times 8\frac{1}{2}$) prints horizontally across the page and is used

Option buttons indicate mutually exclusive options

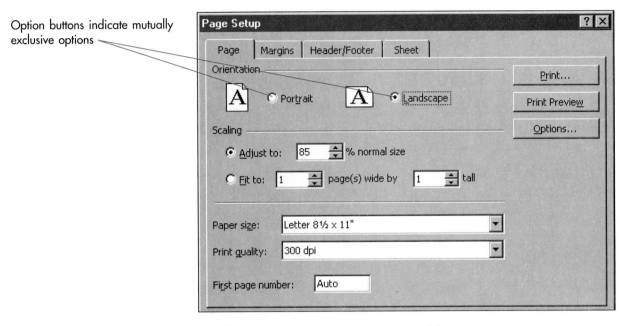

(a) The Page Tab

Set margins explicitly

Center worksheet on printed page

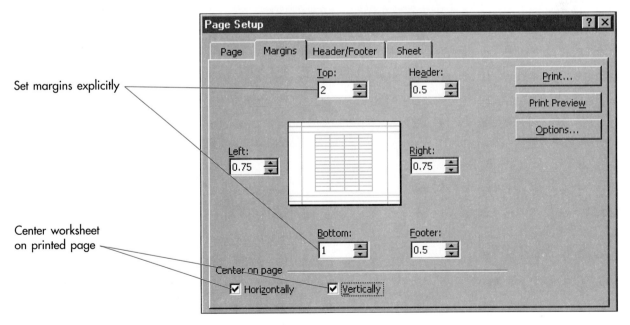

(b) The Margins Tab

FIGURE 1.10   The Page Setup Command

when the worksheet is too wide to fit on a portrait page. The option buttons indicate mutually exclusive items, one of which *must* be selected; that is, a worksheet must be printed in either portrait or landscape orientation. Option buttons are also used to choose the scaling factor. You can reduce (enlarge) the output by a designated scaling factor, or you can force the output to fit on a specified number of pages. The latter option is typically used to force a worksheet to fit on a single page.

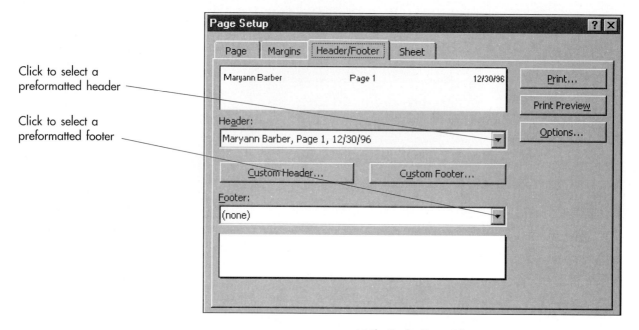

(c) The Header/Footer Tab

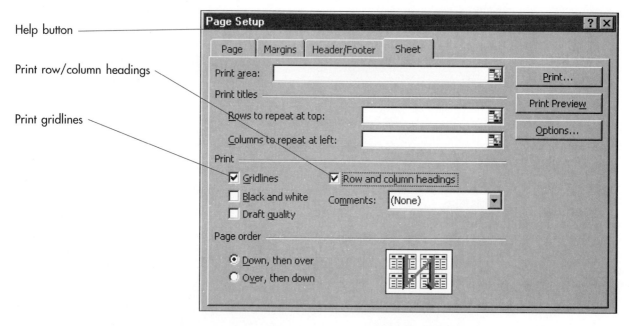

(d) The Sheet Tab

FIGURE 1.10   The Page Setup Command (continued)

The Margins tab in Figure 1.10b not only controls the margins, but will also center the worksheet horizontally and/or vertically. Check boxes are associated with the centering options and indicate that multiple options can be chosen; for example, horizontally and vertically are both selected. The Margins tab also determines the distance of the header and footer from the edge of the page.

The Header/Footer tab in Figure 1.10c lets you create a header (and/or footer) that appears at the top (and/or bottom) of every page. The pull-down list boxes let you choose from several preformatted entries, or alternatively, you can click the appropriate command button to customize either entry.

The Sheet tab in Figure 1.10d offers several additional options. The Gridlines option prints lines to separate the cells within the worksheet. The Row and Column Headings option displays the column letters and row numbers. Both options should be selected for most worksheets. Information about the additional entries can be obtained by clicking the Help button.

HANDS-ON EXERCISE 2

Modifying a Worksheet

Objective: To open an existing workbook; to insert and delete rows and columns in a worksheet; to print cell formulas and displayed values; to use the Page Setup command to modify the appearance of a printed workbook. Use Figure 1.11 as a guide in doing the exercise.

STEP 1: Open the Workbook

➤ Open the grade book as you did in the previous exercise. Pull down the **File menu** and click **Open** (or click the **Open button** on the Standard toolbar) to display the Open dialog box.

➤ Click the **drop-down arrow** on the Look In list box. Click the appropriate drive, drive C or drive A, depending on the location of your data. Double click the **Exploring Excel folder** to make it the active folder (the folder in which you will save the workbook).

➤ Click the **down scroll arrow** until you can select (click) the **Grade Book** workbook. Click the **Open button** to open the workbook and begin the exercise.

THE MOST RECENTLY OPENED FILE LIST

The easiest way to open a recently used workbook is to select the workbook directly from the File menu. Pull down the File menu, but instead of clicking the Open command, check to see if the workbook appears on the list of the most recently opened workbooks located at the bottom of the menu. If it does, you can click the workbook name rather than having to make the appropriate selections through the Open dialog box.

STEP 2: The Save As Command

➤ Pull down the **File menu.** Click **Save As** to display the dialog box shown in Figure 1.11a.

➤ Enter **Finished Grade Book** as the name of the new workbook. (A filename may contain up to 255 characters. Spaces and commas are allowed in the filename.)

➤ Click the **Save button.** Press the **Esc key** or click the **Close button** if you see a Properties dialog box.

➤ There are now two identical copies of the file on disk: "Grade Book," which is the completed workbook from the previous exercise, and "Finished Grade Book," which you just created. The title bar shows the latter name, which is the workbook currently in memory.

Click Save button

Click to select drive/folder

Enter filename

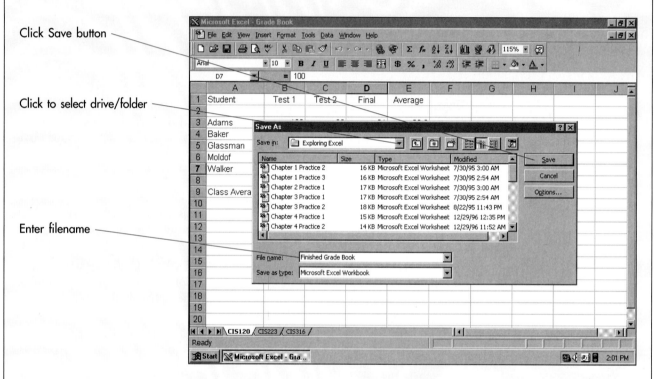

(a) Save As Command (step 2)

FIGURE 1.11 Hands-on Exercise 2

INCOMPATIBLE FILE TYPES

The file format for Excel 97 is incompatible with the format for Excel 95. The newer release (Excel 97) can open a workbook created in its predecessor (Excel 95), but the reverse is not true; that is, you cannot open a workbook created in Excel 97 in Excel 95. You can, however, maintain compatibility with the earlier version by using the Save As command to specify a dual file type (Microsoft Excel 97 & 5.0/95 format). (You will lose formatting features unique to Excel 97.)

STEP 3: Delete a Row

➤ Click any cell in **row 6** (the row you will delete). Pull down the **Edit menu.** Click **Delete** to display the dialog box in Figure 1.11b. Click **Entire Row.** Click **OK** to delete row 6.

➤ Moldof has disappeared from the grade book, and the class averages (now in row 8) have been updated automatically to reflect the fact that Moldof is gone.

Click any cell in row 6

Select Entire Row

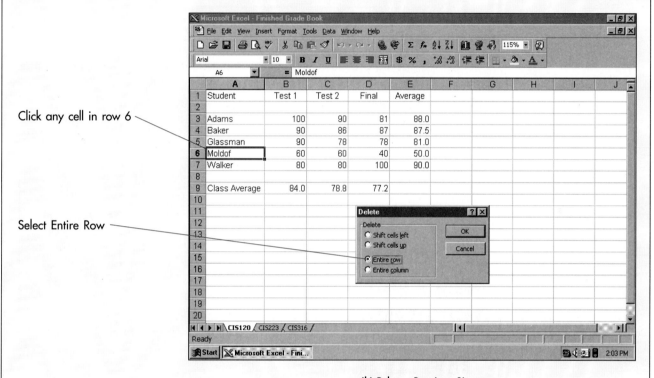

(b) Delete a Row (step 3)

FIGURE 1.11   Hands-on Exercise 2 (continued)

ERASING VERSUS DELETING

The Edit Delete command deletes the selected cell, row, or column from the worksheet. It is very different from the Edit Clear command, which erases the contents (and/or formatting) of the selected cells, but does not delete the cells from the worksheet. The Edit Delete command causes Excel to adjust cell references throughout the worksheet. The Edit Clear command does not adjust cell references as no cells are moved.

THE "WHAT'S THIS" BUTTON

Pull down the Help menu and click the What's This button command (or press the Shift+F1 key). Point to any button on any toolbar (the mouse pointer changes to an arrow with a question mark), then click the button to display a Help balloon to explain the function of that button. Press the Esc key to close the balloon and return the mouse pointer to normal.

STEP 4: The Undo Command

➤ Pull down the **Edit menu** and click **Undo Delete** (or click the **Undo button** on the Standard toolbar) to reverse the last command.

➤ The row for Moldof has been put back in the worksheet.

➤ Click any cell in **row 6,** and this time delete the entire row for good.

16 LEVELS OF UNDO

One of the best enhancements in Excel 97 is the multiple-level Undo command. Excel now enables you to reverse the last 16 changes to a workbook (as opposed to a single change in Excel 95). Click the drop-down arrow next to the Undo button to produce a list of your previous actions, then click the action you want to undo, which also undoes all of the preceding commands. Undoing the fifth command in the list, for example, will also undo the preceding four commands.

STEP 5: Insert a Row

➤ Click any cell in **row 5** (the row containing Glassman's grades).

➤ Pull down the **Insert menu.** Click **Rows** to add a new row above the current row. Row 5 is now blank (it is the newly inserted row), and Glassman (who was in row 5) is now in row 6.

➤ Enter the data for the new student in row 5 as shown in Figure 1.11c:

- Click in **cell A5.** Type **Coulter.** Press the **right arrow key** or click in **cell B5.**
- Type **85.** Press the **right arrow key** or click in **cell C5.**
- Type **95.** Press the **right arrow key** or click in **cell D5.**
- Type **100.** Press the **right arrow key** or click in **cell E5.**
- Enter the formula to compute the semester average, **=(B5+C5+2*D5)/4.** Be sure to begin the formula with an equal sign. Press **enter.**
- Click the **Save button** on the Standard toolbar, or pull down the **File menu** and click **Save** to save the changes made to this point.

Save button

Enter the formula
for the new student

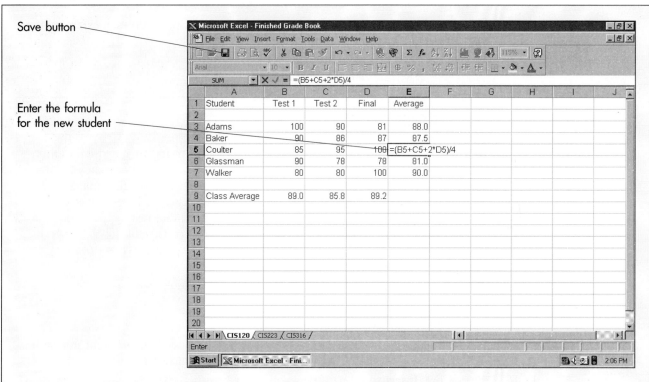

(c) Insert a Row (step 5)

FIGURE 1.11 Hands-on Exercise 2 (continued)

INSERTING (DELETING) ROWS AND COLUMNS

The fastest way to insert or delete a row is to point to the row number, then click the right mouse button to simultaneously select the row and display a shortcut menu. Click Insert to add a row above the selected row, or click Delete to delete the selected row. Use a similar technique to insert or delete a column, by pointing to the column heading, then clicking the right mouse button to display a shortcut menu from which you can select the appropriate command.

STEP 6: Insert a Second Row

➤ Point to the row heading for **row 6** (which now contains Glassman's grades), then click the **right mouse button** to select the row and display a shortcut menu. Click **Insert** to insert a new row 6, which moves Glassman to row 7.

➤ Click in **cell A6.** Type **C,** the first letter in "Courier," which also happens to be the first letter in "Coulter," a previous entry in column A. If the Auto-Complete feature is on (see boxed tip), Coulter's name will be automatically inserted in cell A6 with "oulter" selected. Type **ourier** (the remaining letters in "Courier," which replace "oulter."

➤ Enter Courier's grades in the appropriate cells (75, 75, and 85 in cells B6, C6, and D6, respectively).

➤ Click in **cell E6.** Enter the formula to compute the semester average, **=(B6+C6+2*D6)/4.** Press **enter.**

➤ Save the workbook.

AUTOCOMPLETE

The *AutoComplete* feature is Excel's way of trying to speed data entry. As soon as you begin typing a label into a cell, Excel searches for and (automatically) displays any other label in that column that matches the letters you typed. It's handy if you want to repeat a label, but it can be distracting if you want to enter a different label that just happens to begin with the same letter. To turn the feature on (off), pull down the Tools menu, click Options, then click the Edit tab. Check (clear) the box to enable the AutoComplete feature.

STEP 7: Insert a Column

➤ Point to the column heading for column B, then click the **right mouse button** to display a shortcut menu as shown in Figure 1.11d.

➤ Click **Insert** to insert a new column, which becomes the new column B. All existing columns have been moved to the right.

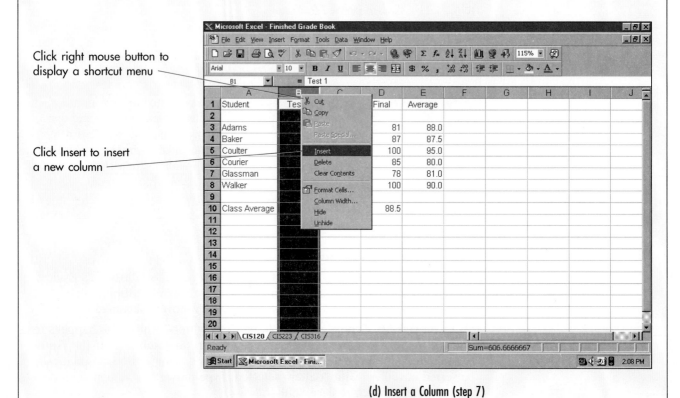

(d) Insert a Column (step 7)

FIGURE 1.11   Hands-on Exercise 2 (continued)

- ➤ Click in **cell B1.** Type **Major.**
- ➤ Click in **cell B3.** Enter **CIS** as Adams's major. Press the **down arrow** to move automatically to the major for the next student.
- ➤ Type **MKT** in cell B4. Press the **down arrow.** Type **ACC** in cell B5. Press the **down arrow.** Type **FIN** in cell B6.
- ➤ Press the **down arrow** to move to cell B7. Type **C** (AutoComplete will automatically enter "IS" to complete the entry). Press the **down arrow** to move to cell B8. Type **C** (the AutoComplete feature again enters "IS"), then press **enter** to complete the entry.
- ➤ Save the workbook.

THE RIGHT MOUSE BUTTON

Point to any object in a worksheet—a cell, a row or column heading, a worksheet tab, or a toolbar—then click the right mouse button to display a context-sensitive menu with commands appropriate to the object you are pointing to. Click the left mouse button to select a command from the menu, or press the Esc key (or click outside the menu) to close the menu without executing a command.

STEP 8: Display the Cell Formulas
- ➤ Pull down the **Tools menu.** Click **Options** to display the Options dialog box. Click the **View tab.** Check the box for **Formulas.** Click **OK.**
- ➤ The worksheet should display the cell formulas as shown in Figure 1.11e. If necessary, click the **right scroll arrow** on the horizontal scroll bar until column F, the column containing the formulas to compute the semester averages, comes into view.
- ➤ If necessary (i.e., if the formulas are not completely visible), double click the border between the column headings for columns F and G. This increases the width of column F to accommodate the widest entry in that column.

DISPLAY CELL FORMULAS

A worksheet should always be printed twice, once to show the computed results, and once to show the cell formulas. The fastest way to toggle (switch) between cell formulas and displayed values is to use the Ctrl+` keyboard shortcut. (The ` is on the same key as the ~ at the upper left of the keyboard.) Press Ctrl+` to switch from displayed values to cell formulas. Press Ctrl+` a second time and you are back to the displayed values.

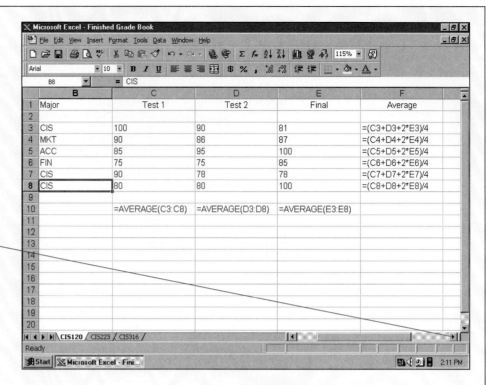

If necessary, click right scroll arrow to see column F

(e) Display the Cell Formulas (step 8)

FIGURE 1.11 Hands-on Exercise 2 (continued)

STEP 9: The Page Setup Command

➤ Pull down the **File menu.** Click the **Page Setup command** to display the Page Setup dialog box as shown in Figure 1.11f.

- Click the **Page tab.** Click the **Landscape option button.** Click the option button to **Fit to 1 page.**

- Click the **Margins tab.** Check the box to center the worksheet horizontally.

- Click the **Header/Footer tab.** Click the **drop-down arrow** on the Footer list box. Scroll to the top of the list and click **(none)** to remove the footer.

- Click the **Sheet tab.** Check the boxes to print Row and Column Headings and Gridlines.

➤ Click **OK** to exit the Page Setup dialog box. Save the workbook.

KEYBOARD SHORTCUTS—THE DIALOG BOX

Press Tab or Shift+Tab to move forward (backward) between fields in a dialog box, or press the Alt key plus the underlined letter to move directly to an option. Use the space bar to toggle check boxes on or off and the up (down) arrow keys to move between options in a list box. Press enter to activate the highlighted command button and Esc to exit the dialog box without accepting the changes.

Print Preview button

Click Landscape

Click Fit to 1 page

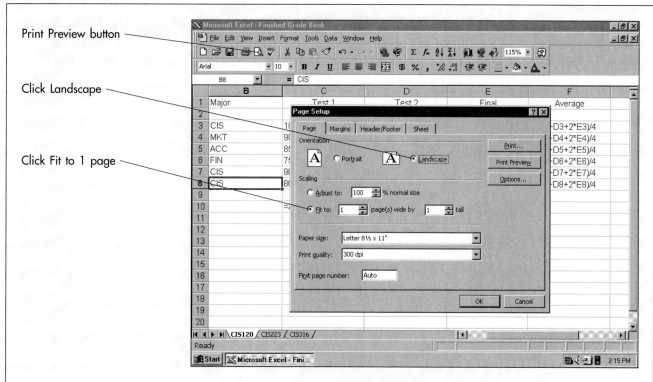

(f) The Page Setup Command (step 9)

FIGURE 1.11   Hands-on Exercise 2 (continued)

STEP 10: The Print Preview Command

➤ Pull down the **File menu** and click **Print Preview** (or click the **Print Preview button** on the Standard toolbar). Your monitor should match the display in Figure 1.11g.

➤ Click the **Print command button** to display the Print dialog box, then click **OK** to print the worksheet.

➤ Press **Ctrl+`** to switch to displayed values rather than cell formulas. Click the **Print button** on the Standard toolbar to print the worksheet without displaying the Print dialog box.

➤ Pull down the **File menu.** Click **Exit** to leave Excel. Click **Yes** if asked to save the workbook.

TIPS FROM THE OFFICE ASSISTANT

The Office Assistant indicates it has a suggestion by displaying a lightbulb. Click the lightbulb to display the tip, then click the Back or Next buttons as appropriate to view additional tips. The Assistant will not, however, repeat a tip from an earlier session unless you reset it at the start of a new session. This is especially important in a laboratory situation where you are sharing a computer with many students. To reset the tips, click the Assistant to display a balloon asking what you want to do, click the Options button in the balloon, click Options, then click the button to Reset My Tips.

Click Print command button

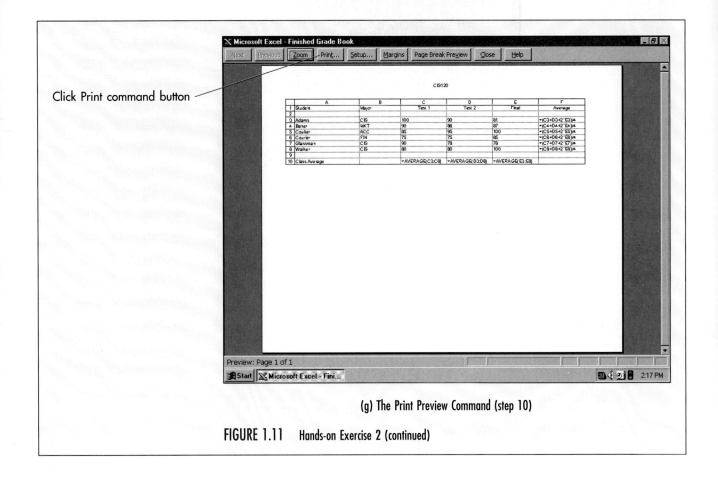

(g) The Print Preview Command (step 10)

FIGURE 1.11   Hands-on Exercise 2 (continued)

SUMMARY

A spreadsheet is the computerized equivalent of an accountant's ledger. It is divided into rows and columns, with each row and column assigned a heading. The intersection of a row and column forms a cell.

Spreadsheet is a generic term. Workbook and worksheet are Excel specific. An Excel workbook contains one or more worksheets.

Every cell in a worksheet (spreadsheet) contains either a formula or a constant. A formula begins with an equal sign; a constant does not. A constant is an entry that does not change and may be numeric or descriptive text. A formula is a combination of numeric constants, cell references, arithmetic operators, and/or functions that produces a new value from existing values.

The Insert and Delete commands add or remove rows or columns from a worksheet. The Open command brings a workbook from disk into memory. The Save command copies the workbook in memory to disk.

The Page Setup command provides complete control over the printed page, enabling you to print a worksheet with or without gridlines or row and column headings. The Page Setup command also controls margins, headers and footers, centering, and orientation. The Print Preview command shows the worksheet as it will print and should be used prior to printing.

A worksheet should always be printed twice, once with displayed values and once with cell formulas. The latter is an important tool in checking the accuracy of a worksheet, which is far more important than its appearance.

Active cell	Formula	Save command
AutoComplete	Formula bar	ScreenTip
AVERAGE function	Function	Spreadsheet
Cell	Insert command	Standard toolbar
Cell contents	Landscape orientation	Status bar
Cell reference	Name box	Text box
Close command	Office Assistant	Toolbar
Constant	Open command	Undo command
Delete command	Page Setup command	Value
Exit command	Portrait orientation	Workbook
File menu	Print command	Worksheet
Formatting toolbar	Print Preview command	

PRACTICE WITH EXCEL 97

1. Your professor is very impressed with the way you did the hands-on exercises in the chapter and has hired you as his grading assistant to handle all of his classes this semester. He would like you to take the Finished Grade Book that you used in the chapter, and save it as *Chapter 1 Practice 1 Solution*. Make the following changes in the new workbook:

    a. Click the worksheet tab for CIS120. Add Milgrom as a new student majoring in Finance with grades of 88, 80, and 84, respectively. Delete Baker. Be sure that the class averages adjust automatically for the insertion and deletion of these students.

    b. Click the worksheet tab for CIS223. Enter the formulas to compute the class averages on all tests as well as each student's semester average. All tests count equally.

    c. Click the worksheet tab for CIS316 to move to this worksheet. Insert a new column for the Final, then enter the following grades for the students in this class (Bippen, 90; Freeman, 75; Manni, 84; Peck, 93; Tanney, 87).

    d. Enter the formulas to compute the semester average for each student in the class. (Tests 1, 2, and 3 each count 20%. The final counts 40%.)

    e. Enter the formulas to compute the class average on each test and the final.

    f. Enter the label *Grading Assistant* followed by your name on each worksheet. Print the entire workbook and submit all three pages of the printout to your instructor as proof that you did this exercise.

2. The worksheet in Figure 1.12 displays last week's sales from the Exotic Gardens Nurseries. There are four locations, each of which divides its sales into three general areas.

    a. Open the partially completed *Chapter 1 Practice 2* workbook on the data disk. Save the workbook as *Finished Chapter 1 Practice 2*.

    b. Enter the appropriate formulas in row 5 of the worksheet to compute the total sales for each location. Use the SUM function to compute the total for each location; for example, type =SUM(B2:B4) in cell B5 (as opposed to =B2+B3+B4) to compute the total sales for the Las Olas location.

c. Insert a new row 4 for a new category of product. Type *Insecticides* in cell A4, and enter $1,000 for each store in this category. The total sales for each store should adjust automatically to include the additional business.

d. Enter the appropriate formulas in column F of the worksheet to compute the total sales for each category.

e. Delete column D, the column containing the sales for the Galleria location. Check to be sure that the totals for each product adjust automatically.

f. Add your name somewhere in the worksheet as the bookkeeper.

g. Print the completed worksheet two times, to show both displayed values and cell formulas. Submit both pages to your instructor.

	A	B	C		E	F
1		Las Olas	Coral Gables	Galleria	Miracle Mile	Total
2	Indoor Plants	1,500	3,000	4,500	800	
3	Accessories	350	725	1,200	128	
4	Landscaping	3,750	7,300	12,000	1,500	
5	Total					
6						
7						
8						

FIGURE 1.12 Spreadsheet for Practice Exercise 2

3. Formatting is not covered until Chapter 2, but we think you are ready to try your hand at basic formatting now. Most formatting operations are done in the context of select-then-do. You select the cell or cells you want to format, then you execute the appropriate formatting command, most easily by clicking the appropriate button on the Formatting toolbar. The function of each button should be apparent from its icon, but you can simply point to a button to display a ScreenTip that is indicative of the button's function.

Open the unformatted version of the *Chapter 1 Practice 3* workbook on the data disk, and save it as *Chapter 1 Practice 3 Solution.* Add a new row 6 and enter data for Hume Hall as shown in Figure 1.13. Format the remainder of the worksheet so that it matches the completed worksheet in Figure 1.13. Add your name in bold italics somewhere in the worksheet as the Residence Hall Coordinator, then print the completed worksheet and submit it to your instructor.

Residential Colleges						
	Freshmen	Sophomores	Juniors	Seniors	Graduates	Totals
Broward Hall	176	143	77	29	13	438
Graham Hall	375	112	37	23	7	554
Hume Hall	212	108	45	43	12	420
Jennings Hall	89	54	23	46	23	235
Rawlings Hall	75	167	93	145	43	523
Tolbert Hall	172	102	26	17	22	339
Totals	1099	686	301	303	120	2509

FIGURE 1.13 Spreadsheet for Practice Exercise 3

4. Create a worksheet that shows your income and expenses for a typical semester according to the format in Figure 1.14. Enter your budget rather than ours by entering your name in cell A1.

    a. Enter at least five different expenses in consecutive rows, beginning in A6, and enter the corresponding amounts in column B.

    b. Enter the text *Total Expenses* in the row immediately below your last expense item and then enter the formula to compute the total in the corresponding cells in columns B through E.

    c. Skip one blank row and then enter the text *What's Left For Fun* in column A and the formula to compute how much money you have left at the end of the month in columns B through E.

    d. Insert a new row 8. Add an additional expense that you left out, entering the text in A8 and the amount in cells B8 through E8. Do the formulas for total expenses reflect the additional expense? If not, change the formulas so they adjust automatically.

    e. Save the workbook as *Chapter 1 Practice 4 Solution*. Center the worksheet horizontally, then print the worksheet two ways, to show cell formulas and displayed values. Submit both printed pages to your instructor.

	A	B	C	D	E
1	Maryann Barber's Budget				
2		Sept	Oct	Nov	Dec
3	Monthly Income	$1,000	$1,000	$1,000	$1,400
4					
5	Monthly Expenses				
6	Food	$250	$250	$250	$250
7	Rent	$350	$350	$350	$350
8	Cable	$40	$40	$40	$40
9	Utilities	$100	$100	$125	$140
10	Phone	$30	$30	$30	$20
11	Gas	$40	$40	$40	$75
12	Total Expenses	$810	$810	$835	$875
13					
14	What's Left for Fun	$190	$190	$165	$525

FIGURE 1.14   Spreadsheet for Practice Exercise 4

GAINING PROFICIENCY: COPYING, FORMATTING, AND ISOLATING ASSUMPTIONS

OBJECTIVES

After reading this chapter you will be able to:

1. Explain the importance of isolating assumptions and initial conditions within a worksheet.
2. Define a cell range; select and deselect ranges within a worksheet.
3. Copy and/or move cells within a worksheet; differentiate between relative, absolute, and mixed addresses.
4. Format a worksheet to include boldface, italics, shading, and borders; change the font and/or alignment of a selected entry.
5. Describe the different types of numeric formats.
6. Change the width of a column; explain what happens if a column is too narrow to display the computed result.

OVERVIEW

This chapter continues the grade book example of Chapter 1. It is perhaps the most important chapter in the entire text as it describes the basic commands to create a worksheet. We begin with the definition of a cell range and the commands to build a worksheet without regard to its appearance. We focus on the Copy command and the difference between relative and absolute addresses. We stress the importance of isolating the assumptions within a worksheet so that alternative strategies may be easily evaluated.

The second half of the chapter presents formatting commands to improve the appearance of a worksheet after it has been created. You will be pleased with the dramatic impact you can achieve with a few simple commands, but we emphasize that accuracy in a worksheet is much more important than appearance.

The hands-on exercises are absolutely critical if you are to master the material. As you do the exercises, you will realize that there are many different ways to accomplish the same task. Our approach is to present the most basic way first and the shortcuts later. You will like the shortcuts better, but you may not remember them all. Do not be concerned because it is much more important to understand the underlying concepts. You can always find the necessary command from the appropriate menu, and if you don't know which menu, you can always look to online help.

A BETTER GRADE BOOK

Figure 2.1 contains a much improved version of the professor's grade book over the one from the previous chapter. The most obvious difference is in the appearance of the worksheet, as a variety of formatting commands have been used to make it more attractive. The exam scores and semester averages are centered under the appropriate headings. The exam weights are formatted with percentages, and all averages are displayed with exactly one decimal point. Boldface and italics are used for emphasis. Shading and borders are used to highlight various areas of the worksheet. The title has been centered over the worksheet and is set in a larger typeface.

The most *significant* differences, however, are that the weight of each exam is indicated within the worksheet, and that the formulas to compute the students' semester averages reference these cells in their calculations. The professor can change the contents of the cells containing the exam weights and see immediately the effect on the student averages.

The isolation of cells whose values are subject to change is one of the most important concepts in the development of a spreadsheet. This technique lets the professor explore alternative grading strategies. He or she may notice, for example, that the class did significantly better on the final than on either of the first two exams. The professor may then decide to give the class a break and increase the weight of the final relative to the other tests. But before the professor says anything to the class, he or she wants to know the effect of increasing the weight of the final to 60%. What if the final should count 70%? The effect of these and other changes can be seen immediately by entering the new exam weights in the appropriate cells at the bottom of the worksheet.

Title is centered and in a larger typeface

Boldface, italics, shading, and borders are used for emphasis

Exam scores are centered

Exam weights are used to calculate the students' semester averages

	A	B	C	D	E
1	CIS 120 - Spring 1997				
2					
3	Student	Test 1	Test 2	Final	Average
4	Costa, Frank	70	80	90	82.5
5	Ford, Judd	70	85	80	78.8
6	Grauer, Jessica	90	80	98	91.5
7	Howard, Lauren	80	78	98	88.5
8	Krein, Darren	85	70	95	86.3
9	Moldof, Adam	75	75	80	77.5
10					
11	Class Averages	78.3	78.0	90.2	
12					
13	Exam Weights	25%	25%	50%	

FIGURE 2.1   A Better Grade Book

CELL RANGES

Every command in Excel operates on a rectangular group of cells known as a *range*. A range may be as small as a single cell or as large as the entire worksheet. It may consist of a row or part of a row, a column or part of a column, or multiple rows and/or columns. The cells within a range are specified by indicating the diagonally opposite corners, typically the upper-left and lower-right corners of the rectangle. Many different ranges could be selected in conjunction with the worksheet of Figure 2.1. The exam weights, for example, are found in the range B13:D13. The students' semester averages are found in the range E4:E9. The student data is contained in the range A4:E9.

The easiest way to select a range is to click and drag—click at the beginning of the range, then press and hold the left mouse button as you drag the mouse to the end of the range where you release the mouse. Once selected, the range is highlighted and its cells will be affected by any subsequent command. The range remains selected until another range is defined or until you click another cell anywhere on the worksheet.

COPY COMMAND

The *Copy command* duplicates the contents of a cell, or range of cells, and saves you from having to enter the contents of every cell individually. It is much easier, for example, to enter the formula to compute the class average once (for test 1), then copy it to obtain the average for the remaining tests, rather than explicitly entering the formula for every test.

Figure 2.2 illustrates how the Copy command can be used to duplicate the formula to compute the class average. The cell(s) that you are copying from, cell B11, is called the *source range*. The cells that you are copying to, cells C11 and D11, are the *destination* (or target) *range*. The formula is not copied exactly, but is adjusted as it is copied, to compute the average for the pertinent test.

The formula to compute the average on the first test was entered in cell B11 as =AVERAGE(B4:B9). The range in the formula references the cell seven rows above the cell containing the formula (i.e., cell B4 is seven rows above cell B11) as well as the cell two rows above the formula (i.e., cell B9). When the formula in cell B11 is copied to C11, it is adjusted so that the cells referenced in the new formula are in the same relative position as those in the original formula; that is, seven and two rows above the formula itself. Thus, the formula in cell C11

	A	B	C	D	E
1			CIS 120 - Spring 1997		
2					
3	Student	Test 1	Test 2	Final	Average
4	Costa, Frank	70	80	90	=$B$13*B4+$C$13*C4+$D$13*D4
5	Ford, Judd	70	85	80	=$B$13*B5+$C$13*C5+$D$13*D5
6	Grauer, Jessica	90	80	98	=$B$13*B6+$C$13*C6+$D$13*D6
7	Howard, Lauren	80	78	98	=$B$13*B7+$C$13*C7+$D$13*D7
8	Krein, Darren	85	70	95	=$B$13*B8+$C$13*C8+$D$13*D8
9	Moldof, Adam	75	75	80	=$B$13*B9+$C$13*C9+$D$13*D9
10					
11	Class Averages	=AVERAGE(B4:B9)	=AVERAGE(C4:C9)	=AVERAGE(D4:D9)	
12					
13	Exam Weights	25%	25%	50%	

FIGURE 2.2   The Copy Command

becomes =AVERAGE(C4:C9). In similar fashion, the formula in cell D11 becomes =AVERAGE(D4:D9).

Figure 2.2 also illustrates how the Copy command is used to copy the formula for a student's semester average, from cell E4 (the source range) to cells E5 through E9 (the destination range). This is slightly more complicated than the previous example because the formula is based on a student's grades, which vary from one student to the next, and on the exam weights, which do not. The cells referring to the student's grades should adjust as the formula is copied, but the addresses referencing the exam weights should not.

The distinction between cell references that remain constant versus cell addresses that change is made by means of a dollar sign. An ***absolute reference*** remains constant throughout the copy operation and is specified with a dollar sign in front of the column and row designation, for example, $B$13. A ***relative reference***, on the other hand, adjusts during a copy operation and is specified without dollar signs; for example, B4. (A ***mixed reference*** uses a single dollar sign to make the column absolute and the row relative; for example, $A5. Alternatively, you can make the column relative and the row absolute as in A$5.)

Consider, for example, the formula to compute a student's semester average as it appears in cell E4 of Figure 2.2:

=$B$13*B4+$C$13*C4+$D$13*D4

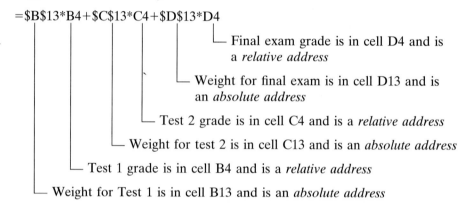

Final exam grade is in cell D4 and is a *relative address*

Weight for final exam is in cell D13 and is an *absolute address*

Test 2 grade is in cell C4 and is a *relative address*

Weight for test 2 is in cell C13 and is an *absolute address*

Test 1 grade is in cell B4 and is a *relative address*

Weight for Test 1 is in cell B13 and is an *absolute address*

The formula in cell E4 uses a combination of relative and absolute addresses to compute the student's semester average. Relative addresses are used for the exam grades (found in cells B4, C4, and D4) and change automatically when the formula is copied to the other rows. Absolute addresses are used for the exam weights (found in cells B13, C13, and D13) and remain constant from student to student.

The copy operation is implemented by using the Windows ***clipboard*** and a combination of the ***Copy*** and ***Paste commands*** from the Edit menu. The contents of the source range are copied to the clipboard, from where they are pasted to the destination range. The contents of the clipboard are replaced with each subsequent Copy command but are unaffected by the Paste command. Thus, you can execute the Paste command several times in succession to paste the contents of the clipboard to multiple locations.

MIXED REFERENCES

Most spreadsheets can be developed using only absolute or relative references such as $A1$1 or A, respectively. Mixed references, where only the row ($A1) or column (A$1) changes, are more subtle, and thus are typically not used by beginners. Mixed references are necessary in more sophisticated worksheets and add significantly to the power of Excel. See practice exercise 4 at the end of the chapter.

MOVE OPERATION

The ***move operation*** is not used in the grade book, but its presentation is essential for the sake of completeness. The move operation transfers the contents of a cell (or range of cells) from one location to another. After the move is completed, the cells where the move originated (that is, the source range) are empty. This is in contrast to the Copy command, where the entries remain in the source range and are duplicated in the destination range.

A simple move operation is depicted in Figure 2.3a, in which the contents of cell A3 are moved to cell C3, with the formula in cell C3 unchanged after the move. In other words, the move operation simply picks up the contents of cell A3 (a formula that adds the values in cells A1 and A2) and puts it down in cell C3. The source range, cell A3, is empty after the move operation has been executed.

Figure 2.3b depicts a situation where the formula itself remains in the same cell, but one of the values it references is moved to a new location; that is, the

Source range
is empty after move

	A	B	C
1	5		
2	2		
3	=A1+A2		

	A	B	C
1	5		
2	2		
3			=A1+A2

(a) Example 1 (only cell A3 is moved)

Cell reference is adjusted
to follow moved entry

	A	B	C
1	5		
2	2		
3	=A1+A2		

	A	B	C
1			5
2	2		
3	=C1+A2		

(b) Example 2 (only cell A1 is moved)

Both cell references adjust
to follow moved entries

	A	B	C
1	5		
2	2		
3	=A1+A2		

	A	B	C
1			5
2			2
3			=C1+C2

(c) Example 3 (all three cells in column A are moved)

Cell reference adjusts to
follow moved entry

Moved formula
is unchanged

	A	B	C
1	5	=A3*4	
2	2		
3	=A1+A2		

	A	B	C
1	5	=C3*4	
2	2		
3			=A1+A2

(d) Example 4 (dependent cells)

FIGURE 2.3   The Move Command

Cell reference adjusts to
follow moved entry ──────

	A	B	C
1	5	=$A$3*4	
2	2		
3	=$A$1+$A$2		

	A	B	C
1		=$C$3*4	5
2			2
3			=$C$1+$C$2

Both cell references adjust
to follow moved entries ────

(e) Example 5 (absolute cell addresses)

FIGURE 2.3   The Move Command (continued)

entry in A1 is moved to C1. The formula in cell A3 is adjusted to follow the moved entry to its new location; that is, the formula is now =C1+A2.

The situation is different in Figure 2.3c as the contents of all three cells—A1, A2, and A3—are moved. After the move has taken place, cells C1 and C2 contain the 5 and the 2, respectively, with the formula in cell C3 adjusted to reflect the movement of the contents of cells A1 and A2. Once again the source range (A1:A3) is empty after the move is completed.

Figure 2.3d contains an additional formula in cell B1, which is *dependent* on cell A3, which in turn is moved to cell C3. The formula in cell C3 is unchanged after the move because *only* the formula was moved, *not* the values it referenced. The formula in cell B1 changes because cell B1 refers to an entry (cell A3) that was moved to a new location (cell C3).

Figure 2.3e shows that the specification of an absolute reference has no meaning in a move operation, because the cell addresses are adjusted as necessary to reflect the cells that have been moved. Moving a formula that contains an absolute reference does not adjust the formula. Moving a value that is specified as an absolute reference, however, adjusts the formula to follow the cell to its new location. Thus all of the absolute references in Figure 2.3e are changed to reflect the entries that were moved.

The move operation is a convenient way to improve the appearance of a worksheet after it has been developed. It is subtle in its operation, and we suggest you think twice before moving cell entries because of the complexities involved.

The move operation is implemented by using the Windows clipboard and a combination of the **Cut** and **Paste commands** from the Edit menu. The contents of the source range are transferred to the clipboard, from which they are pasted to the destination range. (Executing a Paste command after a Cut command empties the clipboard. This is different from pasting after a Copy command, which does not affect the contents of the clipboard.)

LEARNING BY DOING

As we have already indicated, there are many different ways to accomplish the same task. You can execute commands using a pull-down menu, a shortcut menu, a toolbar, or the keyboard. In the exercise that follows we emphasize pull-down menus (the most basic technique) but suggest various shortcuts as appropriate.

Realize, however, that while the shortcuts are interesting, it is far more important to focus on the underlying concepts in the exercise, rather than specific key strokes or mouse clicks. The professor's grade book was developed to emphasize the difference between relative and absolute cell references. The grade book also illustrates the importance of isolating assumptions so that alternative strategies (e.g., different exam weights) can be considered.

Creating a Workbook

Objective: To create a new workbook; to develop a formula containing relative and absolute references; to use the Copy command within a worksheet. Use Figure 2.4 as a guide.

STEP 1: Create a New Workbook

➤ Start Microsoft Excel as described in Chapter 1. Close the Office Assistant if it appears.

➤ Click in **cell A1.** Enter the title of the worksheet, **CIS120 - Spring 1997** as in Figure 2.4a. (The Save As dialog box is not yet visible.)

➤ Press the **down arrow key** to move to cell A3. Type **Student.**

➤ Press the **right arrow key** to move to cell B3. Type **Test 1.**

➤ Press the **right arrow key** to move to cell C3. Type **Test 2.**

➤ Press the **right arrow key** to move to cell D3. Type **Final.**

➤ Press the **right arrow key** to move to cell E3. Type **Average.** Press **enter.**

STEP 2: Save the Workbook

➤ Pull down the **File menu** and click **Save** (or click the **Save button** on the Standard toolbar) to display the Save As dialog box.

➤ Click the **drop-down arrow** on the Save In list box. Click the appropriate drive, drive C or drive A, depending on where you are saving your Excel workbook.

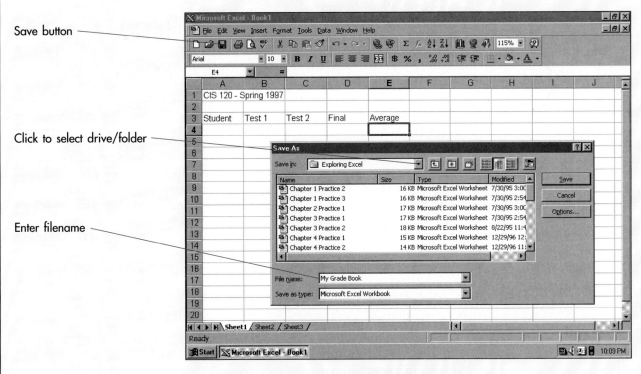

(a) Create the Workbook (steps 1 and 2)

FIGURE 2.4   Hands-on Exercise 1

> ➤ Double click the **Exploring Excel folder** to make it the active folder (the folder in which you will save the document).

> ➤ Click and drag to select **Book1** (the default entry) in the File name text box. Type **My Grade Book** as the name of the workbook. Press the **enter key.**

> ➤ The title bar changes to reflect the name of the workbook.

LONG FILENAMES

Windows 95 allows filenames of up to 255 characters (spaces and commas are permitted). Anyone using Windows 95 for the first time will take descriptive names such as *My Grade Book* for granted, but veterans of MS-DOS and Windows 3.1 will appreciate the improvement over the earlier 8.3 naming convention (an eight-character name followed by a three-letter extension to indicate the file type).

STEP 3: Enter Student Data

> ➤ Click in **cell A4** and type **Costa, Frank.** Move across row 4 and enter Frank's grades on the two tests and the final. Use Figure 2.4b as a guide.
>   - Do *not* enter Frank's average in cell E4 as that will be entered as a formula in step 5.
>   - Do *not* be concerned that you cannot see Frank's entire name because the default width of column A is not wide enough to display the entire name.

> ➤ Enter the names and grades for the other students in rows 5 through 9. Do *not* enter their averages.

> ➤ Complete the entries in column A by typing **Class Averages** and **Exam Weights** in cells **A11** and **A13,** respectively.

> ➤ Click the **Save button** on the Standard toolbar to save the workbook.

SAVE YOUR WORK

We cannot overemphasize the importance of periodically saving a workbook, so if something goes wrong you won't lose everything. Nothing is more frustrating than to lose two hours of effort due to an unexpected problem in Windows or to a temporary loss of power. Save your work frequently, at least once every 15 minutes. Click the Save button on the Standard toolbar or pull down the File menu and click Save. Do it!

STEP 4: Enter Exam Weights

> ➤ Click in **cell B13** and enter **.25** (the weight for the first exam).

> ➤ Press the **right arrow key** to move to cell C13 and enter **.25** (the weight for the second exam).

> ➤ Press the **right arrow key** to move to cell D13 and enter **.5** (the weight for the final). Press **enter.** Do *not* be concerned that the exam weights do not

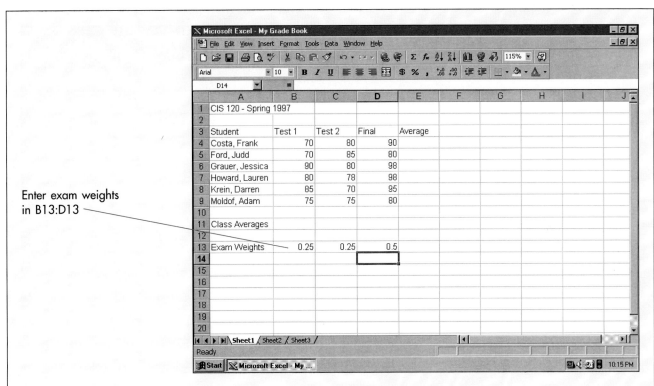

Enter exam weights in B13:D13

(b) Enter Student Data (steps 3 and 4)

FIGURE 2.4   Hands-on Exercise 1 (continued)

appear as percentages; they will be formatted in the second exercise later in the chapter.

➤ The worksheet should match Figure 2.4b except that column A is too narrow to display the entire name of each student.

STEP 5: Compute the Semester Average

➤ Click in **cell E4** and type the formula **=$B$13*B4+$C$13*C4+$D$13*D4** as shown in Figure 2.4c. Press the **enter key** when you have completed the formula.

➤ Check that the displayed value in cell E4 is 82.5, which indicates you entered the formula correctly. Correct the formula if necessary.

➤ Save the workbook.

CORRECTING MISTAKES

The most basic way to correct an erroneous entry is to click in the cell, then re-enter the cell contents in their entirety. It's faster, however, to edit the cell contents rather than retyping them. Click in the cell whose contents you want to change, then make the necessary changes in the formula bar near the top of the Excel window. Use the mouse or arrow keys to position the insertion point. You can also press the Home and End keys to move to the first and last character in the cell, respectively. Make the necessary correction(s), then press the enter key.

Formula bar shows
the contents of cell E4

Cell E4 shows
displayed value

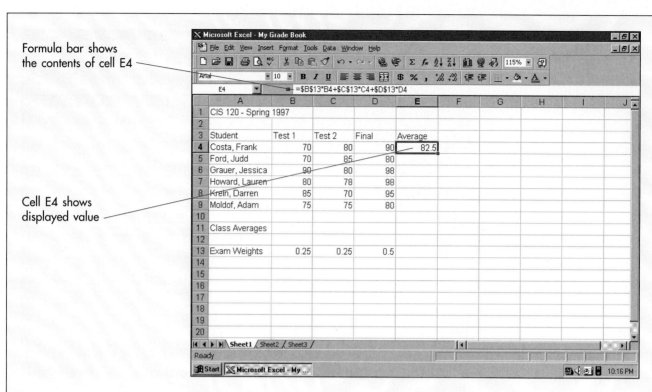

(c) Compute the Semester Average (step 5)

FIGURE 2.4   Hands-on Exercise 1 (continued)

STEP 6: Copy the Semester Average

➤ Click in **cell E4.** Pull down the **Edit menu** and click **Copy** (or click the **copy button** on the standard toolbar). A moving border will surround cell E4, indicating that its contents have been copied to the clipboard.

➤ Click **cell E5.** Drag the mouse over cells **E5** through **E9** to select the destination range as in Figure 2.4d.

➤ Pull down the **Edit menu** and click **Paste** to copy the contents of the clipboard to the destination range. You should see the semester averages for the other students in cells E5 through E9.

➤ Press **Esc** to remove the moving border around cell E4. Click anywhere in the worksheet to deselect cells E5 through E9.

CUT, COPY AND PASTE

Ctrl+X (the X is supposed to remind you of a pair of scissors), Ctrl+C, and Ctrl+V are keyboard equivalents to cut, copy, and paste, respectively, and apply to Excel, Word, PowerPoint and Access, as well as Windows applications in general. (The keystrokes are easier to remember when you realize that the operative letters, X, C, and V, are next to each other at the bottom-left side of the keyboard.) Alternatively, you can use the Cut, Copy, and Paste buttons on the Standard toolbar, which are also found on the Standard toolbar in the other Office applications.

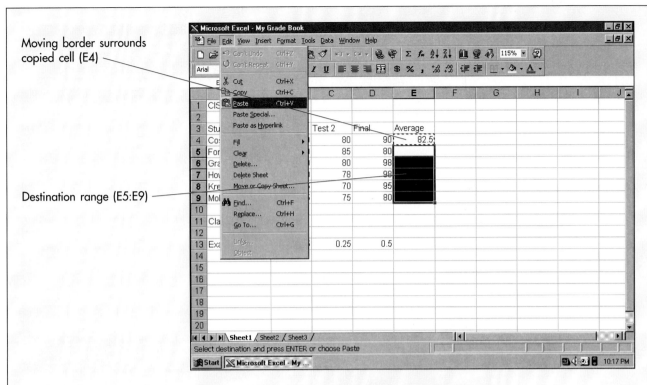

Moving border surrounds
copied cell (E4)

Destination range (E5:E9)

(d) Copy the Semester Average (step 6)

FIGURE 2.4   Hands-on Exercise 1 (continued)

➤ Click in **cell E5** and look at the formula. The cells that reference the grades have changed to B5, C5, and D5. The cells that reference the exam weights—$B$13, $C$13, and $D$13—are the same as in cell E4.

➤ Save the workbook.

STEP 7: Compute Class Averages

➤ Click in **cell B11** and type the formula **=AVERAGE(B4:B9)** to compute the class average on the first test. Press the **enter key** when you have completed the formula.

➤ Point to **cell B11,** then click the **right mouse button** to display the shortcut menu in Figure 2.4e. Click **Copy,** which produces the moving border around cell B11.

➤ Click **cell C11.** Drag the mouse over cells **C11** and **D11,** the destination range for the Copy command.

THE RIGHT MOUSE BUTTON

Point to a cell (or cell range), a worksheet tab, or a toolbar, then click the right mouse button to display a context-sensitive menu with commands appropriate to the item you are pointing to. Right clicking a cell, for example, displays a menu with selected commands from the Edit, Insert, and Format menus. Right clicking a toolbar displays a menu that lets you display (hide) additional toolbars. Right clicking a worksheet tab enables you to rename, move, copy, or delete the worksheet.

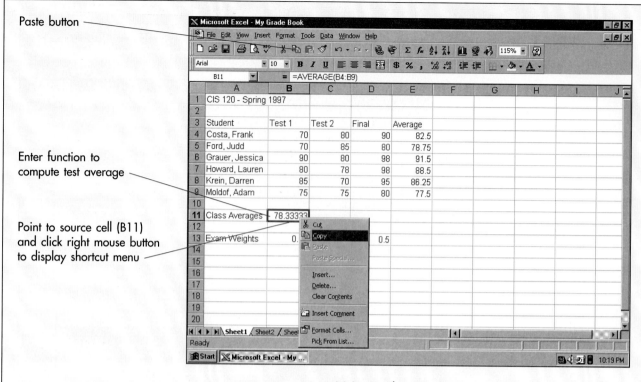

Paste button

Enter function to compute test average

Point to source cell (B11) and click right mouse button to display shortcut menu

(e) Compute Class Averages (step 7)

FIGURE 2.4 Hands-on Exercise 1 (continued)

➤ Click the **Paste button** on the Standard toolbar (or press Ctrl+V) to paste the contents of the clipboard to the destination range.

➤ Press **Esc** to remove the moving border. Click anywhere in the worksheet to deselect cells C11 through D11.

STEP 8: What If? Change Exam Weights

➤ Change the entries in cells B13 and C13 to **.20** and the entry in cell D13 to **.60.** The semester average for every student changes automatically; for example, Costa and Moldof change to 84 and 78, respectively.

➤ The professor decides this does not make a significant difference and wants to go back to the original weights. Click the **Undo button** three times to reverse the last three actions. You should see .25, .25, and .50 in cells B13, C13, and D13, respectively.

➤ Click the **Save button.** Exit Excel if you are not ready to begin the next exercise at this time.

FORMATTING

In this chapter the professor's grade book is developed in two stages, as shown in Figure 2.5. The exercise just completed created the grade book, but paid no attention to its appearance. It had you enter the data for every student, develop the formulas to compute the semester average for every student based on the exam weights at the bottom of the worksheet, and finally, develop the formulas to compute the class averages for each exam.

Figure 2.5a shows the grade book as it exists at the end of the first hands-on exercise. Figure 2.5b shows the grade book at the end of the second exercise after it has been formatted. The differences between the two are due entirely to formatting. Consider:

- The exam weights are formatted as percentages in Figure 2.5b, as opposed to decimals in Figure 2.5a. The class and semester averages are displayed with a single decimal place in Figure 2.5b.
- Boldface and italics are used for emphasis, as are shading and borders.
- Exam grades and computed averages are centered under their respective headings.
- The worksheet title is centered across all five columns.
- The width of column A has been increased so that the students' names are completely visible.

Column A is too narrow ⟶

Class averages are
not uniformly formatted ⟶

	A	B	C	D	E
1	CIS 120 - Spring 1997				
2					
3	Student	Test 1	Test 2	Final	Average
4	Costa, Fran	70	80	90	82.5
5	Ford, Judd	70	85	80	78.75
6	Grauer, Jes:	90	80	98	91.5
7	Howard, Lat	80	78	98	88.5
8	Krein, Darre	85	70	95	86.25
9	Moldof, Ada	75	75	80	77.5
10					
11	Class Avera	78.33333	78	90.16667	
12					
13	Exam Weigl	.25	.25	.50	

(a) At the End of Hands-on Exercise 1

Title is centered across
the worksheet and set in
larger typeface ⟶

Boldface, italics, shading, and
borders used for emphasis ⟶

Grades are centered in column ⟶

Results are displayed
with 1 decimal place ⟶

Exam weights are
formatted as % ⟶

Column A is wider

	A	B	C	D	E
1		*CIS 120 - Spring 1997*			
2					
3	*Student*	*Test 1*	*Test 2*	*Final*	*Average*
4	Costa, Frank	70	80	90	82.5
5	Ford, Judd	70	85	80	78.8
6	Grauer, Jessica	90	80	98	91.5
7	Howard, Lauren	80	78	98	88.5
8	Krein, Darren	85	70	95	86.3
9	Moldof, Adam	75	75	80	77.5
10					
11	*Class Averages*	*78.3*	*78.0*	*90.2*	
12					
13	*Exam Weights*	*25%*	*25%*	*50%*	

(b) At the End of Hands-on Exercise 2

FIGURE 2.5 Developing the Grade Book

Column Widths

A column is often too narrow to display the contents of one or more cells in that column. When this happens, the display depends on whether the cell contains a text or numeric entry, and if it is a text entry, on whether or not the adjacent cell is empty.

The student names in Figure 2.5a, for example, are partially hidden because column A is too narrow to display the entire name. Cells A4 through A9 contain the complete names of each student, but because the adjacent cells in column B contain data, the displayed entries in column A are truncated (cut off) at the cell width. The situation is different for the worksheet title in cell A1. This time the adjacent cell (cell B1) is empty, so that the contents of cell A1 overflow into that cell and are completely visible.

Numbers are treated differently from text and do not depend on the contents of the adjacent cell. Excel displays a series of number signs (######) when a cell containing a numeric entry is too narrow to display the entry in its current format. You may be able to correct the problem by changing the format of the number (e.g., display the number with fewer decimal places). Alternatively, you can increase the **column width** by using the **Column command** in the Format menu.

Row Heights

The **row height** changes automatically as the font size is increased. Row 1 in Figure 2.5b, for example, has a greater height than the other rows to accommodate the larger font size in the title of the worksheet. The row height can also be changed manually through the **Row command** in the Format menu.

FORMAT CELLS COMMAND

The **Format Cells command** controls the formatting for numbers, alignment, fonts, borders, and patterns (color). Execution of the command produces a tabbed dialog box in which you choose the particular formatting category, then enter the desired options. (Many of the formatting options can also be specified from the Formatting toolbar.)

All formatting is done within the context of **select-then-do.** You select the cells to which the formatting is to apply, then you execute the Format Cells command or click the appropriate button on the Formatting toolbar.

> ### FORMATS VERSUS VALUES
>
> Changing the format of a number changes the way the number is displayed but does *not* change its value. If, for example, you entered 1.2345 into a cell but displayed the number as 1.23, the actual value (1.2345) would be used in all calculations involving that cell.

Numeric Formats

General format is the default format for numeric entries and displays a number according to the way it was originally entered. Numbers are shown as integers (e.g., 123), decimal fractions (e.g., 1.23), or in scientific notation (e.g., 1.23E+10) if the number exceeds 11 digits. You can also display a number in one of several formats as shown in Figure 2.6a:

- *Number format,* which displays a number with or without the 1000 separator (e.g., a comma) and with any number of decimal places. Negative numbers are displayed with parentheses and/or can be shown in red.
- *Currency format,* which displays a number with the 1000 separator and an optional dollar sign (which is placed immediately to the left of the number). Negative values are preceded by a minus sign or are shown in red.
- *Accounting format,* which displays a number with the 1000 separator, an optional dollar sign (at the left of the cell that vertically aligns the dollar signs within a column), negative values in parentheses, and zero values as hyphens.
- *Date format,* which displays the date in different ways, such as March 4, 1994, 3/4/94, or 4-Mar-94.
- *Time format,* which displays the time in different formats, such as 10:50 PM or the equivalent 22:50 (24-hour time).
- *Percentage format,* whereby the number is multiplied by 100 for display purposes only, a percent sign is included, and any number of decimal places can be specified.
- *Fraction format,* which displays a number as a fraction, and is appropriate when there is no exact decimal equivalent, for example, ⅓.
- *Scientific format,* which displays a number as a decimal fraction followed by a whole number exponent of 10; for example, the number 12345 would

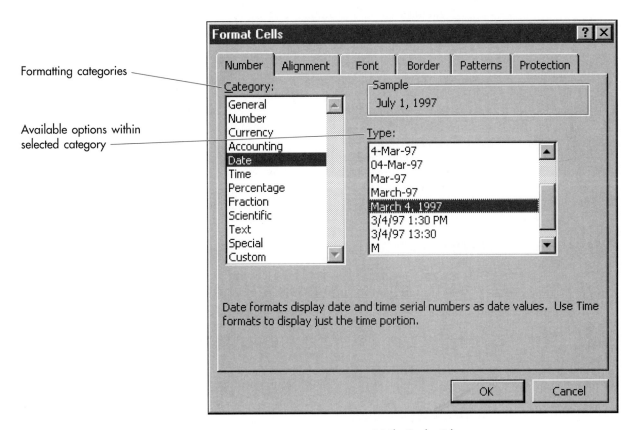

Formatting categories

Available options within selected category

(a) The Number Tab

FIGURE 2.6 The Format Cells Command

appear as 1.2345E+04. The exponent, +04 in the example, is the number of places the decimal point is moved to the left (or right if the exponent is negative). Very small numbers have negative exponents; for example, the entry .0000012 would be displayed as 1.2E−06. Scientific notation is used only with very large or very small numbers.

- **Text format,** which left aligns the entry and is useful for numerical values that have leading zeros and should be treated as text, such as ZIP codes.
- **Special format,** which displays a number with editing characters, such as hyphens in a social security number or parentheses around the area code of a telephone number.
- **Custom format,** which allows you to develop your own formats.

DATES VERSUS FRACTIONS

A fraction may be entered into a cell by preceding the fraction with an equal sign, for example, =1/3. The fraction is converted to its decimal equivalent and displayed in that format in the worksheet. Omission of the equal sign causes Excel to treat the entry as a date; that is, 1/3 will be stored as January 3 (of the current year).

Alignment

The contents of a cell (whether text or numeric) may be aligned horizontally and/or vertically as indicated by the dialog box of Figure 2.6b. The default horizontal alignment is general, which left-aligns text and right-aligns date and numbers. You can also center an entry across a range of selected cells, as in the professor's grade book, which centered the title that was entered in cell A1 across columns A through E. The Fill option duplicates the characters in the cell across the entire width of that cell.

Vertical alignment is important only if the row height is changed and the characters are smaller than the height of the row. Entries may be vertically aligned at the top, center, or bottom (the default) of a cell.

It is also possible to wrap the text within a cell to emulate the word wrap of a word processor. And finally, you can achieve some very interesting effects by rotating text up to 90° in either direction.

Fonts

You can use the same fonts (typefaces) in Excel as you can in any other Windows application. Windows itself includes a limited number of fonts (Arial, Times New Roman, Courier New, Symbol, and Wingdings) to provide variety in creating documents. (Additional fonts are also installed with Microsoft Office.) All fonts are WYSIWYG (What You See Is What You Get), meaning that the worksheet you see on the monitor will match the worksheet produced by the printer.

Any entry in a worksheet may be displayed in any font, style, or point size as indicated by the dialog box of Figure 2.6c. The example shows Arial, Bold Italic, and 14 points, and corresponds to the selection for the worksheet title in the improved grade book. Special effects, such as subscripts or superscripts, are also possible. You can even select a different color, but you will need a color printer to see the effect on the printed page. The Preview box shows the text as it will appear in the worksheet.

Horizontal alignment options

Vertical alignment options

Click to wrap text within a cell

Click and drag to rotate text 90°

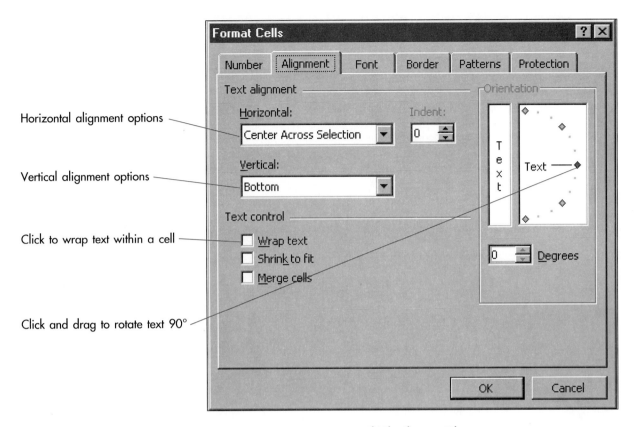

(b) The Alignment Tab

List of available fonts

Preview of selected font

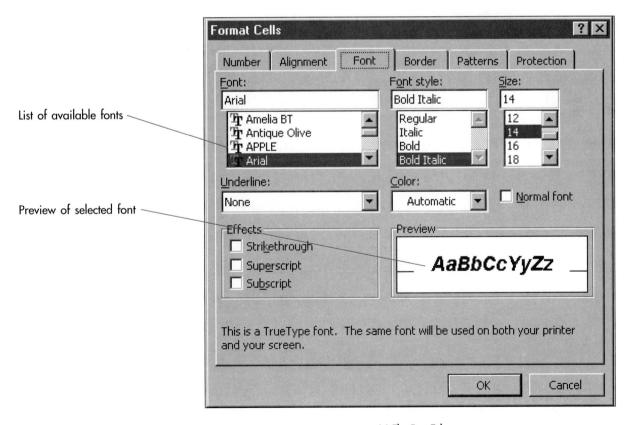

(c) The Font Tab

FIGURE 2.6   The Format Cells Command (continued)

Borders, Patterns, and Shading

The **Border tab** in Figure 2.6d enables you to create a border around a cell (or cells) for additional emphasis. You can outline the entire selection, or you can choose the specific side or sides; for example, thicker lines on the bottom and right sides produce a drop shadow, which is very effective. You can also specify a different color for the border, but you will need a color printer to see the effect on the printed output.

The **Patterns tab** in Figure 2.6e lets you choose a different color in which to shade the cell and further emphasize its contents. The Pattern drop-down list box lets you select an alternate pattern, such as dots or slanted lines.

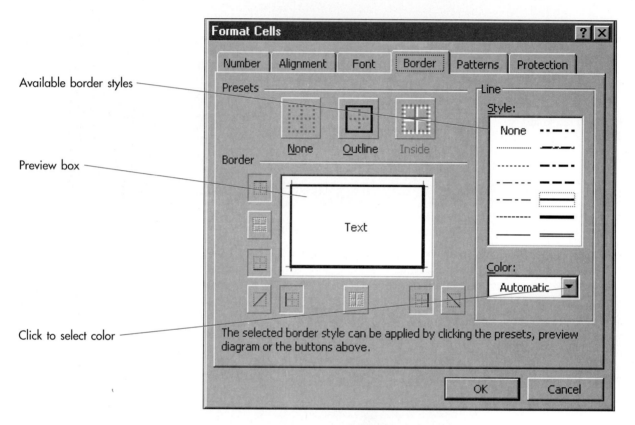

(d) The Border Tab

FIGURE 2.6   The Format Cells Command (continued)

USE RESTRAINT

More is not better, especially in the case of too many typefaces and styles, which produce cluttered worksheets that impress no one. Limit yourself to a maximum of two typefaces per worksheet, but choose multiple sizes and/or styles within those typefaces. Use boldface or italics for emphasis, but do so in moderation, because if you emphasize too many elements, the effect is lost.

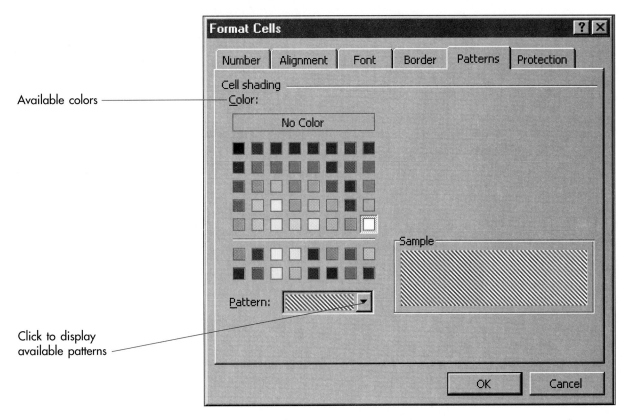

Available colors

Click to display
available patterns

(e) The Patterns Tab

FIGURE 2.6   The Format Cells Command (continued)

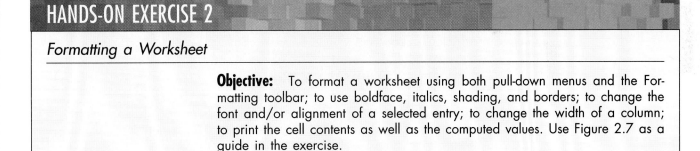

HANDS-ON EXERCISE 2

Formatting a Worksheet

Objective: To format a worksheet using both pull-down menus and the Formatting toolbar; to use boldface, italics, shading, and borders; to change the font and/or alignment of a selected entry; to change the width of a column; to print the cell contents as well as the computed values. Use Figure 2.7 as a guide in the exercise.

STEP 1: Center Across Selection

➤ Open **My Grade Book** from the previous exercise.

➤ Click in **cell A1** to select the cell containing the title of the worksheet.

➤ Pull down the **Format menu.** Click **Cells.** If necessary, click the **Font tab.** Click **Arial** in the Font list box, **Bold Italic** in the Font Style box, and then scroll to select **14** from the Size box. Click **OK.**

➤ Click and drag to select cells **A1** through **E1,** which represents the width of the entire worksheet.

➤ Pull down the **Format menu** a second time. Click **Cells.** Click the **Alignment tab.** Click the **down arrow** in the Horizontal list box, then click **Center Across**

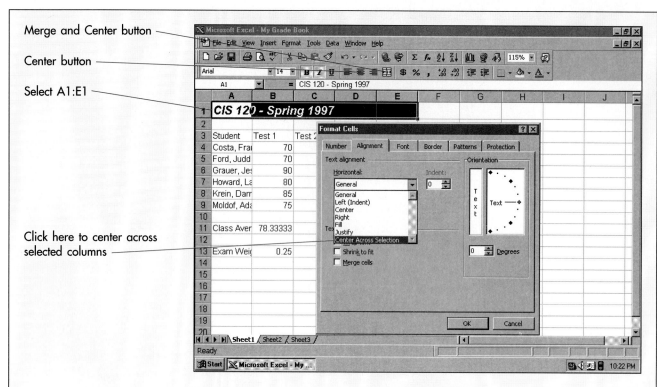

Merge and Center button

Center button

Select A1:E1

Click here to center across selected columns

(a) Center across Selection (step 1)

FIGURE 2.7   Hands-on Exercise 2

Selection as in Figure 2.7a. (You can also click the **Merge and Center button** on the Formatting toolbar.) Click **OK**.

➤ Click and drag over cells **B3** through **E13.** Click the **Centering button** on the Formatting toolbar.

CHANGE THE DEFAULT FILE LOCATION

The *default file location* is the folder Excel uses to open (save) a workbook unless it is otherwise instructed. To change the default location, pull down the Tools menu, click Options, and click the General tab. Type the name of the new folder (e.g., C:\Exploring Excel) in the Default File Location text box, then click OK. The next time you access the Open or Save commands from the File menu, the Look In text box will reflect the change.

STEP 2: Increase the Width of Column A

➤ Click in **cell A4.** Drag the mouse over cells **A4** through **A13.**

➤ Pull down the **Format menu,** click **Column,** then click **AutoFit Selection** as shown in Figure 2.7b. The width of the selected cells increases to accommodate the longest entry in the selected range.

➤ Save the workbook.

Select A4:A13

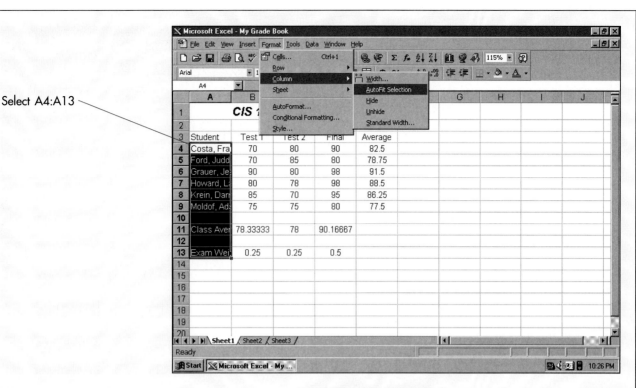

(b) Changing Column Widths (step 2)

FIGURE 2.7 Hands-on Exercise 2 (continued)

COLUMN WIDTHS AND ROW HEIGHTS

Drag the border between column headings to change the column width; for example, to increase (decrease) the width of column A, drag the border between column headings A and B to the right (left). Double click the right boundary of a column heading to change the column width to accommodate the widest entry in that column. Use the same techniques to change the row heights.

STEP 3: Format the Exam Weights

➤ Click and drag to select cells **B13** through **D13.** Point to the selected cells and click the **right mouse button** to display the shortcut menu in Figure 2.7c. Click **Format Cells** to produce the Format Cells dialog box.

➤ If necessary, click the **Number tab.** Click **Percentage** in the Category list box. Click the **down arrow** in the Decimal Places box to reduce the number of decimals to zero, then click **OK.** The exam weights are displayed with percent signs and no decimal places.

➤ Click the **Undo button** on the Standard toolbar to cancel the formatting command.

➤ Click the **% button** on the Formatting toolbar to reformat the exam weights as percentages. (This is an alternate and faster way to change to the percent format.)

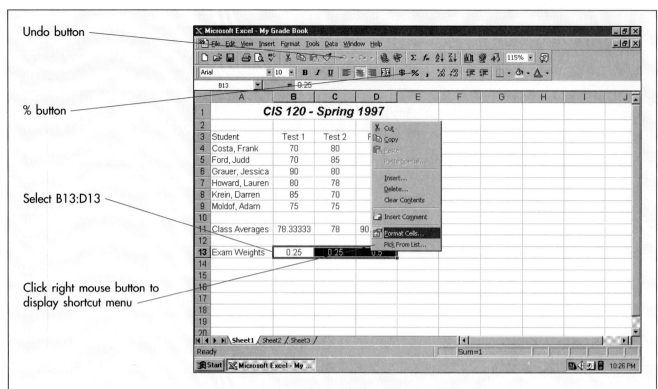

Undo button

% button

Select B13:D13

Click right mouse button to display shortcut menu

(c) Format Exam Weights (step 3)

FIGURE 2.7 Hands-on Exercise 2 (continued)

AUTOMATIC FORMATTING

Excel converts any number entered with a beginning dollar sign to currency format, and any number entered with an ending percent sign to percentage format. The automatic formatting enables you to save a step by typing $100,000 or 7.5% directly into a cell, rather than entering 100000 or .075 and having to format the number. The formatting is applied to the cell and affects any subsequent numbers in that cell.

STEP 4: Noncontiguous Ranges

➤ Select cells **B11** through **D11,** the cells that contain the class averages for the three exams.

➤ Press *and* hold the **Ctrl key** as you click and drag to select cells **E4** through **E9.** Release the **Ctrl key.**

➤ You will see two noncontiguous (nonadjacent) ranges highlighted, cells B11:D11 and cells E4:E9 as in Figure 2.7d. Format the selected cells using either the Formatting toolbar or the Format menu:

• To use the Formatting toolbar, click the appropriate button to increase or decrease the number of decimal places to one.

• To use the Format menu, pull down the **Format menu,** click **Cells,** click the **Number tab,** then click **Number** in the Category list box. Click the **down arrow** in the Decimal Places text box to reduce the decimal places to one. Click **OK.**

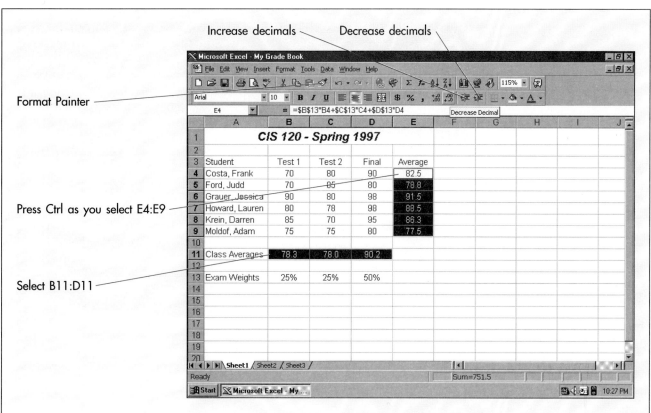

Increase decimals — Decrease decimals

Format Painter

Press Ctrl as you select E4:E9

Select B11:D11

(d) Noncontiguous Ranges (step 4)

FIGURE 2.7   Hands-on Exercise 2 (continued)

THE FORMAT PAINTER

The *Format Painter* copies the formatting of the selected cell to other cells in the worksheet. Click the cell whose formatting you want to copy, then double click the Format Painter button on the Standard toolbar. The mouse pointer changes to a paintbrush to indicate that you can copy the current formatting; just click and drag the paintbrush over the additional cells to which you want to apply the formatting. Repeat the painting process as often as necessary, then click the Format Painter button a second time to return to normal editing.

STEP 5: Borders

➤ Click and drag to select cells **A3** through **E3.** Press *and* hold the **Ctrl key** as you click and drag to select the range **A11:E11.** Continue to press the **Ctrl key** as you click and drag to select cells **A13:E13.**

➤ Pull down the **Format menu** and click **Cells** (or click the **right mouse button** to produce a shortcut menu, then click **Format Cells**). Click the **Border tab** to access the dialog box in Figure 2.7e.

➤ Choose a line width from the Style section. Click the **Top** and **Bottom** boxes in the Border section. Click **OK** to exit the dialog box and return to the worksheet.

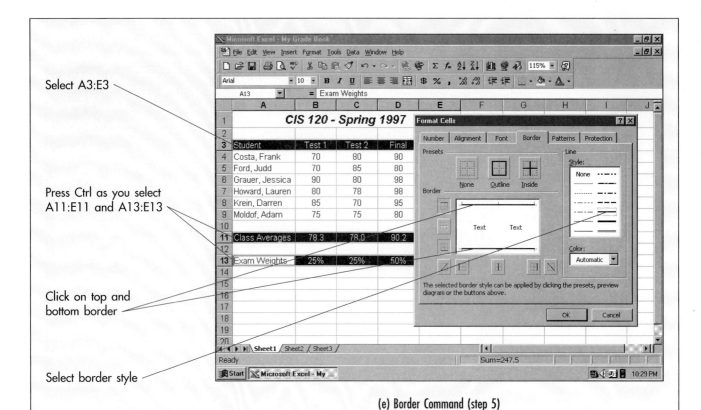

Select A3:E3

Press Ctrl as you select
A11:E11 and A13:E13

Click on top and
bottom border

Select border style

(e) Border Command (step 5)

FIGURE 2.7 Hands-on Exercise 2 (continued)

SELECTING NONCONTIGUOUS RANGES

Dragging the mouse to select a range always produces some type of rectangle; that is, a single cell, a row or column, or a group of rows and columns. You can, however, select *noncontiguous* (nonadjacent) *ranges* by selecting the first range in the normal fashion, then pressing and holding the Ctrl key as you select the additional range(s). This is especially useful when the same command is to be applied to multiple ranges within a worksheet.

STEP 6: Color

➤ Check that all three ranges are still selected (A3:E3, A11:E11, *and* A13:E13).

➤ Click the **down arrow** on the **Fill Color button** on the Formatting toolbar. Click yellow (or whatever color appeals to you) as shown in Figure 2.7f.

➤ Click the **boldface** and **italics buttons** on the Formatting toolbar. Click outside the selected cells to see the effects of the formatting change.

➤ Save the workbook.

Color button

Bold button

Italics button

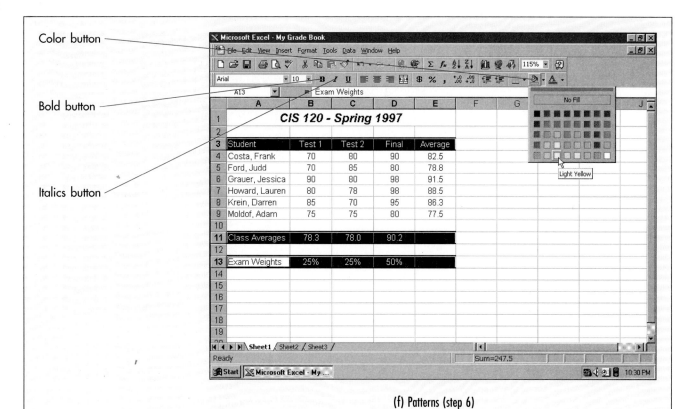

(f) Patterns (step 6)

FIGURE 2.7 Hands-on Exercise 2 (continued)

DESELECTING A RANGE

The effects of a formatting change are often difficult to see when the selected cells are highlighted. Thus, you may need to deselect the range by clicking elsewhere in the worksheet to see the results of a formatting command.

STEP 7: Enter Your Name and Social Security Number

➤ Click in **cell A15.** Type **Grading Assistant.** Press the **down arrow key.** Type your name, press the **down arrow key,** and enter your social security number *without* the hyphens. Press **enter.**

➤ Point to **cell A17,** then click the **right mouse button** to display a shortcut menu. Click **Format Cells** to display the dialog box in Figure 2.7g.

➤ Click the **Number tab,** click **Special** in the Category list box, then click **Social Security Number** in the Type list box. Click **OK.** Hyphens have been inserted into your social security number.

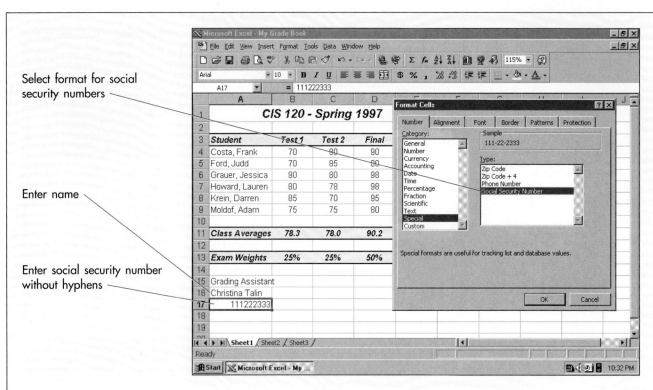

Select format for social
security numbers

Enter name

Enter social security number
without hyphens

(g) Add Your Name and Social Security Number (step 7)

FIGURE 2.7   Hands-on Exercise 2 (continued)

STEP 8: The Page Setup Command

➤ Pull down the **File menu.** Click **Page Setup** to display the Page Setup dialog box.

  • Click the **Margins tab.** Check the box to center the worksheet Horizontally.

  • Click the **Sheet tab.** Check the boxes to print Row and Column Headings and Gridlines.

  • Click **OK** to exit the Page Setup dialog box.

➤ Click the **Print Preview button** to preview the worksheet before printing:

  • If you are satisfied with the appearance of the worksheet, click the **Print button** within the Preview window, then click **OK** to print the worksheet.

  • If you are not satisfied with the appearance of the worksheet, click the **Setup button** within the Preview window to make the necessary changes, after which you can print the worksheet.

➤ Save the workbook.

THE INSERT COMMENT COMMAND

You can add a comment, which displays a ScreenTip, to any cell in a worksheet. Click in the cell, pull down the Insert menu, and click Comment to display a box in which you enter the comment. Click outside the box when you have completed the entry. Point to the cell (which should have a tiny red triangle) and you will see the ScreenTip you just created. (If you do not see the triangle or the tip, pull down the Tools menu, click Options, click the View tab, then click the options button for Comment Indicator Only in the Comments area.)

STEP 9: Print the Cell Formulas

➤ Pull down the **Tools menu,** click **Options,** click the **View tab,** check the box for **Formulas,** then click **OK** (or use the keyboard shortcut **Ctrl+`**). The worksheet should display the cell formulas.

➤ If necessary, click the arrow to the right of the horizontal scroll box so that column E, the column containing the cell formulas, comes into view.

➤ Double click the border between the column headings for columns E and F to increase the width of column E to accommodate the widest entry in the column.

➤ Pull down the **File menu.** Click the **Page Setup** command to display the Page Setup dialog box.

  • Click the **Page tab.** Click the **Landscape orientation button.**

  • Click the option button to **Fit to 1 page.** Click **OK** to exit the Page Setup dialog box.

➤ Click the **Print Preview button** to preview the worksheet before printing. It should match the display in Figure 2.7h:

  • If you are satisfied with the appearance of the worksheet, click the **Print button** within the Preview window, then click **OK** to print the worksheet.

  • If you are not satisfied with the appearance of the worksheet, click the **Setup button** within the Preview window to make the necessary changes, after which you can print the worksheet.

➤ Pull down the **File menu.** Click **Close.** Click **No** if prompted to save changes.

➤ Exit Excel if you do not want to continue with the next exercise at this time.

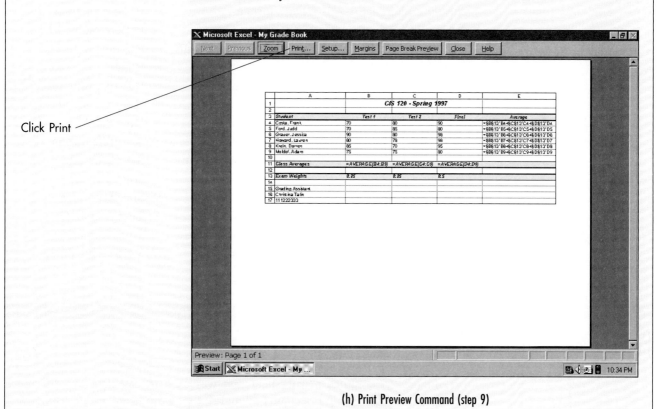

Click Print

(h) Print Preview Command (step 9)

FIGURE 2.7 Hands-on Exercise 2 (continued)

All worksheet commands operate on a cell or group of cells known as a range. A range is selected by dragging the mouse to highlight the range. The range remains selected until another range is defined or you click another cell in the worksheet. Noncontiguous (nonadjacent) ranges may be selected in conjunction with the Ctrl key.

The formulas in a cell or range of cells may be copied or moved anywhere within a worksheet. An absolute reference remains constant throughout a copy operation, whereas a relative address is adjusted for the new location. Absolute and relative references have no meaning in a move operation. The copy and move operations are implemented through the Copy and Paste commands, and the Cut and Paste commands, respectively.

Formatting is done within the context of select-then-do; that is, select the cell or range of cells, then execute the appropriate command. The Format Cells command controls the formatting for Numbers, Alignment, Fonts, Borders, and Patterns (colors). The Formatting toolbar simplifies the formatting process.

A spreadsheet is first and foremost a tool for decision making, and as such, the subject of continual what-if speculation. It is critical, therefore, that the initial conditions and assumptions be isolated and clearly visible, and further that all formulas in the body of the spreadsheet be developed using these cells.

KEY WORDS AND CONCEPTS

Absolute reference	Date format	Paste command
Accounting format	Destination range	Patterns tab
Alignment	Format cells command	Percentage format
Assumptions	Format menu	Range
Automatic formatting	Format Painter	Relative reference
Border tab	Formatting toolbar	Row command
Cell formulas	Fraction format	Row height
Clipboard	General format	Scientific format
Column command	Horizontal alignment	Select-then-do
Column width	Initial conditions	Source range
Copy command	Mixed reference	Special format
Currency format	Move operation	Text format
Custom format	Noncontiguous range	Time format
Cut command	Number format	Vertical alignment

PRACTICE WITH EXCEL 97

1. Figure 2.8 contains a worksheet that was used to calculate the difference between the Asking Price and Selling Price on various real estate listings that were sold during June, as well as the commission paid to the real estate agency as a result of selling those listings. Complete the worksheet, following the steps on the next page.

	A	B	C	D	E	F
1	Coaches Realty - Sales for June					
2						
3						
4	Customer	Address	Asking Price	Selling Price	Difference	Commission
5	Landry	122 West 75 Terr.	450000	350000		
6	Spurrier	4567 S.W. 95 Street	750000	648500		
7	Shula	123 Alamo Road	350000	275000		
8	Lombardi	9000 Brickell Place	275000	250000		
9	Johnson	5596 Powerline Road	189000	189000		
10	Erickson	8900 N.W. 89 Street	456000	390000		
11	Bowden	75 Maynada Blvd.	300000	265000		
12						
13		Totals:				
14						
15	Commission %:	0.035				

FIGURE 2.8   Spreadsheet for Practice Exercise 1

a. Open the partially completed *Chapter 2 Practice 1* workbook on the data disk, then save the workbook as *Chapter 2 Practice 1 Solution.*

b. Click cell E5 and enter the formula to calculate the difference between the asking price and the selling price for the property belonging to Mr. Landry.

c. Click cell F5 and enter the formula to calculate the commission paid to the agency as a result of selling the property. (Pay close attention to the difference between relative and absolute cell references.)

d. Select cells E5:F5 and copy the formulas to E6:F11 to calculate the difference and commission for the rest of the properties.

e. Click cell C13 and enter the formula to calculate the total asking price, which is the sum of the asking prices for the individual listings.

f. Copy the formula in C13 to the range D13:F13 to calculate the other totals.

g. Select the range C5:F13 and format the numbers so that they display with dollar signs and commas, and no decimal places (e.g., $450,000).

h. Click cell B15 and format the number as a percentage.

i. Click cell A1 and center the title across the width of the worksheet. With the cell still selected, select cells A2:F4 as well and change the font to 12 point Arial bold italic.

j. Select cells A4:F4 and create a bottom border to separate the headings from the data. Select cells F5:F11 and shade the commissions.

k. Add your name as the realtor in cell B.

l. Print the worksheet and submit it to your instructor.

2. The Sales Invoice: Use Figure 2.9 as the basis for a sales invoice that you will create and submit to your instructor. Your spreadsheet should follow the general format shown in the figure with respect to including a uniform discount for each item. Your spreadsheet should also include the sales tax. The discount percentage and sales tax percentage should be entered in a separate area so that they can be easily modified.

Use your imagination and sell any product at any price. You must, however, include at least four items in your invoice. Formatting is important, but you need not follow our format exactly. See how creative you can be, then submit your completed invoice to your instructor for inclusion in a class contest for the best invoice. Be sure your name appears somewhere on the worksheet as a sales associate. If you are really ambitious, you might include an object from the Microsoft Clip Gallery.

	A	B	C	D	E	F
1		Bargain Basement Shopping				
2						
3	Item	Quantity	List Price	Discount	Your Price	Total
4	US Robotics ISDN V.34 Fax/Modem	2	$293.14	$58.63	$234.51	$469.02
5	NEC 8X CD-ROM	6	$151.71	$30.34	$121.37	$728.21
6	Seagate 2.1 Gb Hard Drive	4	$299.95	$59.99	$239.96	$959.84
7	Iomega Zip Drive	10	$199.95	$39.99	$159.96	$1,599.60
8						
9	Subtotal					$3,756.67
10	Tax					$244.18
11	Amount Due					$3,512.49
12						
13	Discount Percentage	20.0%				
14	Sales Tax Percentage	6.5%				
15	Sales Associate	Conner Smith				

FIGURE 2.9   Spreadsheet for Practice Exercise 2

3. The Probability Expert: How much would you bet *against* two people in your class having the same birthday? Don't be too hasty, for the odds of two classmates sharing the same birthday (month and day) are much higher than you would expect. For example, there is a fifty percent chance (.5063) in a class of 23 students that two people will have been born on the same day, as shown in Figure 2.10. The probability jumps to seventy percent (.7053) in a class of 30, and to ninety percent (.9025) in a class of 41. Don't take our word for it, but try the experiment in your class.

You need a basic knowledge of probability to create the spreadsheet. In essence you calculate the probability of individuals not having the same birthday, then subtract this number from one, to obtain the probability of the event coming true. In a group of two people, for example, the probability of not being born on the same day is 365/366; i.e., the second person can be born on any of 365 days and still have a different birthday. The probability of two people having the same birthday becomes $1 - 365/366$.

	A	B	C
1		The Birthday Problem	
2	Number of People	Probability of Different Birthdays	Probability of the Same Birthday
3	2	99.73%	0.27%
4	3	99.18%	0.82%
5	4	98.37%	1.63%
6	5	97.29%	2.71%
7	6	95.96%	4.04%
8	7	94.39%	5.61%
9	8	92.59%	7.41%
10	9	90.56%	9.44%
11	10	88.34%	11.66%
	.	.	.
24	23	49.37%	50.63%
	.	.	.
42	41	9.75%	90.25%
	.	.	.
51	50	2.99%	97.01%

FIGURE 2.10   Spreadsheet for Practice Exercise 3

The probability for different birthdays in a group of three is (365/366)*(364/366); the probability of not having different birthdays—that is, of two people having the same birthday, is one minus this number. Each row in the spreadsheet is calculated from the previous row. It's not as hard as it looks, and the results are quite interesting! As you can see, there is a 97% probability that two people in a group of 50 will have the same birthday.

4. Help for Your Sibling: Develop the multiplication table for a younger sibling shown in Figure 2.11. Creating the row and column headings is easy in that you can enter the numbers manually, or you can use online help to learn about the AutoFill feature. The hard part is creating the formulas in the body of the worksheet (we don't want you to enter the numbers manually). The trick is to use mixed references for the formula in cell B4, then copy that single cell to the remainder of the table.

Add your name to the worksheet and submit it to your instructor. Remember, this worksheet is for a younger sibling, and so formatting is important. Print the cell formulas as well so that you can see how the mixed reference changes throughout the worksheet. Submit the complete assignment (title page, displayed values, and cell formulas) to your instructor. Using mixed references correctly is challenging, but once you arrive at the correct solution, you will have learned a lot about this very powerful spreadsheet feature.

	A	B	C	D	E	F	G	H	I	J	K	L	M
1	A Multiplication Table for My Younger Sister												
2													
3		1	2	3	4	5	6	7	8	9	10	11	12
4	1	1	2	3	4	5	6	7	8	9	10	11	12
5	2	2	4	6	8	10	12	14	16	18	20	22	24
6	3	3	6	9	12	15	18	21	24	27	30	33	36
7	4	4	8	12	16	20	24	28	32	36	40	44	48
8	5	5	10	15	20	25	30	35	40	45	50	55	60
9	6	6	12	18	24	30	36	42	48	54	60	66	72
10	7	7	14	21	28	35	42	49	56	63	70	77	84
11	8	8	16	24	32	40	48	56	64	72	80	88	96
12	9	9	18	27	36	45	54	63	72	81	90	99	108
13	10	10	20	30	40	50	60	70	80	90	100	110	120
14	11	11	22	33	44	55	66	77	88	99	110	121	132
15	12	12	24	36	48	60	72	84	96	108	120	132	144

FIGURE 2.11 Spreadsheet for Practice Exercise 4

5. Figure 2.12 illustrates how a spreadsheet can be used to compute a payroll for hourly employees. A partially completed version of the worksheet can be found in the file *Chapter 2 Practice 5*. Your job is to complete the worksheet by developing the entries for the first employee, then copying those entries to the remaining rows. (An employee receives time and a half for overtime.)

To receive full credit for this assignment, the formulas for the withholding and Social Security taxes must reference the percentages in cells C12 and C13, respectively. Format the worksheet after it has been completed. Add your name anywhere in the worksheet, then print it two ways, once with displayed values and once with cell contents; then submit both pages to your instructor.

	A	B	C	D	E	F	G	H
1	Employee Name	Hourly Wage	Regular Hours	Overtime Hours	Gross Pay	Withholding Tax	Soc Sec Tax	Net Pay
2								
3	Jones	$8.00	40	10	$440.00	$123.20	$28.60	$288.20
4	Smith	$9.00	35	0	$315.00	$88.20	$20.48	$206.33
5	Baker	$7.20	40	0	$288.00	$80.64	$18.72	$188.64
6	Barnard	$7.20	40	8	$374.40	$104.83	$24.34	$245.23
7	Adams	$10.00	40	4	$460.00	$128.80	$29.90	$301.30
8								
9	Totals				$1,877.40	$525.67	$122.03	$1,229.70
10								
11	Assumptions							
12	Withholding tax		28.0%					
13	FICA		6.5%					

FIGURE 2.12   Spreadsheet for Practice Exercise 5

GRAPHS AND CHARTS: DELIVERING A MESSAGE

3

OBJECTIVES

After reading this chapter you will be able to:

1. Distinguish between the different types of charts, stating the advantages and disadvantages of each.
2. Distinguish between a chart embedded in a worksheet and one in a separate chart sheet.
3. Explain how multiple charts can be associated with the same worksheet.
4. Use the Chart Wizard to create and/or modify a chart; explain how the Office Assistant can help in creating a chart.
5. Enhance a chart by using arrows and text.
6. Differentiate between data series specified in rows and data series specified in columns.
7. Create a compound document consisting of a word processing memo, a worksheet, and a chart.

OVERVIEW

Business has always known that the graphic representation of data is an attractive, easy-to-understand way to convey information. Indeed, business graphics has become one of the most exciting Windows applications, whereby charts (graphs) are easily created from a worksheet, with just a few simple keystrokes or mouse clicks.

The chapter begins by emphasizing the importance of determining the message to be conveyed by a chart. It describes the different types of charts available within Excel and how to choose among them. It explains how to create a chart using the Chart Wizard, how to embed a chart within a worksheet, and how to create a chart in a separate chart sheet. It also describes how to enhance a chart with arrows and additional text.

The second half of the chapter explains how one chart can plot multiple sets of data, and how several charts can be based on the same worksheet. It also describes how to create a compound document, in which a chart and its associated worksheet are dynamically linked to a memo created by a word processor. All told, we think you will find this to be one of the most enjoyable chapters in the text.

CHART TYPES

A *chart* is a graphic representation of data in a worksheet. The chart is based on descriptive entries called *category labels,* and on numeric values called *data points.* The data points are grouped into one or more *data series* that appear in row(s) or column(s) on the worksheet. In every chart there is exactly one data point, in each data series, for each value of the category label.

The worksheet in Figure 3.1 will be used throughout the chapter as the basis for the charts we will create. Your manager believes that the sales data can be understood more easily from charts than from the strict numerical presentation of a worksheet. You have been given the assignment of analyzing the data in the worksheet and are developing a series of charts to convey that information.

	A	B	C	D	E	F
1	Superior Software Sales					
2						
3		Miami	Denver	New York	Boston	Total
4	Word Processing	$50,000	$67,500	$9,500	$141,000	$268,000
5	Spreadsheets	$44,000	$18,000	$11,500	$105,000	$178,500
6	Database	$12,000	$7,500	$6,000	$30,000	$55,500
7	Total	$106,000	$93,000	$27,000	$276,000	$502,000

FIGURE 3.1   Superior Software

The sales data in the worksheet can be presented several ways—for example, by city, by product, or by a combination of the two. Ask yourself which type of chart is best suited to answer the following questions:

- What percentage of total revenue comes from each city? from each product?
- What is the dollar revenue produced by each city? by each product?
- What is the rank of each city with respect to sales?
- How much revenue does each product contribute in each city?

In every instance realize that a chart exists only to deliver a message, and that you cannot create an effective chart unless you are sure of what that message is. The next several pages discuss various types of business charts, each of which is best suited to a particular type of message.

KEEP IT SIMPLE

Keep it simple. This rule applies to both your message and the means of conveying that message. Excel makes it almost too easy to change fonts, styles, type sizes, and colors, but such changes will often detract from, rather than enhance, a chart. More is not necessarily better, and you do not have to use the features just because they are there. Remember that a chart must ultimately succeed on the basis of content, and content alone.

Pie Charts

A *pie chart* is the most effective way to display proportional relationships. It is the type of chart to select whenever words like *percentage* or *market share* appear in the message to be delivered. The pie, or complete circle, denotes the total amount. Each slice of the pie corresponds to its respective percentage of the total.

The pie chart in Figure 3.2a divides the pie representing total sales into four slices, one for each city. The size of each slice is proportional to the percentage of total sales in that city. The chart depicts a single data series, which appears in cells B7 through E7 on the associated worksheet. The data series has four data points corresponding to the total sales in each city.

To create the pie chart, Excel computes the total sales ($502,000 in our example), calculates the percentage contributed by each city, and draws each slice of the pie in proportion to its computed percentage. Boston's sales of $276,000 account for 55 percent of the total, and so this slice of the pie is allotted 55 percent of the area of the circle.

An *exploded pie chart,* as shown in Figure 3.2b, separates one or more slices of the pie for emphasis. Another way to achieve emphasis in a chart is to choose a title that reflects the message you are trying to deliver. The title in Figure 3.2a, for example, *Revenue by Geographic Area*, is neutral and leaves the reader to develop his or her own conclusion about the relative contribution of each area. By contrast, the title in Figure 3.2b, *New York Accounts for Only 5% of Revenue,* is more suggestive and emphasizes the problems in this office. Alternatively, the title could be changed to *Boston Exceeds 50% of Total Revenue* if the intent were to emphasize the contribution of Boston.

Three-dimensional pie charts may be created in exploded or nonexploded format as shown in Figures 3.2c and 3.2d, respectively. Excel also enables you to add arrows and text for emphasis.

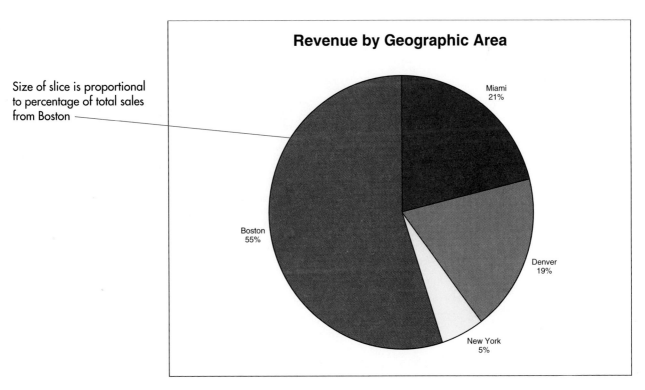

Size of slice is proportional to percentage of total sales from Boston

(a) Simple Pie Chart

FIGURE 3.2   Pie Charts

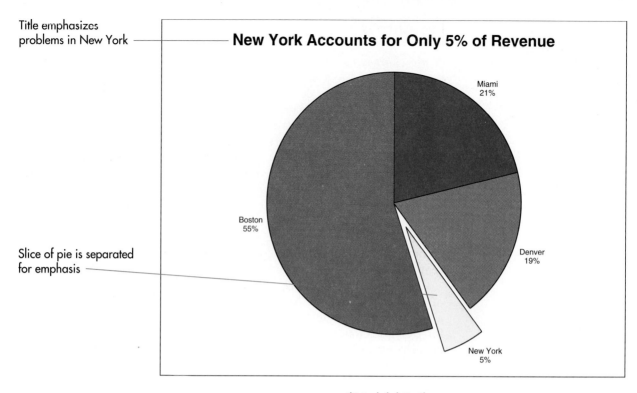

(b) Exploded Pie Chart

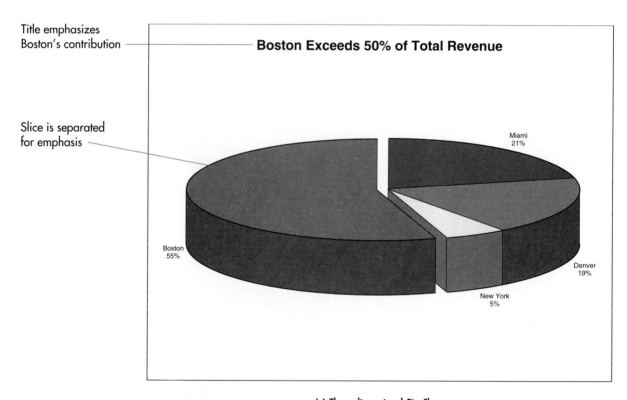

(c) Three-dimensional Pie Chart

FIGURE 3.2   Pie Charts (continued)

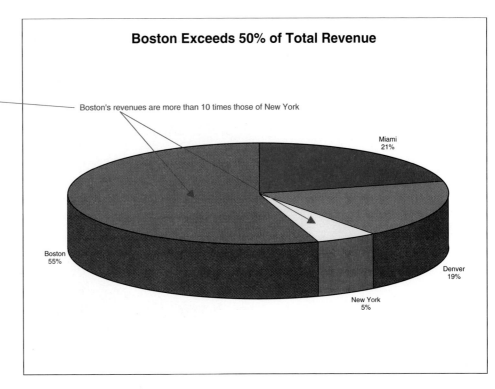

Boston Exceeds 50% of Total Revenue

Arrows and text added for emphasis

Boston's revenues are more than 10 times those of New York

Miami
21%

Boston
55%

Denver
19%

New York
5%

(d) Enhanced Pie Chart

FIGURE 3.2   Pie Charts (continued)

A pie chart is easiest to read when the number of slices is limited (i.e., not more than six or seven), and when small categories (percentages less than five) are grouped into a single category called "Other."

EXPLODED PIE CHARTS

Click and drag wedges out of a pie chart to convert an ordinary pie chart to an exploded pie chart. For best results pull the wedge out only slightly from the main body of the pie.

Column and Bar Charts

A *column chart* is used when there is a need to show actual numbers rather than percentages. The column chart in Figure 3.3a plots the same data series as the earlier pie chart, but displays it differently. The category labels (Miami, Denver, New York, and Boston) are shown along the *X* (horizontal) *axis.* The data points (monthly sales) are plotted along the *Y* (vertical) *axis,* with the height of each column reflecting the value of the data point.

A column chart can be given a horizontal orientation and converted to a *bar chart* as in Figure 3.3b. Some individuals prefer the bar chart over the corresponding column chart because the longer horizontal bars accentuate the difference between the items. Bar charts are also preferable when the descriptive labels are long to eliminate the crowding that can occur along the horizontal axis of a

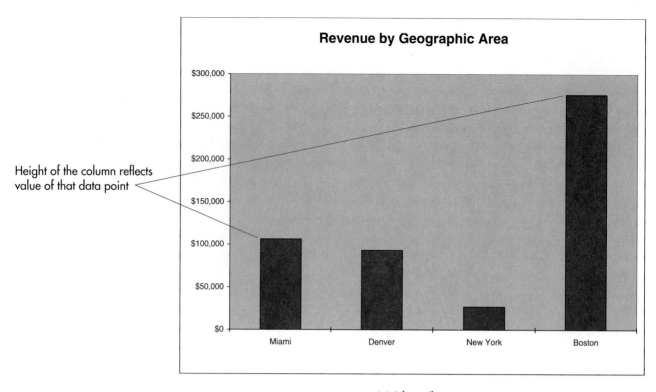

Height of the column reflects
value of that data point

(a) Column Chart

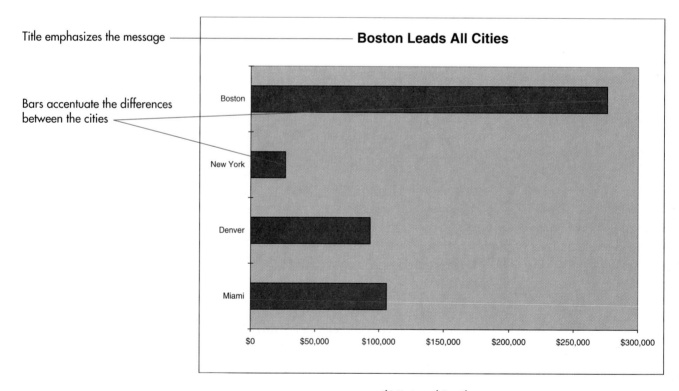

Title emphasizes the message

Bars accentuate the differences
between the cities

(b) Horizontal Bar Chart

FIGURE 3.3   Column/Bar Charts

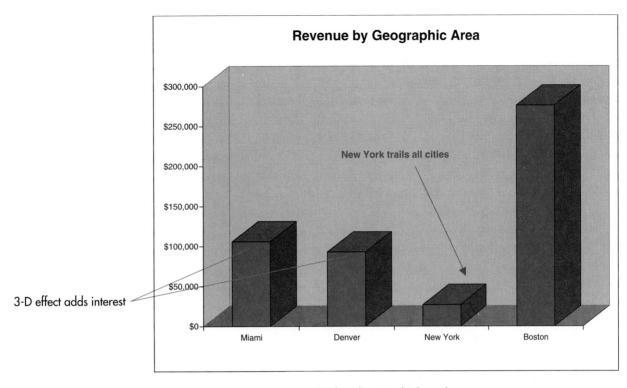

3-D effect adds interest

(c) Three-dimensional Column Chart

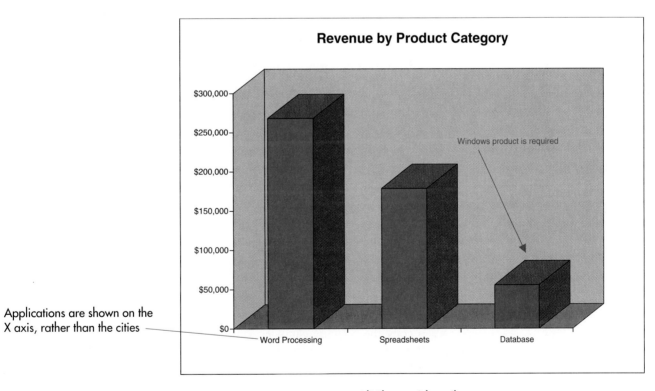

Applications are shown on the X axis, rather than the cities

(d) Alternate Column Chart

FIGURE 3.3   Column/Bar Charts (continued)

column chart. As with the pie chart, a title can lead the reader and further emphasize the message, as with *Boston Leads All Cities* in Figure 3.3b.

A three-dimensional effect can produce added interest as shown in Figures 3.3c and 3.3d. Figure 3.3d plots a different set of numbers than we have seen so far (the sales for each product, rather than the sales for each city). The choice between the charts in Figures 3.3c and 3.3d depends on the message you want to convey—whether you want to emphasize the contribution of each city or each product. The title can be used to emphasize the message. Arrows and text can be added to either chart to enhance the message.

As with a pie chart, column and bar charts are easiest to read when the number of categories is relatively small (seven or fewer). Otherwise the columns (bars) are plotted so close together that labeling becomes impossible.

CREATING A CHART

There are two ways to create a chart in Excel. You can embed the chart in a worksheet, or you can create the chart in a separate *chart sheet.* Figure 3.4a displays an embedded column chart. Figure 3.4b shows a pie chart in its own chart sheet. Both techniques are valid. The choice between the two depends on your personal preference.

Regardless of where it is kept (embedded in a worksheet or in its own chart sheet), a chart is linked to the worksheet on which it is based. The charts in Figure 3.4 plot the same data series (the total sales for each city). Change any of these data points on the worksheet, and both charts will be updated automatically to reflect the new data.

Both charts are part of the same workbook (Software Sales) as indicated in the title bar of each figure. The tabs within the workbook have been renamed to indicate the contents of the associated sheet. Additional charts may be created and embedded in the worksheet and/or placed on their own chart sheets. And, as previously stated, if you change the worksheet, the chart (or charts) based upon it will also change.

Study the column chart in Figure 3.4a to see how it corresponds to the worksheet on which it is based. The descriptive names on the X axis are known as *category labels* and match the entries in cells B3 through E3. The quantitative values (data points) are plotted on the Y axis and match the total sales in cells B7 through E7. Even the numeric format matches; that is, the currency format used in the worksheet appears automatically on the scale of the Y axis.

The *sizing handles* on the embedded chart indicate it is currently selected and can be sized, moved, or deleted the same way as any other Windows object:

- To size the selected chart, point to a sizing handle (the mouse pointer changes to a double arrow), then drag the handle in the desired direction.
- To move the selected chart, point to the chart (the mouse pointer is a single arrow), then drag the chart to its new location.
- To copy the selected chart, click the Copy button to copy the chart to the clipboard, click in the workbook where you want the copied chart to go, then click the Paste button to paste the chart at that location.
- To delete the selected chart, press the Del key.

The same operations apply to any of the objects within the chart (e.g., its title), as will be discussed in the section on enhancing a chart. Note, too, that both figures contain a chart toolbar that enables you to modify a chart after it has been created.

Workbook name

Sizing handles

Data points are plotted on the Y
axis and reflect entries in B7:E7

Descriptive names (category
labels) match entries in B3:E3

Tabs renamed to reflect
content of sheet

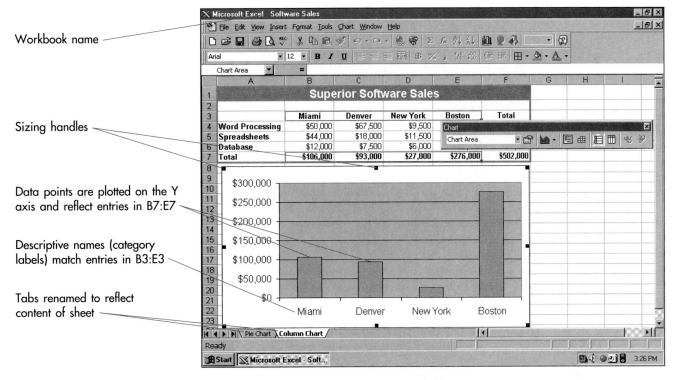

(a) Embedded Chart

Workbook name

Chart toolbar

Selected sheet

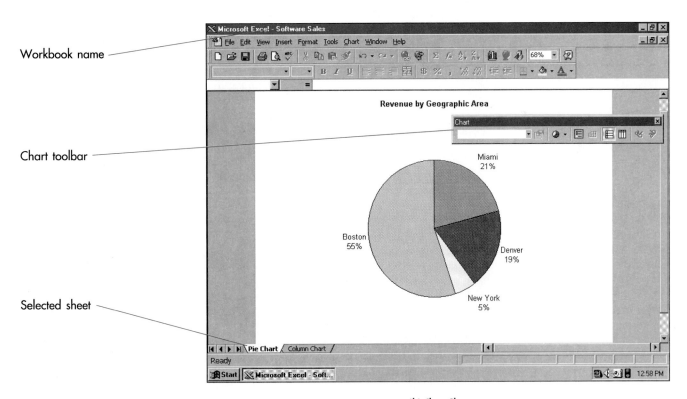

(b) Chart Sheet

FIGURE 3.4   Creating a Chart

The Chart Wizard

The **Chart Wizard** is the easiest way to create a chart. Just select the cells that contain the data as shown in Figure 3.5a, click the Chart Wizard button on the Standard toolbar, and let the wizard do the rest. The process is illustrated in Figure 3.5, which shows how the Wizard creates a column chart to plot total sales by geographic area (city).

The steps in Figure 3.5 appear automatically as you click the Next command button to move from one step to the next. You can retrace your steps at any time by pressing the Back command button, access the Office Assistant for help with the Chart Wizard, or abort the process with the Cancel command button.

Step 1 in the Chart Wizard (Figure 3.5b) asks you to choose one of the available chart types. Step 2 (Figure 3.5c) shows you a preview of the chart and enables you to confirm (and, if necessary, change) the data series specified earlier. (Only one data series is plotted in this example. Multiple data series are illustrated later in the chapter.) Step 3 (Figure 3.5d) asks you to complete the chart by entering its title and specifying additional options (such as the position of a legend and gridlines). And finally, step 4 (Figure 3.5e) has you choose whether the chart is to be created as an embedded chart (an object) within a specific worksheet, or whether it is to be created in its own chart sheet. The entire process takes but a few minutes.

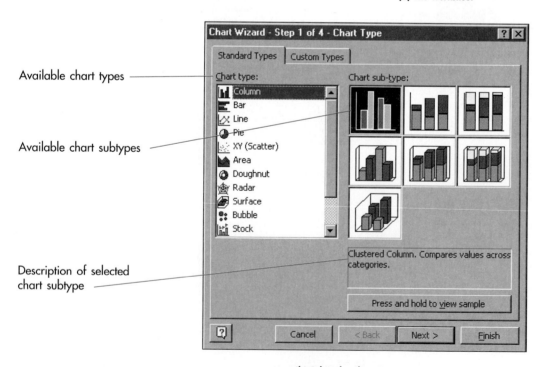

Selected cells (B3:E3 and B7:E7)

	A	B	C	D	E	F
1		Superior Software Sales				
2						
3		Miami	Denver	New York	Boston	Total
4	Word Processing	$50,000	$67,500	$9,500	$141,000	$268,000
5	Spreadsheets	$44,000	$18,000	$11,500	$105,000	$178,500
6	Database	$12,000	$7,500	$6,000	$30,000	$55,500
7	Total	$106,000	$93,000	$27,000	$276,000	$502,000

(a) The Worksheet

Available chart types

Available chart subtypes

Description of selected chart subtype

(b) Select the Chart Type (step 1)

FIGURE 3.5 The Chart Wizard

Preview of chart

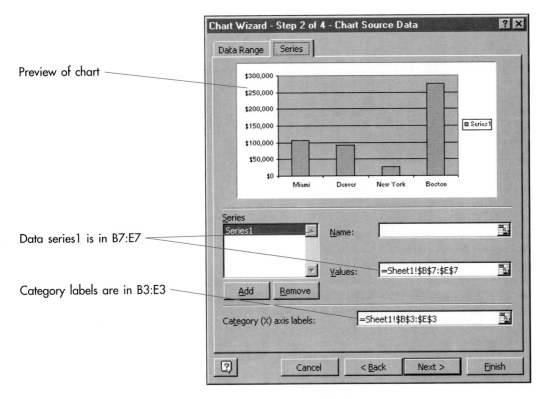

Data series1 is in B7:E7

Category labels are in B3:E3

(c) Check the Data Series (step 2)

Enter chart title

Click tabs to specify
other chart options

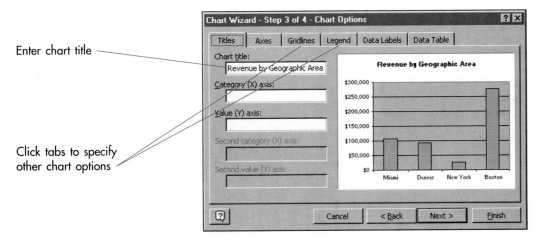

(d) Complete the Chart Options (step 3)

Name of worksheet

Chart will be embedded as an
object on worksheet

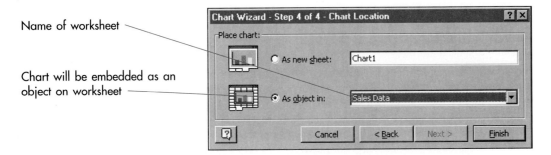

(e) Choose the Location (step 4)

FIGURE 3.5   The Chart Wizard (continued)

Enhancing a Chart

After a chart is created, it can be enhanced in several ways. You can change the chart type, add (or remove) a legend, and/or add (or remove) gridlines by executing the appropriate command from the Chart menu. You can change the font, size, color, and style of existing text anywhere in the chart, by selecting the text, then changing its format. You can also use the ***Drawing toolbar*** to add arrows and other objects to a chart for added emphasis.

Figure 3.6 shows an enhanced version of the column chart created earlier. The ***Chart toolbar*** is displayed automatically whenever any object of a chart is selected. Note, too, the drop-down list box on the Chart toolbar, which enables you to select the component(s) to modify. The Drawing toolbar appears at the bottom of the window and contains various tools to further enhance the chart (or any Office document). The use of both toolbars is explained further in the following hands-on exercise.

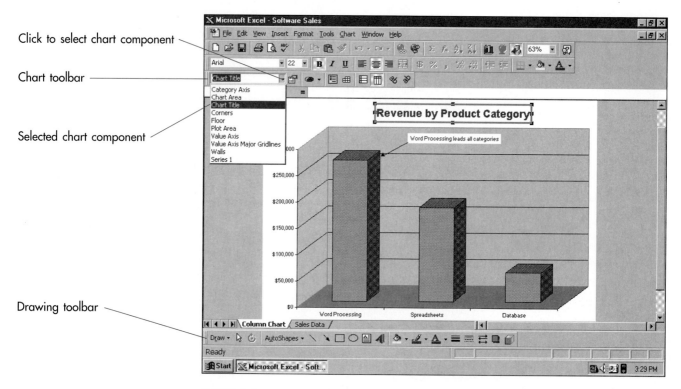

FIGURE 3.6 Enhancing a Chart

SET A TIME LIMIT

Excel enables you to customize virtually every aspect of every object within a chart. You can change the color, shape, or pattern of a data series or the font and style of text anywhere in the chart. It's fun to experiment, but the gain is often minimal. Set a time limit and stop when you reach the allocated time. The default settings are usually adequate to convey your message, and further experimentation is often counter productive.

Objective: To create and modify a chart by using the Chart Wizard; to embed a chart within a worksheet; to enhance a chart to include arrows and text. Use Figure 3.7 as a guide in the exercise.

STEP 1: Start the Chart Wizard

➤ Start Excel. Open the **Software Sales** workbook in the **Exploring Excel** folder. Save the workbook as **Finished Software Sales.**

➤ Drag the mouse over cells **B3 through E3** to select the category labels (the names of the cities). Press and hold the **Ctrl key** as you drag the mouse over cells **B7 through E7** to select the data series (the cells containing the total sales for the individual cities).

➤ Check that cells B3 through E3 and B7 through E7 are selected. Click the **Chart Wizard button** on the Standard toolbar to start the wizard.

➤ You should see the dialog box for step 1 as shown in Figure 3.7a. The **Column** chart type and **Clustered column** subtype are selected by default. Click **Next** to continue.

Chart Wizard button

Select the category labels (B3:E3)

Select the data series (B7:E7)

Column chart is selected

Clustered column subtype is selected

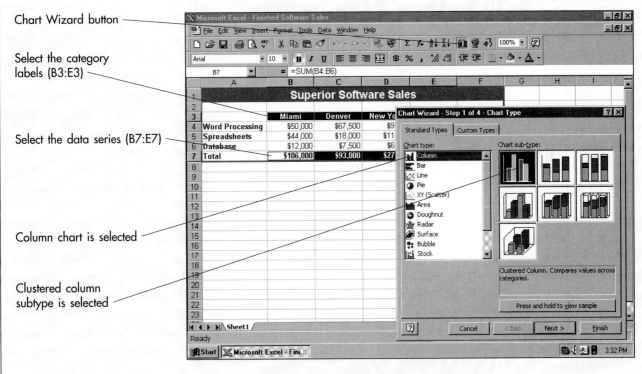

(a) Start the Chart Wizard (step 1)

FIGURE 3.7 Hands-on Exercise 1

STEP 2: Start the Chart Wizard (continued)

➤ You should see step 2 of the Chart Wizard. Click the **Series tab** in the dialog box so that your screen matches Figure 3.7b. Note that the values (the data being plotted) are in cells B7 through E7, and that the Category labels for the X axis are in cells B3 through E3. Click **Next** to continue.

➤ You should see step 3 of the Chart Wizard. If necessary, click the **Titles tab,** then click in the text box for the Chart title. Type **Revenue by Geographic Area.** Click the **Legend tab** and clear the box to show a legend. Click **Next.**

➤ You should see step 4 of the Chart Wizard. If necessary, click the option button to place the chart **As object** in Sheet1 (the name of the worksheet in which you are working). Click **Finish.**

RETRACE YOUR STEPS

The Chart Wizard guides you every step of the way, but what if you make a mistake or change your mind? Click the Back command button at any time to return to a previous screen in order to enter different information, then continue working with the wizard.

STEP 3: Move and Size the Chart

➤ You should see the completed chart as shown in Figure 3.7c. The sizing handles indicate that the chart is selected and will be affected by subsequent commands. The Chart toolbar is displayed automatically whenever a chart is selected.

➤ Move and/or size the chart just as you would any other Windows object:

• To move the chart, click the chart (background) area to select the chart (a ScreenTip, "Chart Area," is displayed), then click and drag (the mouse pointer changes to a four-sided arrow) to move the chart.

• To size the chart, drag a corner handle (the mouse pointer changes to a double arrow) to change the length and width of the chart simultaneously, keeping the chart in proportion as it is resized.

➤ Click outside the chart to deselect it. The sizing handles disappear and the Chart toolbar is no longer visible.

EMBEDDED CHARTS

An embedded chart is treated as an object that can be moved, sized, copied, or deleted just as any other Windows object. To move an embedded chart, click the background of the chart to select the chart, then drag it to a new location in the worksheet. To size the chart, select it, then drag any of the eight sizing handles in the desired direction. To delete the chart, select it, then press the Del key. To copy the chart, select it, click the Copy button on the Standard toolbar to copy the chart to the clipboard, click elsewhere in the workbook where you want the copied chart to go, then click the Paste button.

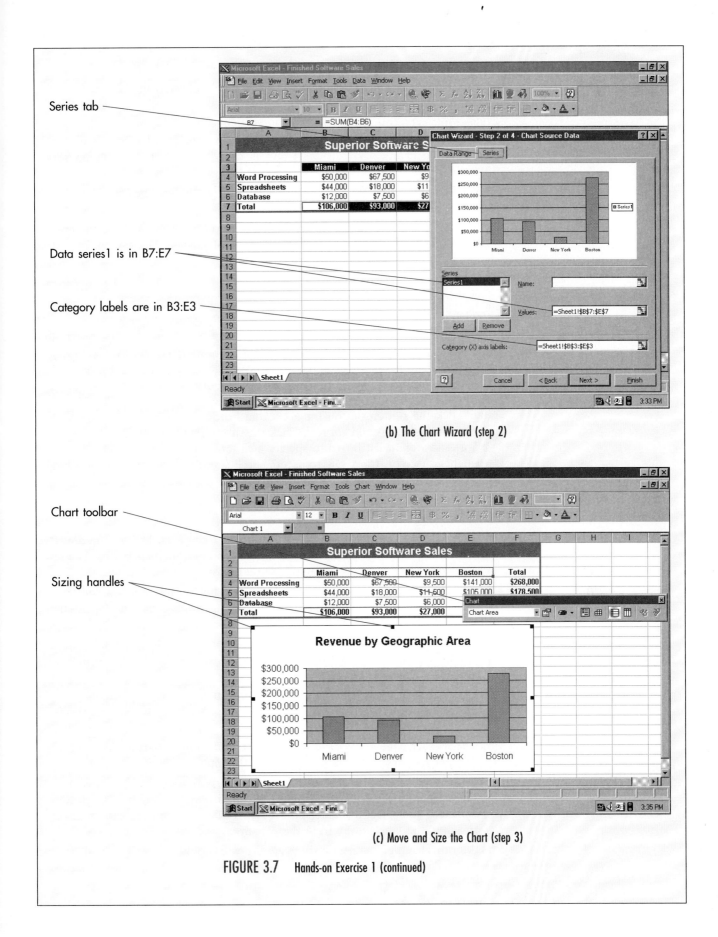

Series tab

Data series1 is in B7:E7

Category labels are in B3:E3

(b) The Chart Wizard (step 2)

Chart toolbar

Sizing handles

(c) Move and Size the Chart (step 3)

FIGURE 3.7   Hands-on Exercise 1 (continued)

STEP 4: Change the Worksheet

➤ Any changes in a worksheet are automatically reflected in the associated chart. Click in cell **B4,** change the entry to **$400,000,** and press the **enter key.**

➤ The total sales for Miami in cell B7 change automatically to reflect the increased sales for word processing, as shown in Figure 3.7d. The column for Miami also changes in the chart and is now larger than the column for Boston.

➤ Click in cell **B3.** Change the entry to **Chicago.** Press **enter.** The category label on the X axis changes automatically.

➤ Click the **Undo button** to change the city back to Miami. Click the **Undo button** a second time to return to the initial value of $50,000. The worksheet and chart are restored to their earlier values.

CREATE AN ATTRACTIVE CHART BORDER

Dress up an embedded chart by changing its border. Point to the chart area (the white background area near the border), click the right mouse button to display a shortcut menu, then click Format Chart Area to display the Format Chart Area dialog box. If necessary, click the Patterns tab, click the option button for a Custom border, then check the boxes for a shadow and round corners. Click the drop-down arrows in the style, color, and weight list boxes to specify a different border style, thickness (weight), or color. Click OK to accept these settings.

STEP 5: Change the Chart Type

➤ Click the chart (background) area to select the chart, click the **drop-down arrow** on the Chart type button on the Chart toolbar, then click the **3-D Pie Chart icon.** The chart changes to a three-dimensional pie chart.

➤ Point to the chart area, click the **right mouse button** to display a shortcut menu, then click the **Chart Options command** to display the Chart Options dialog box shown in Figure 3.7e.

➤ Click the **Data Labels tab,** then click the option button to **Show label and percent.** Click **OK** to accept the settings and close the Chart Options dialog box.

➤ The pie chart changes to reflect the options you just specified, although the chart may not appear exactly as you would like. Accordingly, you can modify each component as necessary:

• Select (click) the (gray) **Plot area.** Click and drag the sizing handles to increase the size of the plot area within the embedded chart.

• Point to any of the labels, click the **right mouse button** to display a shortcut menu, and click **Format Data Labels** to display a dialog box. Click the **Font tab,** and select a smaller point size. It may also be necessary to click and drag the labels away from the plot area.

➤ Make other changes as necessary. Save the workbook.

Undo button

Change entry to $400,000

Total sales changes

Chart reflects increased
sales in Miami

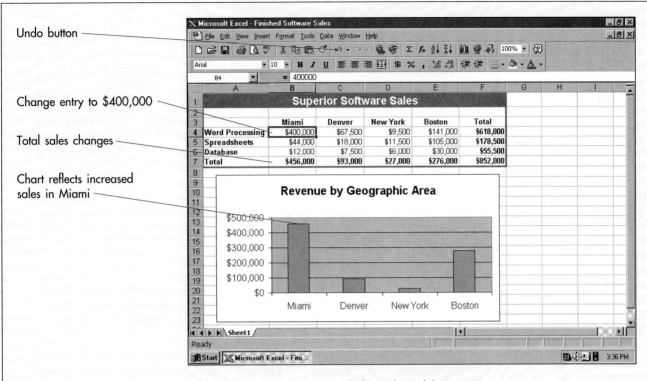

(d) Change the Worksheet (step 4)

Chart Type button

Data Labels tab

Click option to show
label and percent

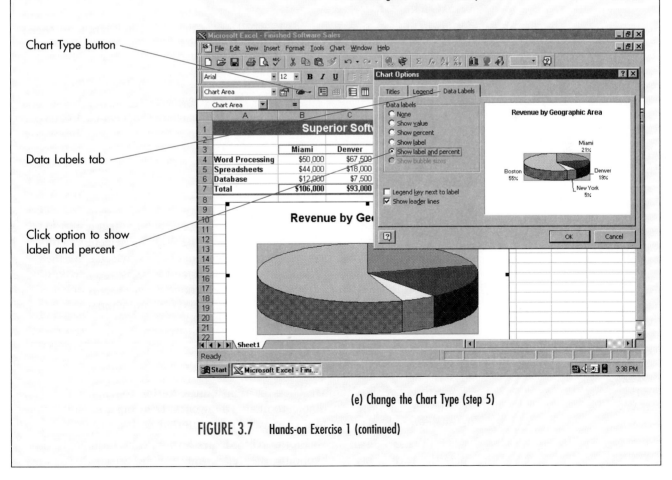

(e) Change the Chart Type (step 5)

FIGURE 3.7   Hands-on Exercise 1 (continued)

ANATOMY OF A CHART

A chart is composed of multiple components (objects), each of which can be selected and changed separately. Point to any part of a chart to display a ScreenTip indicating the name of the component, then click the mouse to select that component and display the sizing handles. You can then click and drag the object within the chart and/or click the right mouse button to display a shortcut menu with commands pertaining to the selected object.

STEP 6: Create a Second Chart

➤ Click and drag to select cells **A4 through A6** in the worksheet. Press and hold the **Ctrl key** as you drag the mouse over cells **F4 through F6** to select the data series.

➤ Click the **Chart Wizard button** on the Standard toolbar to start the Chart Wizard and display the dialog box for step 1 as shown in Figure 3.7f. The Column Chart type is already selected. Click the **Clustered column with a 3-D visual effect subtype.** Click **Next.**

➤ Click the **Series tab** in the dialog box for step 2 to confirm that you selected the correct data points. The values for series1 should consist of cells F4 through F6. The Category labels for the X axis should be cells A4 through A6. Click **Next.**

➤ You should see step 3 of the Chart Wizard. Click the **Titles tab,** then click in the text box for the Chart title. Type **Revenue by Product Category.** Click the **Legend tab** and clear the box to show a legend. Click **Next.**

➤ You should see step 4 of the Chart Wizard. Select the option button to create the chart **As new sheet** (Chart1). Click **Finish.**

➤ The 3-D column chart has been created in the chart sheet labeled Chart1. Save the workbook.

SELECTING NONCONTIGUOUS RANGES

Any time you select a cell or cell range (a row or column, or a group of rows and columns) you automatically deselect the previous selection. You can, however, select noncontiguous (nonadjacent) ranges by selecting the first range in the normal fashion, then pressing and holding the Ctrl key as you select the additional range(s). This technique is very useful in conjunction with the Chart Wizard, or when the same command is to be applied to multiple ranges within a worksheet.

STEP 7: Enhance the Chart

➤ Point to any visible toolbar, click the **right mouse button** to display a shortcut menu listing the available toolbars, then click **Drawing** to display the Drawing toolbar. (Your toolbar may be in a different position from ours.)

➤ Click the **drop-down arrow** on the **AutoShapes button,** click **Callouts** to display the various styles of callouts, then click **Line Callout 2** (No Border) as shown in Figure 3.7g.

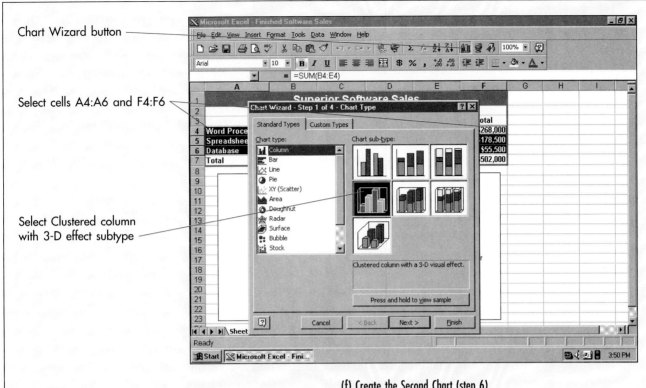

Chart Wizard button

Select cells A4:A6 and F4:F6

Select Clustered column
with 3-D effect subtype

(f) Create the Second Chart (step 6)

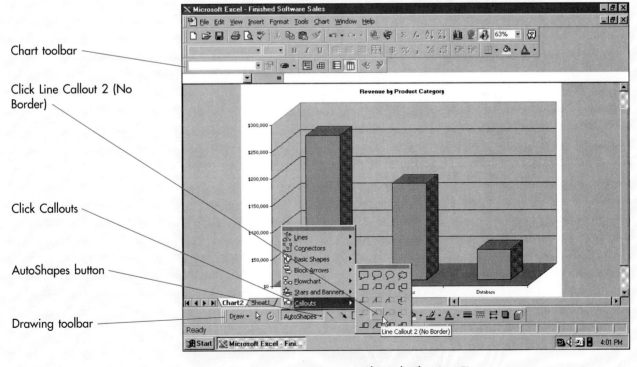

Chart toolbar

Click Line Callout 2 (No
Border)

Click Callouts

AutoShapes button

Drawing toolbar

(g) Enhance the Chart (step 7)

FIGURE 3.7   Hands-on Exercise 1 (continued)

- The mouse pointer changes to a thin crosshair. Click the column representing the sales for word processing (the point in the chart where you want the callout to begin), then drag the mouse to create a line from the callout to the associated text. Release the mouse. Enter the text of the callout (e.g., Word Processing leads all categories). Size the text box as necessary, then click outside the text box.

- Click the title of the chart. You will see sizing handles around the title to indicate it has been selected.

- Click the **drop-down arrow** in the Font Size box on the Formatting toolbar. Click **18** to increase the size of the title.

- Use the **Text Box tool** on the Drawing toolbar to add your name somewhere in the chart so that your instructor will know the assignment is from you.

FLOATING TOOLBARS

Any toolbar can be docked along the edge of the application window or it can be displayed as a floating toolbar within the application window. To move a docked toolbar, drag the toolbar background. To move a floating toolbar, drag its title bar. To size a floating toolbar, drag any border in the direction you want to go. Double click the background of any toolbar to toggle between a floating toolbar and a docked (fixed) toolbar.

STEP 8: Format the Data Series

- Click any of the columns to select the data series. (All three columns will be selected. You can also click a column after the data series has been selected to select only that column and deselect the others.) Be sure that all three columns are selected.

- Point to any column and click the **right mouse button** to display a shortcut menu, then click **Format Data Series** to display the Format Data Series dialog box as shown in Figure 3.7h. Click the **Patterns tab,** select (click) a different color, then click **OK** to accept the change and close the dialog box.

- Save the workbook. Exit Excel if you do not want to continue with the next exercise at this time.

THE EXCEL WORKBOOK

An Excel workbook is the electronic equivalent of a three-ring binder. A workbook contains one or more worksheets and/or chart sheets, each of which is identified by a tab at the bottom of the document window. (Click the appropriate tab to go from one sheet to another.) The sheets in a workbook are typically related to one another. One worksheet, for example, may contain data for several charts, each of which appears on a separate chart sheet in the workbook. The advantage of a workbook is that all of its sheets are stored in a single file, which is accessed as a unit.

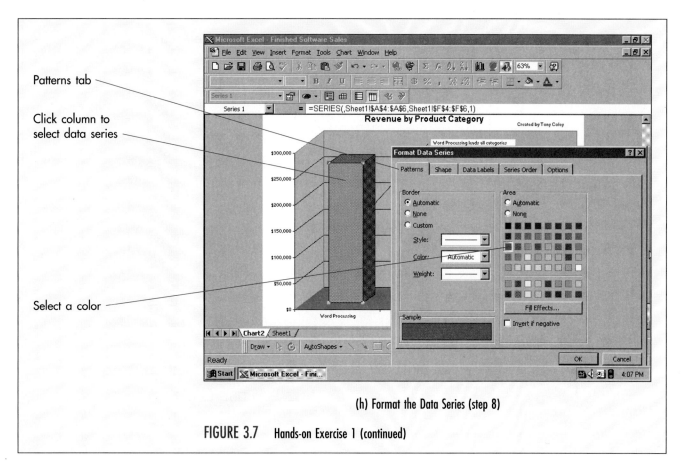

Patterns tab

Click column to
select data series

Select a color

(h) Format the Data Series (step 8)

FIGURE 3.7   Hands-on Exercise 1 (continued)

MULTIPLE DATA SERIES

The charts presented so far displayed only a single data series—for example, the total sales by location or the total sales by product category. Although such charts are useful, it is often necessary to view **multiple data series** on the same chart.

Figure 3.8a displays the sales in each location according to product category. We see how the products compare within each city, and further, that word processing is the leading application in three of the four cities. Figure 3.8b plots the identical data but in **stacked columns** rather than side-by-side.

The choice between the two types of charts depends on your message. If, for example, you want your audience to see the individual sales in each product category, the side-by-side columns are more appropriate. If, on the other hand, you want to emphasize the total sales for each city, the stacked columns are preferable. Note, too, the different scale on the Y axis in the two charts. The side-by-side columns in Figure 3.8a show the sales of each product category and so the Y axis goes only to $160,000. The stacked columns in Figure 3.8b, however, reflect the total sales for each city and thus the scale goes to $300,000.

The biggest difference is that the stacked column explicitly totals the sales for each city while the side-by-side column does not. The advantage of the stacked column is that the city totals are clearly shown and can be easily compared, and further the relative contributions of each product category within each city are apparent. The disadvantage is that the segments within each column do not start at the same point, making it difficult to determine the actual sales for the individual product categories or to compare the product categories among cities.

Realize, too, that for a stacked column chart to make sense, its numbers must be additive. This is true in Figure 3.8b, where the stacked columns consist of three

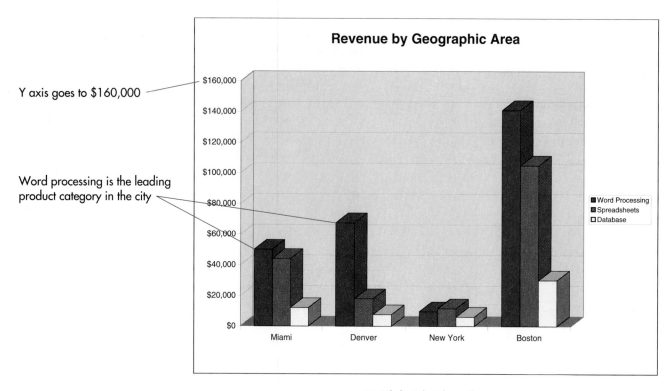

Y axis goes to $160,000

Word processing is the leading product category in the city

(a) Side-by-Side Column Chart

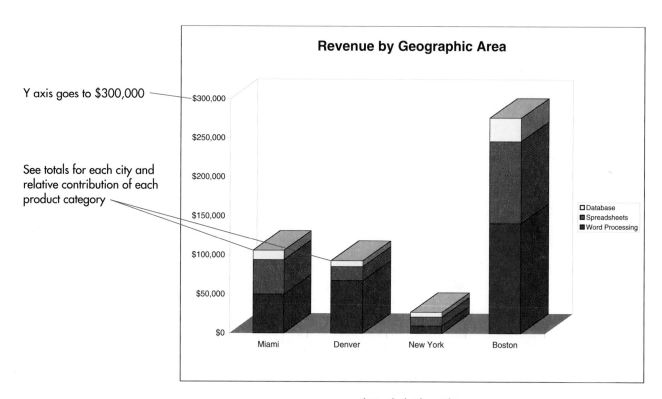

Y axis goes to $300,000

See totals for each city and relative contribution of each product category

(b) Stacked Column Chart

FIGURE 3.8   Column Charts

components, each of which is measured in dollars, and which can be logically added together to produce a total. You shouldn't, however, automatically convert a side-by-side column chart to its stacked column equivalent. It would not make sense, for example, to convert a column chart that plots unit sales and dollar sales side-by-side, into a stacked column chart that adds the two, because units and dollars represent different physical concepts and are not additive.

Rows versus Columns

Figure 3.9 illustrates a critical concept associated with multiple data series—whether the data series are in rows or columns. Figure 3.9a displays the worksheet with multiple data series selected. (Column A and Row 3 are included in the selection to provide the category labels and legend.) Figure 3.9b contains the chart when the data series are in rows (B4:E4, B5:E5, and B6:E6). Figure 3.9c displays the chart based on data series in columns (B4:B6, C4:C6, D4:D6, and E4:E6).

Both charts plot a total of twelve data points (three product categories for each of four locations), but they group the data differently. Figure 3.9b displays the data by city; that is, the sales of three product categories are shown for each of four cities. Figure 3.9c is the reverse and groups the data by product category; this time the sales in the four cities are shown for each of the three product categories. The choice between the two depends on your message and whether you want to emphasize revenue by city or by product category. It sounds complicated, but it's not, and Excel will create either chart for you according to your specifications.

- If the data series are in rows (Figure 3.9b), the Wizard will:
  - Use the first row (cells B3 through E3) in the selected range for the category labels on the X axis
  - Use the first column (cells A4 through A6) for the legend text
- If the data series are in columns (Figure 3.9c), the Wizard will:
  - Use the first column (cells A4 through A6) in the selected range for the category labels on the X axis
  - Use the first row (cells B3 through E3) for the legend text

Stated another way, the data series in Figure 3.9b are in rows. Thus, there are three data series (B4:E4, B5:E5, and B6:E6), one for each product category. The first data series plots the word processing sales in Miami, Denver, New York, and Boston; the second series plots the spreadsheet sales for each city, and so on.

The data series in Figure 3.9c are in columns. This time there are four data series (B4:B6, C4:C6, D4:D6, and E4:E6), one for each city. The first series plots the Miami sales for word processing, spreadsheets, and database; the second series plots the Denver sales for each software category, and so on.

A3:E6 is selected

	A	B	C	D	E	F
1	Superior Software Sales					
2						
3		Miami	Denver	New York	Boston	Total
4	Word Processing	$50,000	$67,500	$9,500	$141,000	$268,000
5	Spreadsheets	$44,000	$18,000	$11,500	$105,000	$178,500
6	Database	$12,000	$7,500	$6,000	$30,000	$55,500
7	Total	$106,000	$93,000	$27,000	$276,000	$502,000

(a) The Worksheet

FIGURE 3.9   Multiple Data Series

Legend reflects entries in first column of selection (A4:A6)

Category labels reflect entries in first row of selection (B3:E3)

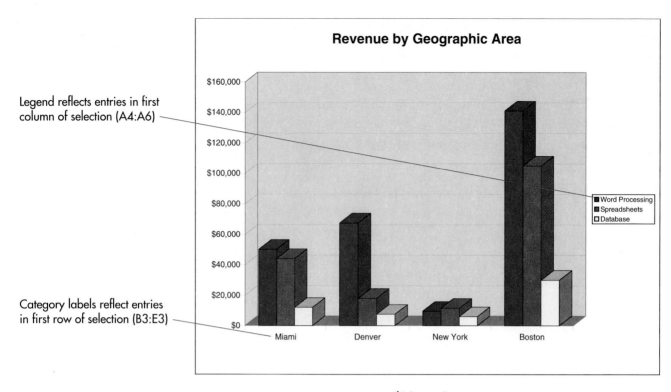

(b) Data in Rows

Legend reflects entries in first row of selection (B3:E3)

Category labels reflect entries in first column of selection (A4:A6)

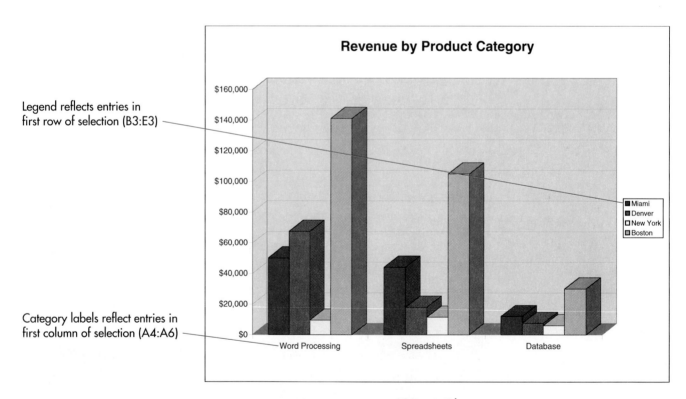

(c) Data in Columns

FIGURE 3.9   Multiple Data Series (continued)

Multiple Data Series

Objective: To plot multiple data series in the same chart; to differentiate between data series in rows and columns; to create and save multiple charts associated with the same worksheet. Use Figure 3.10 as a guide in the exercise.

STEP 1: Rename the Worksheets

➤ Open the **Finished Software Sales** workbook from the previous exercise as shown in Figure 3.10a. The workbook contains an embedded chart and a separate chart sheet.

➤ Point to the workbook tab labeled **Sheet1,** click the **right mouse button** to display a shortcut menu, then click the **Rename** command. The name of the worksheet (Sheet1) is selected. Type **Sales Data** to change the name of the worksheet to the more descriptive name. Press the **enter key.**

➤ Point to the tab labeled **Chart1** (which contains the three-dimensional column chart created in the previous exercise). Click the **right mouse button** to display a shortcut menu, click **Rename,** then enter **Column Chart** as the name of the chart sheet. Press the **enter key.**

➤ Save the workbook.

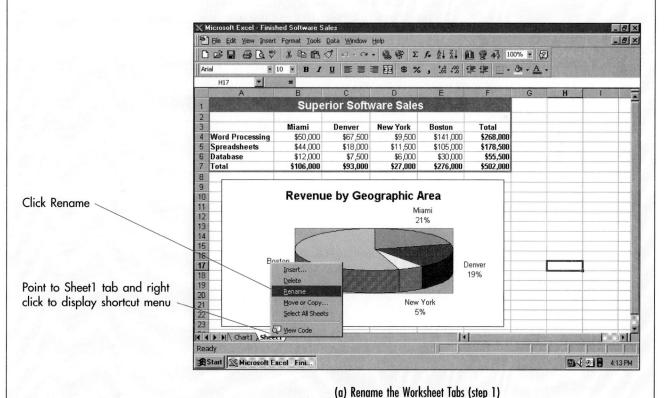

(a) Rename the Worksheet Tabs (step 1)

FIGURE 3.10   Hands-on Exercise 2

THE RIGHT MOUSE BUTTON

Point to a cell (or group of selected cells), a chart or worksheet tab, a toolbar, or chart (or a selected object on the chart), then click the right mouse button to display a shortcut menu. All shortcut menus are context-sensitive and display commands appropriate for the selected item. Right clicking a toolbar, for example, enables you to display (hide) additional toolbars. Right clicking a sheet tab enables you to rename, move, copy, or delete the sheet.

STEP 2: The Office Assistant

➤ Click the **Sales Data tab,** then click and drag to select cells **A3 through E6.** Click the **Chart Wizard button** on the Standard toolbar to start the wizard and display the dialog box shown in Figure 3.10b.

➤ If necessary, click the **Office Assistant button** in the Chart Wizard dialog box to display the Office Assistant and the initial help screen. Click the option button for **Help with this feature.**

➤ The display for the Assistant changes to offer help about the various chart types available. (It's up to you whether you want to explore the advice at this time. You can close the Assistant, or leave it open and drag the title bar out of the way.)

➤ Select **Column** as the chart type and **3-D visual effect Clustered column** as the subtype. Click **Next** to continue with the Chart Wizard.

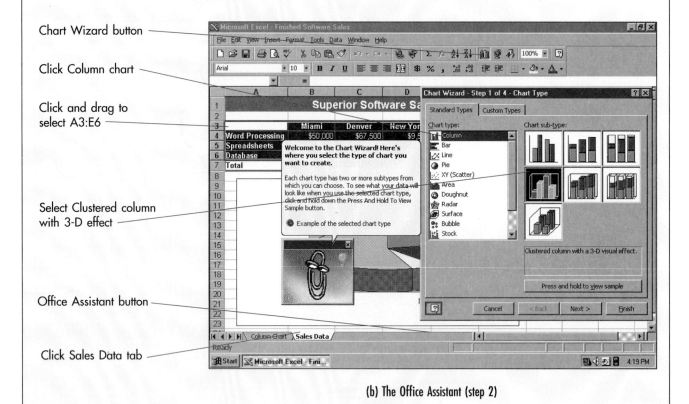

(b) The Office Assistant (step 2)

FIGURE 3.10   Hands-on Exercise 2 (continued)

STEP 3: View the Data Series

➤ You should see step 2 of the Chart Wizard as shown in Figure 3.10c. The help supplied by the Office Assistant changes automatically with the steps in the Chart Wizard.

➤ The data range should be specified as **Sales Data!$A$3:$E$6** as shown in Figure 3.10c. The option button for **Series in Rows** should be selected. To appreciate the concept of data series in rows (versus columns), click the **Series tab:**

• The series list box shows three data series (Word Processing, Spreadsheets, and Database) corresponding to the legends for the chart.

• The **Word Processing** series is selected by default. The legend in the sample chart shows that the data points in the series are plotted in blue. The values are taken from cells B4 through E4 in the Sales Data Worksheet.

• Click **Spreadsheets** in the series list box. The legend shows that the series is plotted in red. The values are taken from cells B5 through E5 in the Sales Data worksheet.

• Click **Database** in the series list box. The legend shows that the series is plotted in yellow. The values are taken from cells B6 through E6 in the Sales Data worksheet.

STEP 4: Complete the Chart

➤ Click **Next** to continue creating the chart. You should see step 3 of the Chart Wizard. Click the **Titles tab.** Click the text box for Chart title. Type **Revenue by City.** Click **Next.**

➤ You should see step 4 of the Chart Wizard. Click the option button for **As new sheet.** Type **Revenue by City** in the associated text box to give the chart sheet a meaningful name. Click **Finish.**

➤ Excel creates the new chart in its own sheet named Revenue by City. Close the Assistant. Save the workbook.

Series tab

Help Text changes

Selected range is A3:E6

Data series is in the rows

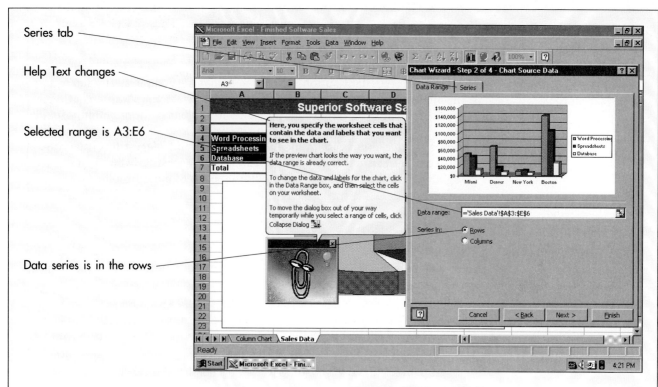

(c) View the Data Series (step 3)

FIGURE 3.10   Hands-on Exercise 2 (continued)

THE F11 KEY

The F11 key is the fastest way to create a chart in its own sheet. Select the data, including the legends and category labels, then press the F11 key to create the chart according to the default format built into the Excel column chart. After the chart has been created, you can use the menu bar, Chart toolbar, or shortcut menus to choose a different chart type and/or customize the formatting.

STEP 5: Copy the Chart Sheet

➤ Point to the tab named **Revenue by City.** Click the **right mouse button.** Click **Move or Copy** to display the dialog box in Figure 3.10d.

➤ Click **Sales Data** in the Before Sheet list box. Check the box to **Create a Copy.** Click **OK.**

A duplicate worksheet called Revenue by City(2) is created and appears before (to the left of) the Sales Data worksheet.

➤ Rename the copied sheet **Revenue by Product.** Save the workbook.

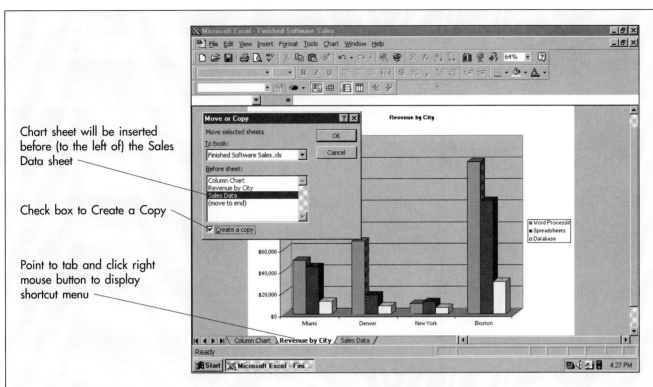

Chart sheet will be inserted before (to the left of) the Sales Data sheet

Check box to Create a Copy

Point to tab and click right mouse button to display shortcut menu

(d) Copy the Chart (step 5)

FIGURE 3.10   Hands-on Exercise 2 (continued)

MOVING AND COPYING A CHART SHEET

The fastest way to move or copy a chart sheet is to drag its tab. To move a sheet, point to its tab, then click and drag the tab to its new position. To copy a sheet, press and hold the Ctrl key as you drag the tab to the desired position for the second sheet. Rename the copied sheet (or any sheet for that matter) by pointing to its tab and clicking the right mouse button to produce a shortcut menu. Click Rename, then enter the new name.

STEP 6: Change the Source Data

➤ Click the **Revenue by Product tab** to make it the active sheet. Click anywhere in the title of the chart, drag the mouse over the word **City** to select the text, then type **Product Category** to replace the selected text. Click outside the title to deselect it.

➤ Pull down the **Chart menu.** Click **Source Data** (you will see the Sales Data worksheet), then click the **Columns option button** so that your screen matches Figure 3.10e. Click the **Series tab** and note the following:

• The current chart (outside the dialog box) plots the data in rows. There are three data series (one series for each product). Each data series has four data points, one point for each city.

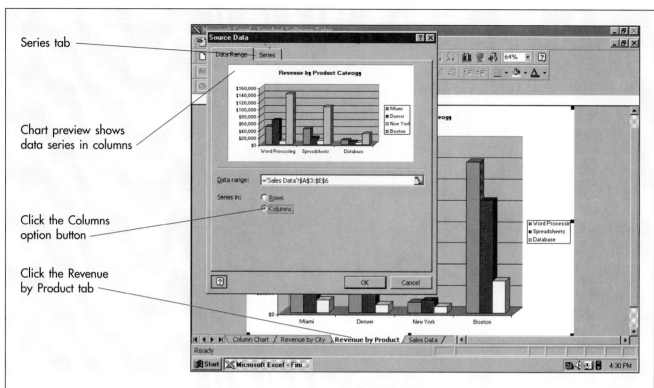

Series tab

Chart preview shows
data series in columns

Click the Columns
option button

Click the Revenue
by Product tab

(e) Change the Source Data (step 6)

FIGURE 3.10   Hands-on Exercise 2 (continued)

- The new chart (shown in the dialog box) plots the data in columns. There are four data series (one series for each city as indicated in the Series list box). Each data series has three data points, one point for each product.
➤ Click **OK** to close the Source Data dialog box and plot the data in columns. Save the workbook.

THE HORIZONTAL SCROLL BAR

The horizontal scroll bar contains four scrolling buttons to scroll through the sheet tabs in a workbook. Click ◄ or ► to scroll one tab to the left or right. Click |◄ or ►| to scroll to the first or last tab in the workbook. Once the desired tab is visible, click the tab to select it.

STEP 7: The Stacked Column Chart
➤ Point to the chart area, click the **right mouse button** to display a shortcut menu, then click the **Chart Type** command to display the Chart Type dialog box.
➤ Select the **3-D visual effect Stacked Column chart** (the middle entry in the second row). Click **OK.** The chart changes to a stacked column chart as shown in Figure 3.10f. Save the workbook.

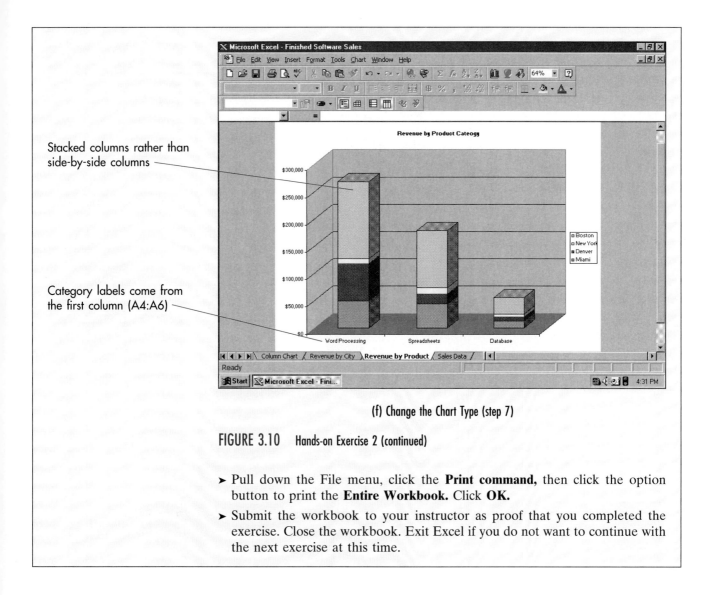

Stacked columns rather than side-by-side columns

Category labels come from the first column (A4:A6)

(f) Change the Chart Type (step 7)

FIGURE 3.10   Hands-on Exercise 2 (continued)

➤ Pull down the File menu, click the **Print command,** then click the option button to print the **Entire Workbook.** Click **OK.**

➤ Submit the workbook to your instructor as proof that you completed the exercise. Close the workbook. Exit Excel if you do not want to continue with the next exercise at this time.

OBJECT LINKING AND EMBEDDING

One of the primary advantages of the Windows environment is the ability to create a ***compound document*** that contains data ***(objects)*** from multiple applications. The memo in Figure 3.11 is an example of a compound document. The memo was created in Microsoft Word, and it contains objects (a worksheet and a chart) that were developed in Microsoft Excel. ***Object Linking and Embedding*** (***OLE,*** pronounced "oh-lay") is the means by which you create the compound document.

The essential difference between linking and embedding is whether the object is stored within the compound document ***(embedding)*** or in its own file ***(linking).*** An ***embedded object*** is stored in the compound document, which in turn becomes the only client for that object. A ***linked object*** is stored in its own file, and the compound document is one of many potential clients for that object. The compound document does not contain the linked object per se, but only a representation of the object as well as a pointer (link) to the file containing the object. The advantage of linking is that any document that is linked to the object is updated automatically if the object is changed.

The choice between linking and embedding depends on how the object will be used. Linking is preferable if the object is likely to change and the compound

Superior Software

Miami, Florida

To: Mr. White
                Chairman, Superior Software

From: Heather Bond
                Vice President, Marketing

Subject: May Sales Data

The May sales data clearly indicate that Boston is outperforming our other geographic areas. It is my feeling that Ms. Brown, the office supervisor, is directly responsible for its success and that she should be rewarded accordingly. In addition, we may want to think about transferring her to New York, as they are in desperate need of new ideas and direction. I will be awaiting your response after you have time to digest the information presented.

Superior Software Sales

	Miami	Denver	New York	Boston	Total
Word Processing	$50,000	$67,500	$9,500	$141,000	**$268,000**
Spreadsheets	$44,000	$18,000	$11,500	$105,000	**$178,500**
Database	$12,000	$7,500	$6,000	$30,000	**$55,500**
Total	**$106,000**	**$93,000**	**$27,000**	**$276,000**	**$502,000**

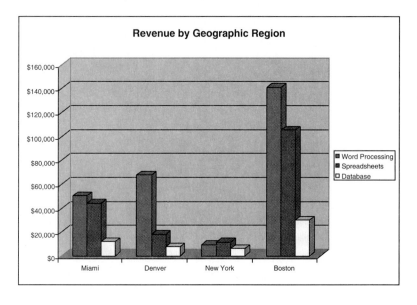

FIGURE 3.11   A Compound Document

document requires the latest version. Linking should also be used when the same object is placed in many documents, so that any change to the object has to be made in only one place. Embedding should be used if you need to take the object with you—for example, if you intend to edit the compound document on a different computer.

The following exercise uses linking to create a Word document containing an Excel worksheet and chart. As you do the exercise, both applications (Word and Excel) will be open, and it will be necessary to switch back and forth between the two. This in turn demonstrates the ***multitasking*** capability within Windows 95 and the use of the Windows 95 taskbar to switch between the open applications.

Objective: To create a compound document consisting of a memo, worksheet, and chart. Use Figure 3.12 as a guide in the exercise.

STEP 1: Open the Software Memo

➤ Click the **Start button** on the taskbar to display the Start menu. Click (or point to) the **Programs menu,** then click **Microsoft Word** to start the program. Close the Office Assistant if it appears.

➤ Word is now active, and the taskbar contains a button for Microsoft Word. It may (or may not) contain a button for Microsoft Excel, depending on whether or not you closed Excel at the end of the previous exercise.

➤ If necessary, click the **Maximize button** in the application window so that Word takes the entire desktop as shown in Figure 3.12a. (The Open dialog box is not yet visible.) Click the **Maximize button** in the document window (if necessary) so that the document window is as large as possible.

➤ Pull down the **File menu** and click **Open** (or click the **Open button** on the Standard toolbar).

• Click the **drop-down arrow** in the Look In list box. Click the appropriate drive, drive C or drive A, depending on the location of your data.

• Double click the **Exploring Excel folder** (we placed the Word memo in the Exploring Excel folder) to open the folder. Double click the **Software Memo** to open the document.

• Save the document as **Finished Software Memo.**

➤ Pull down the **View menu.** Click **Page Layout** to change to the Page Layout view. Pull down the **View menu.** Click **Zoom.** Click **Page Width.**

OBJECT LINKING AND EMBEDDING

Object Linking and Embedding (OLE) enables you to create a compound document containing objects (data) from multiple Windows applications. The two techniques, linking and embedding, can be implemented in different ways. Although OLE is one of the major benefits of working in the Windows environment, it would be impossible to illustrate all of the techniques in a single exercise. Accordingly, we have created the icon at the left to help you identify the many examples of object linking and embedding that appear throughout the *Exploring Windows* series.

STEP 2: Copy the Worksheet

➤ Open (or return to) the **Finished Software Sales workbook** from the previous exercise.

• If you did not close Microsoft Excel at the end of the previous exercise, you will see its button on the taskbar. Click the **Microsoft Excel button** to return to or open the Finished Software Sales workbook.

• If you closed Microsoft Excel, click the **Start button** to start Excel, then open the Finished Software Sales workbook.

➤ The taskbar should now contain a button for both Microsoft Word and Microsoft Excel. Click either button to move back and forth between the open applications. End by clicking the Microsoft Excel button so that you see the Finished Software Sales workbook.

➤ Click the tab for **Sales Data.** Click and drag to select **A1** through **F7** to select the entire worksheet as shown in Figure 3.12b.

➤ Point to the selected area and click the **right mouse button** to display the shortcut menu. Click **Copy.** A moving border appears around the entire worksheet, indicating that it has been copied to the clipboard.

Click to select appropriate drive/folder

Double click to open Software Memo

Taskbar has a button for Microsoft Word

Click Start button to display Start menu

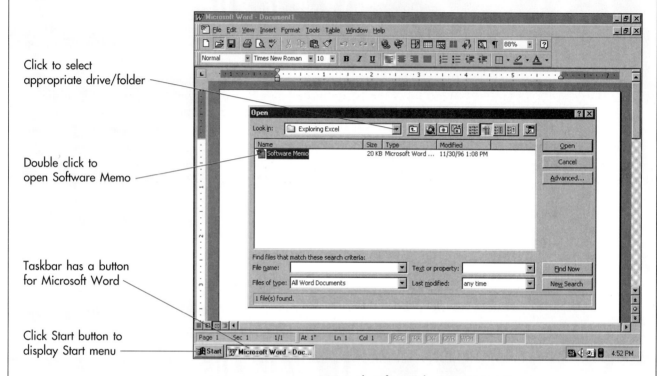

(a) Open the Software Sales Document (step 1)

FIGURE 3.12   Hands-on Exercise 3

THE WINDOWS 95 TASKBAR

Multitasking, the ability to run multiple applications at the same time, is one of the primary advantages of the Windows environment. Each button on the taskbar appears automatically when its application or folder is opened, and disappears upon closing. (The buttons are resized automatically according to the number of open windows.) The taskbar can be moved to the left or right edge of the desktop, or to the top of the desktop, by dragging a blank area of the taskbar to the desired position.

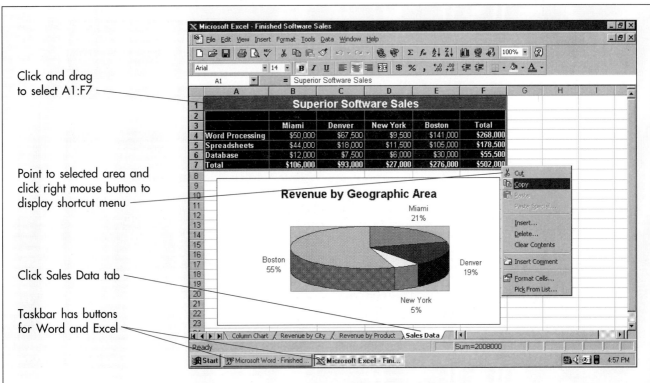

Click and drag
to select A1:F7

Point to selected area and
click right mouse button to
display shortcut menu

Click Sales Data tab

Taskbar has buttons
for Word and Excel

(b) Copy the Worksheet (step 2)

FIGURE 3.12   Hands-on Exercise 3 (continued)

STEP 3: Create the Link

➤ Click the **Microsoft Word button** on the taskbar to return to the memo as shown in Figure 3.12c. Press **Ctrl+End** to move to the end of the memo, which is where you will insert the Excel worksheet.

➤ Pull down the **Edit menu.** Click **Paste Special** to display the dialog box in Figure 3.12c.

➤ Click **Microsoft Excel Worksheet Object** in the As list. Click the **Paste Link option button.** Click **OK** to insert the worksheet into the document.

➤ Click and drag to center the worksheet between the margins. Save the memo.

THE COMMON USER INTERFACE

The common user interface provides a sense of familiarity from one Windows application to the next. Even if you have never used Microsoft Word, you will recognize many of the elements present in Excel. The applications share a common menu structure with consistent ways to execute commands from those menus. The Standard and Formatting toolbars are present in both applications. Many keyboard shortcuts are also common, such as Ctrl+Home and Ctrl+End to move to the beginning and end of a document.

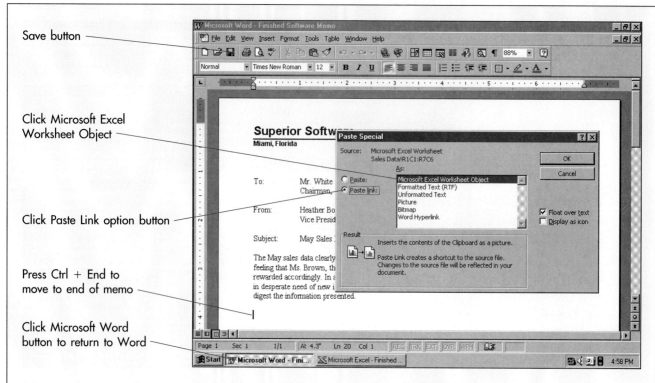

Save button

Click Microsoft Excel
Worksheet Object

Click Paste Link option button

Press Ctrl + End to
move to end of memo

Click Microsoft Word
button to return to Word

(c) Create the Link (step 3)

FIGURE 3.12   Hands-on Exercise 3 (continued)

STEP 4: Copy the Chart

➤ Click the **Microsoft Excel button** on the taskbar to return to the worksheet. Click outside the selected area (cells A1 through F7) to deselect the cells. Press **Esc** to remove the moving border.

➤ Click the **Revenue by City tab** to select the chart sheet. Point to the chart area, then click the left mouse button to select the chart. Be sure you have selected the entire chart and that you see the same sizing handles as in Figure 3.12d.

➤ Pull down the **Edit menu** and click **Copy** (or click the **Copy button** on the Standard toolbar). A moving border appears around the entire chart.

ALT+TAB STILL WORKS

Alt+Tab was a treasured shortcut in Windows 3.1 that enabled users to switch back and forth between open applications. The shortcut also works in Windows 95. Press and hold the Alt key while you press and release the Tab key repeatedly to cycle through the open applications, whose icons are displayed in a small rectangular window in the middle of the screen. Release the Alt key when you have selected the icon for the application you want.

Copy button

Click Revenue by City tab

Click Microsoft Excel
button to return to Excel

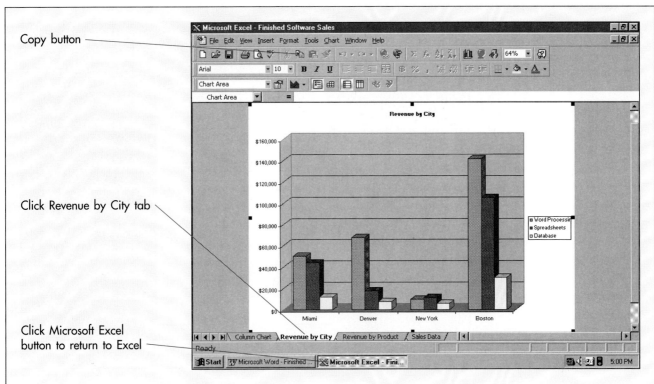

(d) Copy the Chart to the Clipboard (step 4)

FIGURE 3.12   Hands-on Exercise 3 (continued)

STEP 5: Add the Chart

➤ Click the **Microsoft Word button** on the taskbar to return to the memo. If necessary, press **Ctrl+End** to move to the end of the Word document. Press the **enter key** to add a blank line.

➤ Pull down the **Edit menu.** Click **Paste Special.** Click the **Paste Link** option button. If necessary, click **Microsoft Excel Chart Object.** Click **OK** to insert the chart into the document.

➤ Zoom to **Whole Page** to facilitate moving and sizing the chart. You need to reduce its size so that it fits on the same page as the memo. Thus, click on the chart to select it and display the sizing handles as shown in Figure 3.12e. Click and drag a corner sizing handle inward to make the chart smaller, then center it on the page.

➤ Zoom to **Page Width.** Look carefully at the worksheet and chart in the document. The sales for Word Processing in New York are currently $9,500, and the chart reflects this amount. Save the memo.

➤ Point to the **Microsoft Excel button** on the taskbar and click the **right mouse button** to display a shortcut menu. Click **Close** to close Excel. Click **Yes** if prompted whether to save the changes to the Finished Software Sales workbook.

➤ The Microsoft Excel button disappears from the taskbar, indicating that Excel has been closed. Word is now the only open application.

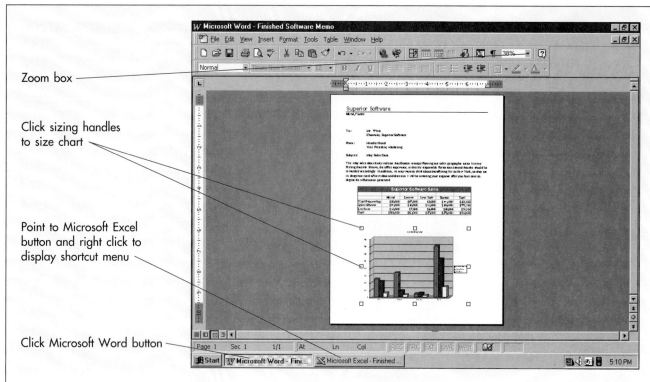

Zoom box

Click sizing handles
to size chart

Point to Microsoft Excel
button and right click to
display shortcut menu

Click Microsoft Word button

(e) Add the Chart (step 5)

FIGURE 3.12   Hands-on Exercise 3 (continued)

LINKING VERSUS EMBEDDING

A linked object maintains its connection to the source file. An embedded object does not. Thus, a linked object can be placed in any number of destination files, each of which maintains a pointer (link) to the same source file. Any change to the object in the source file is reflected automatically in every destination file containing that object.

STEP 6: Modify the Worksheet

➤ Click anywhere in the worksheet to select the worksheet and display the sizing handles as shown in Figure 3.12f.

➤ The status bar indicates that you can double click to edit the worksheet. Double click anywhere within the worksheet to reopen Excel in order to change the data.

➤ The system pauses as it loads Excel and reopens the Finished Software Sales workbook. If necessary, click the **Maximize button** to maximize the Excel window. Close the Office Assistant if it appears.

➤ If necessary, click the **Sales Data tab** within the workbook. Click in **cell D4.** Type **$200,000.** Press **enter.**

➤ Click the **|◄ button** to scroll to the first tab. Click the **Revenue by City tab** to select the chart sheet. The chart has been modified automatically and reflects the increased sales for New York.

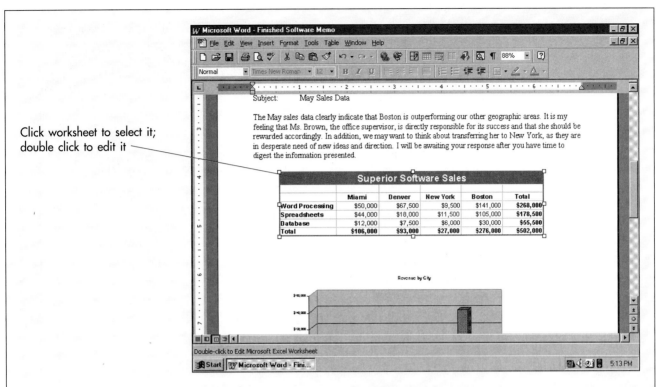

Click worksheet to select it; double click to edit it

Subject: May Sales Data

The May sales data clearly indicate that Boston is outperforming our other geographic areas. It is my feeling that Ms. Brown, the office supervisor, is directly responsible for its success and that she should be rewarded accordingly. In addition, we may want to think about transferring her to New York, as they are in desperate need of new ideas and direction. I will be awaiting your response after you have time to digest the information presented.

Superior Software Sales

	Miami	Denver	New York	Boston	Total
Word Processing	$50,000	$67,500	$9,500	$141,000	$268,000
Spreadsheets	$44,000	$18,000	$11,500	$105,000	$178,500
Database	$12,000	$7,500	$6,000	$30,000	$55,500
Total	$106,000	$93,000	$27,000	$276,000	$502,000

Revenue by City

Double-click to Edit Microsoft Excel Worksheet

(f) Modify the Worksheet (step 6)

FIGURE 3.12   Hands-on Exercise 3 (continued)

STEP 7: Update the Links

➤ Click the **Microsoft Word button** on the taskbar to return to the Software memo. The links for the worksheet and chart should be updated automatically. If not:

- Pull down the **Edit menu.** Click **Links to** display the Links dialog box in Figure 3.12g.
- Select the link(s) to update. (You can press and hold the **Ctrl key** to select multiple links simultaneously.)
- Click the **Update Now button** to update the selected links.
- Close the Links dialog box.

➤ The worksheet and chart should both reflect $200,000 for word processing sales in New York. Save the Word document.

UPDATE LINKS BEFORE PRINTING

Word will automatically update any linked information prior to printing a document, provided the options are set properly. Pull down the Tools menu, click the Options command, click the Print tab, then check the Update links check box.

Click Update Now button

Select the link to update

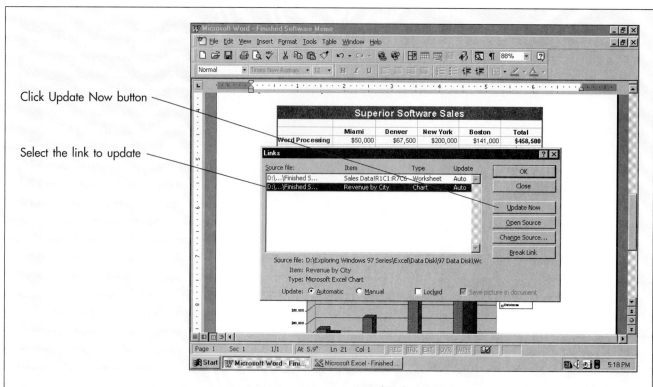

(g) Update the Links (step 7)

FIGURE 3.12 Hands-on Exercise 3 (continued)

STEP 8: The Finishing Touches

➤ Point to the chart, click the **right mouse button** to display a shortcut menu, then click the **Format Object command** to display the Format Object dialog box in Figure 3.12h.

➤ Click the **Colors and Lines Tab,** click the **drop-down arrow** in the Line Color box, then click **black** to display a line (border) around the worksheet. Click **OK.** Deselect the chart to see the border.

➤ Zoom to the **Whole Page** to view the completed document. Click and drag the worksheet and/or the chart within the memo to make any last minute changes. Save the memo a final time.

➤ Print the completed memo and submit it to your instructor. Exit Word. Exit Excel. Save the changes to the Finished Software Sales workbook.

➤ Congratulations on a job well done.

TO CLICK OR DOUBLE CLICK

Clicking an object selects the object and displays the sizing handles, which let you move and/or size the object or change its properties. Double clicking an object starts the application that created the object and enables you to change underlying data. Any changes to the object in the source file (e.g., the worksheet) are automatically reflected in the object in the destination file (e.g., the Word document) provided the two are properly linked to one another.

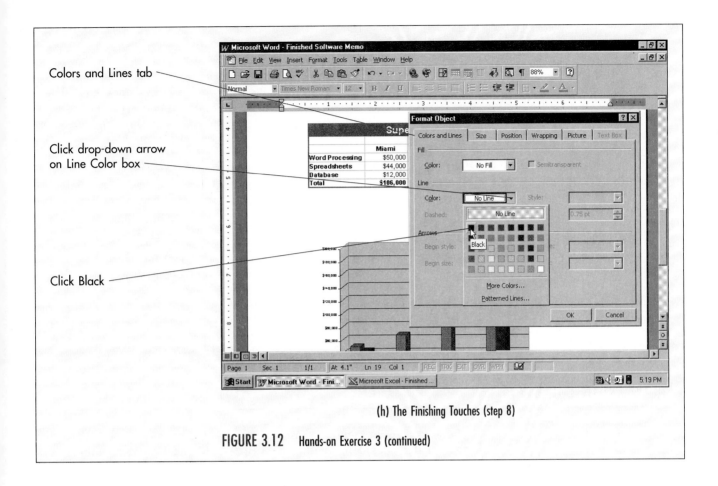

Colors and Lines tab

Click drop-down arrow
on Line Color box

Click Black

(h) The Finishing Touches (step 8)

FIGURE 3.12 Hands-on Exercise 3 (continued)

SUMMARY

A chart is a graphic representation of data in a worksheet. The type of chart chosen depends on the message to be conveyed. A pie chart is best for proportional relationships. A column or bar chart is used to show actual numbers rather than percentages.

The Chart Wizard is the easiest way to create a chart. Once created, a chart can be enhanced with arrows and text boxes found on the Drawing toolbar. The title of a chart can be used to emphasize the intended message.

A chart may be embedded in a worksheet or created in a separate chart sheet. An embedded chart may be moved within a worksheet by selecting it and dragging it to its new location. An embedded chart may be sized by selecting it and dragging any of the sizing handles in the desired direction.

Multiple data series may be specified in either rows or columns. If the data is in rows, the first row is assumed to contain the category labels, and the first column is assumed to contain the legend. Conversely, if the data is in columns, the first column is assumed to contain the category labels, and the first row the legend. The Chart Wizard makes it easy to switch from rows to columns and vice versa.

Object Linking and Embedding enables the creation of a compound document containing data (objects) from multiple applications. The essential difference between linking and embedding is whether the object is stored within the compound document (embedding) or in its own file (linking). An embedded object is stored in the compound document, which in turn becomes the only user (client) of that object. A linked object is stored in its own file, and the compound document is one of many potential clients of that object.

Bar chart	Docked toolbar	Object Linking and
Category label	Drawing toolbar	Embedding (OLE)
Chart	Embedded chart	Pie chart
Chart sheet	Embedded object	Sizing handles
Chart toolbar	Embedding	Stacked columns
Chart type	Exploded pie chart	Taskbar
Chart Wizard	Floating toolbar	Three-dimensional
Column chart	Legend	column chart
Common user interface	Linked object	Three-dimensional pie
Compound document	Linking	chart
Data point	Multiple data series	X axis
Data series	Multitasking	Y axis
Default chart	Object	

PRACTICE WITH EXCEL 97

1. The worksheet in Figure 3.13 is to be used as the basis of several charts that analyze the sales data for the chain of four Michael Moldof clothing boutiques. The worksheet is found on the data disk in the *Brief Chapter 3 Practice 1 Workbook.* Use the worksheet to develop the following charts:

   a. A pie chart showing the percentage of total sales attributed to each store.

   b. A column chart showing the total sales for each store.

   c. A stacked column chart showing total sales for each store, broken down by clothing category.

   d. A stacked column chart showing total dollars for each clothing category, broken down by store.

   e. Create each chart in its own chart sheet. Rename the various chart sheets to reflect the charts they contain.

   f. Title each chart appropriately and enhance each chart as you see fit.

   g. Print the entire workbook (the worksheet and all four chart sheets).

   h. Add a title page with your name and date, then submit the completed assignment to your instructor.

	A	B	C	D	E	F
1	Michael Moldof Men's Boutique					
2	January Sales					
3						
4		Store 1	Store 2	Store 3	Store 4	Total
5	Slacks	$25,000	$28,750	$21,500	$9,400	$84,650
6	Shirts	$43,000	$49,450	$36,900	$46,000	$175,350
7	Underwear	$18,000	$20,700	$15,500	$21,000	$75,200
8	Accessories	$7,000	$8,050	$8,000	$4,000	$27,050
9						
10	Total	$93,000	$106,950	$81,900	$80,400	$362,250

FIGURE 3.13   Spreadsheet for Practice Exercise 1

2. The worksheet in Figure 3.14 is to be used by the corporate marketing manager in a presentation in which she describes sales over the past four years. The manager has placed the worksheet on the data disk (in the *Brief Chapter 3 Practice 2 Workbook*) and would like you, her student intern, to do all of the following:

a. Format the worksheet attractively so that it can be used as part of the presentation. Include your name somewhere in the worksheet.

b. Create any chart(s) you think appropriate to emphasize the successful performance enjoyed by the London office.

c. Use the same data and chart type(s) as in part (a) but modify the title (and/or callouts) to emphasize the disappointing performance of the Paris office.

d. Print the worksheet together with all charts and submit them to your instructor. Be sure to title all charts appropriately and to use the text and arrow tools to add the required emphasis.

	A	B	C	D	E	F
1	Unique Boutiques					
2	Sales for 1993-1996					
3						
4	Store	1993	1994	1995	1996	Totals
5	Miami	1500000	2750000	3000000	3250000	10500000
6	London	4300000	5500000	6700000	13000000	29500000
7	Paris	2200000	1800000	1400000	1000000	6400000
8	Rome	2000000	3000000	4000000	5000000	14000000
9	Totals	10000000	13050000	15100000	22250000	60400000

FIGURE 3.14   Spreadsheet for Practice Exercise 2

3. The worksheet in Figure 3.15 is to be used as the basis for several charts depicting information on hotel capacities. Each of the charts is to be created in its own chart sheet within the *Brief Chapter 3 Practice 3 Workbook* on the data disk. We describe the message we want to convey, but it is up to you to determine the appropriate chart and associated data range(s). Accordingly, you are to create a chart that:

a. Compares the total capacity of the individual hotels to one another.

b. Shows the percent of total capacity for each hotel.

c. Compares the number of standard and deluxe rooms for all hotels, with the number of standard and deluxe rooms side-by-side for each hotel.

d. Compares the standard and deluxe room rates for all hotels, with the two different rates side-by-side for each hotel.

e. Add your name to the worksheet as the Hotel Manager, then print the complete workbook, which will consist of the original worksheet plus the four chart sheets you created.

	A	B	C	D	E	F
1		Hotel Capacities and Room Rates				
2						
3	Hotel	No. of Standard Rooms	Standard Rate	No. of Deluxe Rooms	Deluxe Rate	Total Number of Rooms
4	Holiday Inn	300	100	100	150	400
5	Hyatt	225	120	50	175	275
6	Ramada Inn	150	115	35	190	185
7	Sheraton	175	95	25	150	200
8	Marriott	325	100	100	175	425
9	Hilton	250	80	45	120	295
10	Best Western	150	75	25	125	175
11	Days Inn	100	50	15	100	115

FIGURE 3.15   Spreadsheet for Practice Exercise 3

4. A partially completed version of the worksheet in Figure 3.16 can be found on the data disk in the file *Brief Chapter 3 Practice 4.* Open the workbook and make all necessary entries so that your worksheet matches the one in Figure 3.16. Next, create a memo to your instructor containing the worksheet and a chart that plots the sales data in columns to emphasize the contribution of each salesperson. Use any wording you think is appropriate for the memo. Print the completed memo, add your name, and submit it to your instructor as proof you did this exercise.

	A	B	C	D	E	F
1	**Ralph Cordell Sporting Goods**					
2	Quarterly Sales Report					
3						
4	**Salesperson**	**1st Qtr**	**2nd Qtr**	**3rd Qtr**	**4th Qtr**	**Total**
5	Powell	$50,000	$55,000	$62,500	$85,400	$252,900
6	Blaney	$34,000	$48,500	$62,000	$62,000	$206,500
7	Rego	$49,000	$44,000	$42,500	$41,000	$176,500
8	**Total**	$133,000	$147,500	$167,000	$188,400	$635,900

FIGURE 3.16   Worksheet for Practice Exercise 4

5. Object Linking and Embedding: The compound document in Figure 3.17 contains a memo and combination chart. (The worksheet is contained in the *Brief Chapter 3 Practice 5 Workbook.* The text of the memo is in the *Brief Chapter 3 Practice 5 Memo,* which exists as a Word document in the Exploring Excel folder on the data disk.) You are to complete the compound document and submit it to your instructor by completing the following steps:

   a. Create a letterhead for the memo containing your name, address, phone number, and any other information you deem appropriate.

   b. Create the combination chart that appears in the memo. Select the data for the Chart Wizard in the usual fashion. You must, however, specify the custom chart type (Line–Column on 2 Axis) as opposed to a standard line or column chart. (Click the Custom Types tab in step 1 of the Chart Wizard.)

   c. Link the chart to the memo.

   d. Print the compound document and submit it to your instructor as proof you did this exercise.

6. Create the compound document in Figure 3.18, which is based on the partially completed worksheet in *Brief Chapter 3 Practice 6.* You need to enter the text of the memo yourself, and in addition, create an interesting letterhead using Microsoft WordArt. You need not duplicate our letterhead exactly. This exercise gives you the opportunity to practice a variety of skills. The Format Picture command in Microsoft Word enables you to position the chart and worksheet within the memo.

Steven Stocks

Financial Investments   •   100 Century Tower   •   New York, NY 10020

To: Carlos Rosell

From: Steven Stocks

Subject: Status Report on National Widgets

I have uncovered some information that I feel is important to the overall health of your investment portfolio. The graph below clearly shows that while revenues for National Widgets have steadily increased since 1992, profits have steadily decreased. In addition, the stock price is continuing to decline. Although at one time I felt that a turnaround was imminent, I am no longer so optimistic and am advising you to cut your losses and sell your National Widgets stock as soon as possible.

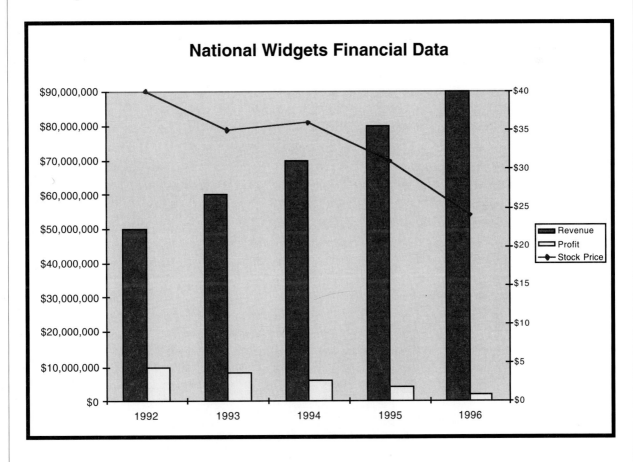

FIGURE 3.17   Compound Document for Practice Exercise 5

Office of Residential Living

University of Miami   •   P.O. Box 248904   •   Coral Gables, FL 33124

January 10, 1998

Mr. Jeffrey Redmond, President
Dynamic Dining Services
4329 Palmetto Lane
Miami, FL 33157

Dear Jeff,

As per our conversation, occupancy is projected to be back up from last year. I have enclosed a spreadsheet and chart that show the total enrollment for the past four school years. Please realize, however, that the 1997-1998 figures are projections, as the Spring 1998 numbers are still incomplete. The final 1997-1998 numbers should be confirmed within the next two weeks. I hope that this helps with your planning. If you need further information, please contact me at the above address.

Dorm Occupancy				
	94-95	95-96	96-97	97-98
Beatty	330	285	270	250
Broward	620	580	620	565
Graham	450	397	352	420
Rawlings	435	470	295	372
Tolbert	550	554	524	635
Totals	2385	2286	2061	2242

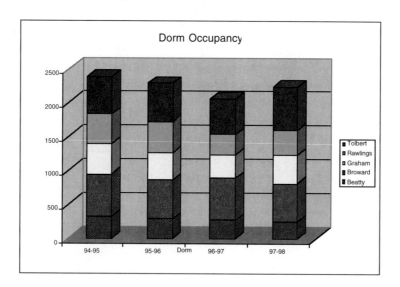

FIGURE 3.18   Compound Document for Practice Exercise 6

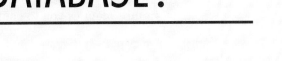

INTRODUCTION TO MICROSOFT ACCESS: WHAT IS A DATABASE?

1

OBJECTIVES

After reading this chapter you will be able to:

1. Define the terms *field, record, table,* and *database.*
2. Start Microsoft Access; describe the Database window and the objects in an Access database
3. Describe the different views associated with a table and the purpose of each.
4. Add, edit, and delete records within a table.
5. Use the Find command to locate a specific record; describe several parameters associated with the Find and Replace commands.
6. Describe the record selector; explain when changes are saved to a table.
7. Explain the importance of data validation in table maintenance.
8. Open an existing database and run its queries and reports.

OVERVIEW

All businesses and organizations maintain data of one kind or another. Companies store data about their employees. Schools and universities store data about their students and faculties. Magazines and newspapers store data about their subscribers. The list goes on and on, and while each of these examples refers to different types of data, they all operate under the same basic principles of database management.

This chapter provides a broad-based introduction to database management through the example of a college bookstore. We begin by showing how the mechanics of manual record keeping can be extended to a computerized system. We discuss the basic operations in maintaining data and stress the importance of data validation.

The chapter also introduces you to Microsoft Access, the fourth major application in the Microsoft Office Professional suite. We describe the objects within an Access database and show you how to add, edit, and delete records in an Access table.

The hands-on exercises in the chapter enable you to apply all of the material at the computer, and are indispensable to the learn-by-doing philosophy we follow throughout the text. As you do the exercises, you may recognize many commands from other Windows applications, all of which share a common user interface and consistent command structure.

CASE STUDY: THE COLLEGE BOOKSTORE

Imagine, if you will, that you are the manager of a college bookstore and that you maintain data for every book in the store. Accordingly, you have recorded the specifics of each book (the title, author, publisher, price, and so on) in a manila folder, and have stored the folders in one drawer of a file cabinet.

One of your major responsibilities is to order books at the beginning of each semester, which in turn requires you to contact the various publishers. You have found it convenient, therefore, to create a second set of folders with data about each publisher such as the publisher's phone number, address, discount policy, and so on. You also found it necessary to create a third set of folders with data about each order such as when the order was placed, the status of the order, which books were ordered, how many copies, and so on.

Normal business operations will require you to make repeated trips to the filing cabinet to maintain the accuracy of the data and keep it up to date. You will have to create a new folder whenever a new book is received, whenever you contract with a new publisher, or whenever you place a new order. Each of these folders must be placed in the proper drawer in the filing cabinet. In similar fashion, you will have to modify the data in an existing folder to reflect changes that occur, such as an increase in the price of a book, a change in a publisher's address, or an update in the status of an order. And, lastly, you will need to remove the folder of any book that is no longer carried by the bookstore, or of any publisher with whom you no longer have contact, or of any order that was canceled.

The preceding discussion describes the bookstore of 40 years ago—before the advent of computers and computerized databases. The bookstore manager of today needs the same information as his or her predecessor. Today's manager, however, has the information readily available, at the touch of a key or the click of a mouse, through the miracle of modern technology. The concepts are identical in both the manual and computerized systems.

You can think of the file cabinet, which contains the various sets of folders, as a *database.* Each set of folders in the file cabinet corresponds to a *table* within the database. In our example the bookstore database consists of three separate tables—for books, publishers, and orders. Each table, in turn, consists of multiple *records,* corresponding to the folders in the file cabinet. The Books table, for example, contains a record for every book title in the store. The Publishers table has a record for each publisher, just as the Orders table has a record for each order.

Each fact (or data element) that is stored within a record is called a *field.* In our example each book record consists of six fields—ISBN (a unique identifying number for the book), title, author, year of publication, price, and publisher. The table is constructed in such a way that every record has the same fields in the same order. In similar fashion, every record in the Publishers table will have the same fields for each publisher, just as every record in the Orders table has the same fields for each order. This terminology (field, record, table, and database) is extremely important and will be used throughout the text.

Microsoft Access, the fourth major application in the Microsoft Office, is used to create and manage a database such as the one for the college bookstore. Consider now Figure 1.1, which shows how Microsoft Access appears on the desktop. Our discussion assumes a basic familiarity with Windows 95 and the user interface that is common to all Windows applications. You should recognize, therefore, that the desktop in Figure 1.1 has two open windows—an application window for Microsoft Access and a document (database) window for the database that is currently open.

Each window has its own title bar and Minimize, Maximize (or Restore), and Close buttons. The title bar in the application window contains the name of the application (Microsoft Access). The title bar in the document (database) window contains the name of the database that is currently open (Bookstore). The application window for Access has been maximized to take up the entire desktop, and hence the Restore button is visible. The database window has not been maximized.

A menu bar appears immediately below the application title bar. A toolbar (similar to those in other Office applications) appears below the menu bar and offers alternative ways to execute common commands. The Windows 95 taskbar appears at the bottom of the screen and shows the open applications.

The Database Window

The *Database window* displays the various objects in an Access database. There are six types of objects—tables, queries, forms, reports, macros, and modules. Every database must contain at least one table, and it may contain any or all (or

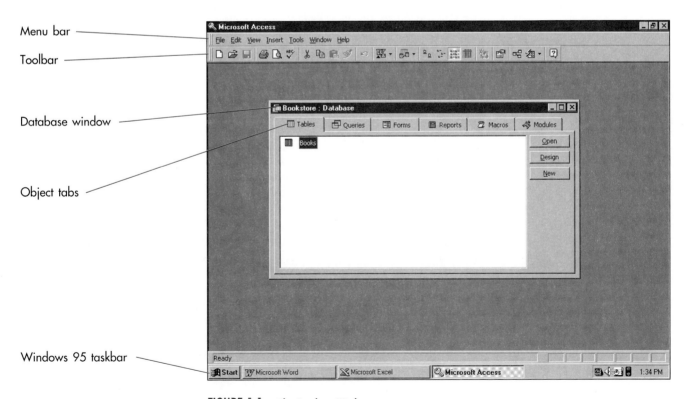

Menu bar

Toolbar

Database window

Object tabs

Windows 95 taskbar

FIGURE 1.1   The Database Window

none) of the other objects. Each object type is accessed through the appropriate tab within the Database window. In this chapter we concentrate on tables, but we briefly describe the other types of objects as a preview of what you will learn as you read our book.

- A *table* stores data about an entity (a person, place, or thing) and is the basic element in any database. A table is made up of records, which in turn are made up of fields. It is columnar in appearance, with each record in a separate row of the table and each field in a separate column.
- A *form* provides a more convenient and attractive way to enter, display, and/or print the data in a table. Forms are discussed in Chapter 2.
- A *query* answers a question about the database. The most common type of query specifies a set of criteria, then searches the database to retrieve the records that satisfy the criteria. Queries are introduced in Chapter 3.
- A *report* presents the data in a table or query in attractive fashion on the printed page. Reports are described in Chapter 3.
- A *macro* is analogous to a computer program and consists of commands that are executed automatically one after the other. Macros are used to automate the performance of any repetitive task.
- A *module* provides a greater degree of automation through programming in Access Basic. Modules are beyond the scope of this text.

ONE FILE HOLDS ALL

All of the objects in an Access database (tables, forms, queries, reports, macros, and modules) are stored in a single file on disk. The database itself is opened through the Open command in the File menu or by clicking the Open button on the Database toolbar. The individual objects within a database are opened through the database window.

Tables

A table (or set of tables) is the heart of any database, as it contains the actual data. In Access a table is displayed in one of two views—the Design view or the Datasheet view. The *Design view* is used to define the table initially and to specify the fields it will contain. It is also used to modify the table definition if changes are subsequently necessary. The Design view is discussed in detail in Chapter 2. The *Datasheet view*—the view you use to add, edit, or delete records—is the view on which we focus in this chapter.

Figure 1.2 shows the Datasheet view for the Books table in our bookstore. The first row in the table contains the *field names.* Each additional row contains a record (the data for a specific book). Each column represents a field (one fact about a book). Every record in the table contains the same fields in the same order: ISBN Number, Title, Author, Year, List Price, and Publisher.

The status bar at the bottom of Figure 1.2a indicates that there are five records in the table and that you are positioned on the first record. This is the record you are working on and is known as the *current record.* (You can work on only one record at a time.) There is a *record selector symbol* (either a triangle or a pencil) next to the current record to indicate its status.

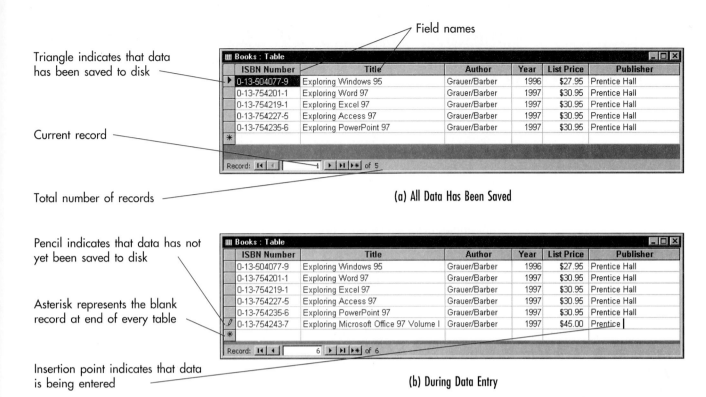

Field names

Triangle indicates that data
has been saved to disk

Current record

Total number of records

(a) All Data Has Been Saved

Pencil indicates that data has not
yet been saved to disk

Asterisk represents the blank
record at end of every table

Insertion point indicates that data
is being entered

(b) During Data Entry

FIGURE 1.2 Tables

A *triangle* indicates that the record has been saved to disk. A *pencil* indicates that you are working on the record and that the changes have not yet been saved. As soon as you move to the next record, however, the pencil changes to a triangle to indicate that the record on which you were working has been saved. (Access, unlike other Office applications, automatically saves changes made to a record without your having to execute the Save command.) An *asterisk* appears next to the blank record at the end of every table.

Figure 1.2a shows the table as it would appear immediately after you opened it. The first field in the first record is selected (highlighted), and anything you type at this point will replace the selected data. (This is the same convention as in any other Windows application.) The triangle next to the current record (record 1) indicates that changes have not yet been made. An asterisk appears as the record selector symbol next to the blank record at the end of the table. The blank record is used to add a record to the table and is not counted in determining the number of records in the table.

Figure 1.2b shows the table as you are in the process of entering data for a new record at the end of the table. The current record is now record 6. The *insertion point* (a flashing vertical bar) appears at the point where text is being entered. The record selector for the current record is a pencil, indicating that the record has not yet been saved. The asterisk has moved to the blank record at the end of the table, which now contains one more record than the table in Figure 1.2a.

Note, too, that each table in a database must have a field (or combination of fields) known as the *primary key,* which is unique for every record in the table. The ISBN (International Standard Book Number) is the primary key in our example, and it ensures that each record in the Books table is different from every other record. (Other fields may also have a unique value for every record, but only one field is designated as the primary key.)

Introduction to Microsoft Access

Objective: To open an existing database; to add a record to a table within the database. Use Figure 1.3 as a guide in the exercise.

STEP 1: Welcome to Windows

➤ Turn on the computer and all of its peripherals. The floppy drive should be empty prior to starting your machine. This ensures that the system starts by reading from the hard disk, which contains the Windows files, as opposed to a floppy disk, which does not.

➤ Your system will take a minute or so to get started, after which you should see the desktop in Figure 1.3a. Do not be concerned if the appearance of your desktop is different from ours. If necessary, click the **Close button** to close the Welcome window.

TAKE THE WINDOWS 95 TOUR

Windows 95 greets you with a Welcome window that contains a command button to take you on a 10-minute tour. Click the command button and enjoy the show. If you do not see the Welcome window, click the Start button, click Run, type WELCOME in the Open text box, and press enter. Windows 97 was not available when we went to press, but we expect it to have a similar option.

(a) Welcome to Windows (step 1)

FIGURE 1.3   Hands-on Exercise 1

STEP 2: Obtain the Practice Files:

➤ We have created a series of practice files for you to use throughout the text. Your instructor will make these files available to you in a variety of ways:

- You can download the files from our Web site if you have access to the Internet and World Wide Web (see boxed tip).

- The files may be on a network drive, in which case you use the Windows Explorer to copy the files from the network to a floppy disk.

- There may be an actual "data disk" that you are to check out from the lab in order to use the Copy Disk command to duplicate the disk.

➤ Check with your instructor for additional information.

DOWNLOAD THE PRACTICE FILES

You can download the practice files for any book in the *Exploring Windows* series from Bob Grauer's home page (www.bus.miami.edu/~rgrauer). Use any Web browser to get to Bob's page, then click the link to the *Exploring Windows* series where you choose the appropriate book and download the file. Be sure to read the associated "read me" file, which provides additional information about downloading the file.

STEP 3: Start Microsoft Access

➤ Click the **Start button** to display the Start menu. Click (or point to) the **Programs menu,** then click **Microsoft Access** to start the program. Close the Office Assistant if it appears. (The Office Assistant is described in the next hands-on exercise.)

➤ You should see the Microsoft Access dialog box with the option button to **Open an Existing Database** already selected. Click **More Files,** then click **OK** to display the Open dialog box in Figure 1.3b.

➤ Click the **Details button** to change to the Details view. Click and drag the vertical border between columns to increase (or decrease) the size of a column.

➤ Click the **drop-down arrow** on the Look In list box. Click the appropriate drive (drive C is recommended rather than drive A), depending on the location of your data. Double click the **Exploring Access folder.**

➤ Click the **down scroll arrow** until you can click the **Bookstore database.** Click the **Open command button** to open the database.

WORK ON DRIVE C

Even in a lab setting it is preferable to work on the local hard drive, as opposed to a floppy disk. The hard drive is much faster, which becomes especially important when working with the large file sizes associated with Access. Use the Windows Explorer to copy the database from the network drive to the local hard drive prior to the exercise, then work on drive C throughout the exercise. Once you have completed the exercise, use the Explorer a second time to copy the modified database to a floppy disk that you can take with you.

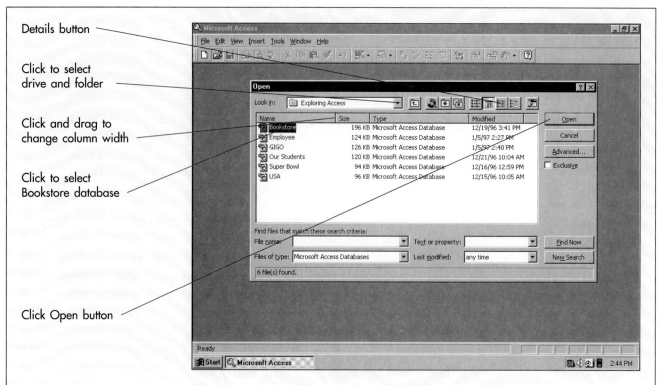

Details button

Click to select
drive and folder

Click and drag to
change column width

Click to select
Bookstore database

Click Open button

(b) Open an Existing Database (step 3)

FIGURE 1.3   Hands-on Exercise 1 (continued)

STEP 4: Open the Books Table

➤ You should see the database window for the Bookstore database with the **Tables tab** already selected. Double click the icon next to **Books** to open the table as shown in Figure 1.3c.

➤ Click the **Maximize button** so that the Books table fills the Access window and reduces the clutter on the screen.

➤ If necessary, click the **Maximize button** in the application window so that Access takes the entire desktop.

A SIMPLER DATABASE

The real power of Access is derived from a database with multiple tables that are related to one another. For the time being, however, we focus on a database with only one table so that you can learn the basics of Access. After you are comfortable working with a single table, we will show you how to work with multiple tables and how to relate them to one another.

STEP 5: Moving within a Table

➤ Click in any field in the first record. The status bar at the bottom of the Books Table indicates record 1 of 22.

➤ The triangle symbol in the record selector indicates that the record has not changed since it was last saved.

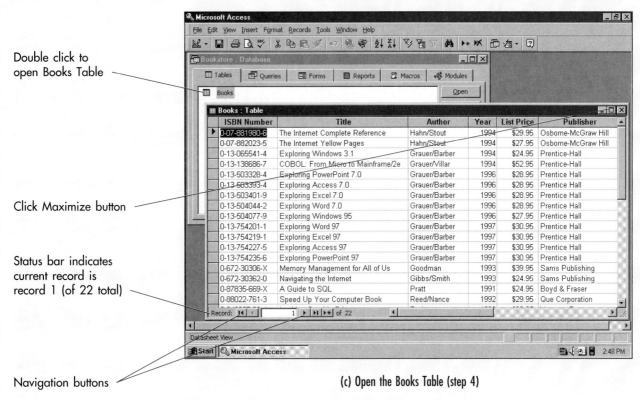

Double click to
open Books Table

Click Maximize button

Status bar indicates
current record is
record 1 (of 22 total)

Navigation buttons

(c) Open the Books Table (step 4)

FIGURE 1.3   Hands-on Exercise 1 (continued)

➤ You can move from record to record (or field to field) using either the mouse or the arrow keys:

• Click in any field in the second record. The status bar indicates record 2 of 22.

• Press the **down arrow key** to move to the third record. The status bar indicates record 3 of 22.

• Press the **left and right arrow keys** to move from field to field within the third record.

➤ You can also use the navigation buttons above the status bar to move from one record to the next:

• Click |◄ to move to the first record in the table.

• Click ► to move forward in the table to the next record.

• Click ◄ to move back in the table to the previous record.

MOVING FROM FIELD TO FIELD

Press the Tab key, the right arrow key, or the enter key to move to the next field in the current record (or the first field in the next record if you are already in the last field of the current record). Press Shift+Tab or the left arrow key to return to the previous field in the current record (or the last field in the previous record if you are already in the first field of the current record).

- Click ▶| to move to the last record in the table.
- Click ▶* to move beyond the last record in order to insert a new record.
➤ Click |◀ to return to the first record in the table.

STEP 6: Add a Record

➤ Pull down the **Insert menu** and click **New Record** (or click the **New Record button** on the Table Datasheet toolbar). The record selector moves to the last record (now record 23). The insertion point is positioned in the first field (ISBN Number).

➤ Enter data for the new record as shown in Figure 1.3d. The record selector changes to a pencil as soon as you enter the first character in the new record.

➤ Press the **enter key** when you have entered the last field for the record. The new record is saved, and the record selector changes to a triangle and moves automatically to the next record.

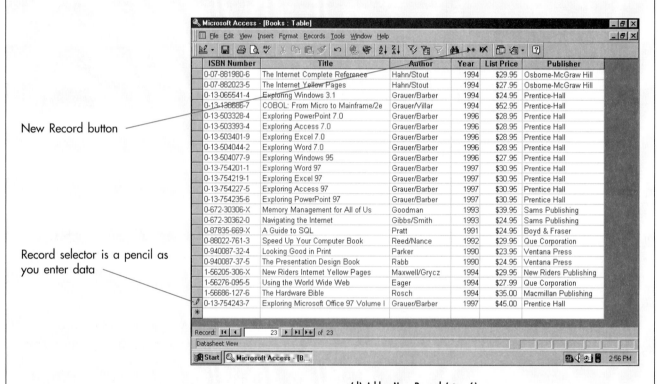

(d) Add a New Record (step 6)

FIGURE 1.3   Hands-on Exercise 1 (continued)

WHEN IS DATA SAVED?

There is one critical difference between Access and other Office applications such as Word for Windows or Microsoft Excel. *Access automatically saves any changes in the current record as soon as you move to the next record or when you close the table.* In other words, you do *not* have to execute the Save command explicitly to save the data in the table.

STEP 7: Add a Second Record

➤ The record selector is at the end of the table where you can add another record. Enter **0-13-271693-3** as the ISBN number for this record. Press the **Tab, enter,** or **right arrow key** to move to the Title field.

➤ Enter the title of this book as **Exploring teh Internet/2nd Edition** (deliberately misspelling the word "the"). Try to look at the monitor as you type to see the AutoCorrect feature (common to all Office applications) in action. Access will correct the misspelling and change *teh* to *the.*

➤ If you did not see the correction being made, press the **backspace key** several times to erase the last several characters in the title, then re-enter the title.

➤ Complete the entry for this book. Enter **Grauer/Marx** for the author. Enter **1997** for the year of publication. Enter **28.95** for the list price. Enter **Prentice Hall** for the publisher, then press **enter.**

CREATE YOUR OWN SHORTHAND

Use the AutoCorrect feature that is common to all Office applications to expand abbreviations such as "PH" for Prentice Hall. Pull down the Tools menu, click AutoCorrect, type the abbreviation in the Replace text box and the expanded entry in the With text box. Click the Add command button, then click OK to exit the dialog box and return to the document. The next time you type PH (in upper- or lowercase) as you enter a record, it will automatically be expanded to Prentice Hall.

STEP 8: Print the Table

➤ Pull down the **File menu.** Click **Page Setup** to display the Page Setup dialog box in Figure 1.3e.

➤ Click the **Page tab.** Click the **Landscape option button.** Click **OK** to accept the settings and close the dialog box.

➤ Click the **Print button** on the toolbar to print the table. Alternatively, you can pull down the **File menu,** click **Print** to display the Print dialog box, click the **All options button,** then click **OK.**

ABOUT MICROSOFT ACCESS

Pull down the Help menu and click About Microsoft Access to display the specific release number as well as other licensing information, including the product serial number. This help screen also contains two very useful command buttons, System Info and Tech Support. The first button displays information about the hardware installed on your system, including the amount of memory and available space on the hard drive. The Tech Support button provides telephone numbers for technical assistance.

Print button

Click Page tab

Select Landscape

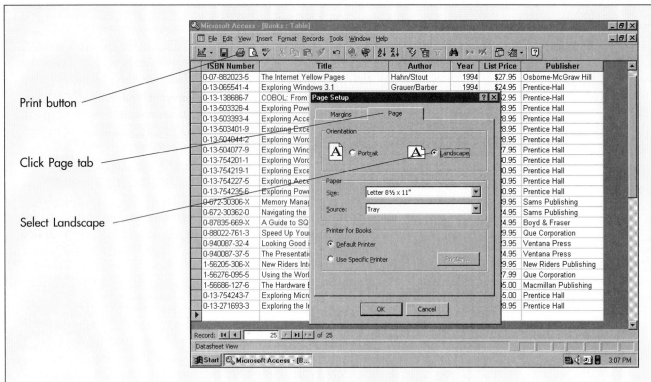

(e) Print the Table (step 8)

FIGURE 1.3 Hands-on Exercise 1 (continued)

STEP 9: Exit Access

➤ You need to close both the Books table and the Bookstore database:

• Pull down the **File menu** and click **Close** (or click the **Close button**) to close the Books table. Answer **Yes** if asked to save changes to the layout of the table.

• Pull down the **File menu** and click **Close** (or click the **Close button**) to close the Bookstore database.

➤ Pull down the **File menu** and click **Exit** to close Access if you do not want to continue with the next exercise at this time.

OUR FAVORITE BOOKSTORE

This exercise has taken you through our hypothetical bookstore database. It's more fun, however, to go to a real bookstore. Amazon Books (www.amazon.com), with a virtual inventory of more than one million titles, is one of our favorite sites on the Web. You can search by author, subject, or title, read reviews written by other Amazon visitors, or contribute your own review. It's not as cozy as your neighborhood bookstore, but you can order any title for mail-order delivery. And you never have to leave home.

The exercise just completed showed you how to open an existing table and add records to that table. You will also need to edit and/or delete existing records in order to maintain the data as changes occur. These operations require you to find the specific record and then make the change. You can search the table manually, or more easily through the Find and Replace commands.

Find and Replace Commands

The Find and Replace commands are similar in function to the corresponding commands in all other Office applications. The ***Find command*** in Microsoft Access enables you to locate a specific record(s) by searching a table for a particular value. You could, for example, search the Books table for the title of a book as in Figure 1.4a, then move to the appropriate field to change its price. The ***Replace command*** incorporates the Find command and allows you to locate and optionally replace (one or more occurrences of) one value with another. The Replace command in Figure 1.4b, for example, searches for *PH* in order to substitute *Prentice Hall.*

Searches can be made more efficient by making use of the various options. A case-sensitive search, for example, matches not only the specific characters, but also the use of upper- and lowercase letters. Thus, *PH* is different from *ph,* and a case-sensitive search on one will not identify the other. A case-insensitive search (where Match Case is *not* selected) will find both *PH* and *ph.* Any search may specify a match on whole fields to identify *Davis,* but not *Davison.* And finally, a

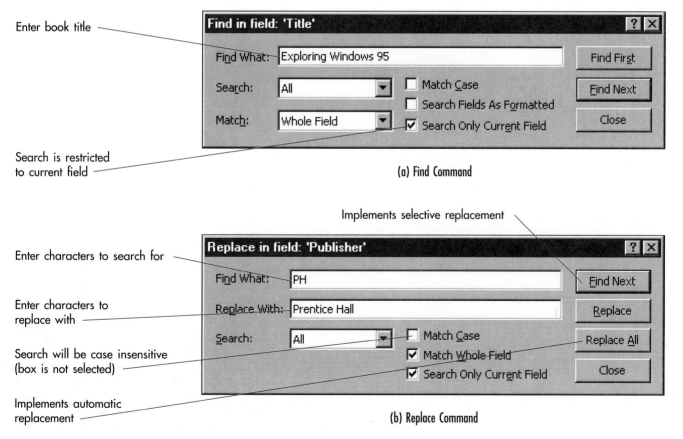

Enter book title

Search is restricted to current field

(a) Find Command

Implements selective replacement

Enter characters to search for

Enter characters to replace with

Search will be case insensitive (box is not selected)

Implements automatic replacement

(b) Replace Command

FIGURE 1.4 Find and Replace Commands

search can also be made more efficient by restricting it to the current field (e.g., Publisher), as opposed to searching every field.

The replacement can be either selective or automatic. Selective replacement lets you examine each successful match in context and decide whether to replace it. Automatic replacement makes the substitution without asking for confirmation (and is generally not recommended). Selective replacement is implemented by clicking the Find Next command button, then clicking (or not clicking) the Replace button to make (or not make) the substitution. Automatic replacement (through the entire table) is implemented by clicking the Replace All button.

Data Validation

It is unwise to simply add (edit or delete) a record without adequate checks on the validity of the data. Ask yourself, for example, whether a search for all books by Prentice Hall (without a hyphen) will also return all books by *Prentice-Hall* (with a hyphen). The answer is *no* because the publisher's name is spelled differently and a search for one will not locate the other. *You* know the publisher is the same in both instances, but the computer does not.

Data validation is a crucial part of any system. Good systems will anticipate errors you might make and reject those errors prior to accepting data. Access automatically implements certain types of data validation. It will not, for example, let you enter letters where a numeric value is expected (such as the Year and List Price fields in our example.) More sophisticated types of validation are implemented by the user when the table is created. You may decide, for example, to reject any record that omits the title or author. Data validation is described more completely in Chapter 2.

GARBAGE IN, GARBAGE OUT (GIGO)

A computer does exactly what you tell it to do, which is not necessarily what you want it to do. It is absolutely critical, therefore, that you validate the data that goes into a system, or else the associated information may not be correct. No system, no matter how sophisticated, can produce valid output from invalid input. In other words: *garbage in, garbage out.*

FORMS, QUERIES, AND REPORTS

As previously indicated, an Access database can contain as many as six different types of objects. Thus far we have concentrated on tables, but now we extend the discussion to include forms, queries, and reports as illustrated in Figure 1.5.

Figure 1.5a contains the Books table as it exists after the first hands-on exercise. There are 24 records in the table and six fields for each record. The status bar indicates that you are currently positioned in the first record. You can enter new records in the table as was done in the previous exercise. You can also edit or delete an existing record, as will be illustrated in the next exercise.

Figure 1.5b displays a form that is based on the table of Figure 1.5a. A form provides a friendlier interface than does a table and is easier to understand and use. Note, for example, the command buttons in the form to add a new record, or to find and/or delete an existing record. The status bar at the bottom of the form indicates that you are on the first of 24 records, and is identical to the status bar for the table in Figure 1.5a.

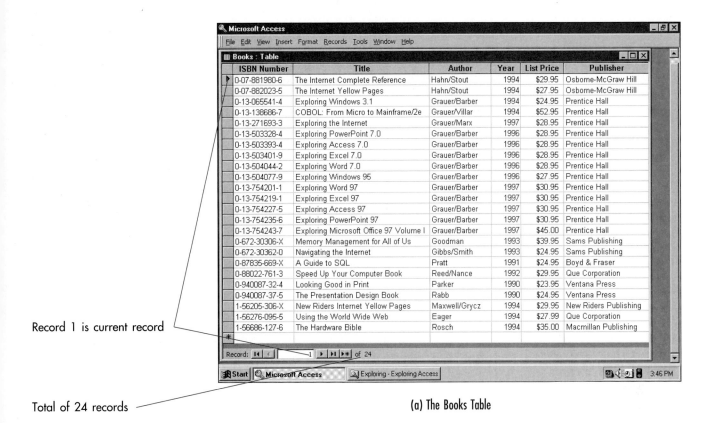

Record 1 is current record

Total of 24 records

(a) The Books Table

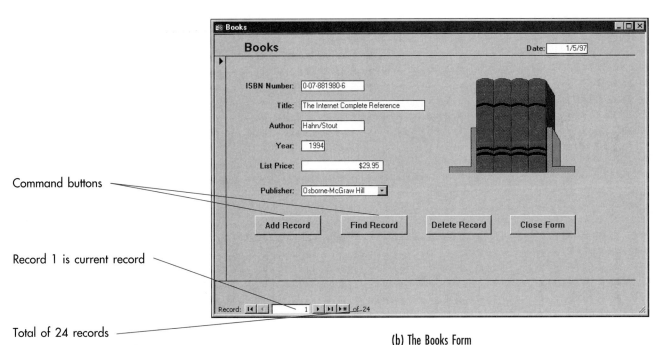

Command buttons

Record 1 is current record

Total of 24 records

(b) The Books Form

FIGURE 1.5 The Objects in a Database

Figure 1.5c displays a query to list the books for a particular publisher (Prentice Hall in this example). A query consists of a question (e.g., enter the publisher name) and an answer (the records that satisfy the query). The results of the query are similar in appearance to the underlying table, except that the query contains selected records and/or selected fields for those records. The query may also list the records in a different sequence from that of the table.

Books are in sequence by author, and within the same author, by title

Publisher	Author	Title	ISBN Number	Year	List Price
Prentice Hall	Grauer/Barber	Exploring Access 7.0	0-13-503393-4	1996	$28.95
Prentice Hall	Grauer/Barber	Exploring Access 97	0-13-754227-5	1997	$30.95
Prentice Hall	Grauer/Barber	Exploring Excel 7.0	0-13-503401-9	1996	$28.95
Prentice Hall	Grauer/Barber	Exploring Excel 97	0-13-754219-1	1997	$30.95
Prentice Hall	Grauer/Barber	Exploring Microsoft Office 97 Volume I	0-13-754243-7	1997	$45.00
Prentice Hall	Grauer/Barber	Exploring PowerPoint 7.0	0-13-503328-4	1996	$28.95
Prentice Hall	Grauer/Barber	Exploring PowerPoint 97	0-13-754235-6	1997	$30.95
Prentice Hall	Grauer/Barber	Exploring Windows 3.1	0-13-065541-4	1994	$24.95
Prentice Hall	Grauer/Barber	Exploring Windows 95	0-13-504077-9	1996	$27.95
Prentice Hall	Grauer/Barber	Exploring Word 7.0	0-13-504044-2	1996	$28.95
Prentice Hall	Grauer/Barber	Exploring Word 97	0-13-754201-1	1997	$30.95
Prentice Hall	Grauer/Marx	Exploring the Internet	0-13-271693-3	1997	$28.95
Prentice Hall	Grauer/Villar	COBOL: From Micro to Mainframe/2e	0-13-138686-7	1994	$52.95

Record: 1 of 13

(c) The Publisher Query

Publisher's Report

05-Jan-97

Publisher	Author	Title	ISBN Number	Year	List Price
Prentice Hall	Grauer/Barber	Exploring Access 7.0	0-13-503393-4	1996	$28.95
Prentice Hall	Grauer/Barber	Exploring Access 97	0-13-754227-5	1997	$30.95
Prentice Hall	Grauer/Barber	Exploring Excel 7.0	0-13-503401-9	1996	$28.95
Prentice Hall	Grauer/Barber	Exploring Excel 97	0-13-754219-1	1997	$30.95
Prentice Hall	Grauer/Barber	Exploring Microsoft Office 97 Volume I	0-13-754243-7	1997	$45.00
Prentice Hall	Grauer/Barber	Exploring PowerPoint 7.0	0-13-503328-4	1996	$28.95
Prentice Hall	Grauer/Barber	Exploring PowerPoint 97	0-13-754235-6	1997	$30.95
Prentice Hall	Grauer/Barber	Exploring Windows 3.1	0-13-065541-4	1994	$24.95
Prentice Hall	Grauer/Barber	Exploring Windows 95	0-13-504077-9	1996	$27.95
Prentice Hall	Grauer/Barber	Exploring Word 7.0	0-13-504044-2	1996	$28.95
Prentice Hall	Grauer/Barber	Exploring Word 97	0-13-754201-1	1997	$30.95
Prentice Hall	Grauer/Marx	Exploring the Internet	0-13-271693-3	1997	$28.95
Prentice Hall	Grauer/Villar	COBOL: From Micro to Mainframe/2e	0-13-138686-7	1994	$52.95

(d) The Publisher Report

FIGURE 1.5 The Objects in a Database (continued)

Figure 1.5d illustrates a report that includes only the books from Prentice Hall. A report provides presentation-quality output and is preferable to printing the results of a table or query. Note, too, that a report may be based on either a table or a query. You could, for example, base the report in Figure 1.5d on the Books table, in which case it would list every book in the table. Alternatively, the report could be based on a query, as in Figure 1.5d, and list only the books that satisfy the criteria within the query.

Later chapters discuss forms, queries, and reports in depth. The exercise that follows is intended only as a brief introduction to what can be accomplished in Access.

Maintaining the Database

Objective: To add, edit, and delete a record; to demonstrate data validation; to introduce forms, queries, and reports. Use Figure 1.6 as a guide in doing the exercise.

STEP 1: Open the Bookstore Database

➤ Start Access. The Bookstore database should appear within the list of recently opened databases as shown in Figure 1.6a.

➤ Select the **Bookstore database** (its drive and folder may be different from that in Figure 1.6a). Click **OK** to open the database.

➤ Close the Office Assistant if it appears.

Select the Bookstore database

Close the Office Assistant

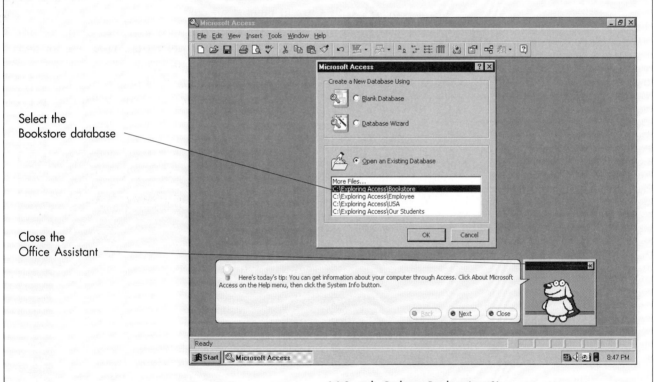

(a) Open the Bookstore Database (step 1)

FIGURE 1.6   Hands-on Exercise 2

CHOOSE YOUR OWN ASSISTANT

You can choose your own personal assistant from one of several available images. Click the Office Assistant button on any visible toolbar to display the Assistant, click the Options button to display the Office Assistant dialog box, click the Gallery tab, then click the Next button repeatedly to cycle through the available images. Click OK to select the character and close the dialog box. (The Office 97 CD is required for certain characters.)

STEP 2: The Find Command

➤ Click the **Tables tab** in the Database window. Double click the icon for the **Books table** to open the table from the previous exercise.

➤ You should see the Books table in Figure 1.6b. (The Find dialog box is not yet displayed).

➤ If necessary, click the **Maximize button** to maximize the Books table within the Access window.

➤ Exploring Office 95 and Exploring the Internet, the books you added in the previous exercise, appear in sequence according to the ISBN number because this field is the primary key for the Books table.

➤ Click in the **Title field** for the first record. Pull down the **Edit menu** and click **Find** (or click the **Find button** on the toolbar) to display the dialog box in Figure 1.6b. (You are still positioned in the first record.)

➤ Enter **Exploring Windows 95** in the Find What text box. Check that the other parameters for the Find command match the dialog box in Figure 1.6b. Be sure that **Search Only Current Field** is selected.

➤ Click the **Find First command button.** Access moves to record 10, the record containing the designated character string, and selects the Title field for that record. Click **Close** to close the Find dialog box.

➤ Press the **tab key** three times to move from the Title field to the List Price field. The current price ($27.95) is already selected. Type **28.95,** then press the **enter key** to change the price to $28.95.

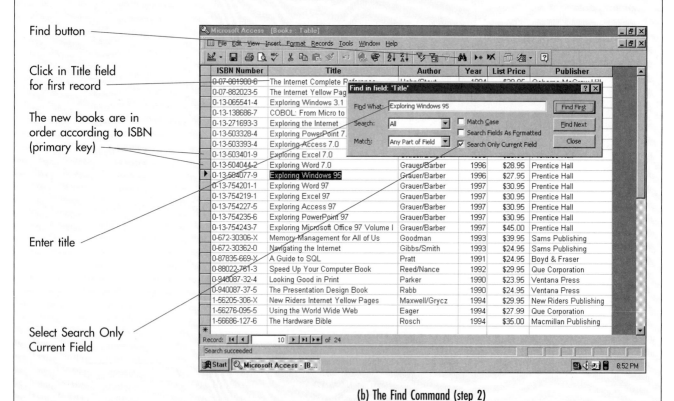

(b) The Find Command (step 2)

FIGURE 1.6   Hands-on Exercise 2 (continued)

EDITING A RECORD

The fastest way to replace the value in an existing field is to select the field, then type the new value. Access automatically selects the field for you when you use the keyboard (Tab, enter, or arrow keys) to move from one field to the next. Click the mouse within the field (to deselect the field) if you are replacing only one or two characters rather than the entire field.

STEP 3: The Undo Command

➤ Pull down the **Edit menu** and click **Undo Current Field/Record** (or click the **Undo button** on the toolbar). The price for Exploring Windows 95 returns to its previous value.

➤ Pull down the **Edit menu** a second time. The Undo command is dim (as is the Undo button on the toolbar), indicating that you can no longer undo any changes. Press **Esc.**

➤ Correct the List Price field a second time and move to the next record to save your change.

THE UNDO COMMAND

The Undo command is common to all Office applications, but is implemented differently from one application to the next. Microsoft Word, for example, enables you to undo the last 100 operations. Access, however, because it saves changes automatically as soon as you move to the next record, enables you to undo only the most recent command.

STEP 4: The Delete Command

➤ Click any field in the record for **A Guide to SQL.** (You can also use the **Find command** to search for the title and move directly to its record.)

➤ Pull down the **Edit menu.** Click **Select Record** to highlight the entire record.

➤ Press the **Del key** to delete the record. You will see a dialog box as shown in Figure 1.6c, indicating that you are about to delete a record and asking you to confirm the deletion. Click **Yes.**

➤ Pull down the **Edit menu.** The Undo command is dim, indicating that you cannot undelete a record. Press **Esc** to continue working.

THE RECORD SELECTOR

Click the record selector (the box immediately to the left of the first field in a record) to select the record without having to use a pull-down menu. Click and drag the mouse over the record selector for multiple rows to select several sequential records at the same time.

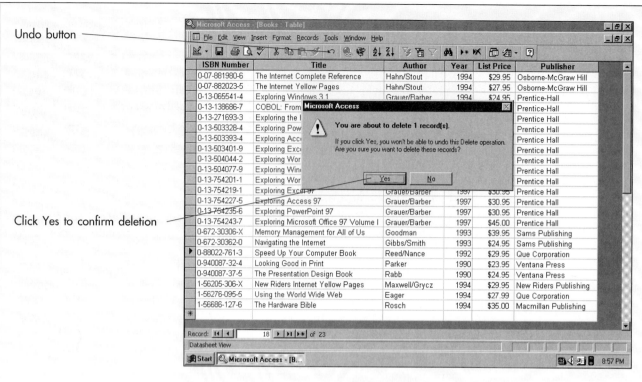

Undo button

Click Yes to confirm deletion

(c) The Delete Command (step 4)

FIGURE 1.6   Hands-on Exercise 2 (continued)

STEP 5: Data Validation

➤ Click the **New Record button** on the toolbar. The record selector moves to the last record (record 24).

➤ Add data as shown in Figure 1.6d, being sure to enter an invalid price **(XXX)** in the List Price field. Press the **Tab key** to move to the next field.

➤ Access displays the dialog box in Figure 1.6d, indicating that the value you entered (XXX) is inappropriate for the List Price field; in other words, you cannot enter letters when Access is expecting a numeric entry.

➤ Click the **OK command button** to close the dialog box and return to the table. Drag the mouse to select XXX, then enter the correct price of **$39.95.**

➤ Press the **Tab key** to move to the Publisher field. Type **IDG Books World-wide.** Press the **Tab key, right arrow key,** or **enter key** to complete the record.

➤ Click the **Close button** to close the Books table.

STEP 6: Open the Books Form

➤ Click the **Forms tab** in the Database window. Double click the **Books form** to open the form as shown in Figure 1.6e, then (if necessary) maximize the form so that it takes the entire window.

➤ Click the **Add Record command button** to move to a new record. The status bar shows record 25 of 25.

➤ Click in the text box for **ISBN number,** then use the **Tab key** to move from field to field as you enter data for the book as shown in Figure 1.6e.

➤ Click the **drop-down arrow** on the Publisher's list box to display the available publishers and to select the appropriate one. The use of a list box ensures that you cannot misspell a publisher's name.

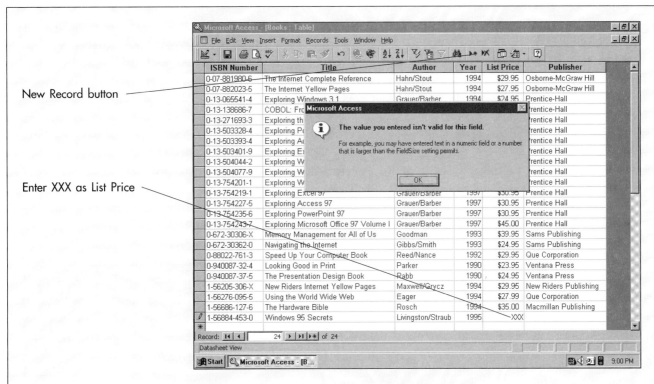

New Record button

Enter XXX as List Price

(d) Data Validation (step 5)

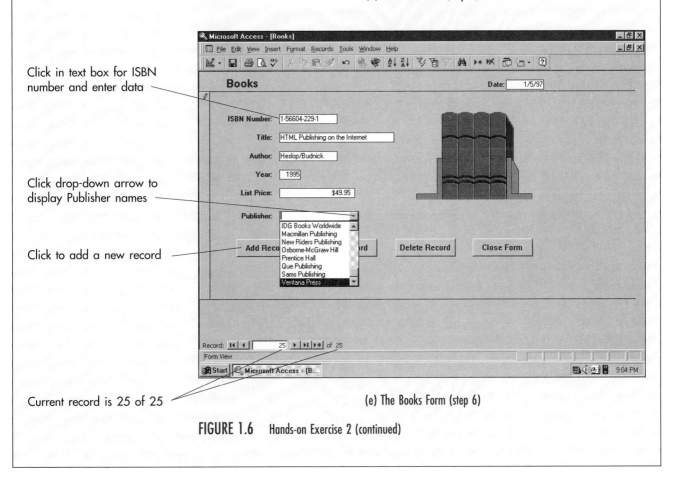

Click in text box for ISBN number and enter data

Click drop-down arrow to display Publisher names

Click to add a new record

Current record is 25 of 25

(e) The Books Form (step 6)

FIGURE 1.6   Hands-on Exercise 2 (continued)

STEP 7: The Replace Command

➤ Pull down the **View menu.** Click **Datasheet** to switch from the Form view to the Datasheet view to display the table on which the form is based.

➤ Press **Ctrl+Home** to move to the first record in the Books table, then click in the **Publisher field** for that record. Pull down the **Edit menu.** Click **Replace** to display the dialog box in Figure 1.6f.

➤ Enter the parameters as they appear in Figure 1.6f, then click the **Find Next button** to move to the first occurrence of Prentice-Hall.

➤ Click **Replace** to make the substitution in this record and move to the next occurrence.

➤ Click **Replace** to make the second (and last) substitution, then close the dialog box when Access no longer finds the search string.

➤ Click the **Close button** to close the table.

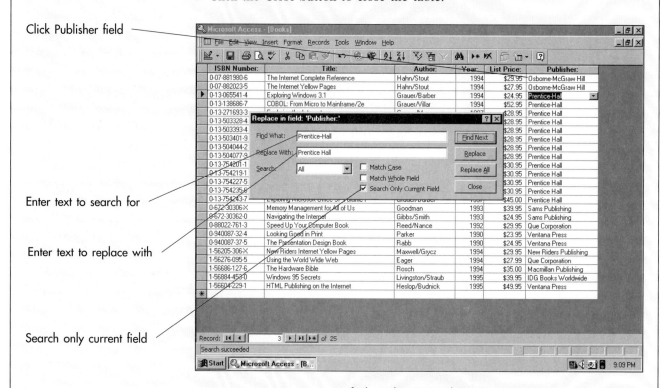

Click Publisher field

Enter text to search for

Enter text to replace with

Search only current field

(f) The Replace Command (step 7)

FIGURE 1.6   Hands-on Exercise 2 (continued)

THE COMMON USER INTERFACE

Ctrl+Home and Ctrl+End are keyboard shortcuts that apply universally to virtually every Windows application and move to the beginning and end of a document, respectively. Microsoft Access is no exception. Press Ctrl+Home to move to the first field in the first record of a table. Press Ctrl+End to move to the last field in the last record. Press Home and End to move to the first and last fields in the current record, respectively. Other common shortcuts you may find useful are Ctrl+X, Ctrl+C, and Ctrl+V to cut, copy, and paste, respectively.

STEP 8: Run a Query

➤ Click the **Queries tab** in the Database window. Double click the **Publisher query** to run the query.

➤ You will see the Enter Parameter Value dialog box in Figure 1.6g. Type **Prentice Hall**, then press **enter** to see the results of the query, which should contain 13 books by Prentice Hall. (If you do not see all of the books, it is probably because you failed to replace Prentice-Hall with Prentice Hall in step 7.)

➤ Click the **Close button** to close the query, which returns you to the Database window.

Click Queries tab

Double click Publisher query

Enter Prentice Hall

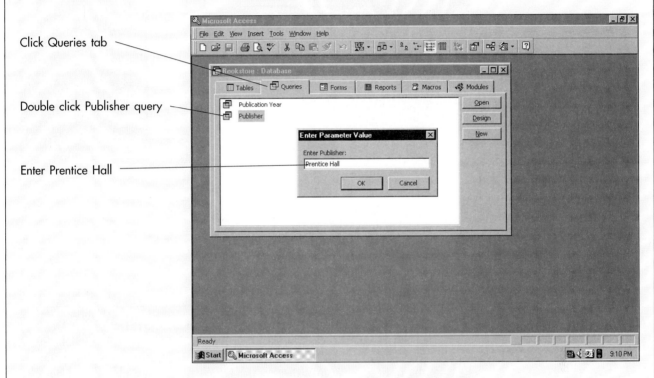

(g) Run a Query (step 8)

FIGURE 1.6 Hands-on Exercise 2 (continued)

STEP 9: Print a Report

➤ Click the **Reports tab** in the Database window to display the available reports.

➤ Double click the icon for the **Publisher report.** Type **Prentice Hall** (or the name of any other publisher) in the Parameter dialog box. Press **enter** to create the report.

➤ If necessary, click the **Maximize button** in the Report Window so that the report takes the entire screen as shown in Figure 1.6h.

➤ Click the **arrow** on the Zoom box on the Report toolbar, then click **Fit** to display the whole page. Note that all of the books in the report are published by Prentice Hall, which is consistent with the parameter you entered earlier.

➤ Click the **Print button** on the Report toolbar.

➤ Click the **Close Window button** to close the Report window.

Print button ——————

Click down arrow
on Zoom box ——————

Close Window button ——————

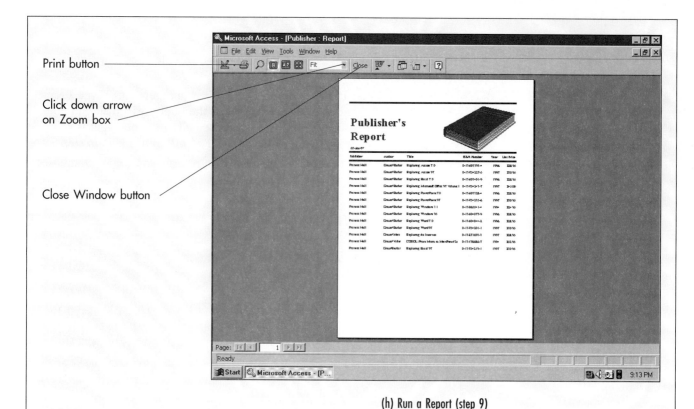

(h) Run a Report (step 9)

FIGURE 1.6   Hands-on Exercise 2 (continued)

TIP OF THE DAY

You can set the Office Assistant to greet you with a "Tip of the Day" whenever you start Access. If the Office Assistant is not visible, click the Office Assistant button on the Standard toolbar to start the Assistant, then click the options button to display the Office Assistant dialog box. Check the Show the Tip of the Day at startup box, then click OK. The next time you start Access, the Assistant will greet you with a tip of the day.

STEP 10: The Office Assistant

➤ Click the **Office Assistant button** on the Standard toolbar to display the Office Assistant. (You may see a different character than the one we have selected.)

➤ Enter your question, for example, **What is a table** as shown in Figure 1.6i, then click the **Search button** to look for the answer.

➤ The size of the dialog box expands as the Assistant suggests several topics that may be appropriate to answer your question.

➤ Click the topic **Tables: What they are and how they work** to display a help screen that reviews (and extends) much of the material in this chapter.

➤ There are three help screens in this topic, each of which contains several graphic elements. You go from one screen to the next by clicking the number (1, 2, or 3) at the upper left of the Help Window.

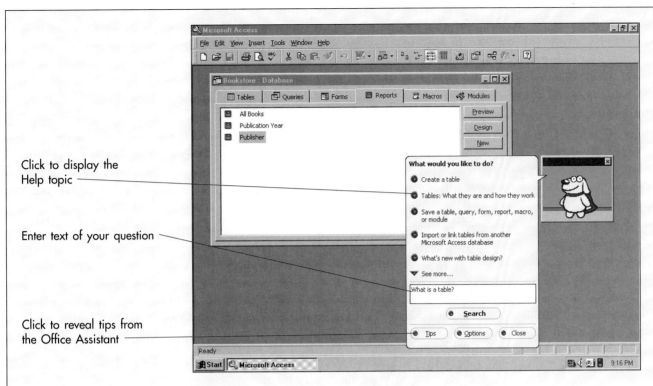

Click to display the
Help topic

Enter text of your question

Click to reveal tips from
the Office Assistant

(i) The Office Assistant (step 10)

FIGURE 1.6 Hands-on Exercise 2 (continued)

➤ These help screens also contain a series of screen tips (indicated by a red border). Point to any tip (the mouse pointer changes to a hand), then click to display additional information.

➤ Continue to read the help screen(s), then close the Help Window.

ADVICE FROM THE OFFICE ASSISTANT

The Office Assistant indicates it has a suggestion by displaying a lightbulb. Click the lightbulb to display the tip, then click the Back or Next buttons as appropriate to view additional tips. The Assistant will not, however, repeat a tip from an earlier session unless you reset it at the start of a new session. To reset the tips, click the Assistant to display a balloon asking what you want to do, click the Options button in the balloon, click the Options tab, then click the button to Reset My Tips.

STEP 11: Exit Access

➤ Pull down the **File menu.** Click **Exit** to close the Bookstore database and also exit from Access.

➤ Remember to use the Windows Explorer to copy the Bookstore database from drive C to a floppy disk that you will keep as backup.

A database consists of multiple tables that are related to each other. Each table in the database is composed of records, and each record is in turn composed of fields. Every record in a given table has the same fields in the same order.

An Access database has six types of objects—tables, forms, queries, reports, macros, and modules. The database window displays these objects and enables you to open an existing object or create a new object.

A table is displayed in one of two views—the Design view or the Datasheet view. The Design view is used to define the table initially and to specify the fields it will contain. The Datasheet view is the view you use to add, edit, or delete records.

A record selector symbol is displayed next to the current record and signifies the status of that record. A triangle indicates that the record has been saved. A pencil indicates that the record has not been saved and that you are in the process of entering (or changing) the data. An asterisk appears next to the blank record present at the end of every table, where you add a new record to the table.

Access automatically saves any changes in the current record as soon as you move to the next record or when you close the table. The Undo Current Record command cancels (undoes) the changes to the previously saved record.

No system, no matter how sophisticated, can produce valid output from invalid input. Data validation is thus a critical part of any system. Access automatically imposes certain types of data validation during data entry. Additional checks can be implemented by the user.

The Office Assistant is new to Office 97 and is activated by clicking the Office Assistant button on the Standard toolbar, by pulling down the Help menu and requesting Word help, or by pressing the F1 function key. The Assistant enables you to ask a question in English, then it returns a series of topics that attempt to answer your question.

KEY WORDS AND CONCEPTS

Asterisk (record selector) symbol	Find command	Query
	Form	Record
AutoCorrect	GIGO (garbage in, garbage out)	Record selector symbol
Current record		Relational database
Data validation	Insertion point	Replace command
Database	Macro	Report
Database window	Microsoft Access	Table
Datasheet view	Module	Triangle (record selector) symbol
Design view	Pencil (record selector) symbol	Undo command
Field		
Field name	Primary key	

PRACTICE WITH ACCESS 97

1. Do the two hands-on exercises in the chapter, then modify the Bookstore database to accommodate the following:
   a. Add the book *Welcome to CompuServe* (ISBN: 1-55828-353-6), written by Banks, published in 1994 by MIS Press, and selling for $24.95.

b. Change the price of *Memory Management for All of Us* to $29.95.

c. Delete *The Presentation Design Book*.

d. Print the *All Books Report* after these changes have been made.

2. The table in Figure 1.7 exists within the Employee database on the data disk. Open the table and do the following:

a. Add a new record for yourself. You have been hired as a trainee earning $25,000 in Boston.

b. Delete the record for Kelly Marder.

c. Change Pamela Milgrom's salary to $59,500.

d. Use the Replace command to change all occurrences of "Manager" to "Supervisor".

e. Print the table after making the changes in parts a through d.

f. Print the Employee Census Report after making the changes in parts a through d.

g. Create a cover page (in Microsoft Word), then submit the output from parts e and f to your instructor.

Employees : Table

SocialSecurityNumber	LastName	FirstName	Location	Title	Salary	Sex
000-01-0000	Milgrom	Pamela	Boston	Manager	$57,500.00	F
000-02-2222	Adams	Jennifer	Atlanta	Trainee	$19,500.00	F
111-12-1111	Johnson	James	Chicago	Account Rep	$47,500.00	M
123-45-6789	Coulter	Tracey	Atlanta	Manager	$100,000.00	F
222-23-2222	Marlin	Billy	Miami	Manager	$125,000.00	M
222-52-5555	James	Mary	Chicago	Account Rep	$42,500.00	F
333-34-3333	Manin	Ann	Boston	Account Rep	$49,500.00	F
333-43-4444	Smith	Frank	Atlanta	Account Rep	$65,000.00	M
333-66-1234	Brown	Marietta	Atlanta	Trainee	$18,500.00	F
444-45-4444	Frank	Vernon	Miami	Manager	$75,000.00	M
555-22-3333	Rubin	Patricia	Boston	Account Rep	$45,000.00	F
555-56-5555	Charles	Kenneth	Boston	Account Rep	$40,000.00	M
776-67-6666	Adamson	David	Chicago	Manager	$52,000.00	M
777-78-7777	Marder	Kelly	Chicago	Account Rep	$38,500.00	F

Record: 1 of 14

FIGURE 1.7 Screen for Practice Exercise 2

3. Figure 1.8 displays a table from the United States (USA) database that is one of our practice files. The database contains statistical data about all 50 states and enables you to produce various reports such as the 10 largest states in terms of population.

a. Open the USA database, then open the USstates table. Click anywhere in the Population field, then click the Sort Descending button to list the states in descending order. Click and drag to select the first ten records so that you have selected the ten most populous states.

b. Pull down the File menu, click the Print command, then click the option button to print the selected records. Be sure to print in Landscape mode so that all of the data fits on one page. (Use the Page Setup command in the File menu prior to printing.)

c. Repeat the procedure in steps a and b, but this time print the ten states with the largest area.

d. Repeat the procedure once again to print the first thirteen states admitted to the Union. (You have to sort in ascending rather than descending sequence.)

e. Submit all three pages together with a title page (created in Microsoft Word) to your instructor.

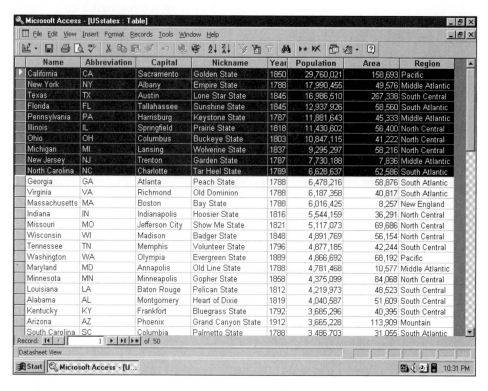

FIGURE 1.8   Screen for Practice Exercise 3

4. Filtering and Sorting: A filter is a set of criteria that is applied to a table in order to display a subset of that table. Access has four types of filters, the easiest of which, Filter by Selection, is illustrated in Figure 1.9.

a. Open the Super Bowl database on the data disk and display the table in Figure 1.9. Our data stops with the 1996 Super Bowl and is no longer current. Thus, the first thing you need to do is update our table.

b. Pull down the View menu, click Toolbars, then toggle the Web toolbar on. Enter the address of the NFL home page (www.nfl.com) in the Address bar, then click the link to the Super Bowl. Follow the links that will allow you to determine the teams and score of any game(s) not included in our table.

c. Click the New Record button and enter the additional data in the table. The additional data will be entered at the end of the table, and hence you need to sort the data after it is entered. Click anywhere in the Year field, then click the Descending Sort button to display the most recent Super Bowl first.

d. Select the winner in any year (e.g., NFC in 1996 as shown in Figure 1.9). Click the Filter by Selection button to display only those records (i.e., the years in which the NFC won the game). Print these records.

e. Click the Remove Filter button. Select any year in which the AFC won, then click the Filter by Selection button to display the years in which the AFC won. Print these records. Remove the filter.

f. Create one additional filter (e.g., the years in which your team won the big game). Print these records as well.

g. Create a cover sheet, then submit all three reports to your instructor.

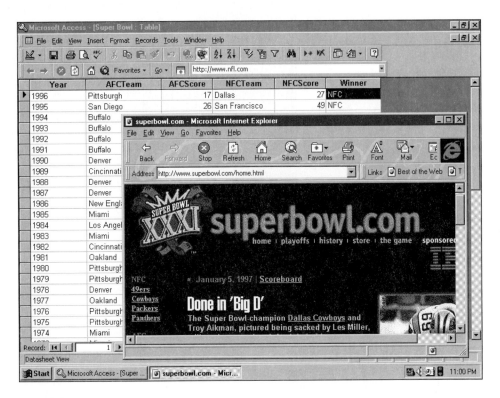

FIGURE 1.9 Screen for Practice Exercise 4

5. This problem is different from the other exercises in that it does not require you to work with a specific database. Instead, we ask you to use the Help facility to review the conceptual information in the chapter.

a. Start the Office Assistant and ask the question, "What is a database?" Select the topic, "Databases: What they are and how they work", to display the screen in Figure 1.10

b. Click the numbers in the upper left corner to read the additional help pages as shown on the screen of Figure 1.10. This will review (and extend) the information about a relational database that was presented at the end of the chapter. The help topic contains a total of seven screens, all of which present helpful information.

c. Was this a useful review? Did you learn anything new that was not covered directly in the chapter? Bring your comments to the next class to discuss your impression with your instructor and classmates.

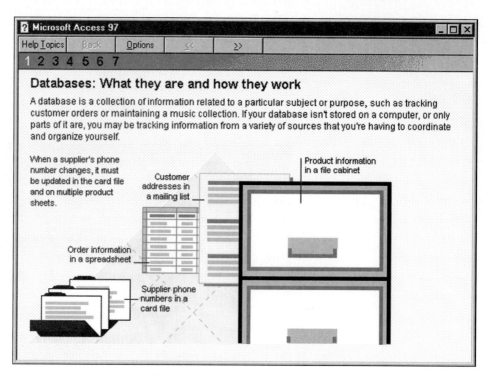

FIGURE 1.10   Screen for Practice Exercise 5

TABLES AND FORMS: DESIGN, PROPERTIES, VIEWS, AND WIZARDS

2

OBJECTIVES

After reading this chapter you will be able to:

1. Describe in general terms how to design a table; discuss three guidelines you can use in the design process.
2. Describe the data types and properties available within Access and the purpose of each; set the primary key for a table.
3. Use the Table Wizard to create a table; add and delete fields in an existing table.
4. Discuss the importance of data validation and how it is implemented in Access.
5. Use the Form Wizard to create one of several predefined forms.
6. Distinguish between a bound control, an unbound control, and a calculated control; explain how each type of control is entered on a form.
7. Modify an existing form to include a combo box, command buttons, and color.
8. Switch between the Form view, Design view, and Datasheet view; use a form to add, edit, and delete records in a table.

OVERVIEW

This chapter introduces a new case study, that of a student database, which we use to present the basic principles of table and form design. Tables and forms are used to input data into a system from which information can be produced. The value of that information depends entirely on the quality of the underlying data, which must be both complete and accurate. We begin, therefore, with a conceptual discussion emphasizing the importance of proper design and develop essential guidelines that are used throughout the book.

After the design has been developed, we turn our attention to implementing that design in Access. We show you how to create a table using the Table Wizard, then show you how to refine its design by changing the properties of various fields within the table. We also stress the importance of data validation during data entry.

The second half of the chapter introduces forms as a more convenient way to enter and display data. We introduce the Form Wizard to create a basic form, then show you how to modify that form to include command buttons, a list box, a check box, and an option group.

As always, the hands-on exercises in the chapter enable you to apply the conceptual material at the computer. This chapter contains three exercises, after which you will be well on your way toward creating a useful database in Access.

CASE STUDY: A STUDENT DATABASE

As a student you are well aware that your school maintains all types of data about you. They have your social security number. They have your name and address and phone number. They know whether or not you are receiving financial aid. They know your major and the number of credits you have completed.

Think for a moment about the information your school requires, then write down all of the data needed to produce that information. This is the key to the design process. You must visualize the output the end user will require to determine the input to produce that output. Think of the specific fields you will need. Try to characterize each field according to the type of data it contains (such as text, numbers, or dates) as well as its size (length).

Our solution is shown in Figure 2.1, which may or may not correspond to what you have written down. The order of the fields within the table is not significant. Neither are the specific field names. What is important is that the table contain all necessary fields so that the system can perform as intended.

Field Name	Type
SSN	Text
FirstName	Text
LastName	Text
Address	Text
City	Text
State	Text
PostalCode	Text
PhoneNumber	Text
Major	Text
BirthDate	Date/Time
FinancialAid	Yes/No
Gender	Text
Credits	Number
QualityPoints	Number

FIGURE 2.1   The Students Table

Figure 2.1 may seem obvious upon presentation, but it does reflect the results of a careful design process based on three essential guidelines:

1. Include all of the necessary data
2. Store data in its smallest parts
3. Do not use calculated fields

Each guideline is discussed in turn. As you proceed through the text, you will be exposed to many applications that help you develop the experience necessary to design your own systems.

Include the Necessary Data

How do you determine the necessary data? The best way is to create a rough draft of the reports you will need, then design the table so that it contains the fields necessary to create those reports. In other words, ask yourself what information will be expected from the system, then determine the data required to produce that information.

Consider, for example, the type of information that can and cannot be produced from the table in Figure 2.1:

- You can contact a student by mail or by telephone. You cannot, however, contact the student's parents if the student lives on campus or has an address different from his or her parents.
- You can calculate a student's grade point average (GPA) by dividing the quality points by the number of credits. You cannot produce a transcript listing the courses a student has taken.
- You can calculate a student's age from his or her date of birth. You cannot determine how long the student has been at the university because the date of admission is not in the table.

Whether or not these omissions are important depends on the objectives of the system. Suffice it to say that you must design a table carefully, so that you are not disappointed when it is implemented. *You must be absolutely certain that the data entered into a system is sufficient to provide all necessary information;* otherwise the system is almost guaranteed to fail.

DESIGN FOR THE NEXT 100 YEARS

Your system will not last 100 years, but it is prudent to design as though it will. It is a fundamental law of information technology that systems evolve continually and that information requirements will change. Try to anticipate the future needs of the system, then build in the flexibility to satisfy those demands. Include the necessary data at the outset and be sure that the field sizes are large enough to accommodate future expansion.

Store Data in Its Smallest Parts

Figure 2.1 divides a student's name into two fields (first name and last name) to reference each field individually. You might think it easier to use a single field consisting of both the first and last name, but that approach is inadequate. Consider, for example, the following list in which the student's name is stored as a single field:

Allison Foster
Brit Reback
Carrie Graber
Danielle Ferrarro

The first problem in this approach is one of flexibility, in that you cannot separate a student's first name from her last name. You could not, for example, create a salutation of the form "Dear Allison" or "Dear Ms. Foster" because the first and last name are not accessible individually.

A second difficulty is that the list of students cannot be put into alphabetical order because the last name begins in the middle of the field. Indeed, whether you realize it or not, the names in the list are already in alphabetical order (according to the design criteria of a single field) because sorting always begins with the leftmost position in a field. Thus the "A" in Allison comes before the "B" in Brit, and so on. The proper way to sort a file is on the last name, which can be done only if the last name is stored as a separate field.

CITY, STATE, AND ZIP CODE: ONE FIELD OR THREE?

The city, state, and zip code should always be stored as separate fields. Any type of mass mailing requires you to sort on zip code to take advantage of bulk mail. Other applications may require you to select records from a particular state or zip code, which can be done only if the data is stored as separate fields. The guideline is simple—store data in its smallest parts.

Avoid Calculated Fields

A *calculated field* is a field whose value is derived from a formula or function that references an existing field or combination of fields. Calculated fields should not be stored in a table because they are subject to change, waste space, and are otherwise redundant.

The Grade Point Average (GPA) is an example of a calculated field as it is computed by dividing the number of quality points by the number of credits. It is both unnecessary and undesirable to store GPA in the Students table, because the table contains the fields on which the GPA is based. In other words, Access is able to calculate the GPA from these fields whenever it is needed, which is much more efficient than doing it manually. Imagine, for example, having to manually recalculate the GPA for 10,000 students each semester.

BIRTHDATE VERSUS AGE

A person's age and date of birth provide equivalent information, as one is calculated from the other. It might seem easier, therefore, to store the age rather than the birth date, and thus avoid the calculation. That would be a mistake because age changes continually (and would need to be updated continually), whereas the date of birth remains constant. Similar reasoning applies to an employee's length of service versus date of hire.

There are two ways to create a table. The easier way is to use the **Table Wizard,** an interactive coach that lets you choose from several predefined tables. The Table Wizard asks you questions about the fields you want to include in your table, then creates the table for you. Alternatively, you can create a table yourself by defining every field in the table. Regardless of how a table is created, you can modify it to include a new field or to delete an existing field.

Every field has a **field name** to identify the data that is entered into the field. The field name should be descriptive of the data and can be up to 64 characters in length, including letters, numbers, and spaces. We do not, however, use spaces in our field names, but use uppercase letters to distinguish the first letter of a new word. This is consistent with the default names provided by Access in its predefined tables.

Every field also has a **data type** that determines the type of data that can be entered and the operations that can be performed on that data. Access recognizes nine data types: Number, Text, Memo, Date/Time, Currency, Yes/No, OLE Object, AutoNumber, and Hyperlink.

- A **Number field** contains a value that can be used in a calculation such as the number of quality points or credits a student has earned. The contents of a number field are restricted to numbers, a decimal point, and a plus or minus sign.
- A **Text field** stores alphanumeric data such as a student's name or address. It can contain alphabetic characters, numbers, and/or special characters (e.g., an apostrophe in O'Malley). Fields that contain only numbers but are not used in a calculation (e.g., social security number, telephone number, or zip code) should be designated as text fields for efficiency purposes. A text field can hold up to 255 characters.
- A **Memo field** can be up to 64,000 characters long. Memo fields are used to hold descriptive data (several sentences or paragraphs).
- A **Date/Time field** holds formatted dates or times (e.g., mm/dd/yy) and allows the values to be used in date or time arithmetic.
- A **Currency field** can be used in a calculation and is used for fields that contain monetary values.
- A **Yes/No field** (also known as a Boolean or Logical field) assumes one of two values such as Yes or No, or True or False.
- An **OLE field** contains an object created by another application. OLE objects include pictures, sounds, or graphics.
- An **AutoNumber field** is a special data type that causes Access to assign the next consecutive number each time you add a record. The value of an AutoNumber field is unique for each record in the file, and thus AutoNumber fields are frequently used as the primary key.
- A **Hyperlink field** stores a Web address (URL). All Office 97 documents are Web-enabled so that you can click a hyperlink within an Access database and display the associated Web page, provided that you have access to the Internet.

Primary Key

The **primary key** is a field (or combination of fields) that uniquely identifies a record. There can be only one primary key per table and, by definition, every record in the table must have a different value for the primary key.

A person's name is not used as the primary key because names are not unique. A social security number, on the other hand, is unique and is a frequent choice for the primary key as in the Students table in this chapter. The primary key emerges naturally in many applications such as a part number in an inventory system, or the ISBN in the Books table of Chapter 1. If there is no apparent primary key, a new field can be created with the AutoNumber field type.

Views

A table has two views—the Datasheet view and the Design view. The Datasheet view is the view you used in Chapter 1 to add, edit, and delete records. The Design view is the view you will use in this chapter to create (and modify) a table.

Figure 2.2a shows the Datasheet view corresponding to the table in Figure 2.1. (Not all of the fields are visible.) The **Datasheet view** displays the record selector symbol for the current record (a pencil or a triangle). It also displays an asterisk in the record selector column next to the blank record at the end of the table.

Figure 2.2b shows the Design view of the same table. The **Design view** displays the field names in the table, the data type of each field, and the properties of the selected field. The Design view also displays a key indicator next to the field (or combination of fields) designated as the primary key.

Current record

Blank record

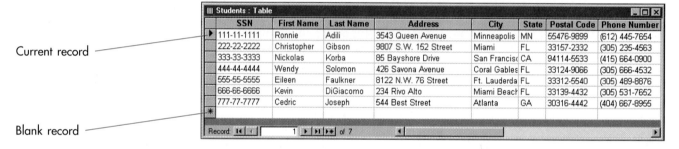

(a) Datasheet View

Key indicates the primary key

Properties of the selected field

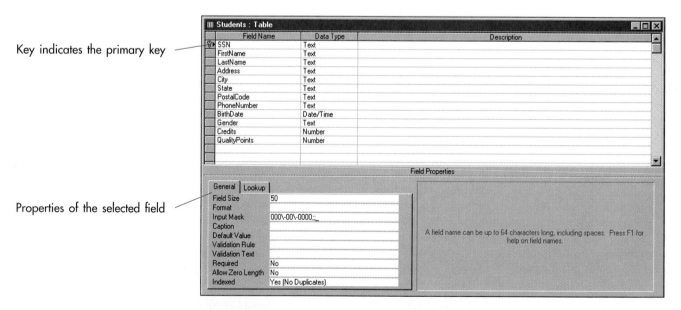

(b) Design View

FIGURE 2.2   The Views of a Table

Properties

A *property* is a characteristic or attribute of an object that determines how the object looks and behaves. Every Access object (tables, forms, queries, and reports) has a set of properties that determine the behavior of that object. The properties for an object are displayed and/or changed in a *property sheet,* which is described in more detail later in the chapter.

Each field has its own set of properties that determine how the data in the field are stored and displayed. The properties are set to default values according to the data type, but can be modified as necessary. The properties are displayed in the Design view and described briefly below:

- The *Field Size property* adjusts the size of a text field or limits the allowable value in a number field. Microsoft Access uses only the amount of space it needs even if the field size allows a greater number.
- The *Format property* changes the way a field is displayed or printed, but does not affect the stored value.
- The *Input Mask property* facilitates data entry by displaying characters, such as hyphens in a social security number or slashes in a date. It also imposes data validation by ensuring that the data entered by the user fits within the mask.
- The *Caption property* specifies a label other than the field name for forms and reports.
- The *Default Value property* automatically assigns a designated (default) value for the field in each record that is added to the table.
- The *Validation Rule property* rejects any record where the data does not conform to the specified rules for data entry.
- The *Validation Text property* specifies the error message that is displayed when the validation rule is violated.
- The *Required property* rejects any record that does not have a value entered for this field.
- The *Allow Zero Length property* allows text or memo strings of zero length.
- The *Indexed property* increases the efficiency of a search on the designated field. (The primary key in a table is always indexed.)

The following exercise has you create a table using the Table Wizard and then modify the table by including additional fields. It also has you change the properties for various fields within the table.

CHANGE THE DEFAULT FOLDER

The default folder is the folder Access uses to retrieve (and save) a database unless it is otherwise instructed. To change the default folder, pull down the Tools menu, click Options, then click the General tab in the Options dialog box. Enter the name of the default database folder (e.g., C:\Exploring Access), then click OK to accept the settings and close the Options dialog box. The next time you access the File menu the default folder will reflect the change.

Creating a Table

Objective: To use the Table Wizard to create a table; to add and delete fields in an existing table; to change the primary key of an existing table; to establish an input mask and validation rule for fields within a table; to switch between the Design and Datasheet views of a table. Use Figure 2.3 as a guide.

STEP 1: Create a New Database

➤ Click the **Start button** to display the Start menu. Click (or point to) the **Programs menu,** then click **Microsoft Access** to start the program.

➤ You should see the Microsoft Access dialog box. Click the option button to create a new database using a **Blank Database.** Click **OK.** You should see the File New Database dialog box shown in Figure 2.3a.

➤ Click the **Details button** to change to the Details view. Click and drag the vertical border between columns to change the size of a column.

➤ Click the **drop-down arrow** on the Save In list box. Click the appropriate drive (e.g., drive C), depending on the location of your data. Double click the **Exploring Access folder** to make it the active folder.

➤ Click in the **File Name text box** and drag to select **db1.** Type **My First Database** as the name of the database you will create. Click the **Create button.**

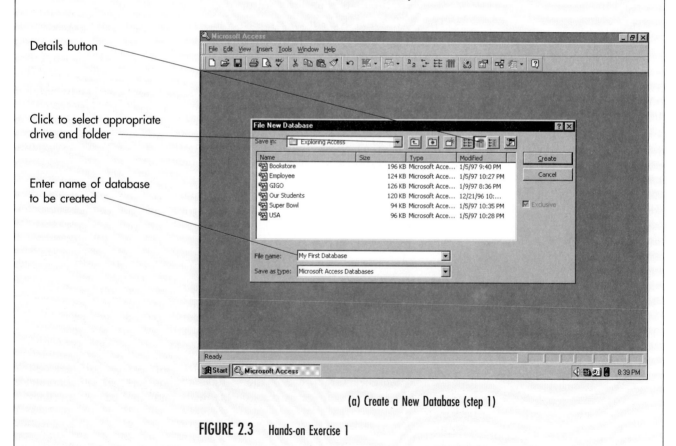

Details button

Click to select appropriate drive and folder

Enter name of database to be created

(a) Create a New Database (step 1)

FIGURE 2.3 Hands-on Exercise 1

STEP 2: Create the Table

➤ The Database window for My First Database should appear on your monitor. The **Tables tab** is selected by default.

➤ Click and drag an edge or border of the Database window to change its size to match that in Figure 2.3b. Click and drag the title bar of the Database window to change its position on the desktop.

➤ Click the **New command button** to display the New Table dialog box shown in Figure 2.3b. Click (select) **Table Wizard** in the New Table dialog box, then click **OK** to start the Table Wizard.

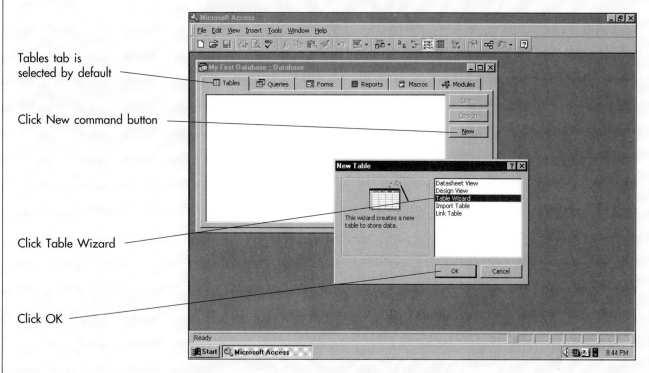

Tables tab is selected by default

Click New command button

Click Table Wizard

Click OK

(b) The Table Wizard (step 2)

FIGURE 2.3   Hands-on Exercise 1 (continued)

STEP 3: The Table Wizard

➤ If necessary, click the **Business option button.** Click the **down arrow** on the **Sample Tables list box** to scroll through the available business tables. Click (select) **Students** within the list of sample tables. The tables are *not* in alphabetical order, and the Students table is found near the very bottom of the list.

➤ The **StudentID field** is already selected in the Sample Fields list box. Click the > **button** to enter this field in the list of fields for the new table as shown in Figure 2.3c.

➤ Enter the additional fields for the new table by selecting the field and clicking the > **button** (or by double clicking the field). The fields to enter are: **FirstName, LastName, Address, City,** and **StateOrProvince** as shown in the figure.

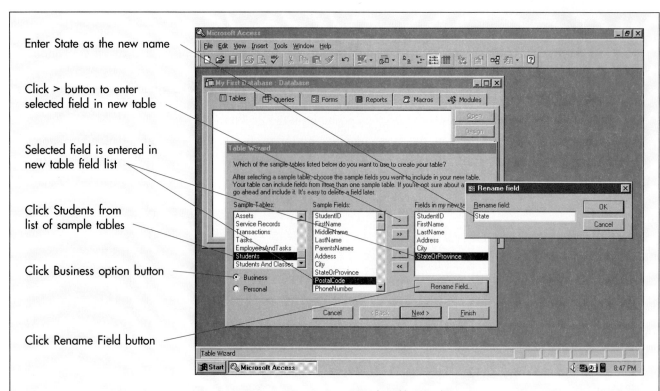

Enter State as the new name

Click > button to enter selected field in new table

Selected field is entered in new table field list

Click Students from list of sample tables

Click Business option button

Click Rename Field button

(c) The Table Wizard (step 3)

FIGURE 2.3   Hands-on Exercise 1 (continued)

➤ Click the **Rename Field command button** after adding the StateOrProvince field to display the Rename Field dialog box. Enter **State** to shorten the name of this field. Click **OK.**

➤ Add **PostalCode** and **PhoneNumber** as the last two fields in the table. Click the **Next command button** when you have entered all the fields.

WIZARDS AND BUTTONS

Many Wizards present you with two open list boxes and expect you to copy some or all fields from the list box on the left to the list box on the right. The > and >> buttons work from left to right. The < and << buttons work in the opposite direction. The > button copies the selected field from the list box on the left to the box on the right. The >> button copies all of the fields. The < button removes the selected field from the list box on the right. The << removes all of the fields.

STEP 4: The Table Wizard (continued)

➤ The next screen in the Table Wizard asks you to name the table and determine the primary key.

• Accept the Wizard's suggestion of **Students** as the name of the table.

• Make sure that the option button **Yes, set a primary key for me** is selected.

• Click the **Next command button** to accept both of these options.

➤ The final screen in the Table Wizard asks what you want to do next.
  - Click the option button to **Modify the table design.**
  - Click the **Finish command button.** The Students table should appear on your monitor.
➤ Pull down the **File menu** and click **Save** (or click the **Save button** on the Table Design toolbar) to save the table.

STEP 5: Add the Additional Fields

➤ Click the **Maximize button** to give yourself more room to work. Click the cell immediately below the last field in the table (PhoneNumber). Type **Birth-Date** as shown in Figure 2.3d.
➤ Press the **Tab key** to move to the Data Type column. Click the **down arrow** on the drop-down list box. Click **Date/Time** as the data type for the Birth-Date field.
➤ Add the remaining fields with the indicated data types to the Students table:
  - Add **Gender** as a Text field.
  - Add **Credits** as a Number field.
  - Add **QualityPoints** as a Number field. (There is no space in the field name.)
➤ Save the table.

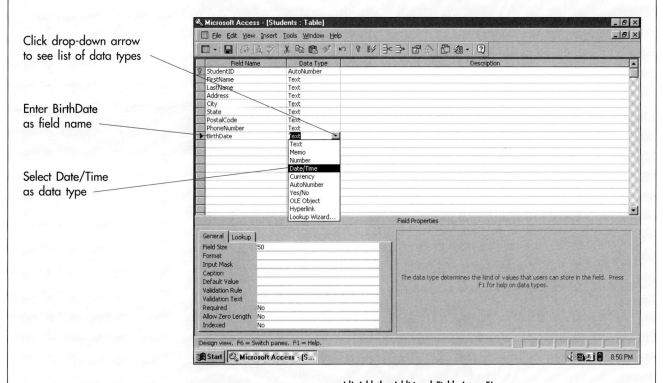

(d) Add the Additional Fields (step 5)

FIGURE 2.3   Hands-on Exercise 1 (continued)

CHOOSING A DATA TYPE

The fastest way to specify the data type is to type the first letter—T for Text, D for Date, N for Number, and Y for Yes/No. Text is the default data type and is entered automatically.

STEP 6: Change the Primary Key

➤ Point to the first row of the table and click the **right mouse button** to display the shortcut menu in Figure 2.3e. Click **Insert Rows.**

➤ Click the **Field Name column** in the newly inserted row. Type **SSN** (for social security number) as the name of the new field. Press **enter.** The data type will be set to Text by default.

➤ Click the **Required box** in the Properties area. Click the drop-down arrow and select **Yes.**

➤ Click in the Field Name column for **SSN,** then click the **Primary Key button** on the Table Design toolbar to change the primary key to social security number. The primary key symbol has moved from the StudentID field to SSN.

➤ Point to the **StudentID field** in the second row. Click the **right mouse button** to display the shortcut menu. Click **Delete Rows** to remove this field from the table definition.

➤ Save the table.

Point to first row and click right mouse button to display the shortcut menu

Click Insert Rows

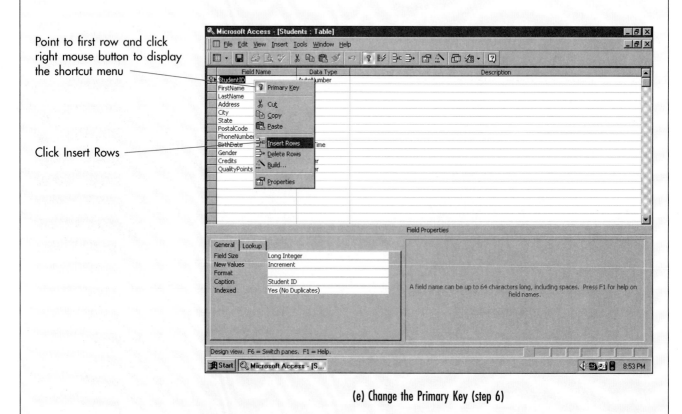

(e) Change the Primary Key (step 6)

FIGURE 2.3 Hands-on Exercise 1 (continued)

INSERTING OR DELETING FIELDS

To insert or delete a field, point to an existing field, then click the right mouse button to display a shortcut menu. Click Insert Row or Delete Row to add or remove a field as appropriate. To insert (or delete) multiple fields, point to the field selector to the left of the field name, click and drag the mouse over multiple rows to extend the selection, then click the right mouse button to display a shortcut menu.

STEP 7: Add an Input Mask

➤ Click the field selector column for **SSN.** Click the **Input Mask box** in the Properties area. (The box is currently empty.)

➤ Click the **Build button** to display the Input Mask Wizard. Click **Social Security Number** in the Input Mask Wizard dialog box as shown in Figure 2.3f.

➤ Click the **Try It** text box and enter a social security number to see how the mask works. If necessary, press the **left arrow key** until you are at the beginning of the text box, then enter a social security number (digits only). Click the **Finish command button** to accept the input mask.

➤ Click the field selector column for **BirthDate,** then follow the steps detailed above to add an input mask. (Choose the **Short Date** format.) Click **Yes** if asked whether to save the table.

➤ Save the table.

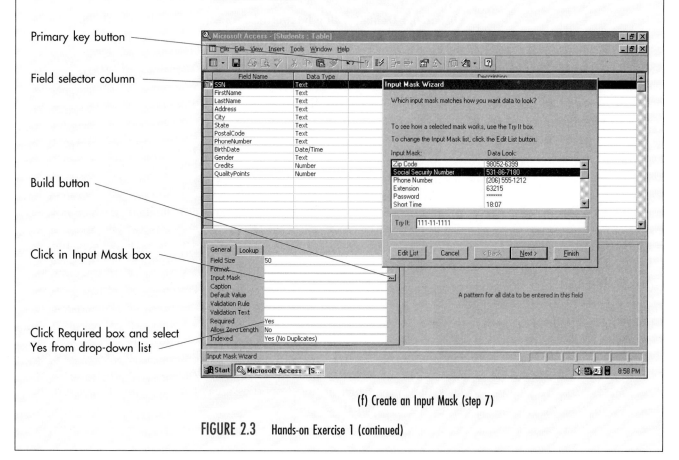

(f) Create an Input Mask (step 7)

FIGURE 2.3   Hands-on Exercise 1 (continued)

STEP 8: Change the Field Properties

➤ Click the field selector column for the **FirstName** field:
- Click the **Field Size box** in the Properties area and change the field size to **25.** (You can press the F6 key to toggle between the field name and the Properties area.)
- Click the **Required box** in the Properties area. Click the **drop-down arrow** and select **Yes.**

➤ Click the field selector column for the **LastName** field:
- Click the **Field Size box** in the Properties area. Change the field size to **25.**
- Click the **Required box** in the Properties area. Click the **drop-down arrow** and select **Yes.**

➤ Click the field selector column for the **State** field.
- Click the **Field Size box** in the Properties area and change the field size to **2,** corresponding to the accepted abbreviation for a state.
- Click the **Format box** in the Properties area. Type a **> sign** to convert the data to uppercase.

➤ Click the field selector column for the **Credits** field:
- Click the **Field Size box** in the Properties area, click the **drop-down arrow** to display the available field sizes, then click **Integer.**
- Click the **Default Value box** in the Properties area. Delete the **0.**

➤ Click the field selector column for the **QualityPoints** field:
- Click the **Field Size box** in the Properties area, click the **drop-down arrow** to display the available field sizes, then click **Integer.**
- Click the **Default Value box** in the Properties area. Delete the **0.**

➤ Save the table.

THE FIELD SIZE PROPERTY

The field size property for a Text or Number field determines the maximum number of characters that can be stored in that field. The property should be set to the smallest possible setting because smaller data sizes are processed more efficiently. A text field can hold from 0 to 255 characters (50 is the default). Number fields (which do not contain a decimal value) can be set to Byte, Integer, or Long Integer field sizes, which hold values up to 255, or 32,767, or 2,147,483,647, respectively. The Single or Double sizes are required if the field is to contain a decimal value, as they specify the precision with which a value will be stored. (See online Help for details.)

STEP 9: Add a Validation Rule

➤ Click the field selector column for the **Gender** field. Click the **Field Size box** and change the field size to **1** as shown in Figure 2.3g.

➤ Click the **Format box** in the Properties area. Type a **> sign** to convert the data entered to uppercase.

➤ Click the **Validation Rule box.** Type **"M" or "F"** to accept only these values on data entry.
➤ Click the **Validation Text box.** Type **You must specify M or F.**
➤ Save the table.

Save button

View button

Click field selector column for Gender

Click Field Size box and enter 1

Click Format box and enter >

Click and enter validation rule

Click and enter validation text

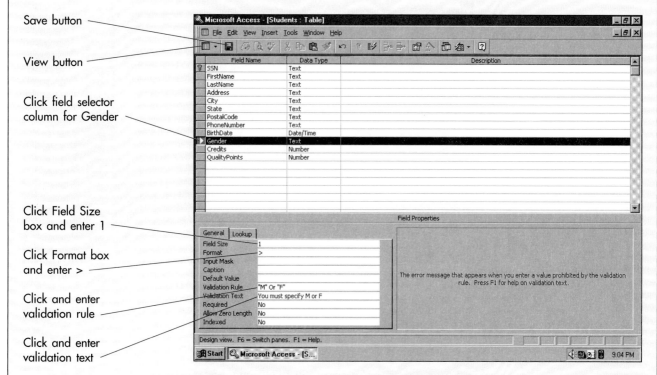

(g) Add a Validation Rule (step 9)

FIGURE 2.3   Hands-on Exercise 1 (continued)

STEP 10: The Datasheet View
➤ Pull down the **View menu** and click **Datasheet View** (or click the **View button** on the toolbar) to change to the Datasheet view as shown in Figure 2.3h.
➤ The insertion point (a flashing vertical line indicating the position where data will be entered) is automatically set to the first field of the first record.
➤ Type **111111111** to enter the social security number for the first record. (The mask will appear as soon as you enter the first digit.)
➤ Press the **Tab key,** the **right arrow key,** or the **enter key** to move to the First-Name field. Enter the data for Ronnie Adili as shown in Figure 2.3h. Make up data for the fields you cannot see.
➤ Scrolling takes place automatically as you move within the record.

CHANGE THE FIELD WIDTH

Drag the border between field names to change the displayed width of a field. Double click the right boundary of a field name to change the width to accommodate the widest entry in that field.

Print button

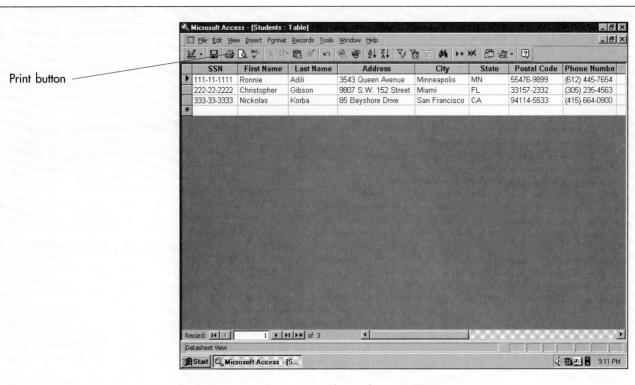

(h) Datasheet View (steps 10 & 11)

FIGURE 2.3   Hands-on Exercise 1 (continued)

STEP 11: Enter Additional Data

➤ Enter data for the two additional students shown in the figure, but enter deliberately invalid data to experiment with the validation capabilities built into Access. Here are some of the errors you may encounter:

- The message, *The value you entered isn't valid for this field,* implies that the data type is wrong—for example, alphabetic characters in a numeric field such as Credits.

- The message, *You must specify M or F,* means you entered a letter other than "M" or "F" in the Gender field (or you didn't enter a value at all).

- The message, *The changes you requested to the table were not successful because they would create duplicate values in the index, primary key, or relationship,* indicates that the value of the primary key is not unique.

- The message, *The field 'Students.LastName' can't contain a Null value,* implies that you left a required field blank.

- If you encounter a data validation error, press **Esc** (or click **OK**), then reenter the data.

STEP 12: Print the Students Table

➤ Pull down the **File menu** and click **Print** (or click the **Print button**). Click the **All option button** to print the entire table. Click **OK.** Do not be concerned if the table prints on multiple pages. (You can, however, use the Page Setup command to change the way the data are printed.)

➤ Pull down the **File menu** and click **Close** to close the Students table. Click **Yes** if asked to save the changes to the table.

➤ Pull down the **File menu** and click the **Close** command to close the database and remain in Access.

➤ Pull down the **File menu** a second time and click **Exit** if you do not want to continue with the next exercise at this time.

THE PAGE SETUP COMMAND

The Page Setup command controls the margins and orientation of the printed page and may enable you to keep all fields for a single record on the same page. Pull down the File menu, click Page Setup, click the Margins tab, then decrease the left and right margins (to .5 inch each) to increase the amount of data that is printed on one line. Be sure to check the box to Print Headings so that the field names appear with the table. Click the Page tab, then click the Landscape option button to change the orientation, which further increases the amount of data printed on one line. Click OK to exit the Page Setup dialog box.

FORMS

A *form* provides an easy way to enter and display the data stored in a table. You type data into a form, such as the one in Figure 2.4, and Access stores the data in the corresponding (underlying) table in the database. One advantage of using a form (as opposed to entering records in the Datasheet view) is that you can see all of the fields in a single record without scrolling. A second advantage is that a form can be designed to resemble a paper form, and thus provide a sense of familiarity for the individuals who actually enter the data.

A form has different views, as does a table. The *Form view* in Figure 2.4a displays the completed form and is used to enter or modify the data in the underlying table. The *Design view* in Figure 2.4b is used to create or modify the form.

Controls

All forms consist of *controls* (objects) that accept and display data, perform a specific action, or add descriptive information. There are three types of controls—bound, unbound, and calculated. A *bound control* (such as the text boxes in Figure 2.4a) has a data source (a field in the underlying table) and is used to enter or modify the data in that table. An *unbound control* has no data source. Unbound controls are used to display titles, labels, lines, graphics, or pictures. Note, too, that every bound control (*text box*) in Figure 2.4a is associated with an unbound control (*label*). The bound control for social security number, for example, is preceded by a label (immediately to the left of the control) that indicates to the user the value that is to be entered.

A *calculated control* has as its data source an expression rather than a field. An *expression* is a combination of operators (e.g., +, −, *, and /), field names, constants, and/or functions. A student's Grade Point Average (GPA in Figure 2.4a) is an example of a calculated control, since it is computed by dividing the number of quality points by the number of credits.

Input mask displays
hyphens automatically

Status bar indicates
record 1 of 4

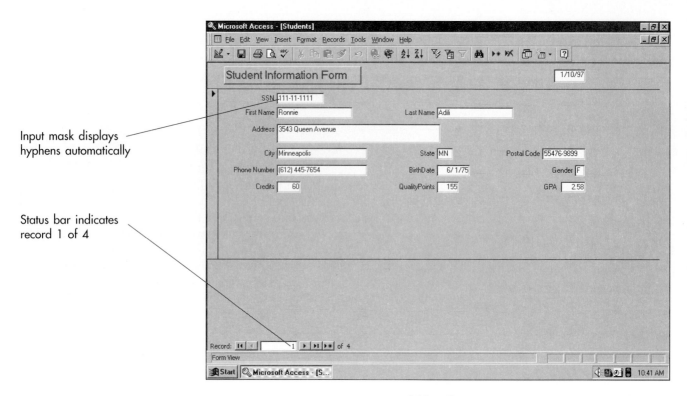

(a) Form View

Bound controls (text boxes)

Unbound controls (labels)

Calculated control (expression)

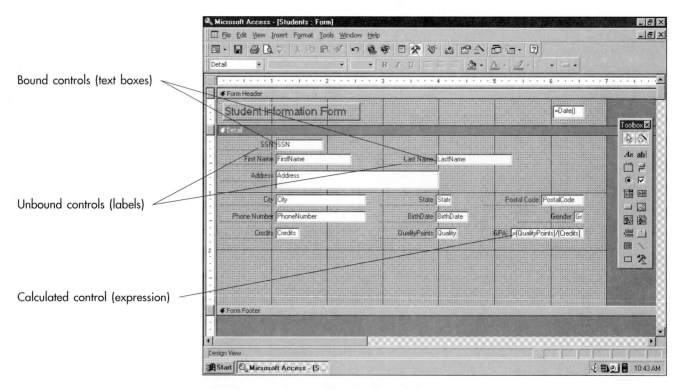

(b) Design View

FIGURE 2.4   Forms

A form is divided into one or more sections. Virtually every form has a detail section to display or enter the records in the underlying table. You can, however, increase the effectiveness or visual appeal of a form by adding a header and/or footer. Either section may contain descriptive information about the form such as a title, instructions for using the form, or a graphic or logo.

Properties

As previously stated, a **property** is a characteristic or attribute of an object that determines how the object looks and behaves. Each control in a form has its own set of properties, just as every field in a table has its own set of properties. The properties for a control are displayed in a **property sheet,** as shown in Figure 2.5.

Figure 2.5a displays the property sheet for the Form Header Label. There are 32 different properties (note the vertical scroll bar) that control every aspect of the label's appearance. The properties are determined automatically as the object is created; that is, as you move and size the label on the form, the properties related to its size and position (Left, Top, Width, and Height in Figure 2.5a) are established for you.

Other actions, such as various formatting commands, set the properties that determine the font name and size (MS Sans Serif and 14 point in Figure 2.5a). You can change the appearance of an object in two ways—by executing a command to change the object on the form, which in turn changes the property sheet, *or* by changing the property within the property sheet, which in turn changes the object's appearance on the form.

Figure 2.5b displays the property sheet for the bound SSN control. The name of the control is SSN. The source for the control is the SSN field in the Students table. Thus, various properties of the SSN control, such as the input mask, are inherited from the SSN field in the underlying table. Note, too, that the list of properties in Figure 2.5b, which reflects a bound control, is different from the list of properties in Figure 2.5a for an unbound control. Some properties, however (such as left, top, width, and height, which determine the size and position of an object), are present for every control and determine its location on the form.

The Form Wizard

The easiest way to create a form is with the **Form Wizard.** The Form Wizard asks a series of questions, then builds a form according to your answers. You can use the form as is, or you can customize it to better suit your needs.

Figure 2.6 displays the New Form dialog box from which you call the Form Wizard. The Form Wizard, in turn, requires that you specify the table or query on which the form will be based. (Queries are discussed in Chapter 3.) The form in this example will be based on the Students table created in the previous exercise. Once you specify the underlying table, you select one or more fields from that table as shown in Figure 2.6b. Each field that is selected is entered automatically on the form as a bound control. The Form Wizard asks you to select a layout (e.g., Columnar in Figure 2.6c) and a style (e.g., Colorful 1 in Figure 2.6d). The Form Wizard then has all of the information it needs, and creates the form for you. You can enter data immediately, or you can modify the form in the Form Design view.

Scroll bar indicates that
more properties exist than
can currently be seen

Properties are set as
object is moved and sized

Properties are determined
as object is formatted

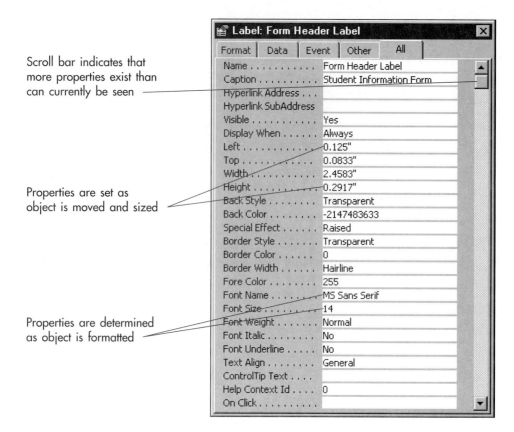

(a) Form Header Label (unbound control)

Name of data source
within underlying table

Properties are inherited
from underlying table

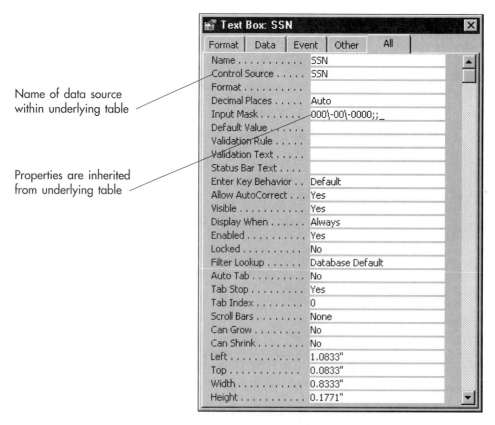

(b) SSN Text Box (bound control)

FIGURE 2.5   Property Sheets

Select underlying table/query

Selected fields for new form

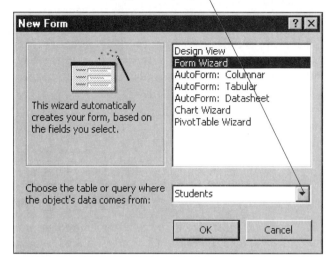

(a) Specify the Underlying Table

(b) Select the Fields

Selected layout

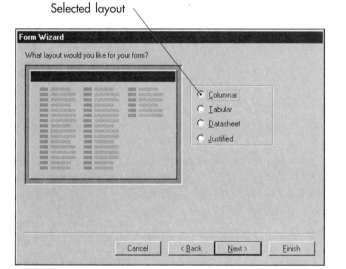

Selected style

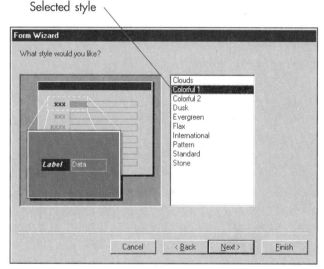

(c) Choose the Layout

(d) Choose the Style

FIGURE 2.6   The Form Wizard

Modifying a Form

The Form Wizard provides an excellent starting point, but you typically need to customize the form by adding other controls (e.g., the calculated control for GPA) and/or by modifying the controls that were created by the Wizard. Each control is treated as an object, and moved or sized like any other Windows object. In essence, you select the control, then click and drag to resize the control or position it elsewhere on the form. You can also change the properties of the control through buttons on the various toolbars or by displaying the property sheet for the control and changing the appropriate property. Consider:

- *To select a bound control and its associated label (an unbound control),* click either the control or the label. If you click the control, the control has sizing handles and a move handle, but the label has only a move handle. If you click the label, the opposite occurs; that is, the label will have both sizing handles and a move handle, but the control will have only a move handle.

- *To size a control,* click the control to select the control and display the sizing handles, then drag the sizing handles in the appropriate direction. Drag the handles on the top or bottom to size the box vertically. Drag the handles on the left or right side to size the box horizontally. Drag the handles in the corner to size both horizontally and vertically.

- *To move a control and its label,* click and drag the border of either object. To move either the control or its label, click and drag the move handle (a tiny square in the upper left corner) of the appropriate object.

- *To change the properties of a control,* point to the control, click the right mouse button to display a shortcut menu, then click Properties to display the property sheet. Click the text box for the desired property, make the necessary change, then close the property sheet.

- *To select multiple controls,* press and hold the Shift key as you click each successive control. The advantage of selecting multiple controls is that you can modify the selected controls at the same time rather than working with them individually.

HANDS-ON EXERCISE 2

Creating a Form

Objective: To use the Form Wizard to create a form; to move and size controls within a form; to use the completed form to enter data into the associated table. Use Figure 2.7 as a guide in the exercise.

STEP 1: Open the Existing Database

➤ Start Access as you did in the previous exercise. Select (click) **My First Database** from the list of recently opened databases, then click **OK.** (Click the **Open Database button** on the Database toolbar if you do not see My First Database.)

➤ Click the **Forms tab** in the Database window. Click the **New command button** to display the New Form dialog box as shown in Figure 2.7a.

➤ Click **Form Wizard** in the list box. Click the **drop-down arrow** to display the available tables and queries in the database on which the form can be based.

➤ Click **Students** to select the Students table from the previous exercise. Click **OK** to start the Form Wizard.

THE MOST RECENTLY OPENED FILE LIST

The easiest way to open a recently used database is to select it from the Microsoft Access dialog box that appears when Access is first started. Check to see if your database appears on the list of the four most recently opened databases, and if so, simply double click the database to open it. The list of the most recently opened databases can also be found at the bottom of the File menu.

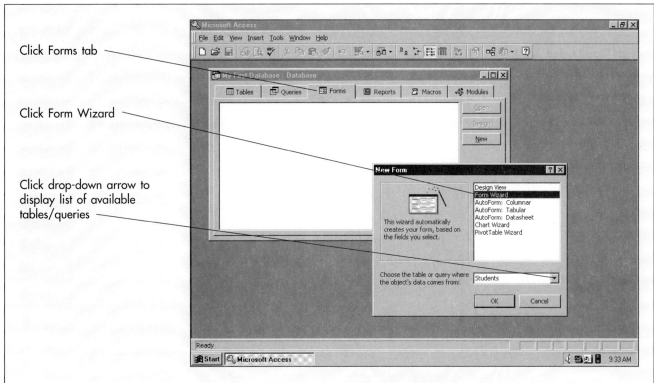

Click Forms tab

Click Form Wizard

Click drop-down arrow to display list of available tables/queries

(a) Create a Form (step 1)

FIGURE 2.7 Hands-on Exercise 2

STEP 2: The Form Wizard

➤ You should see the dialog box in Figure 2.7b, which displays all of the fields in the Students table. Click the **>> button** to enter all of the fields in the table on the form. Click the **Next command button.**

➤ The **Columnar layout** is already selected. Click the **Next command button.**

➤ Click **Standard** as the style for your form. Click the **Next command button.**

➤ The Form Wizard asks you for the title of the form and what you want to do next.

- The Form Wizard suggests **Students** as the title of the form. Keep this entry.
- Click the option button to **Modify the form's design.**

➤ Click the **Finish command button** to display the form in Design view.

FLOATING TOOLBARS

A toolbar is typically docked (fixed) along the edge of the application window, but it can be displayed as a floating toolbar within the application window. To move a docked toolbar, drag the toolbar background. To move a floating toolbar, drag its title bar. To size a floating toolbar, drag any border in the direction you want to go. Double click the background of any toolbar to toggle between a floating toolbar and a docked (fixed) toolbar.

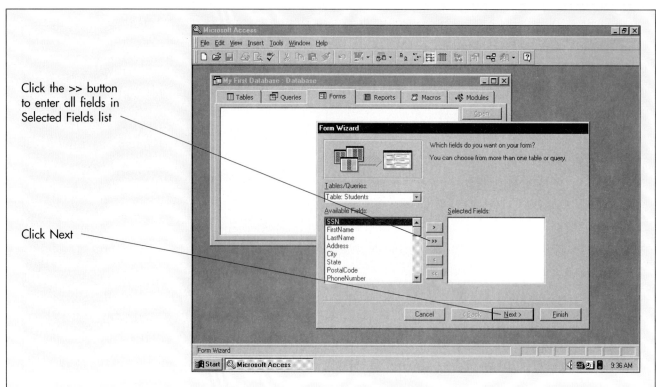

Click the >> button
to enter all fields in
Selected Fields list

Click Next

(b) The Form Wizard (step 2)

FIGURE 2.7   Hands-on Exercise 2 (continued)

STEP 3: Move the Controls

➤ If necessary, click the **Maximize button** so that the form takes the entire screen as shown in Figure 2.7c. The Form Wizard has arranged the controls in columnar format, but you need to rearrange the controls.

➤ Click the **LastName control** to select the control and display the sizing handles. (Be sure to select the text box and *not* the attached label.) Click and drag the **border** of the control (the pointer changes to a hand) so that the LastName control is on the same line as the FirstName control. Use the grid to space and align the controls.

➤ Click and drag the **Address control** under the FirstName control (to take the space previously occupied by the last name).

➤ Click and drag the **border** of the form to **7 inches** so that the City, State, and PostalCode controls will fit on the same line. (Click and drag the title bar of the Toolbox toolbar to move the toolbar out of the way.)

➤ Click and drag the **State control** so that it is next to the City control, then click and drag the **PostalCode control** so that it is on the same line as the other two. Press and hold the **Shift key** as you click the **City, State,** and **PostalCode controls** to select all three, then click and drag the selected controls under the Address control.

➤ Place the controls for **PhoneNumber, BirthDate,** and **Gender** on the same line.

➤ Place the controls for **Credits** and **QualityPoints** on the same line.

➤ Pull down the **File menu** and click **Save** (or click the **Save button**) to save the form.

Click and drag title
bar to move toolbar

Ruler

Click and drag border of
control (pointer is a hand)

Sizing handles

Click and drag border of
form to 7" (as indicated
on ruler)

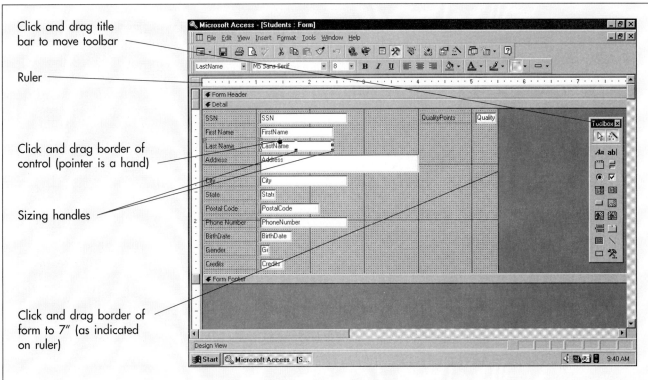

(c) Move the Controls (step 3)

FIGURE 2.7 Hands-on Exercise 2 (continued)

THE UNDO COMMAND

The Undo command is invaluable at any time, and is especially useful
when moving and sizing controls. Pull down the Edit menu and click Undo
(or click the Undo button on the toolbar) immediately to reverse the
effects of the last command.

STEP 4: Add a Calculated Control (GPA)

➤ Click the **Text Box tool** in the toolbox as shown in Figure 2.7d. The mouse
pointer changes to a tiny crosshair with a text box attached.

➤ Click and drag in the form where you want the text box (the GPA control)
to go. Release the mouse. You will see an Unbound control and an attached
label containing a field number (e.g., Text24) as shown in Figure 2.7d.

➤ Click in the **text box** of the control. The word Unbound will disappear, and
you can enter an expression:

• Enter **=[QualityPoints]/[Credits]** to calculate a student's GPA. Do not be
concerned if you cannot see the entire entry as scrolling will take place as
necessary.

• You must enter the field names *exactly* as they were defined in the table;
that is, do *not* include a space between Quality and Points.

➤ Select the attached label (Text24), then click and drag to select the text in
the attached label. Type **GPA** as the label for this control. Size the text box

Save button

Textbox tool

Click and drag to select
text in attached label,
then type GPA

Click and drag to
create control

Click in text box and
enter expression

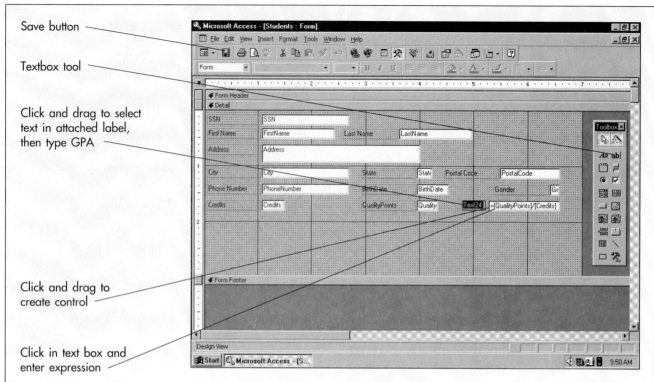

(d) Add a Calculated Control (step 4)

FIGURE 2.7   Hands-on Exercise 2 (continued)

appropriately for GPA. Click the **move handle** on the label so that you can
move the label closer to the text box.

➤ Click the **Save button.**

SIZING OR MOVING A CONTROL AND ITS LABEL

A bound control is created with an attached label. Select (click) the control, and the control has sizing handles and a move handle, but the label
has only a move handle. Select the label (instead of the control), and the
opposite occurs; the control has only a move handle, but the label will
have both sizing handles and a move handle. To move a control and its
label, click and drag the border of either object. To move either the control or its label, click and drag the move handle (a tiny square in the upper
left corner) of the appropriate object.

STEP 5: Modify the Property Sheet

➤ Point to the GPA control and click the **right mouse button** to display a shortcut menu. Click **Properties** to display the Properties dialog box.

➤ If necessary, click the **All tab** as shown in Figure 2.7e. The Control Source
text box contains the entry =[QualityPoints]/[Credits] from the preceding
step.

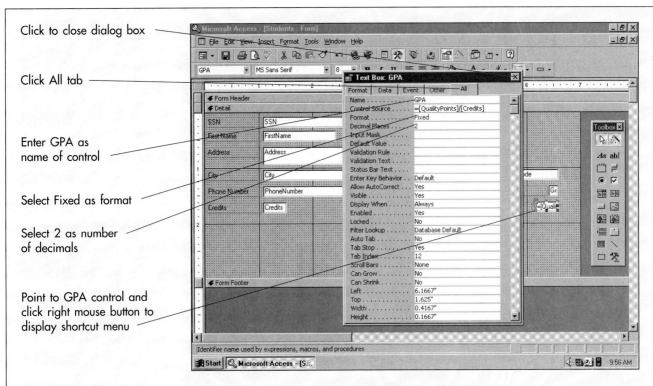

Click to close dialog box

Click All tab

Enter GPA as
name of control

Select Fixed as format

Select 2 as number
of decimals

Point to GPA control and
click right mouse button to
display shortcut menu

(e) Modify the Property Sheet (step 5)

FIGURE 2.7   Hands-on Exercise 2 (continued)

➤ Click the **Name text box.** Replace the original name (e.g., Text24) with **GPA.**
➤ Click the **Format box.** Click the **drop-down arrow,** then scroll until you can select **Fixed.**
➤ Click the box for the **Decimal places.** Click the **drop-down arrow** and select **2** as the number of decimal places.
➤ Close the Properties dialog box to accept these settings and return to the form.

USE THE PROPERTY SHEET

You can change the appearance or behavior of a control in two ways—by changing the actual control on the form itself or by changing the underlying property sheet. Anything you do to the control automatically changes the associated property, and conversely, any change to the property sheet is reflected in the appearance or behavior of the control. In general, you can obtain greater precision through the property sheet, but we find ourselves continually switching back and forth between the two techniques.

STEP 6: Align the Controls

➤ Press and hold the **Shift key** as you click the label for each control on the form. This enables you to select multiple controls at the same time in order to apply uniform formatting to the selected controls.

➤ All labels should be selected as shown in Figure 2.7f. Click the **Align Right button** on the Formatting toolbar to move the labels to the right so that each label is closer to its associated control.

➤ Click anywhere on the form to deselect the controls, then fine-tune the form as necessary to make it more attractive. We moved LastName to align it with State. We also made the SSN and PostalCode controls smaller.

Right-align button

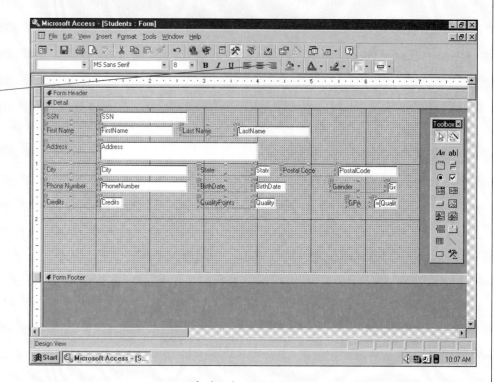

(f) Align the Controls (step 6)

FIGURE 2.7   Hands-on Exercise 2 (continued)

ALIGN THE CONTROLS

To align controls in a straight line (horizontally or vertically), press and hold the Shift key and click the labels of the controls to be aligned. Pull down the Format menu, click Align, then select the edge to align (Left, Right, Top, and Bottom). Click the Undo command if you are not satisfied with the result.

STEP 7: Create the Form Header

➤ Click and drag the line separating the border of the Form Header and Detail to provide space for a header as shown in Figure 2.7g.

➤ Click the **Label tool** on the Toolbox toolbar (the mouse pointer changes to a cross hair combined with the letter A). Click and drag the mouse pointer to create a label within the header. The insertion point (a flashing vertical line) is automatically positioned within the label.

➤ Type **Student Information Form.** Do not be concerned about the size or alignment of the text at this time. Click outside the label when you have completed the entry, then click the control to select it.

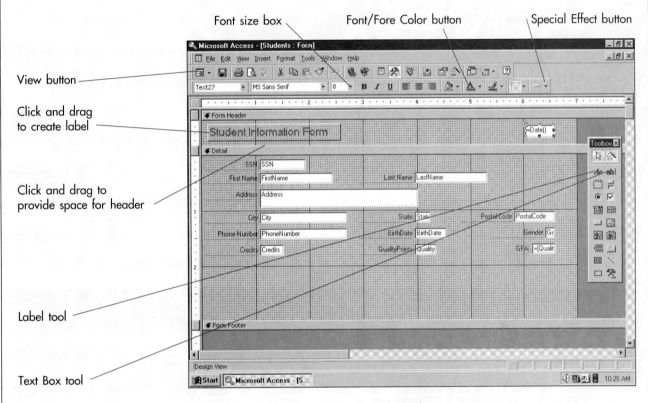

(g) Create the Header (steps 7 & 8)

FIGURE 2.7 Hands-on Exercise 2 (continued)

THE FORMATTING TOOLBAR

The Formatting toolbar contains many of the same buttons that are found on the Formatting toolbars of the other Office applications. These include buttons for boldface, italics, and underlining, as well as left, center, and right alignment. You will find drop-down list boxes to change the font or point size. The Formatting toolbar also contains drop-down palettes to change the foreground or background color, the border color and width, and the special effect.

➤ Click the **drop-down arrow** on the **Font Size list box** on the Formatting tool-bar. Click **14.** The size of the text changes to the larger point size.

➤ Click the **drop-down arrow** next to the **Special Effect button** on the Format-ting toolbar to display the available effects. Click the **Raised button** to high-light the label.

➤ Click the **drop-down arrow** next to the **Font/Fore Color button** on the For-matting toolbar. Click **Red.**

➤ Click outside the label to deselect it. Click the **Save button** to save the form.

STEP 8: Add the Date

➤ Click the **Textbox tool** on the Toolbox toolbar. The mouse pointer changes to a tiny crosshair with a text box attached. Click and drag in the form where you want the text box for the date, then release the mouse.

➤ You will see an Unbound control and an attached label containing a number (e.g., Text27). Click in the text box, and the word Unbound will disappear. Type =**Date().** Click the attached label. Press the **Del key** to delete the label.

STEP 9: The Form View

➤ Click the **Form view button** to switch to the Form view. You will see the first record in the table that was created in the previous exercise.

➤ Click the **New Record button** to move to the end of the table to enter a new record as shown in Figure 2.7h. Enter data for yourself:

• The record selector symbol changes to a pencil as you begin to enter data.

• Press the **Tab key** to move from one field to the next within the form. All properties (masks and data validation) have been inherited from the Stu-dents table created in the first exercise.

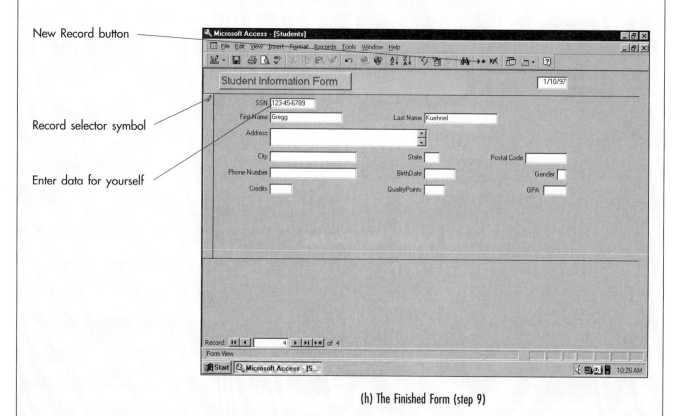

(h) The Finished Form (step 9)

FIGURE 2.7   Hands-on Exercise 2 (continued)

➤ Pull down the **File menu** and click **Close** to close the form. Click **Yes** if asked to save the changes to the form.

➤ Pull down the **File menu** and click **Close** to close the database and remain in Access. Pull down the **File menu** a second time and click **Exit** if you do not want to continue with the next exercise at this time.

ERROR MESSAGES—#NAME? OR #ERROR?

The most common reason for either message is that the control source references a field that no longer exists, or a field whose name is misspelled. Go to the Design view, right click the control, click the Properties command, then click the All tab within the Properties dialog box. Look at the Control Source property and check the spelling of every field. Be sure there are brackets around each field in a calculated control; for example =[QualityPoints]/[Credits].

A MORE SOPHISTICATED FORM

The Form Wizard provides an excellent starting point but stops short of creating the form you really want. The exercise just completed showed you how to add controls to a form that were not in the underlying table, such as the calculated control for the GPA. The exercise also showed how to move and size existing controls to create a more attractive and functional form.

Consider now Figure 2.8, which further improves on the form from the previous exercise. Three additional controls have been added—for major, financial

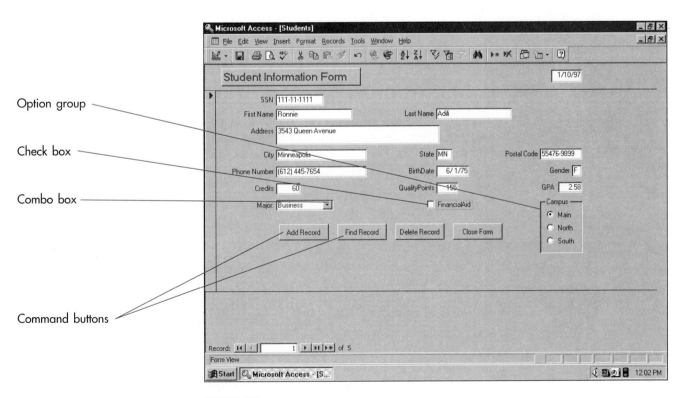

FIGURE 2.8   An Improved Form

aid, and campus—to illustrate other ways to enter data than through a text box. The student's major is selected from a *drop-down list box.* The indication of financial aid (a Yes/No field) is entered through a *check box.* The student's campus is selected from an *option group,* in which you choose one of three mutually exclusive options.

Command buttons have also been added to the bottom of the form to facilitate the way in which the user carries out certain procedures. To add a record, for example, the user simply clicks the Add Record command button, as opposed to having to click the New Record button on the Database toolbar or having to pull down the Insert menu. The next exercise has you retrieve the form you created in Hands-on Exercise 2 in order to add these enhancements.

HANDS-ON EXERCISE 3

A More Sophisticated Form

Objective: To add fields to an existing table; to use the Lookup Wizard to create a combo box; to add controls to an existing form to demonstrate inheritance; to add command buttons to a form. Use Figure 2.9 as a guide in the exercise.

STEP 1: Modify the Table

➤ Open **My First Database** that we have been using throughout the chapter. If necessary, click the **Tables tab** in the Database window. The **Students table** is already selected since that is the only table in the database.

➤ Click the **Design command button** to open the table in Design view as shown in Figure 2.9a. (The FinancialAid, Campus, and Major fields have not yet been added.) Maximize the window.

➤ Click the **Field Name box** under QualityPoints. Enter **FinancialAid** as the name of the new field. Press the **enter (Tab,** or **right arrow) key** to move to the Data Type column. Type **Y** (the first letter in a Yes/No field) to specify the data type.

➤ Click the **Field Name box** on the next row. Type **Campus.** (There is no need to specify the Data Type since Text is the default.)

➤ Press the **down arrow key** to move to the Field Name box on the next row. Enter **Major.** Press the **enter (Tab,** or **right arrow) key** to move to the Data Type column. Click the **drop-down arrow** to display the list of data types as shown in Figure 2.9a. Click **Lookup Wizard.**

STEP 2: The Lookup Wizard

➤ The first screen in the Lookup Wizard asks how you want to look up the data. Click the option button that indicates **I will type in the values that I want.** Click **Next.**

➤ You should see the dialog box in Figure 2.9b. The number of columns is already entered as one. Click the **text box** to enter the first major. Type **Business.** Press **Tab** or the **down arrow key** (do *not* press the enter key) to enter the next major.

➤ Complete the entries shown in Figure 2.9b. Click **Next.** The Wizard asks for a label to identify the column. (Major is already entered.) Click **Finish** to exit the Wizard and return to the Design View.

➤ Click the **Save button** to save the table. Close the table.

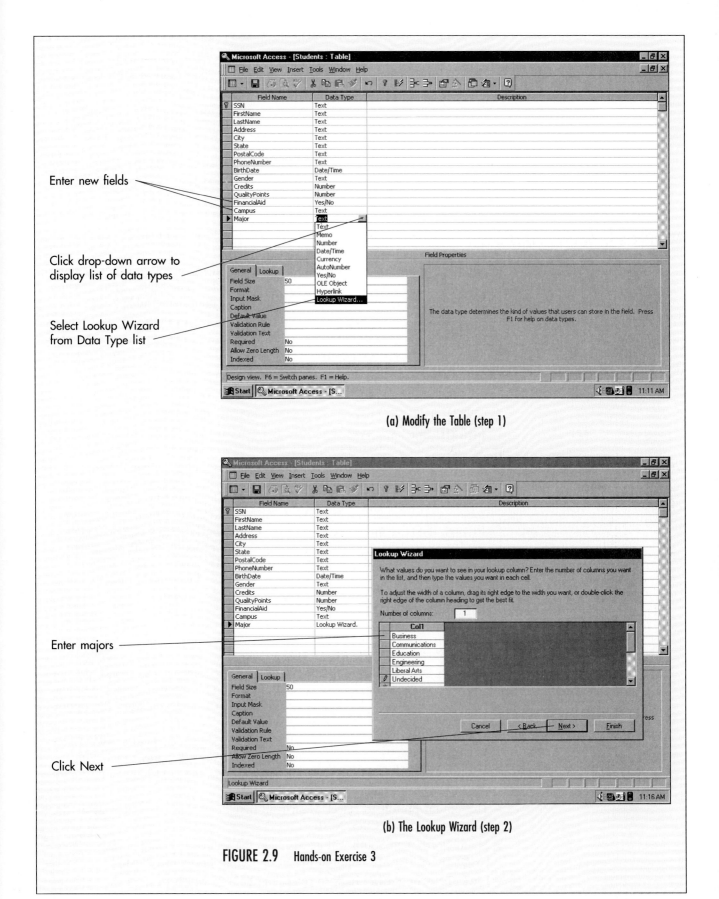

Enter new fields

Click drop-down arrow to display list of data types

Select Lookup Wizard from Data Type list

(a) Modify the Table (step 1)

Enter majors

Click Next

(b) The Lookup Wizard (step 2)

FIGURE 2.9   Hands-on Exercise 3

STEP 3: Add the New Controls

➤ Click the **Forms tab** in the Database window. The Students form is already highlighted since there is only one form in the database.

➤ Click the **Design command button** to open the form from the previous exercise. If necessary, click the **Maximize button** so that the form takes the entire window.

➤ Pull down the **View menu.** Click **Field List** to display the field list for the table on which the form is based. You can move and size the field list just like any other Windows object.

  • Click and drag the **title bar** of the field list to the position in Figure 2.9c.

  • Click and drag a **corner** or **border** of the field list so that you can see all of the fields at the same time.

➤ Fields can be added to the form from the field list in any order. Click and drag the **Major field** from the field list to the form. The Major control is created as a combo box because of the list in the underlying table.

➤ Click and drag the **FinancialAid field** from the list to the form. The FinancialAid control is created as a check box because FinancialAid is a Yes/No field in the underlying table.

➤ Save the form.

INHERITANCE

A bound control inherits the same properties as the associated field in the underlying table. A check box, for example, appears automatically next to any bound control that was defined as a Yes/No field. In similar fashion, a drop-down list will appear next to any bound control that was defined through the Lookup Wizard. Changing the property setting of a field *after* the form has been created will *not* change the property of the associated control. And finally, changing the property setting of a control does *not* change the property setting of the field because the control inherits the properties of the field rather than the other way around.

STEP 4: Create an Option Group

➤ Click the **Option Group button** on the Toolbox toolbar. The mouse pointer changes to a tiny crosshair attached to an option button when you point anywhere in the form. Click and drag in the form where you want the option group to go, then release the mouse.

➤ You should see the Option Group Wizard as shown in Figure 2.9d. Enter **Main** as the label for the first option, then press the **Tab key** to move to the next line. Type **North** and press **Tab** to move to the next line. Enter **South** as the third and last option. Click **Next.**

➤ The option button to select Main (the first label that was entered) as the default is selected. Click **Next.**

➤ Main, North, and South will be assigned the values 1, 2, and 3, respectively. (Numeric entries are required for an option group.) Click **Next.**

➤ Click the **drop-down arrow** to select the field in which to store the value of the option group, then scroll until you can select **Campus.** Click **Next.**

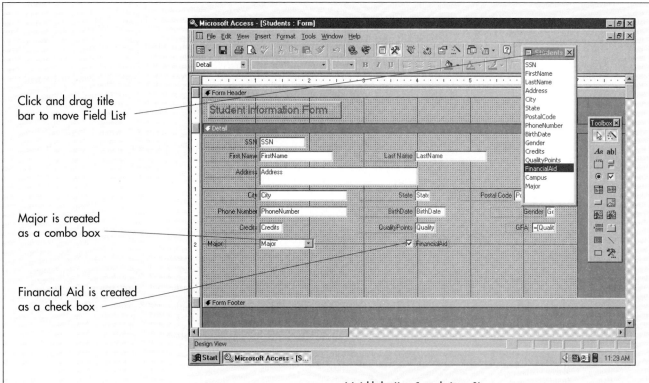

Click and drag title bar to move Field List

Major is created as a combo box

Financial Aid is created as a check box

(c) Add the New Controls (step 3)

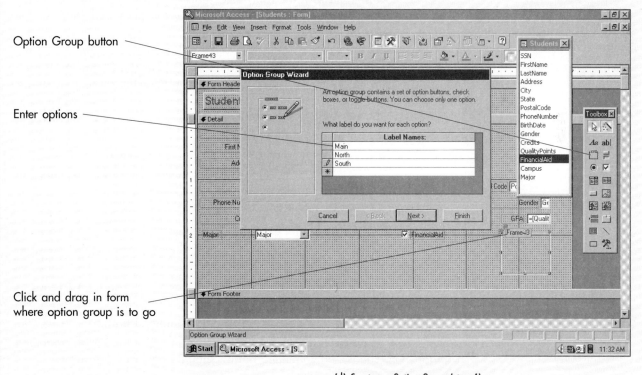

Option Group button

Enter options

Click and drag in form where option group is to go

(d) Create an Option Group (step 4)

FIGURE 2.9   Hands-on Exercise 3 (continued)

➤ Make sure the Option button is selected as the type of control.

➤ Click the option button for the **Sunken style** to match the other controls on the form. Click **Next.**

➤ Enter **Campus** as the caption for the group. Click the **Finish command button** to create the option group on the form. Click and drag the option group to position it on the form under the GPA control.

➤ Point to the border of the option group on the form, click the **right mouse button** to display a shortcut menu, and click **Properties.** Click the **All tab.** Change the name to **Campus.** Close the dialog box. Save the form.

MISSING TOOLBARS

The Form Design, Formatting, and Toolbox toolbars appear by default in the Form Design view, but any (or all) of these toolbars may be hidden at the discretion of the user. Point to any visible toolbar, click the right mouse button to display a shortcut menu, then check the name of any toolbar you want to display. You can also click the Toolbox button on the Form Design toolbar to display (hide) the Toolbox toolbar.

STEP 5: Add a Command Button

➤ Click the **Command Button tool.** The mouse pointer changes to a tiny crosshair attached to a command button when you point anywhere in the form.

➤ Click and drag in the form where you want the button to go, then release the mouse. This draws a button and simultaneously opens the Command Button Wizard as shown in Figure 2.9e. (The number in your button may be different from ours.)

➤ Click **Record Operations** in the Categories list box. Choose **Add New Record** as the operation. Click **Next.**

➤ Click the **Text option button** in the next screen. Click **Next.**

➤ Type **Add Record** as the name of the button, then click the **Finish command button.** The completed command button should appear on your form. Save the form.

STEP 6: Create the Additional Command Buttons

➤ Click the **Command Button tool.** Click and drag on the form where you want the second button to go.

➤ Click **Record Navigation** in the Categories list box. Choose **Find Record** as the operation. Click the **Next command button.**

➤ Click the **Text option button.** Click the **Next command button.**

➤ Type **Find Record** as the name of the button, then click the **Finish command button.** The completed command button should appear on the form.

➤ Repeat these steps to add the command buttons to delete a record (Record Operations) and close the form (Form Operations).

➤ Save the form.

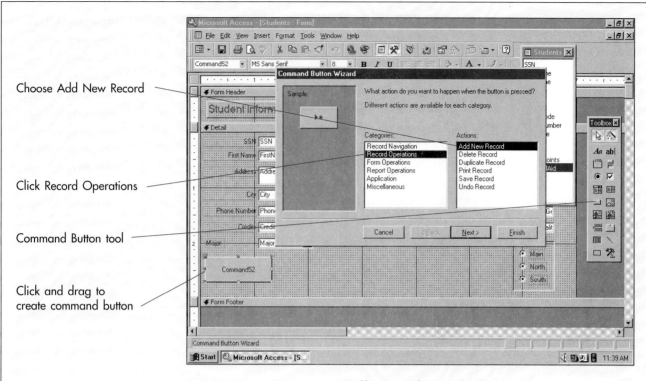

Choose Add New Record

Click Record Operations

Command Button tool

Click and drag to
create command button

(e) Add a Command Button (step 5)

FIGURE 2.9   Hands-on Exercise 3 (continued)

STEP 7: Align the Command Buttons

➤ Select the four command buttons by pressing and holding the **Shift key** as you click each button. Release the Shift key when all buttons are selected.

➤ Pull down the **Format menu.** Click **Size** to display the cascade menu shown in Figure 2.9f. Click **to Widest** to set a uniform width.

➤ Pull down the **Format menu** a second time, click **Size,** then click **to Tallest** to set a uniform height.

➤ Pull down the **Format menu** again, click **Horizontal Spacing,** then click **Make Equal** so that each button is equidistant from the other buttons.

➤ Pull down the **Format menu** a final time, click **Align,** then click **Bottom** to complete the alignment. Drag the buttons to the center of the form.

MULTIPLE CONTROLS AND PROPERTIES

Press and hold the Shift key as you click one control after another to select multiple controls. To view or change the properties for the selected controls, click the right mouse button to display a shortcut menu, then click Properties to display a property sheet. If the value of a property is the same for all selected controls, that value will appear in the property sheet; otherwise the box for that property will be blank. Changing a property when multiple controls are selected changes the property for all selected controls.

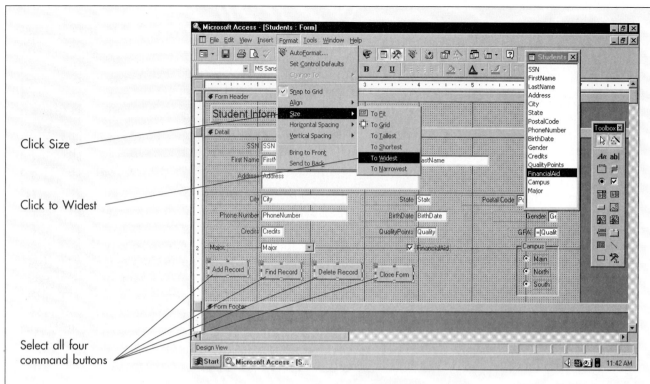

Click Size

Click to Widest

Select all four
command buttons

(f) Align the Buttons (step 7)

FIGURE 2.9   Hands-on Exercise 3 (continued)

STEP 8: Reset the Tab Order

➤ Click anywhere in the Detail section. Pull down the **View menu.** Click **Tab Order** to display the Tab Order dialog box in Figure 2.9g.

➤ Click the **AutoOrder command button** so that the tab key will move to fields in left-to-right, top-to-bottom order as you enter data in the form. Click **OK** to close the Tab Order dialog box.

➤ Check the form one more time in order to make any last-minute changes.

➤ Save the form.

CHANGE THE TAB ORDER

The Tab key provides a shortcut in the finished form to move from one field to the next; that is, you press Tab to move forward to the next field and Shift+Tab to return to the previous field. The order in which fields are selected corresponds to the sequence in which the controls were entered onto the form, and need not correspond to the physical appearance of the actual form. To restore a left-to-right, top-to-bottom sequence, pull down the View menu, click Tab Order, then select AutoOrder. Alternatively, you can specify a custom sequence by clicking the selector for the various controls within the Tab Order dialog box, then moving the row up or down within the list.

View button

Click Auto Order

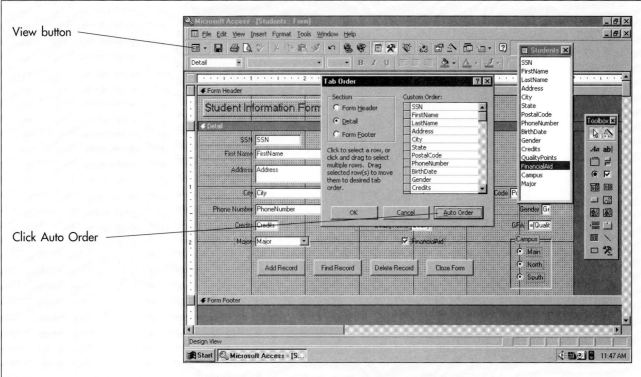

(g) Modify the Tab Order (step 8)

FIGURE 2.9 Hands-on Exercise 3 (continued)

STEP 9: The Page Setup Command

➤ Point to any blank area in the Detail section of the form. Click the **right mouse button** to display a shortcut menu, then click **Properties** to display the Properties dialog box for the Detail section. Click the **All tab.**

➤ Click the text box for **Height.** Enter **3.5** to change the height of the Detail section to three and one-half inches. Close the Properties dialog box.

➤ If necessary, click and drag the **right border** of the form so that all controls are fully visible. Do *not* exceed a width of 7 inches for the entire form.

➤ Pull down the **File menu.** Click **Page Setup** to display the Page Setup dialog box. If necessary, click the **Margins tab.**

➤ Change the left and right margins to **.75** inch. Click **OK** to accept the settings and close the Page Setup dialog box.

CHECK YOUR NUMBERS

The width of the form, plus the left and right margins, cannot exceed the width of the printed page. Thus increasing the width of a form may require a corresponding decrease in the left and right margins or a change to landscape (rather than portrait) orientation. Pull down the File menu and choose the Page Setup command to modify the dimensions of the form prior to printing.

STEP 10: The Completed Form

➤ Click the **View button** to switch to the Form view and display the first record in the table.

➤ Complete the record by adding appropriate data (choose any values you like) for the Major, FinancialAid, and Campus fields that were added to the form in this exercise.

➤ Click the **Add Record command button** to create a new record. Click the text box for **Social Security Number.** Add the record shown in Figure 2.9h. The record selector changes to a pencil as soon as you begin to enter data to indicate the record has not been saved.

➤ Press the **Tab key** or the **enter key** to move from field to field within the record. Click the **arrow** on the drop-down list box to display the list of majors, then click the desired major. Complete all of the information in the form.

➤ Click the **selection area** (the thin vertical column to the left of the form) to select only the current record. The record selector changes from a pencil to an arrow. The selection area is shaded to indicate that the record has been selected.

➤ Pull down the **File menu.** Click **Print** to display the Print dialog box. Click the option button to **print Selected Records**—that is, to print only the one record. Click **OK.**

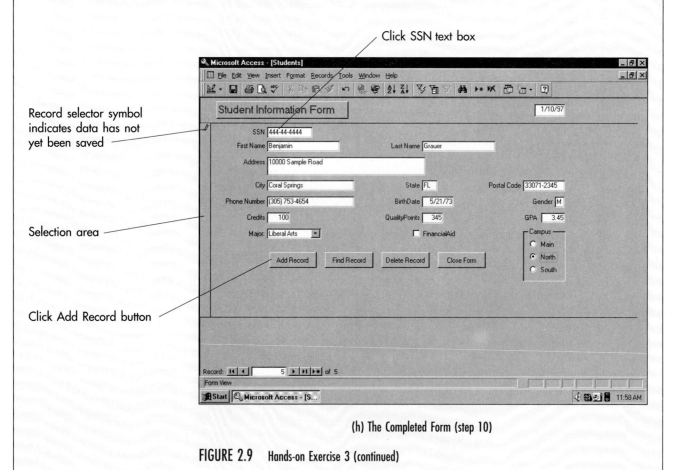

(h) The Completed Form (step 10)

FIGURE 2.9 Hands-on Exercise 3 (continued)

➤ Examine your printed output to be sure that the form fits on a single page. It if doesn't, you need to adjust the margins of the form itself and/or change the margins using the Page Setup command in the File menu, then print the form a second time.

KEYBOARD SHORTCUTS

Press Tab to move from one field to the next in a finished form. Press Shift+Tab to return to the previous field. Type the first letter of an item's name to select the first item in a drop-down list beginning with that letter; for example, type "B" to select the first item in Major beginning with that letter. Type the first two letters quickly—for example, Bu—and you will go directly to Business. Press the space bar to toggle a check box on and off. Press the down arrow key to move from one option to the next within an option group.

STEP 11: Exit Access
➤ Click the **Close Form command button** when you have completed the record. Click **Yes** if you see a message asking to save changes to the form.
➤ Pull down the **File menu.** Click **Exit** to leave Access. Congratulations on a job well done.

SUMMARY

The information produced by a system depends entirely on the underlying data. The design of the database is of critical importance and must be done correctly. Three guidelines were suggested. These are to include the necessary data, to store data in its smallest parts, and to avoid the use of calculated fields in a table.

The Table Wizard is the easiest way to create a table. It lets you choose from a series of business or personal tables, asks you questions about the fields you want, then creates the table for you.

A table has two views—the Design view and the Datasheet view. The Design view is used to create the table and display the fields within the table, as well as the data type and properties of each field. The Datasheet view is used after the table has been created to add, edit, and delete records.

A form provides a user-friendly way to enter and display data, in that it can be made to resemble a paper form. The Form Wizard is the easiest way to create a form. The Design view enables you to modify an existing form.

A form consists of objects called controls. A bound control has a data source such as a field in the underlying table. An unbound control has no data source. A calculated control contains an expression. Controls are selected, moved, and sized the same way as any other Windows object.

A property is a characteristic or attribute of an object that determines how the object looks and behaves. Every Access object (e.g., tables, fields, forms, and controls) has a set of properties that determine the behavior of that object. The properties for an object are displayed in a property sheet.

Allow Zero Length
  property
AutoNumber field
AutoOrder
Bound control
Calculated control
Calculated field
Caption property
Check box
Combo box
Command button
Control
Currency field
Data type
Datasheet view
Date/Time field
Default Value property
Design view

Drop-down list box
Expression
Field name
Field Size property
Form
Form view
Form Wizard
Format property
Hyperlink field
Indexed property
Inheritance
Input Mask property
Label
Lookup Wizard
Memo field
Number field
OLE field
Option group

Page Setup
Primary key
Print Preview
Property
Property sheet
Required property
Selection area
Tab Order
Table Wizard
Text box
Text field
Toolbox toolbar
Unbound control
Validation Rule
  property
Validation Text
  property
Yes/No field

PRACTICE WITH ACCESS 97

1. Modify the Student form created in the hands-on exercises to match the form in Figure 2.10. (The form contains three additional controls that must be added to the Students table.)

   a. Add the DateAdmitted and EmailAddress as a date and a text field, respectively, in the Students table. Add a Yes/No field to indicate whether or not the student is an International student.

   b. Add controls for the additional fields as shown in Figure 2.10.

   c. Modify the State field in the underlying Students table to use the Lookup Wizard, and set CA, FL, NJ, and NY as the values for the list box. (These are the most common states in the Student population.) The control in the form will not, however, inherit the list box because it was added to the table after the form was created. Hence you have to delete the existing control in the form, display the field list, then click and drag the State field from the field list to the form.

   d. Resize the control in the Form Header so that *University of Miami Student Information Form* takes two lines. Press Ctrl+Enter to force a line break within the control. Resize the Form Header.

   e. Change the tab order to reflect the new fields in the form.

   f. Add a graphic as described in problem 2.

2. This exercise is a continuation of problem 1 and describes how to insert a graphic created by another application onto an Access form. (The faster your machine, the more you will enjoy the exercise.)

   a. Open the Students form in My First Database in the Design view. Move the date in the header under the label.

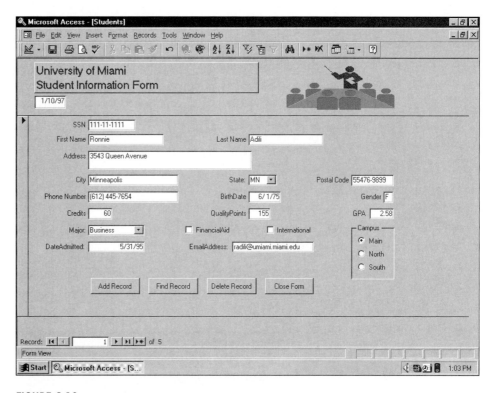

FIGURE 2.10   Screen for Practice Exercises 1 and 2

b. Click the Unbound Object Frame tool on the toolbox. (If you are unsure as to which tool to click, just point to the tool to display the name of the tool.)

c. Click and drag in the Form Header to size the frame, then release the mouse to display an Insert Object dialog box.

d. Click the Create New option button. Select the Microsoft Clip Gallery as the object type. Click OK.

e. Click the Clip Art tab in the Microsoft Clip Gallery dialog box. Choose the category and picture you want from within the Clip Gallery. Click the Insert button to insert the picture into the Access form and simultaneously close the Clip Gallery dialog box. Do *not* be concerned if only a portion of the picture appears on the form.

f. Right click the newly inserted object to display a shortcut menu, then click Properties to display the Properties dialog box. Select (click) the Size Mode property and select Stretch from the associated list. Change the Back Style property to Transparent, the Special Effect property to Flat, and the Border Style property to Transparent. Close the Properties dialog box.

g. You should see the entire clip art image, although it may be distorted because the size and shape of the frame you inserted in steps (b) and (c) do not match the image you selected. Click and drag the sizing handles on the frame to size the object so that its proportions are correct. Click anywhere in the middle of the frame (the mouse pointer changes to a hand) to move the frame elsewhere in the form.

h. If you want to display a different object, double click the clip art image to return to the Clip Gallery in order to select another object.

3. Open the Employee database in the Exploring Access folder to create a form similar to the one in Figure 2.11. (This is the same database that was referenced in problem 2 in Chapter 1.)

    a. The form was created using the Form Wizard and Colorful1 style. The various controls were then moved and sized to match the arrangement in the figure.

    b. The label in the Form Header, date of execution, and command buttons were added after the form was created, using the techniques in the third hands-on exercise.

    c. To add lines to the form, click the Line tool in the toolbox, then click and drag on the form to draw the line. To draw a straight line, press and hold the Shift key as you draw the line.

    d. You need not match our form exactly, and we encourage you to experiment with a different design.

    e. Add a record for yourself (if you have not already done so in Chapter 1), then print the form containing your data. Submit the printed form to your instructor as proof you did this exercise.

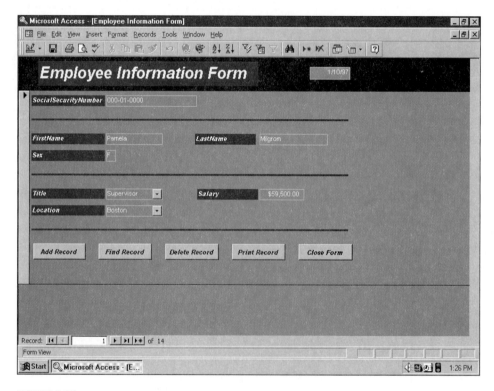

FIGURE 2.11　Screen for Practice Exercise 3

4. Open the USA database found in the Exploring Access folder to create a form similar to the one in Figure 2.12.

    a. The form was created using the Form Wizard and Standard style. The controls were moved and sized to match the arrangement in the figure.

    b. Population density is a calculated control and is computed by dividing the population by the area. Format the density to two decimal places.

    c. You need not match our form exactly, and we encourage you to experiment with different designs.

d. The Find command can be used after the form has been created to search through the table and answer questions about the United States. The dialog box in Figure 2.12, for example, will identify the Empire State.

e. Add the graphic, following the steps in the second exercise.

f. Print the form of your favorite state and submit it to your instructor. Be sure to choose the option to print only the selected record.

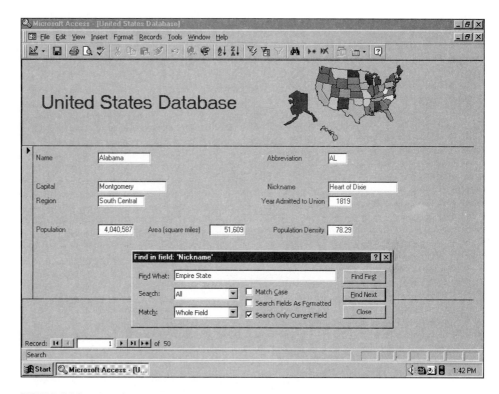

FIGURE 2.12   Screen for Practice Exercise 4

5. Figure 2.13 displays the Design view of a form to maintain an address book of friends and acquaintances. The picture is an added touch and well worth the effort, but it requires you to obtain pictures of your friends in machine-readable form. Each picture is stored initially in its own file (in GIF or JPEG format). The form and underlying table build upon the information in the chapter and should adhere to the following guidelines:

a. Create an Address Book database containing a table and associated form, using Figure 2.13 as a guide. You can add or delete fields as appropriate with the exception of the FriendID field, which is designated as the primary key. The FriendID should be defined as an AutoNumber field whose value is created automatically each time a record is added to the table.

b. Define the postal code as a nine-digit zip code. You can obtain the additional four digits from the U.S. Postal Service as shown in Figure 2.13. Pull down the View menu, click Toolbars, then toggle the Web toolbar on. Enter the address of the Postal Service (www.usps.gov), then click the appropriate link to obtain the complete zip code.

c. Include a logical field (e.g., SendCard) in the underlying table. This will enable you to create a report of those people who are to receive a birthday card (or season's greetings card) once the data have been entered.

d. Include an OLE field in the table, regardless of whether or not you actually have a picture, and be sure to leave space in the form for the picture.

Those records that have an associated picture will display the picture in the form; those records that do not have a picture will display a blank space. To insert a picture into the database, open the table, click in the OLE field, pull down the Insert menu, and click the Object command. Click the Create from File option button, click the Browse button in the associated dialog box, then select the appropriate file name and location.

e. Enter data for yourself in the completed form, then print the associated form to submit to your instructor as proof you did this exercise.

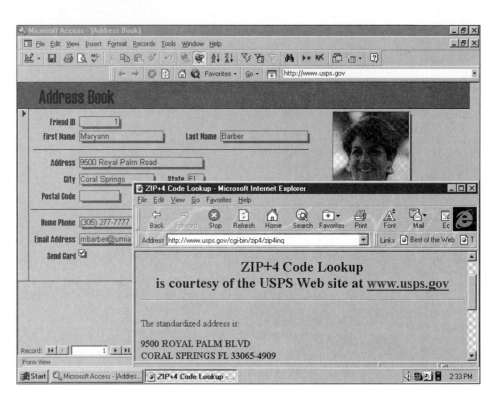

FIGURE 2.13   Screen for Practice Exercise 5

INFORMATION FROM THE DATABASE: REPORTS AND QUERIES

OBJECTIVES

After reading this chapter you will be able to:

1. Describe the various types of reports available through the Report Wizard.
2. Describe the various views in the Report Window and the purpose of each.
3. Describe the similarities between forms and reports with respect to bound, unbound, and calculated controls.
4. List the sections that may be present in a report and explain the purpose of each.
5. Differentiate between a query and a table; explain how the objects in an Access database (tables, forms, queries, and reports) interact with one another.
6. Use the design grid to create and modify a select query.
7. Explain the use of multiple criteria rows within the design grid to implement AND and OR conditions in a query.
8. Describe the various views in the Query window and the purpose of each.

OVERVIEW

Data and information are not synonymous. Data refers to a fact or facts about a specific record, such as a student's name, major, quality points, or number of completed credits. Information can be defined as data that has been rearranged into a more useful format. The individual fields within a student record are considered data. A list of students on the Dean's List, however, is information that has been produced from the data about the individual students.

Chapters 1 and 2 described how to enter and maintain data through the use of tables and forms. This chapter shows how to convert the data to information through queries and reports. Queries enable you to ask questions about the database. Reports provide presentation quality output and display detail as well as summary information about the records in a database.

As you read the chapter, you will see that the objects in an Access database (tables, forms, reports and queries) have many similar characteristics. We use these similarities to build on what you have learned in previous chapters. You already know, for example, that the controls in a form inherit their properties from the corresponding fields in a table. The same concept applies to the controls in a report. And since you know how to move and size controls within a form, you also know how to move and size the controls in a report. As you read the chapter, look for these and other similarities to apply your existing knowledge to the new material.

REPORTS

A *report* is a printed document that displays information from a database. Figure 3.1 shows several sample reports, each of which will be created in this chapter. The reports were created with the Report Wizard and are based on the Students table that was presented in Chapter 2. (The table has been expanded to 24 records.) As you view each report, ask yourself how the data in the table was rearranged to produce the information in the report.

The *columnar (vertical) report* in Figure 3.1a is the simplest type of report. It lists every field for every record in a single column (one record per page) and typically runs for many pages. The records in this report are displayed in the same sequence (by social security number) as the records in the table on which the report is based.

The *tabular report* in Figure 3.1b displays fields in a row rather than in a column. Each record in the underlying table is printed in its own row. Unlike the previous report, only selected fields are displayed, so the tabular report is more concise than the columnar report of Figure 3.1a. Note, too, that the records in the report are listed in alphabetical order rather than by social security number.

The report in Figure 3.1c is also a tabular report, but it is very different from the report in Figure 3.1b. The report in Figure 3.1c lists only a selected set of students (those students with a GPA of 3.50 or higher), as opposed to the earlier reports, which listed every student. The students are listed in descending order according to their GPA.

The report in Figure 3.1d displays the students in groups, according to their major, then computes the average GPA for each group. The report also contains summary information (not visible in Figure 3.1d) for the report as a whole, which computes the average GPA for all students.

DATA VERSUS INFORMATION

Data and information are not synonymous although the terms are often interchanged. Data is the raw material and consists of the table (or tables) that compose a database. Information is the finished product. Data is converted to information by selecting records, performing calculations on those records, and/or changing the sequence in which the records are displayed. Decisions in an organization are made on the basis of information rather than raw data.

Student Roster

SSN	111-11-1111
FirstName	Jared
LastName	Berlin
Address	900 Main Highway
City	Charleston
State	SC
PostalCode	29410-0560
PhoneNumber	(803) 223-7868
BirthDate	1/15/72
Gender	M
Credits	100
QualityPoints	250
FinancialAid	Yes
Campus	1
Major	Engineering

(a) Columnar Report

Student Master List

Last Name	First Name	Phone Number	Major
Adili	Ronnie	(612) 445-7654	Business
Berlin	Jared	(803) 223-7868	Engineering
Camejo	Oscar	(716) 433-3321	Liberal Arts
Coe	Bradley	(415) 235-6543	Undecided
Cornell	Ryan	(404) 755-4490	Undecided
DiGiacomo	Kevin	(305) 531-7652	Business
Faulkner	Eileen	(305) 489-8876	Communications
Frazier	Steven	(410) 995-8755	Undecided
Gibson	Christopher	(305) 235-4563	Business
Heltzer	Peter	(305) 753-4533	Engineering
Huerta	Carlos	(212) 344-5654	Undecided
Joseph	Cedric	(404) 667-8955	Communications
Korba	Nickolas	(415) 664-0900	Education
Ortiz	Frances	(303) 575-3211	Communications
Parulis	Christa	(410) 877-6565	Liberal Arts
Price	Lori	(310) 961-2323	Communications
Ramsay	Robert	(212) 223-9889	Business
Slater	Erica	(312) 545-6978	Communications
Solomon	Wendy	(305) 666-4532	Engineering
Watson	Ana	(305) 595-7877	Liberal Arts
Watson	Ana	(305) 561-2334	Business
Weissman	Kimberly	(904) 388-8605	Liberal Arts
Zacco	Michelle	(617) 884-3434	Undecided
Zimmerman	Kimberly	(713) 225-3434	Education

(b) Tabular Report

Dean's List

First Name	Last Name	Major	Credits	Quality Points	GPA
Peter	Heltzer	Engineering	25	100	4.00
Cedric	Joseph	Communications	45	170	3.78
Erica	Slater	Communications	105	390	3.71
Kevin	DiGiacomo	Business	105	375	3.57
Wendy	Solomon	Engineering	50	175	3.50

(c) Dean's List

GPA by Major

Major	Last Name	First Name	GPA
Business			
	Adili	Ronnie	2.58
	Cornell	Ryan	1.78
	DiGiacomo	Kevin	3.57
	Gibson	Christopher	1.71
	Ramsay	Robert	3.24
	Watson	Ana	2.50
	Average GPA for Major		2.56
Communications			
	Faulkner	Eileen	2.67
	Joseph	Cedric	3.78
	Ortiz	Frances	2.14
	Price	Lori	1.75
	Slater	Erica	3.71
	Average GPA for Major		2.81
Education			
	Korba	Nickolas	1.66
	Zimmerman	Kimberly	3.29
	Average GPA for Major		2.48
Engineering			
	Berlin	Jared	2.50
	Heltzer	Peter	4.00
	Solomon	Wendy	3.50
	Average GPA for Major		3.33
Liberal Arts			
	Camejo	Oscar	2.80
	Parulis	Christa	1.80
	Watson	Ana	2.79
	Weissman	Kimberly	2.63
	Average GPA for Major		2.51

(d) Summary Report

FIGURE 3.1   Report Types

Anatomy of a Report

All reports are based on an underlying table or query within the database. (Queries are discussed later in the chapter, beginning on page 102.) A report, however, displays the data or information in a more attractive fashion because it contains various headings and/or other decorative items that are not present in either a table or a query.

The easiest way to learn about reports is to compare a printed report with its underlying design. Consider, for example, Figure 3.2a, which displays the tabular report, and Figure 3.2b, which shows the underlying design. The latter shows how a report is divided into sections, which appear at designated places when the report is printed. There are seven types of sections, but a report need not contain all seven.

The *report header* appears once, at the beginning of a report. It typically contains information describing the report, such as its title and the date the report was printed. (The report header appears above the page header on the first page of the report.) The *report footer* appears once at the end of the report, above the page footer on the last page of the report, and displays summary information for the report as a whole.

The *page header* appears at the top of every page in a report and can be used to display page numbers, column headings, and other descriptive information. The *page footer* appears at the bottom of every page and may contain page numbers (when they are not in the page header) or other descriptive information.

A *group header* appears at the beginning of a group of records to identify the group. A *group footer* appears after the last record in a group and contains summary information about the group. Group headers and footers are used only when the records in a report are sorted (grouped) according to a common value in a specific field. These sections do not appear in the report of Figure 3.2, but were shown earlier in the report of Figure 3.1d.

The *detail section* appears in the main body of a report and is printed once for every record in the underlying table (or query). It displays one or more fields for each record in columnar or tabular fashion, according to the design of the report.

The Report Wizard

The *Report Wizard* is the easiest way to create a report, just as the Form Wizard is the easiest way to create a form. The Report Wizard asks you questions about the report you want, then builds the report for you. You can accept the report as is, or you can customize it to better suit your needs.

Figure 3.3a displays the New Report dialog box, from which you can select the Report Wizard. The Report Wizard, in turn, requires you to specify the table or query on which the report will be based. The report in this example will be based on an expanded version of the Students table that was created in Chapter 2.

After you specify the underlying table, you select one or more fields from that table, as shown in Figure 3.3b. The Report Wizard then asks you to select a layout (e.g., Tabular in Figure 3.3c.) and a style (e.g., Soft Gray in Figure 3.3d). This is all the information the Report Wizard requires, and it proceeds to create the report for you. The controls on the report correspond to the fields you selected and are displayed in accordance with the specified layout.

Apply What You Know

The Report Wizard provides an excellent starting point, but typically does not create the report exactly as you would like it to be. Accordingly, you can modify a

Report header ——————

Page header ——————

Detail lines ——————

Page footer ——————

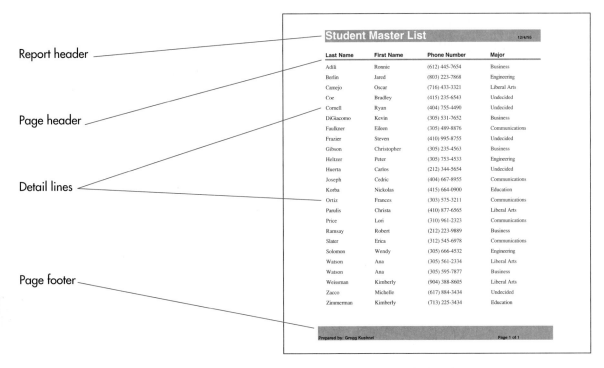

(a) The Printed Report

Report header (title and date) ——————

Page header (column headings) ——————

Detail (data for each record) ——————

Page footer (page number) ——————

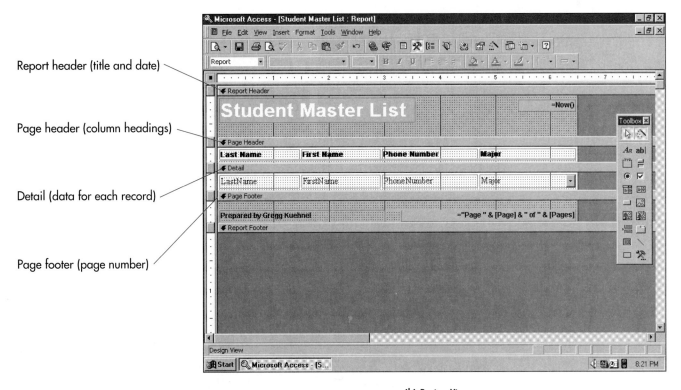

(b) Design View

FIGURE 3.2   Anatomy of a Report

Select the underlying table/query

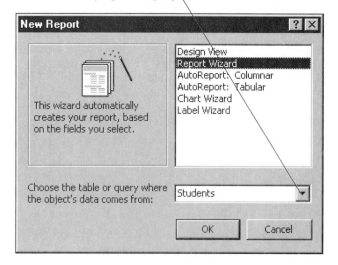

(a) Select the Underlying Table

Selected fields for report

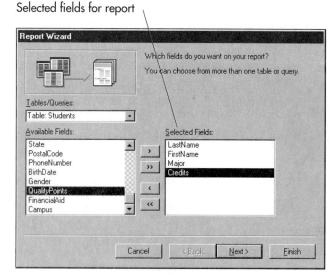

(b) Select the Fields

Selected layout and orientation

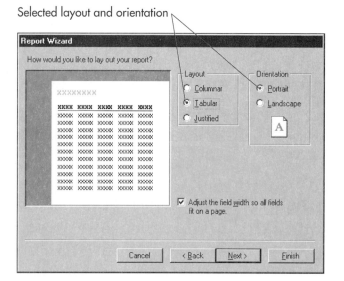

(c) Choose the Layout

Selected style

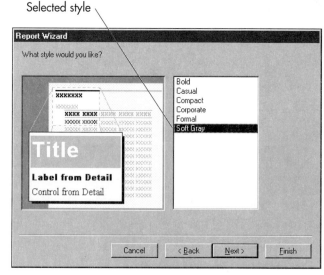

(d) Choose the Style

FIGURE 3.3   The Report Wizard

report created by the Report Wizard, just as you can modify a form created by the Form Wizard. The techniques are the same, and you should look for similarities between forms and reports so that you can apply what you already know. Knowledge of one is helpful in understanding the other.

Controls appear in a report just as they do in a form, and the same definitions apply. A ***bound control*** has as its data source a field in the underlying table. An ***unbound control*** has no data source and is used to display titles, labels, lines, rectangles, and graphics. A ***calculated control*** has as its data source an expression rather than a field. A student's Grade Point Average is an example of a calculated control since it is computed by dividing the number of quality points by the number of credits. The means for selecting, sizing, moving, aligning, and deleting controls are the same, regardless of whether you are working on a form or a report. Thus:

- To select a control, click anywhere on the control. To select multiple controls, press and hold the Shift key as you click each successive control.
- To size a control, click the control to select it, then drag the sizing handles. Drag the handles on the top or bottom to size the box vertically. Drag the handles on the left or right side to size the box horizontally. Drag the handles in the corner to size both horizontally and vertically.
- To move a control, point to any border, but not to a sizing handle (the mouse pointer changes to a hand), then click the mouse and drag the control to its new position.
- To change the properties of a control, point to the control, click the right mouse button to display a shortcut menu, then click Properties to display the property sheet. Click the text box for the desired property, make the necessary change, then close the property sheet.

INHERITANCE

A bound control inherits the same property settings as the associated field in the underlying table. Changing the property setting for a field after the report has been created does *not*, however, change the property of the corresponding control in the report. In similar fashion, changing the property setting of a control in a report does *not* change the property setting of the field in the underlying table.

HANDS-ON EXERCISE 1

The Report Wizard

Objective: To use the Report Wizard to create a new report; to modify an existing report by adding, deleting, and/or modifying its controls. Use Figure 3.4 as a guide in the exercise.

STEP 1: Open the Our Students Database
➤ Start Access. You should see the Microsoft Access dialog box with the option button to **Open an Existing Database** already selected.
➤ Double click the **More Files** selection to display the Open dialog box. Click the **drop-down arrow** on the Look In list box, click the drive containing the **Exploring Access folder,** then open that folder.

THE OUR STUDENTS DATABASE

The Our Students database has the identical design as the database you created in Chapter 2. We have, however, expanded the Students table so that it contains 24 records. The larger table enables you to create more meaningful reports and to obtain the same results as we do in the hands-on exercise.

➤ Click the **down scroll arrow,** if necessary, and select the **Our Students** database. Click the **Open command button** to open the database.

➤ Click the **Reports tab** in the database window, then click the **New command button** to display the New Report dialog box in Figure 3.4a. Select the **Report Wizard** as the means of creating the report.

➤ Click the **drop-down arrow** to display the tables and queries in the database in order to select the one on which the report will be based. Click **Students** (the only table in the database). Click **OK** to start the Report Wizard.

Click Reports tab

Click Report Wizard

Click drop-down arrow to see list of available tables and queries

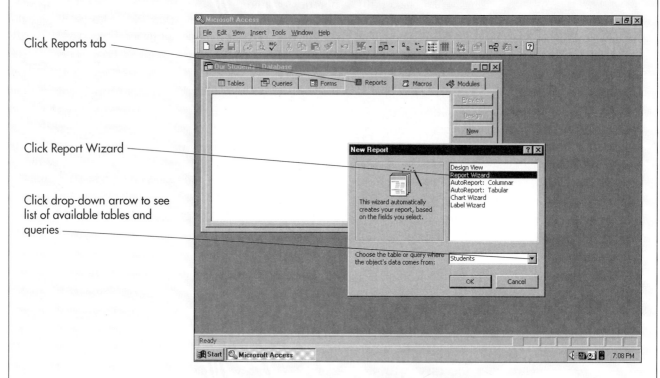

(a) Create a Report (step 1)

FIGURE 3.4   Hands-on Exercise 1

STEP 2: The Report Wizard

➤ You should see the dialog box in Figure 3.4b, which displays all of the fields in the Students table. Click the **LastName field** in the Available Fields list box, then click the **> button** to enter this field in the Selected Fields list, as shown in Figure 3.4b.

➤ Enter the remaining fields (FirstName, PhoneNumber, and Major) one at a time, by selecting the field name, then clicking the **> button.** Click the **Next command button** when you have entered all fields.

WHAT THE REPORT WIZARD DOESN'T TELL YOU

The fastest way to select a field is by double clicking; that is, double click a field in the Available Fields list box, and it is automatically moved to the Selected Fields list for inclusion in the report. The process also works in reverse; that is, you can double click a field in the Selected Fields list to remove it from the report.

Click the > button to move selected field from Available Fields list to Selected Fields list

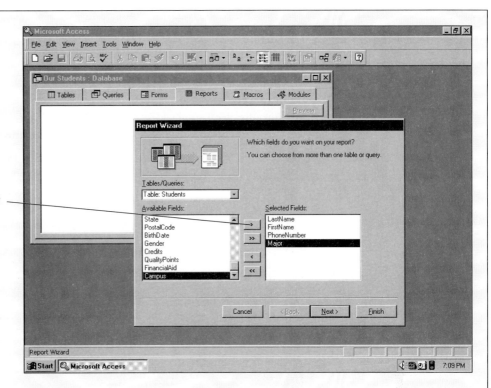

(b) The Report Wizard

FIGURE 3.4   Hands-on Exercise 1 (continued)

STEP 3: The Report Wizard (continued)

➤ The Report Wizard displays several additional screens asking about the report you want to create. The first screen asks whether you want to choose any grouping levels. Click **Next** without specifying a grouping level.

➤ The next screen asks whether you want to sort the records. Click the **drop-down arrow** to display the available fields, then select **LastName.** Click **Next.**

➤ The **Tabular layout** is selected, as is **Portrait orientation.** Be sure the box is checked to **Adjust field width so all fields fit on a page.** Click **Next.**

➤ Choose **Soft Gray** as the style. Click **Next.**

➤ Enter **Student Master List** as the title for your report. The option button to **Preview the Report** is already selected. Click the **Finish command button** to exit the Report Wizard and view the report.

AUTOMATIC SAVING

The Report Wizard automatically saves a report under the name you supply for the title of the report. To verify that a report has been saved, change to the Database window by pulling down the Window menu or by clicking the Database Window button that appears on every toolbar. Once you are in the Database window, click the Reports tab to see the list of existing reports. Note, however, that any subsequent changes must be saved explicitly by clicking the Save button in the Report Design view, or by clicking Yes in response to the warning prompt should you attempt to close the report without saving the changes.

STEP 4: Preview the Report

➤ Click the **Maximize button** so the report takes the entire window as shown in Figure 3.4c. Note the report header at the beginning of the report, the page header (column headings) at the top of the page, and the page footer at the bottom of the page.

➤ Click the **drop-down arrow** on the Zoom Control box so that you can view the report at **75%.** Click the **scroll arrows** on the vertical scroll bar to view the names of additional students.

➤ Click the **Close button** to close the Print Preview window and change to the Report Design view.

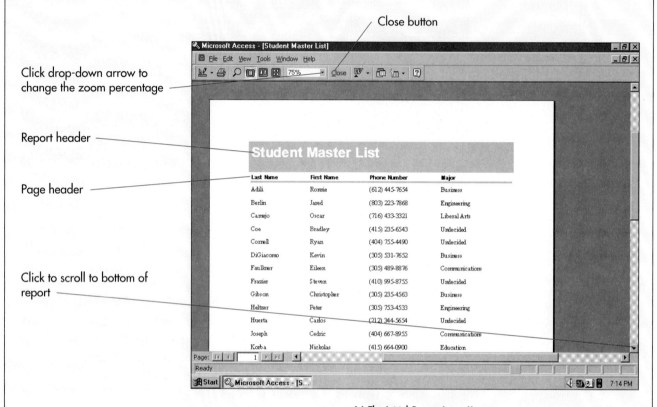

Close button

Click drop-down arrow to change the zoom percentage

Report header

Page header

Click to scroll to bottom of report

(c) The Initial Report (step 4)

FIGURE 3.4   Hands-on Exercise 1 (continued)

THE PRINT PREVIEW WINDOW

The Print Preview window enables you to preview a report in various ways. Click the One Page, Two Page, or Multiple Page buttons for different views of a report. Use the Zoom button to toggle between the full page and zoom (magnified) views, or use the Zoom Control box to choose a specific magnification. The Navigation buttons at the bottom of the Print Preview window enable you to preview a specific page, while the vertical scroll bar at the right side of the window lets you scroll within a page.

STEP 5: Modify an Existing Control

➤ Click and drag the control containing the **Now function** from the report footer to the report header as shown in Figure 3.4d. Size the control as necessary, then check that the control is still selected and click the **Align Right button** on the Formatting toolbar.

➤ Point to the control, then click the **right mouse button** to display a shortcut menu and click **Properties** to display the Properties sheet.

➤ Click the **Format tab** in the Properties sheet, click the **Format property,** then click the **drop-down arrow** to display the available formats. Click **Short Date,** then close the Properties sheet.

➤ Pull down the **File menu** and click **Save** (or click the **Save button**) to save the modified design

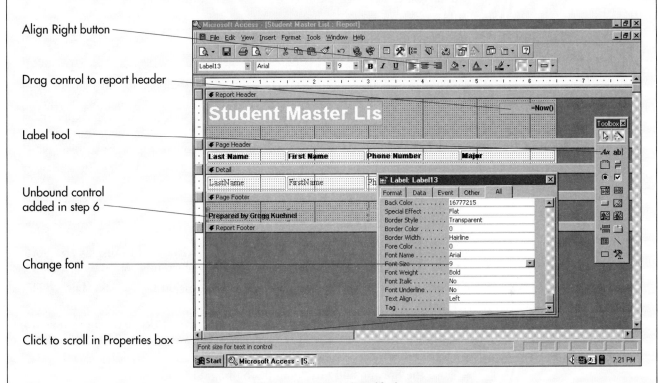

Align Right button

Drag control to report header

Label tool

Unbound control added in step 6

Change font

Click to scroll in Properties box

(d) Modify the Report (steps 5 & 6)

FIGURE 3.4   Hands-on Exercise 1 (continued)

ACCESS FUNCTIONS

Access contains many built-in functions, each of which returns a specific value or the result of a calculation. The Now function, for example, returns the current date and time. The Page and Pages functions return the specific page number and total number of pages, respectively. The Report Wizard automatically adds these functions at appropriate places in a report. You can also add these (or other) functions explicitly, by creating a text box, then replacing the default unbound control by an equal sign, followed by the function name (and associated arguments if any)— for example, =Now( ) to insert the current date and time.

STEP 6: Add an Unbound Control

➤ Click the **Label tool** on the Toolbox toolbar, then click and drag in the report footer where you want the label to go and release the mouse. You should see a flashing insertion point inside the label control. (If you see the word *Unbound* instead of the insertion point, it means you selected the Text box tool rather than the Label tool; delete the text box and begin again.)

➤ Type **Prepared by** followed by your name as shown in Figure 3.4d. Press **enter** to complete the entry and also select the control. Point to the control, click the **right mouse button** to display the shortcut menu, then click **Properties** to display the Properties dialog box.

➤ Click the **down arrow** on the scroll bar, then scroll until you see the Font Size property. Click in the **Font Size box,** click the **drop-down arrow,** then scroll until you can change the font size to **9.** Close the Property sheet.

MISSING TOOLBARS

The Report Design, Formatting, and Toolbox toolbars appear by default in the Report Design view, but any (or all) of these toolbars may be hidden at the discretion of the user. If any of these toolbars do not appear, point to any visible toolbar, click the right mouse button to display a shortcut menu, then click the name of the toolbar you want to display. You can also click the Toolbox button on the Report Design toolbar to display (hide) the Toolbox toolbar.

STEP 7: Change the Sort Order

➤ Pull down the **View menu.** Click **Sorting and Grouping** to display the Sorting and Grouping dialog box. The students are currently sorted by last name.

➤ Click the **drop-down arrow** in the Field Expression box. Click **Major.** (The ascending sequence is selected automatically.)

➤ Click on the next line in the Field Expression box, click the **drop-down arrow** to display the available fields, then click **LastName** to sort the students alphabetically within major as shown in Figure 3.4e.

➤ Close the Sorting and Grouping dialog box. Save the report.

STEP 8: View the Modified Report

➤ Click the **Print Preview button** to preview the finished report. If necessary, click the **Zoom button** on the Print Preview toolbar so that the display on your monitor matches Figure 3.4f. The report has changed so that:

• The date appears in the report header (as opposed to the report footer). The format of the date has changed to a numbered month, and the day of the week has been eliminated.

• The students are listed by major and, within each major, alphabetically according to last name.

• Your name appears in the Report Footer. Click the **down arrow** on the vertical scroll bar to move to the bottom of the page to see your name.

➤ Click the **Print button** to print the report and submit it to your instructor. Click the **Close button** to exit the Print Preview window.

➤ Click the **Close button** in the Report Design window. Click **Yes** if asked whether to save the changes to the Student Master List report.

Print Preview button

Click to close dialog box

Select Major from drop-down list

Select LastName from drop-down list

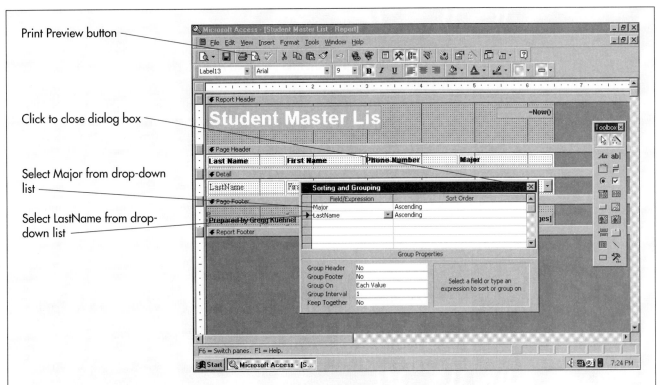

(e) Change the Sort Order (step 7)

Close button

Zoom button

Date is in report header

Students are in alphabetical order within major

Click to scroll to bottom of page

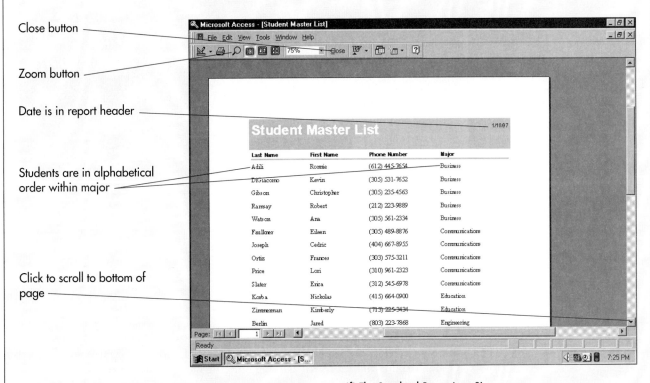

(f) The Completed Report (step 8)

FIGURE 3.4   Hands-on Exercise 1 (continued)

STEP 9: Report Properties

➤ The Database window for the Our Students database should be displayed on the screen as shown in Figure 3.4g. Click the **Restore button** to restore the window to its earlier size.

➤ The **Reports tab** is already selected. Point to the **Student Master List** (the only report in the database), click the **right mouse button** to display a shortcut menu, then click **Properties** to display the Properties dialog box as shown in Figure 3.4g.

➤ Click the **Description text box,** then enter the description shown in the figure. Click **OK** to close the Properties dialog box.

➤ Close the database. Exit Access if you do not wish to continue with the next exercise at this time.

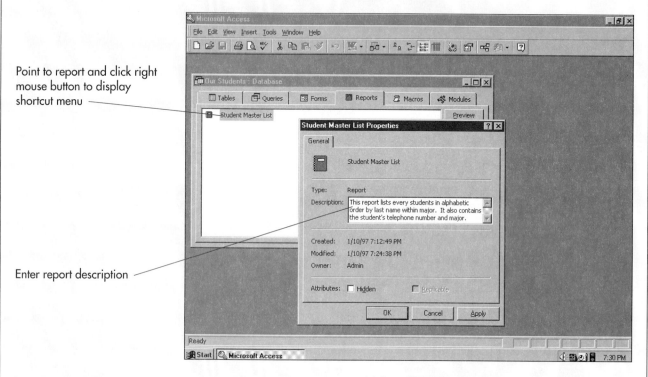

Point to report and click right mouse button to display shortcut menu

Enter report description

(g) Report Properties

FIGURE 3.4   Hands-on Exercise 1 (continued)

DESCRIBE YOUR OBJECTS

A working database will contain many different objects of the same type, making it all too easy to forget the purpose of the individual objects. It is important, therefore, to use meaningful names for the objects themselves, and further to take advantage of the Description property to enter additional information about the object. Once a description has been created, you can right click any object in the Database window, then click the Properties command from the shortcut menu to display the Properties dialog box with the description of the object.

The report you just created displayed every student in the underlying table. What if, however, we wanted to see just the students who are majoring in Business? Or the students who are receiving financial aid? Or the students who are majoring in Business *and* receiving financial aid? The ability to ask questions such as these, and to see the answers to those questions, is provided through a query. Queries represent the real power of a database.

A *query* lets you see the data you want in the sequence that you want it. It lets you select specific records from a table (or from several tables) and show some or all of the fields for the selected records. It also lets you perform calculations to display data that is not explicitly stored in the underlying table(s), such as a student's GPA.

A query represents a question and an answer. The question is developed by using a graphical tool known as the *design grid.* The answer is displayed in a *dynaset,* which contains the records that satisfy the criteria specified in the query.

A dynaset looks and acts like a table, but it isn't a table; it is a *dyna*mic sub-*set* of a table that selects and sorts records as specified in the query. A dynaset is similar to a table in appearance and, like a table, it enables you to enter a new record or modify or delete an existing record. Any changes made in the dynaset are automatically reflected in the underlying table.

Figure 3.5a displays the Students table we have been using throughout the chapter. (We omit some of the fields for ease of illustration.) Figure 3.5b contains the design grid used to select students whose major is "Undecided" and further, to list those students in alphabetical order. (The design grid is explained in the next section.) Figure 3.5c displays the answer to the query in the form of a dynaset.

The table in Figure 3.5a contains 24 records. The dynaset in Figure 3.5c has only five records, corresponding to the students who are undecided about their major. The table in Figure 3.5a has 15 fields for each record (some of the fields are hidden). The dynaset in Figure 3.5c has only four fields. The records in the table are in social security number order (the primary key), whereas the records in the dynaset are in alphabetical order by last name.

The query in Figure 3.5 is an example of a *select query,* which is the most common type of query. A select query searches the underlying table (Figure 3.5a in the example) to retrieve the data that satisfies the query. The data is displayed in a dynaset (Figure 3.5c), which you can modify to update the data in the under-lying table(s). The specifications for selecting records and determining which fields will be displayed for the selected records, as well as the sequence of the selected records, are established within the design grid of Figure 3.5b.

The design grid consists of columns and rows. Each field in the query has its own column and contains multiple rows. The *Field row* displays the field name. The *Sort row* enables you to sort in *ascending* or *descending sequence.* The *Show row* controls whether or not the field will be displayed in the dynaset. The *Criteria row(s)* determine the records that will be selected, such as students with an undecided major.

REPORTS, QUERIES, AND TABLES

Every report is based on either a table or a query. The design of the report may be the same with respect to the fields that are included, but the actual reports will be very different. A report based on a table contains every record in the table and is in sequence by the primary key. A report based on a query contains only the records that satisfy the criteria in the query in the specified sequence.

Records in table are in order by SSN —

SSN	First Name	Last Name	Major	BirthDate	Gender	Credits	QualityPoints
111-11-1111	Jared	Berlin	Engineering	1/15/72	M	100	250
111-22-3333	Christopher	Gibson	Business	3/12/73	M	35	60
112-12-1212	Peter	Heltzer	Engineering	3/8/73	M	25	100
222-22-2222	Cedric	Joseph	Communications	4/12/74	M	45	170
223-34-2323	Kimberly	Zimmerman	Education	4/18/70	F	120	395
233-33-4444	Robert	Ramsay	Business	5/1/74	M	50	162
333-22-1111	Steven	Frazier	Undecided	9/9/68	M	35	45
333-33-3333	Kimberly	Weissman	Liberal Arts	11/11/74	F	63	166
334-44-4444	Christa	Parulis	Liberal Arts	7/15/72	F	50	90
444-44-4444	Oscar	Camejo	Liberal Arts	3/10/75	M	100	280
445-55-4444	Ronnie	Adili	Business	6/1/75	F	60	155
446-66-7777	Ana	Watson	Business	4/18/75	F	30	75
555-55-5555	Ana	Watson	Liberal Arts	8/1/75	F	70	195
556-66-7777	Frances	Ortiz	Communications	2/3/74	F	28	60
666-33-1111	Bradley	Coe	Undecided	8/22/71	M	52	143
666-66-6666	Nickolas	Korba	Education	11/11/71	M	100	166
666-77-7766	Erica	Slater	Communications	5/1/72	F	105	390
777-77-7777	Wendy	Solomon	Engineering	1/31/75	F	50	175
777-88-8888	Ryan	Cornell	Undecided	9/30/74	M	45	80
888-77-7777	Lori	Price	Communications	7/1/72	F	24	42
888-88-8888	Michelle	Zacco	Undecided	10/24/75	F	21	68
888-99-9999	Eileen	Faulkner	Communications	9/12/75	F	30	80
999-11-1111	Kevin	DiGiacomo	Business	5/31/72	M	105	375
999-99-9999	Carlos	Huerta	Undecided	6/18/75	M	15	40

Record: 1 of 24

(a) Students Table

Students will be listed in alphabetical order by LastName —

Only those students with an Undecided major will be included —

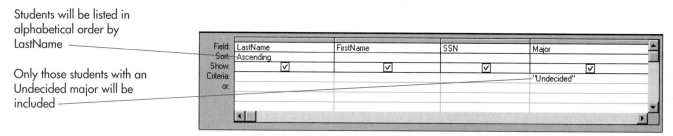

Field:	LastName	FirstName	SSN	Major
Sort:	Ascending			
Show:	✓	✓	✓	✓
Criteria:				"Undecided"
or:				

(b) Design Grid

Records in dynaset are in alphabetical order by LastName —

Only Undecided majors will be included —

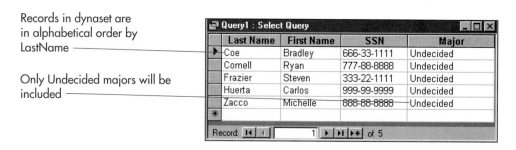

Last Name	First Name	SSN	Major
Coe	Bradley	666-33-1111	Undecided
Cornell	Ryan	777-88-8888	Undecided
Frazier	Steven	333-22-1111	Undecided
Huerta	Carlos	999-99-9999	Undecided
Zacco	Michelle	888-88-8888	Undecided

Record: 1 of 5

(c) Dynaset

FIGURE 3.5   Queries

Query Window

The **Query window** has three views. The **Design view** is displayed by default and is used to create (or modify) a select query. The **Datasheet view** displays the resulting dynaset. The **SQL view** enables you to use SQL (Structured Query Language) statements to modify the query and is beyond the scope of the present

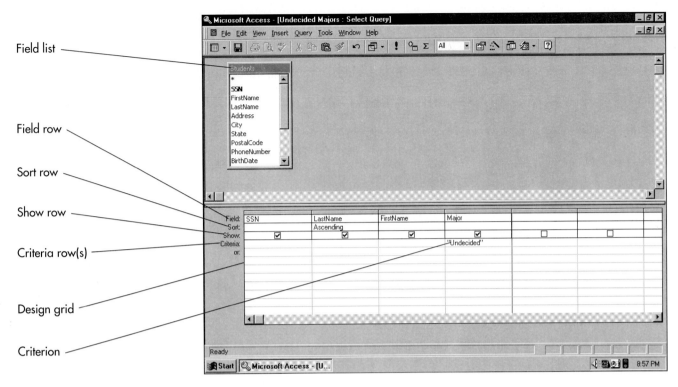

Field list

Field row

Sort row

Show row

Criteria row(s)

Design grid

Criterion

FIGURE 3.6 Query Design View

discussion. The Query Design toolbar contains the buttons to display all three views.

A select query is created in the Design view as shown in Figure 3.6a. The upper portion of the Design view window contains the field list for the table(s) on which the query is based (the Students table in this example). The lower portion of the window displays the design grid, which is where the specifications for the select query are entered. A field is added to the design grid by dragging it from the field list.

The data type of a field determines the way in which the criteria are specified for that field. The criterion for a text field is enclosed in quotation marks. The criteria for number, currency, and counter fields are shown as digits with or without a decimal point. (Commas and dollar signs are not allowed.) Dates are enclosed in pound signs and are entered in the mm/dd/yy format. The criterion for a Yes/No field is entered as Yes (or True) or No (or False).

CONVERSION TO STANDARD FORMAT

Access accepts values for text and date fields in the design grid in multiple formats. The value for a text field can be entered with or without quotation marks (Undecided or "Undecided"). A date can be entered with or without pound signs (1/1/97 or #1/1/97#). Access converts your entries to standard format as soon as you move to the next cell in the design grid. Thus, text entries are always shown in quotation marks, and dates are enclosed in pound signs.

Selection Criteria

To specify selection criteria in the design grid, enter a value or expression in the Criteria row of the appropriate column. Figure 3.7 contains several examples of simple criteria and provides a basic introduction to select queries.

The criterion in Figure 3.7a selects the students majoring in Business. The criteria for text fields are case-insensitive. Thus, "*Business*" is the same as "*business*" or "*BUSINESS*".

Values entered in multiple columns of the same Criteria row implement an **AND condition** in which the selected records must meet *all* of the specified criteria. The criteria in Figure 3.7b select students who are majoring in Business *and* who are from the state of Florida. The criteria in Figure 3.7c select Communications majors who are receiving financial aid.

Values entered in different Criteria rows are connected by an **OR condition** in which the selected records may satisfy *any* of the indicated criteria. The criteria in Figure 3.7d select students who are majoring in Business *or* who are from Florida or both.

Field:	LastName	State	Major	BirthDate	FinancialAid	Credits
Sort:						
Show:	☑	☑	☑	☑	☑	☑
Criteria:			"Business"			
or:						

(a) Business Majors

Field:	LastName	State	Major	BirthDate	FinancialAid	Credits
Sort:						
Show:	☑	☑	☑	☑	☑	☑
Criteria:		"FL"	"Business"			
or:						

(b) Business Majors from Florida

Field:	LastName	State	Major	BirthDate	FinancialAid	Credits
Sort:						
Show:	☑	☑	☑	☑	☑	☑
Criteria:			"Communications"		Yes	
or:						

(c) Communications Majors Receiving Financial Aid

Field:	LastName	State	Major	BirthDate	FinancialAid	Credits
Sort:						
Show:	☑	☑	☑	☑	☑	☑
Criteria:		"FL"				
or:			"Business"			

(d) Business Majors or Students from Florida

FIGURE 3.7   Criteria

Relational operators (>, <, >=, <=, =, and <>) are used with date or number fields to return records within a designated range. The criteria in Figure 3.7e select Engineering majors with fewer than 60 credits. The criteria in Figure 3.7f select Communications majors who were born on or after April 1, 1974.

Field:	LastName	State	Major	BirthDate	FinancialAid	Credits
Sort:						
Show:	☑	☑	☑	☑	☑	☑
Criteria:			"Engineering"			<60
or:						

(e) Engineering Majors with Fewer than 60 Credits

Field:	LastName	State	Major	BirthDate	FinancialAid	Credits
Sort:						
Show:	☑	☑	☑	☑	☑	☑
Criteria:			"Communications"	>=#4/1/74#		
or:						

(f) Communications Majors Born on or after April 1, 1974

Field:	LastName	State	Major	BirthDate	FinancialAid	Credits
Sort:						
Show:	☑	☑	☑	☑	☑	☑
Criteria:			"Engineering"			<60
or:			Communications	>=#4/1/74#		

(g) Engineering Majors with Fewer than 60 Credits or Communications Majors Born on or after April 1, 1974

Field:	LastName	State	Major	BirthDate	FinancialAid	Credits
Sort:						
Show:	☑	☑	☑	☑	☑	☑
Criteria:						Between 60 and 90
or:						

(h) Students with between 60 and 90 Credits

Field:	LastName	State	Major	BirthDate	FinancialAid	Credits
Sort:						
Show:	☑	☑	☑	☑	☑	☑
Criteria:			Not "Liberal Arts"			
or:						

(i) Students with Majors Other Than Liberal Arts

FIGURE 3.7   Criteria (continued)

Criteria can grow more complex by combining multiple AND and OR conditions. The criteria in Figure 3.7g select Engineering majors with fewer than 60 credits *or* Communications majors who were born on or after April 1, 1974.

Other functions enable you to impose still other criteria. The ***Between function*** selects records that fall within a range of values. The criterion in Figure 3.7h selects students who have between 60 and 90 credits. The ***NOT function*** selects records that do not contain the designated value. The criterion in Figure 3.7i selects students with majors other than Liberal Arts.

WILD CARDS

Select queries recognize the question mark and asterisk wild cards that enable you to search for a pattern within a text field. A question mark stands for a single character in the same position as the question mark; thus H?ll will return Hall, Hill, and Hull. An asterisk stands for any number of characters in the same position as the asterisk; for example, S*nd will return Sand, Stand, and Strand.

HANDS-ON EXERCISE 2

Creating a Select Query

Objective: To create a select query using the design grid; to show how changing values in a dynaset changes the values in the underlying table; to create a report based on a query. Use Figure 3.8 as a guide in the exercise.

STEP 1: Open the Existing Database
➤ Start Access as you did in the previous exercise. Our Students (the database you used in the previous exercise) should appear within the list of recently opened databases.
➤ Select (click) **Our Students,** then click **OK** (or simply double click the name of the database) to open the database and display the database window.
➤ Click the **Queries tab** in the database window. Click the **New command button** to display the New Query dialog box as shown in Figure 3.8a.
➤ **Design View** is already selected as the means of creating a query. Click **OK** to begin creating the query.

THE SIMPLE QUERY WIZARD

The Simple Query Wizard is exactly what its name implies—simple. It lets you select fields from an underlying table, but it does not let you enter values or a sort sequence. We prefer, therefore, to bypass the Wizard and to create the query entirely from the Query Design window.

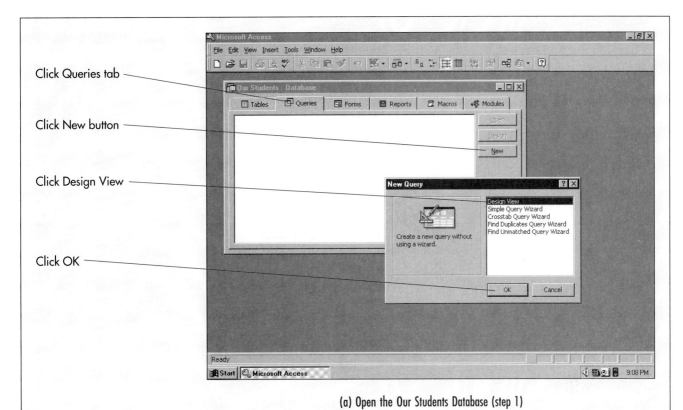

Click Queries tab

Click New button

Click Design View

Click OK

(a) Open the Our Students Database (step 1)

FIGURE 3.8　Hands-on Exercise 2

STEP 2: Add the Students Table

➤ The Show Table dialog box appears as shown in Figure 3.8b, with the **Tables tab** already selected.

➤ Click the **Add button** to add the Students table to the query. (You can also double click the Students table.)

➤ The field list should appear within the Query Design window. Click **Close** to close the Show Table dialog box.

➤ Click the **Maximize button** so that the Query Design window takes up the entire screen.

CUSTOMIZE THE QUERY WINDOW

The Query window displays the field list and design grid in its upper and lower halves, respectively. To increase (decrease) the size of either portion of the window, drag the line dividing the upper and lower sections. Drag the title bar to move a field list. You can also size a field list by dragging a border just as you would size any other window. Press the F6 key to toggle between the upper and lower halves of the Design window.

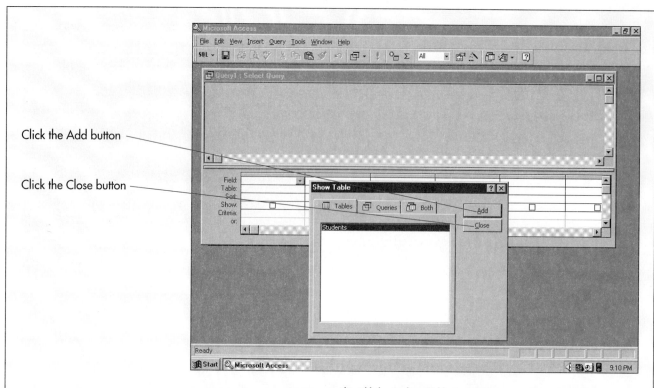

Click the Add button

Click the Close button

(b) Add the Students Table (step 2)

FIGURE 3.8 Hands-on Exercise 2 (continued)

STEP 3: Create the Query

➤ Click and drag the **LastName field** from the Students field list to the Field row in the first column of the QBE grid as shown in Figure 3.8c.

➤ Click and drag the **FirstName, PhoneNumber, Major,** and **Credits fields** (in that order) in similar fashion, dragging each field to the next available column in the Field row.

➤ A check appears in the Show row under each field name to indicate that the field will be displayed in the dynaset. (The show box functions as a toggle switch; thus, you can click the box to clear the check and hide the field in the dynaset. Click the box a second time to display the check and show the field.)

ADDING AND DELETING FIELDS

The fastest way to add a field to the design grid is to double click the field name in the field list. To add more than one field at a time, press and hold the Ctrl key as you click the fields within the field list, then drag the group to a cell in the Field row. To delete a field, click the column selector above the field name to select the column, then press the Del key.

STEP 4: Specify the Criteria

➤ Click the **Criteria row** for Major. Type **Undecided.**

➤ Click the **Sort row** under the LastName field, click the **drop-down arrow,** then select **Ascending** as the sort sequence.

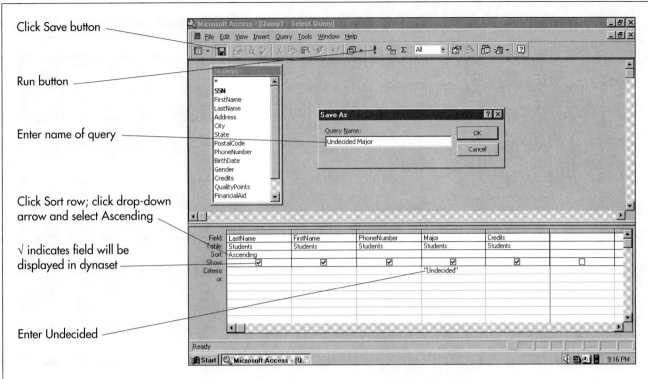

Click Save button

Run button

Enter name of query

Click Sort row; click drop-down arrow and select Ascending

√ indicates field will be displayed in dynaset

Enter Undecided

(c) Create the Query (steps 3 & 4)

FIGURE 3.8   Hands-on Exercise 2 (continued)

➤ Pull down the **File menu** and click **Save** (or click the **Save button**) to display the dialog box in Figure 3.8c.

➤ Type **Undecided Major** as the query name. Click **OK.**

FLEXIBLE CRITERIA

Access offers a great deal of flexibility in the way you enter the criteria for a text field. Quotation marks and/or an equal sign are optional. Thus "Undecided", Undecided, =Undecided, or ="Undecided" are all valid, and you may choose any of these formats. Access will convert your entry to standard format ("Undecided" in this example) after you have moved to the next cell.

STEP 5: Run the Query

➤ Pull down the **Query menu** and click **Run** (or click the **Run button**) to run the query and change to the Datasheet view.

➤ You should see the five records in the dynaset of Figure 3.8d. Change Ryan Cornell's major to Business by clicking in the **Major field,** clicking the **drop-down arrow,** then choosing **Business** from the drop-down list.

➤ Click the **View button** to change the query.

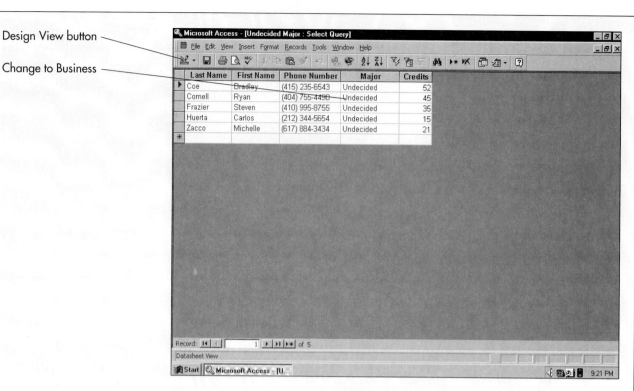

Design View button

Change to Business

(d) Run the Query (step 5)

FIGURE 3.8   Hands-on Exercise 2 (continued)

STEP 6: Modify the Query

➤ Click the **Show check box** in the Major field to remove the check as shown in Figure 3.8e.

➤ Click the **Criteria row** under credits. Type **>30** to select only the Undecided majors with more than 30 credits.

➤ Click the **Save button** to save the revised query. Click the **Run button** to run the revised query. This time there are only two records (Bradley Coe and Steven Frazier) in the dynaset, and the major is no longer displayed.

  • Ryan Cornell does not appear because he has changed his major.

  • Carlos Huerta and Michelle Zacco do not appear because they do not have more than 30 credits.

STEP 7: Create a Report

➤ Pull down the **Window menu** and click **1 Our Students: Database** (or click the **Database window button** on the toolbar). You will see the Database window in Figure 3.8f.

➤ Click the **Reports tab,** then click the **New button** to create a report based on the query you just created. Select **Report Wizard** as the means of creating the report.

➤ Select **Undecided Major** from the drop-down list as shown in Figure 3.8f. Click **OK** to begin the Report Wizard.

➤ You should see the Report Wizard dialog box, which displays all of the visible fields (Major has been hidden) in the Undecided Major query. Click the **>> button** to select all of the fields from the query for the report. Click **Next.**

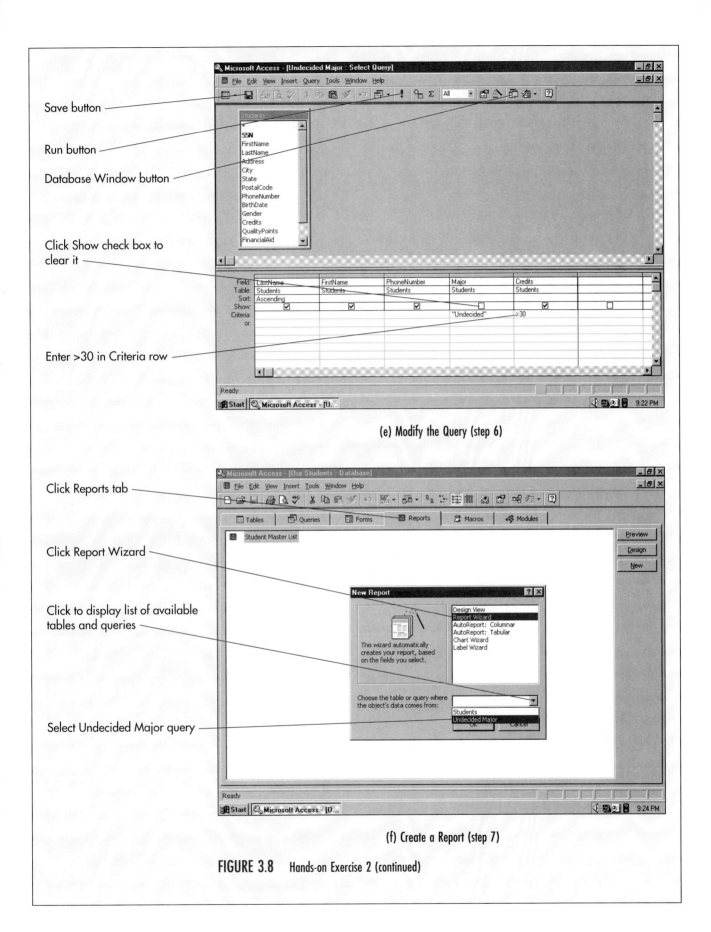

Save button

Run button

Database Window button

Click Show check box to clear it

Enter >30 in Criteria row

(e) Modify the Query (step 6)

Click Reports tab

Click Report Wizard

Click to display list of available tables and queries

Select Undecided Major query

(f) Create a Report (step 7)

FIGURE 3.8   Hands-on Exercise 2 (continued)

➤ You do not want to choose additional grouping levels. Click **Next** to move to the next screen.

➤ There is no need to specify a sort sequence. Click **Next.**

➤ The **Tabular layout** is selected, as is **Portrait orientation.** Be sure the box is checked to **Adjust field width so all fields fit on a page.** Click **Next.**

➤ Choose **Soft Gray** as the style. Click **Next.**

➤ If necessary, enter **Undecided Major** as the title for your report. The option button to **Preview the Report** is already selected. Click the **Finish command button** to exit the Report Wizard and view the report.

THE BACK BUTTON

The Back button is present on every screen within the Report Wizard and enables you to recover from mistakes or simply to change your mind about how you want the report to look. Click the Back button at any time to return to the previous screen, then click it again if you want to return to the screen before that, and continue, if necessary, all the way back to the beginning.

STEP 8: View the Report

➤ If necessary, click the **Maximize button** to see the completed report as shown in Figure 3.8g. Click the **Zoom button** to see the full page.

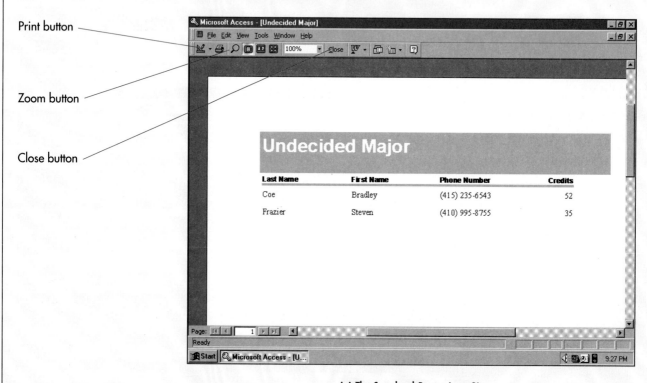

(g) The Completed Report (step 8)

FIGURE 3.8   Hands-on Exercise 2 (continued)

➤ Click the **Print button** to print the report and submit it to your instructor. Click the **Close button** to exit the Print Preview window.

➤ Click the **Close button** in the Report Design window.

➤ If necessary, click the **Database Window button** on the toolbar to return to the Database window. Click the **Maximize button**:

- Click the **Queries tab** to display the names of the queries in the Our Students database. You should see the *Undecided Major* query created in this exercise.

- Click the **Reports tab.** You should see two reports: *Student Master List* (created in the previous exercise) and *Undecided Major* (created in this exercise).

- Click the **Forms tab.** You should see the *Students* form corresponding to the form you created in Chapter 2.

- Click the **Tables tab.** You should see the *Students* table, which is the basis of all other objects in the database.

➤ Close the **Our Students database** and exit Access if you do not wish to continue with the next exercise. Click **Yes** if asked to save changes to any of the objects in the database.

DATABASE PROPERTIES

The tabs within the Database window display the objects within a database, but show only one type of object at a time. You can, for example, see all of the reports or all of the queries, but you cannot see the reports and queries at the same time. There is another way. Pull down the File menu, click Database Properties, then click the Contents tab to display the contents (objects) in the database. You cannot, however, use the Database Properties dialog box to open those objects.

GROUPING RECORDS

The records in a report are often grouped according to the value of a specific field. The report in Figure 3.9a, for example, groups students according to their major, sorts them alphabetically according to last name within each major, then calculates the average GPA for all students in each major. A group header appears before each group of students to identify the group and display the major. A group footer appears at the end of each group and displays the average GPA for students in that major

Figure 3.9b displays the Design view of the report in Figure 3.9a, which determines the appearance of the printed report. Look carefully at the design to relate each section to the corresponding portion of the printed report:

■ The report header contains the title of the report and appears once, at the beginning of the printed report.

■ The page header contains the column headings that appear at the top of each page. The column headings are labels (or unbound controls) and are formatted in bold.

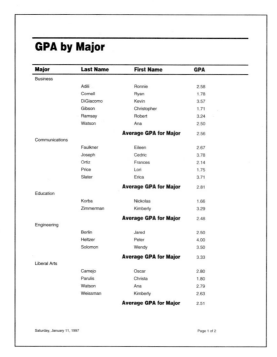
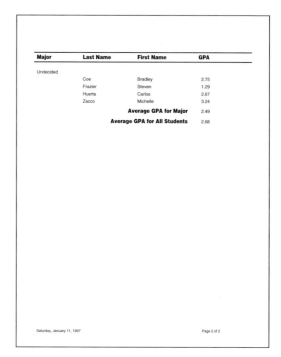

(a) The Printed Columnar Report

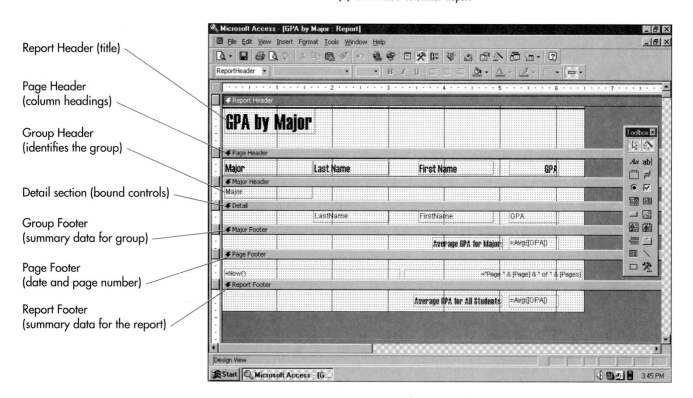

Report Header (title)

Page Header
(column headings)

Group Header
(identifies the group)

Detail section (bound controls)

Group Footer
(summary data for group)

Page Footer
(date and page number)

Report Footer
(summary data for the report)

(b) Design View

FIGURE 3.9   Summary Reports

- The group header consists of a single bound control that displays the value of the major field prior to each group of detail records.
- The detail section consists of bound controls that appear directly under the corresponding heading in the page header. The detail section is printed once for each record in each group.

- The group footer appears after each group of detail records. It consists of an unbound control (Average GPA for Major:) followed by a calculated control that computes the average GPA for each group of students.
- The page footer appears at the bottom of each page and contains the date, page number, and total number of pages in the report.
- The report footer appears at the end of the report. It consists of an unbound control (Average GPA for All Students:) followed by a calculated control that computes the average GPA for all students.

Grouping records within a report enables you to perform calculations on each group of records as was done in the group footer of Figure 3.9. The calculations in our example made use of the *Avg function,* but other types of calculations are possible:

- The *Sum function* computes the total of a specific field for all records in the group.
- The *Min function* determines the minimum value for all records in the group.
- The *Max function* determines the maximum value for all records in the group.
- The *Count function* counts the number of records in the group.

The following exercise has you create the report in Figure 3.9. The report is based on a query containing a calculated control, GPA, which is computed by dividing the QualityPoints field by the Credits field. The Report Wizard is used to design the basic report, but additional modifications are necessary to create the group header and group footer.

HANDS-ON EXERCISE 3

Grouping Records

Objective: To create a query containing a calculated control, then create a report based on that query; to use the Sorting and Grouping command to add a group header and group footer to a report. Use Figure 3.10 as a guide.

STEP 1: Create the Query

➤ Start Access and open the **Our Students database** from the previous exercise.

➤ Click the **Queries tab** in the database window, then click the **New command button** to display the New Query dialog box. **Design View** is already selected as the means of creating a query. Click **OK** to begin creating the query.

➤ The Show Table dialog box appears; the **Tables tab** is already selected, as is the **Students table.**

➤ Click the **Add button** to add the table to the query (the field list should appear within the Query window). Click **Close** to close the Show Table dialog box.

➤ Click the **Maximize button** so that the window takes up the entire screen as shown in Figure 3.10a. Drag the border between the upper and lower portions of the window to give yourself more room in the upper portion. Make the field list larger, to display more fields at one time.

➤ Scroll (if necessary) within the field list, then click and drag the **Major field** from the field list to the query. Click and drag the **LastName, FirstName, QualityPoints,** and **Credits fields** (in that order) in similar fashion.

Click drop-down arrow and
Select Ascending

Click Sort row, then select
Ascending from drop-down list

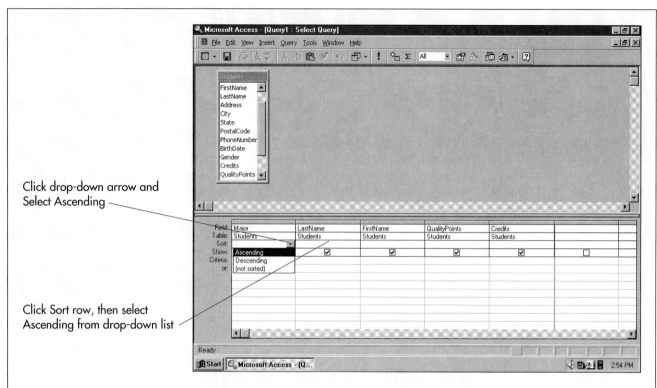

(a) Create the Query (step 1)

FIGURE 3.10   Hands-on Exercise 3

➤ Click the **Sort row** for the Major field. Click the **down arrow** to open the drop-down list box. Click **Ascending.**

➤ Click the **Sort row** for the LastName field. Click the **down arrow** to open the drop-down list box. Click **Ascending.**

SORTING ON MULTIPLE FIELDS

You can sort a query on more than one field, but you must be certain that the fields are in the proper order within the design grid. Access sorts from left to right (the leftmost field is the primary sort key), so the fields must be arranged in the desired sort sequence. To move a field within the design grid, click the column selector above the field name to select the column, then drag the column to its new position.

STEP 2: Add a Calculated Control

➤ Click in the first blank column in the Field row. Enter the expression **=[QualityPoints]/[Credits].** Do not be concerned if you cannot see the entire expression.

➤ Press **enter.** Access has substituted Expr1: for the equal sign you typed initially. Drag the **column selector boundary** so that the entire expression is visible as in Figure 3.10b. (You may have to make some of the columns narrower to see all of the fields in the design grid.)

➤ Pull down the **File menu** and click **Save** (or click the **Save button**) to display the dialog box in Figure 3.10b. Enter **GPA By Major** for the Query Name. Click **OK**.

USE DESCRIPTIVE NAMES

An Access database contains multiple objects—tables, forms, queries, and reports. It is important, therefore, that the name assigned to each object be descriptive of its function so that you can select the proper object from the Database window. The name of an object can contain up to 64 characters and can include any combination of letters, numbers, and spaces. (Names may not, however, include leading spaces, a period, an exclamation mark, or brackets ([ ]).

Save button

Run button

Enter Query Name

Click and drag to adjust column width

Access has substituted Expr1

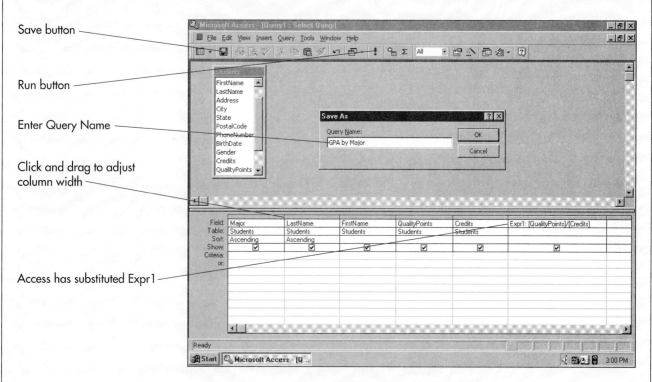

(b) Add a Calculated Control (step 2)

FIGURE 3.10   Hands-on Exercise 3 (continued)

STEP 3: Run the Query

➤ Pull down the **Query menu** and click **Run** (or click the **Run button** on the Query Design toolbar). You will see the dynaset in Figure 3.10c:

• Students are listed by major and alphabetically by last name within major.

• The GPA is calculated to several places (you may not even see the number to the left of the decimal) and appears in the Expr1 field.

➤ Click the **View button** in order to modify the query.

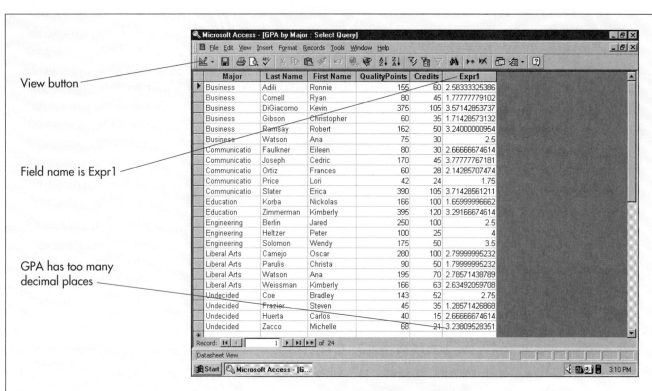

View button

Field name is Expr1

GPA has too many decimal places

(c) Run the Query (step 3)

FIGURE 3.10   Hands-on Exercise 3 (continued)

ADJUST THE COLUMN WIDTH

Point to the right edge of the column you want to resize, then drag the mouse in the direction you want to go; drag to the right to make the column wider or to the left to make it narrower. Alternatively, you can double click the column selector line (right edge) to fit the longest entry in that column. Adjusting the column width in the Design view does not affect the column width in the Datasheet view, but you can use the same technique in both views.

STEP 4: Modify the Query

➤ Click and drag to select **Expr1** in the Field row for the calculated field. (Do not select the colon). Type **GPA** to substitute a more meaningful field name.

➤ Point to the column and click the **right mouse button** to display a shortcut menu. Click **Properties** to display the Field Properties dialog box in Figure 3.10d. Click the **General tab** if necessary:

 • Click the **Description text box.** Enter **GPA** as shown in Figure 3.10d.

 • Click the **Format text box.** Click the **drop-down arrow** to display the available formats. Click **Fixed.**

 • Close the Field Properties dialog box.

➤ Click the **Save button** to save the modified query.

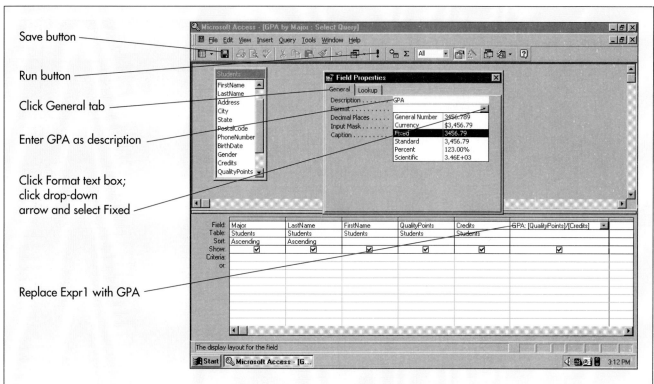

Save button

Run button

Click General tab

Enter GPA as description

Click Format text box;
click drop-down
arrow and select Fixed

Replace Expr1 with GPA

(d) Modify the Query (step 4)

FIGURE 3.10 Hands-on Exercise 3 (continued)

THE TOP VALUES PROPERTY

Can you create a query that lists only the five students with the highest
or lowest GPA? It's easy, if you know about the Top Values property.
First, sort the query according to the desired sequence—for example, students in descending order by GPA to see the students with the highest
GPA. (Remove all other sort keys within the query.) Point anywhere in
the gray area in the upper portion of the Query window, click the right
mouse button to display a shortcut menu, then click Properties to display
the Query Properties sheet. Click the Top Values box and enter the
desired number of students (e.g., 5 for five students, or 5% for the top
five percent). When you run the query you will see only the top five students. (You can see the bottom five instead if you specify ascending rather
than descending as the sort sequence.)

STEP 5: Rerun the Query

➤ Click the **Run button** to run the modified query. You will see a new dynaset
corresponding to the modified query as shown in Figure 3.10e. Resize the column widths (as necessary) within the dynaset.

• Students are still listed by major and alphabetically within major.

• The GPA is calculated to two decimal places and appears under the GPA
field.

Undo button

Field name is GPA

Replace 60 with 70 (GPA changes to 2.00)

GPA has 2 decimal places

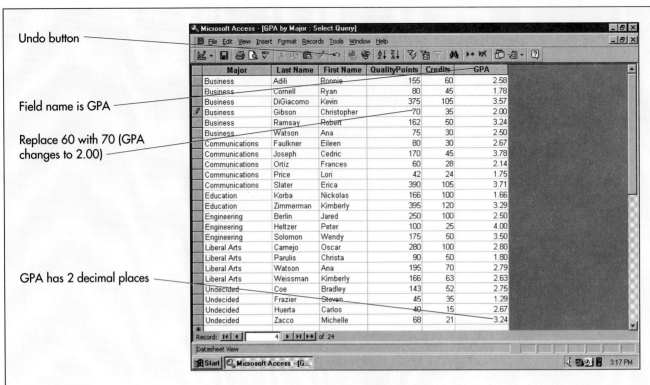

(e) Rerun the Query (step 5)

FIGURE 3.10   Hands-on Exercise 3 (continued)

➤ Click the **QualityPoints field** for Christopher Gibson. Replace 60 with **70.** Press **enter.** The GPA changes automatically to 2.

➤ Pull down the **Edit menu** and click **Undo Current Field/Record** (or click the **Undo button** on the Query toolbar). The GPA returns to its previous value.

➤ Tab to the **GPA field** for Christopher Gibson. Type **2.** Access will beep and prevent you from changing the GPA because it is a calculated field as indicated on the status bar.

➤ Click the **Close button** to close the query and return to the Database window. Click **Yes** if asked whether to save the changes.

THE DYNASET

A query represents a question and an answer. The question is developed by using the design grid in the Query Design view. The answer is displayed in a dynaset that contains the records that satisfy the criteria specified in the query. A dynaset looks and acts like a table but it isn't a table; it is a dynamic subset of a table that selects and sorts records as specified in the query. A dynaset is like a table in that you can enter a new record or modify or delete an existing record. It is dynamic because the changes made to the dynaset are automatically reflected in the underlying table.

STEP 6: The Report Wizard

➤ You should see the Database window. Click the **Reports tab,** then click the **New button** to create a report based on the query you just created. Select **Report Wizard** as the means of creating the report.

➤ Select **GPA By Major** from the drop-down list at the bottom of the dialog box. Click **OK** to begin the Report Wizard. You should see the Report Wizard dialog box, which displays all of the fields in the GPA by Major query.

   • Click the **Major field** in the Available fields list box. Click the **>** button.

   • Add the **LastName, FirstName,** and **GPA fields** one at a time.

   • Do not include the QualityPoints or Credits fields. Click **Next.**

➤ You should see the screen asking whether you want to group the fields. Click (select) the **Major field,** then click the **>** button to display the screen in Figure 3.10f. The Major field appears above the other fields to indicate that the records will be grouped according to the value of the Major field. Click **Next.**

➤ The next screen asks you to specify the order for the detail records. Click the **drop-down arrow** on the list box for the first field. Click **LastName** to sort the records alphabetically by last name within each major. Click **Next.**

➤ The **Stepped Option button** is already selected for the report layout, as is **Portrait orientation.** Be sure the box is checked to **Adjust field width so all fields fit on a page.** Click **Next.**

➤ Choose **Compact** as the style. Click **Next.**

➤ **GPA By Major** (which corresponds to the name of the underlying query) is already entered as the name of the report. Click the Option button to **Modify the report's design.** Click **Finish** to exit the Report Wizard.

Click Reports tab

Major field appears above other fields to indicate that records will be grouped by Major

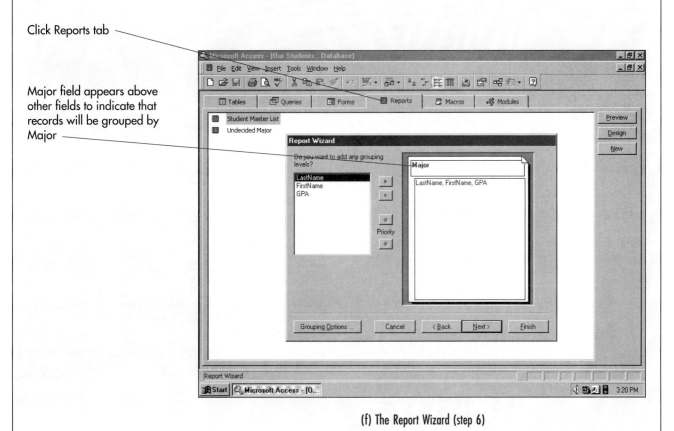

(f) The Report Wizard (step 6)

FIGURE 3.10   Hands-on Exercise 3 (continued)

STEP 7: Sorting and Grouping

➤ You should see the Report Design view as shown in Figure 3.10g. (The Sorting and Grouping dialog box is not yet visible.)

➤ Maximize the Report window (if necessary) so that you have more room in which to work.

➤ Move, size, and align the column headings and bound controls as shown in Figure 3.10g. We made GPA (label and bound control) smaller. We also moved FirstName (label and bound control) to the right.

➤ Pull down the **View menu.** Click **Sorting and Grouping** to display the Sorting and Grouping dialog box.

Save button

Click Group Footer property; click drop-down arrow and select Yes

Click and drag to extend Report Footer section

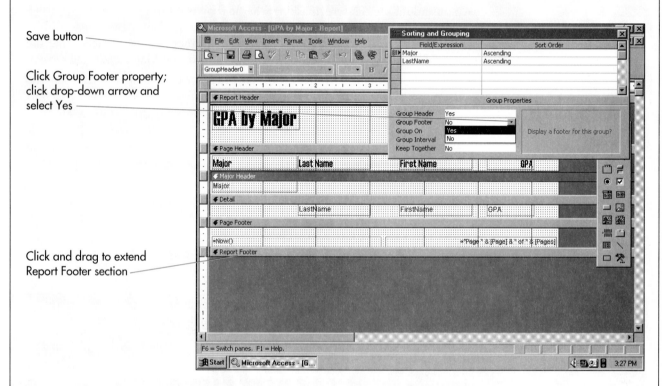

(g) Sorting and Grouping (step 7)

FIGURE 3.10   Hands-on Exercise 3 (continued)

SELECTING MULTIPLE CONTROLS

Select (click) a column heading in the page header, then press and hold the Shift key as you select the corresponding bound control in the Detail section. This selects both the column heading and the bound control and enables you to move and size the objects in conjunction with one another. Continue to work with both objects selected as you apply formatting through various buttons on the Formatting toolbar, or change properties through the property sheet. Click anywhere on the report to deselect the objects when you are finished.

➤ The **Major field** should already be selected. Click the **Group Footer** property, click the **drop-down arrow,** then click **Yes** to create a group footer for the Major field.

➤ Close the dialog box. The Major footer has been added to the report. Click the Save button to save the modified report.

STEP 8: Create the Group Footer

➤ Click the **Text Box button** on the Toolbox toolbar. The mouse pointer changes to a tiny crosshair with a text box attached.

➤ Click and drag in the group footer where you want the text box (which will contain the average GPA) to go. Release the mouse. You will see an Unbound control and an attached label containing a field number (e.g., Text 14).

➤ Click in the **text box** of the control (Unbound will disappear). Enter **=Avg(GPA)** to calculate the average of the GPA for all students in this group as shown in Figure 3.10h.

➤ Click in the attached unbound control, click and drag to select the text (Text14), then type **Average GPA for Major** as the label for this control. Size, move, and align the label as shown in the figure. (See the boxed tip on sizing or moving a control and its label.)

➤ Point to the **Average GPA control,** click the **right mouse button** to display a shortcut menu, then click **Properties** to display the Properties dialog box. If necessary, click the **All tab,** then scroll to the top of the list to view and/or modify the existing properties:

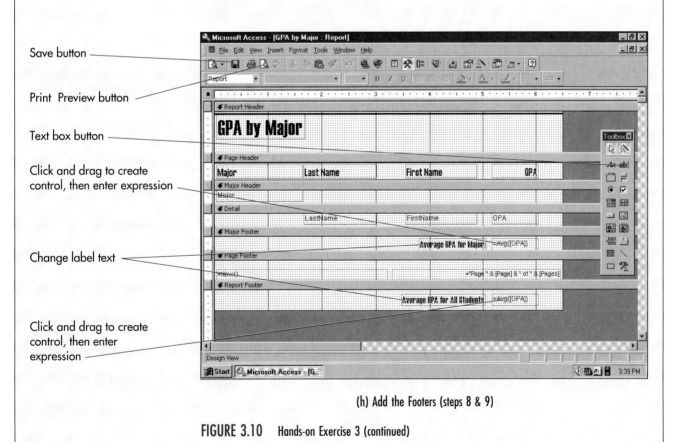

Save button

Print Preview button

Text box button

Click and drag to create control, then enter expression

Change label text

Click and drag to create control, then enter expression

(h) Add the Footers (steps 8 & 9)

FIGURE 3.10   Hands-on Exercise 3 (continued)

- The Control Source text box contains the entry =Avg([GPA]) from the preceding step.
- Click the **Name text box.** Replace the original name (e.g., Text14) with **Average GPA for Major.**
- Click the **Format box.** Click the **drop-down arrow** and select **Fixed.**
- Click the box for the **Decimal places.** Click the **drop-down arrow** and select (click) **2.**
- Close the Properties dialog box to accept these settings and return to the report.

➤ Click the **Save button** on the toolbar.

SIZING OR MOVING A BOUND CONTROL AND ITS LABEL

A bound control is created with an attached label. Select (click) the control, and the control has sizing handles and a move handle, but the label has only a move handle. Select the label (instead of the control), and the opposite occurs: the control has only a move handle, but the label will have both sizing handles and a move handle. To move a control and its label, click and drag the border of either object. To move either the control or its label (but not both), click and drag the move handle (a tiny square in the upper left corner) of the appropriate object. (Use the Undo command if the result is not what you expect; then try again.)

STEP 9: Create the Report Footer

➤ The report footer is created in similar fashion to the group footer. Click and drag the bottom of the report footer to extend the size of the footer as shown in Figure 3.10h.

➤ Click the **Text Box button** on the Toolbox toolbar, then click and drag in the report footer where you want the text box to go. Release the mouse. You will see an Unbound control and an attached label containing a field number (e.g., Text16).

➤ Click in the **text box** of the control (Unbound will disappear). Enter **=Avg(GPA)** to calculate the average of the grade point averages for all students in the report.

➤ Click in the attached label, click and drag to select the text (Text16), then type **Average GPA for All Students** as the label for this control. Move, size, and align the label appropriately.

➤ Size the text box, then format the control:
- Point to the control, click the **right mouse button** to display a shortcut menu, then click **Properties** to display the Properties dialog box. Change the properties to **Fixed Format** with **2 decimal places.** Change the name to **Average GPA for All Students.**
- Close the Properties dialog box to accept these settings and return to the report.

➤ Click the **Save button** on the toolbar.

STEP 10: View the Report

➤ Click the **Print Preview button** to view the completed report as shown in Figure 3.10i. The status bar shows you are on page 1 of the report.

➤ Click the **Zoom button** to see the entire page. Click the **Zoom button** a second time to return to the higher magnification, which lets you read the report.

➤ Click the **Navigation button** to move to the next page (page 2). Click the **Navigation button** to return to page 1.

➤ Be sure that you are satisfied with the appearance of the report and that all controls align properly with their associated labels. If necessary, return to the Design view to modify the report.

➤ Pull down the **File menu** and click **Print** (or click the **Print button**) to display the Print dialog box. The **All option button** is already selected under Print Range. Click **OK** to print the report.

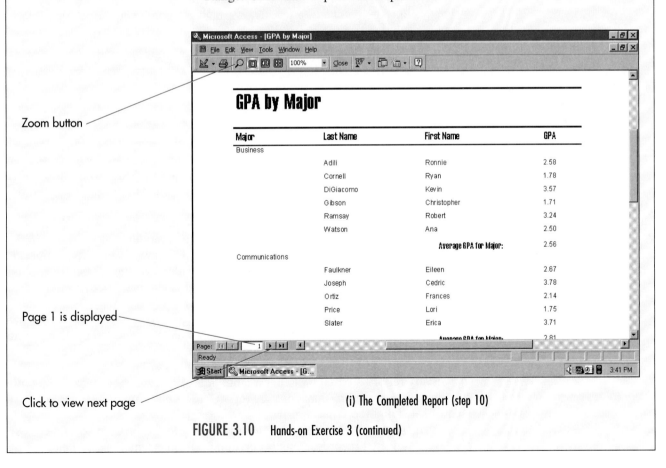

Zoom button

Page 1 is displayed

Click to view next page

(i) The Completed Report (step 10)

FIGURE 3.10   Hands-on Exercise 3 (continued)

THE BORDER PROPERTY

The Border property enables you to display a border around any type of control. Point to the control (in the Design view), click the right mouse button to display a shortcut menu, then click Properties to display the Properties dialog box. Select the Format tab, click the Border Style property, then choose the type of border you want (e.g., solid to display a border or transparent to suppress a border). Use the Border Color and Border Width properties to change the appearance of the border.

STEP 11: Exit Access

➤ Pull down the **File menu** and click **Close** to close the GPA by Major report. Click **Yes** if asked to save design changes to the report.

➤ Close the **Our Students database** and exit Access.

COMPACTING A DATABASE

The size of an Access database is quite large even if the database contains only a limited number of records. It is not surprising to see simple databases, such as the Our Students database in this chapter, grow to 500KB or more. You can, however, reduce the storage requirements by compacting the database, a practice we highly recommend. See the case study at the end of the chapter.

SUMMARY

Data and information are not synonymous. Data refers to a fact or facts about a specific record. Information is data that has been rearranged into a more useful format. Data may be viewed as the raw material, whereas information is the finished product.

A report is a printed document that displays information from the database. Reports are created through the Report Wizard, then modified as necessary in the Design view. A report is divided into sections. The report header (footer) occurs at the beginning (end) of the report. The page header (footer) appears at the top (bottom) of each page. The detail section is found in the main body of the report and is printed once for each record in the report.

Each section is comprised of objects known as controls. A bound control has a data source such as a field in the underlying table. An unbound control has no data source. A calculated control contains an expression. Controls are selected, moved, and sized the same way as any other Windows object.

Every report is based on either a table or a query. A report based on a table contains every record in that table. A report based on a query contains only the records satisfying the criteria in the query.

A query enables you to select records from a table (or from several tables), display the selected records in any order, and perform calculations on fields within the query. A select query is the most common type of query and is created using the design grid. A select query displays its output in a dynaset that can be used to update the data in the underlying table(s).

The records in a report are often grouped according to the value of a specific field within the record. A group header appears before each group to identify the group. A group footer appears at the end of each group and can be used to display the summary information about the group.

All objects (tables, forms, queries, and reports) in an Access database are named according to the same rules. The name can contain up to 64 characters (letters or numbers) and can include spaces. A form and/or a report can have the same name as the table or query on which it is based to emphasize the relationship between the two.

KEY WORDS AND CONCEPTS

AND condition	Dynaset	Relational operators
Ascending sequence	Field row	Report
Avg function	Group footer	Report footer
Between function	Group header	Report header
Bound control	Inheritance	Report Wizard
Calculated control	Label tool	Select query
Columnar report	Max function	Show row
Compacting	Min function	Sort row
Count function	NOT function	Sorting and Grouping
Criteria row	Now function	Sum function
Database Properties	OR condition	Tabular report
Datasheet view	Page footer	Text box tool
Descending sequence	Page header	Top Values property
Design grid	Print Preview	Unbound control
Design view	Query	Wild card
Detail section	Query window	

PRACTICE WITH ACCESS 97

1. Use the Our Students database as the basis for the following queries and reports:

   a. Create a select query for students on the Dean's List (GPA >= 3.50). Include the student's name, major, quality points, credits, and GPA. List the students alphabetically.

   b. Use the Report Wizard to prepare a tabular report based on the query in part a. Include your name in the report header as the academic advisor.

   c. Create a select query for students on academic probation (GPA < 2.00). Include the same fields as the query in part a. List the students in alphabetical order.

   d. Use the Report Wizard to prepare a tabular report similar to the report in part b.

   e. Print both reports and submit them to your instructor as proof that you did this exercise.

2. Use the Employee database in the Exploring Access folder to create the reports listed below. (This is the same database that was used earlier in Chapters 1 and 2.)

   a. A report containing all employees in sequence by location and alphabetically within location. Show the employee's last name, first name, location, title, and salary. Include summary statistics to display the total salaries in each location as well as for the company as a whole.

   b. A report containing all employees in sequence by title and alphabetically within title. Show the employee's last name, first name, location, title, and salary. Include summary statistics to show the average salary for each title as well as the average salary in the company.

   c. Add your name to the report header in the report so that your instructor will know the reports came from you. Print both reports and submit them to your instructor.

3. Use the United States database in the Exploring Access folder to create the report shown in Figure 3.11. (This is the same database that was used in Chapters 1 and 2.) The report lists states by geographic region, and alphabetically within region. It includes a calculated field, Population Density, which is computed by dividing a state's population by its area. Summary statistics are also required as shown in the report.

   Note that the report header contains a map of the United States that was taken from the Microsoft Clip Gallery. The instructions for inserting an object can be found on page 81 in conjunction with an earlier problem. Be sure to include your name in the report footer so that your instructor will know that the report comes from you.

4. Use the Bookstore database in the Exploring Access folder to create the report shown in Figure 3.12. (This is the same database that was used in the hands-on exercises in Chapter 1.)

   The report header in Figure 3.12 contains a graphic object that was taken from the Microsoft Clip Gallery. You are not required to use this specific image, but you are required to insert a graphic. The instructions for inserting an object can be found on page 81 in conjunction with an earlier problem. Be sure to include your name in the report header so that your instructor will know that the report comes from you.

5. Use the Super Bowl database in the Exploring Access folder to create the report in Figure 3.13, which lists the participants and scores in every game played to date. It also displays the Super Bowl logo, which we downloaded from the home page of the NFL (www.nfl.com). Be sure to include your name in the report footer so that your instructor will know that the report comes from you. (See the Super Bowl case study for suggestions on additional reports or queries that you can create from this database.)

6. There are many sources of help for Access as well as every Office application. You can use the regular Help facility or you can go to the Microsoft web site to obtain the latest information. Start Access, pull down the Help menu, click Microsoft on the Web, then click online support to go to the home page for Microsoft Access. Explore the various options that are available, then write a short summary of your findings and submit it to your instructor as proof you did this exercise. Figure 3.14 displays the feature articles that were available when this book went to press and provides an indication of what you can expect to find.

United States
By Region

Region	Name	Capital	Population	Area	Population Density
Middle Atlantic					
	Delaware	Dover	666,168	2,057	323.85
	Maryland	Annapolis	4,781,468	10,577	452.06
	New Jersey	Trenton	7,730,188	7,836	986.50
	New York	Albany	17,990,455	49,576	362.89
	Pennsylvania	Harrisburg	11,881,643	45,333	262.10
	Total for Region:		43,049,922	115,379	
	Average for Region:		8,609,984.40	23,075.80	477.48
Mountain					
	Arizona	Phoenix	3,665,228	113,909	32.18
	Colorado	Denver	3,294,394	104,247	31.60
	Idaho	Boise	1,006,749	83,557	12.05
	Montana	Helena	799,065	147,138	5.43
	Nevada	Carson City	1,201,833	110,540	10.87
	New Mexico	Santa Fe	1,515,069	121,666	12.45
	Utah	Salt Lake City	1,722,850	84,916	20.29
	Wyoming	Cheyenne	453,588	97,914	4.63
	Total for Region:		13,658,776	863,887	
	Average for Region:		1,707,347.00	107,985.88	16.19
New England					
	Connecticut	Hartford	3,287,116	5,009	656.24
	Maine	Augusta	1,227,928	33,215	36.97
	Massachusetts	Boston	6,016,425	8,257	728.65
	New	Concord	1,109,252	9,304	119.22
	Rhode Island	Providence	1,003,464	1,214	826.58
	Vermont	Montpellier	562,758	9,609	58.57
	Total for Region:		13,206,943	66,608	
	Average for Region:		2,201,157.17	11,101.33	404.37

Saturday, January 11, 1997

Page 1 of 3

FIGURE 3.11   Screen for Practice Exercise 3

University of Miami Book Store

Publisher	ISBN Number	Author	Title	List Price
IDG Books Worldwide				
	1-56884-453-0	Livingston/Straub	Windows 95 Secrets	$39.95
			Number of Books:	1
			Average List Price:	$39.95
Macmillan Publishing				
	1-56686-127-6	Rosch	The Hardware Bible	$35.00
			Number of Books:	1
			Average List Price:	$35.00
MIS Press				
	1-55828-353-6	Banks	Welcome to CompuServe	$24.95
			Number of Books:	1
			Average List Price:	$24.95
New Riders Publishing				
	1-56205-306-X	Maxwell/Grycz	New Riders Internet Yellow Pages	$29.95
			Number of Books:	1
			Average List Price:	$29.95
Osborne-McGraw Hill				
	0-07-882023-5	Hahn/Stout	The Internet Yellow Pages	$27.95
	0-07-881980-6	Hahn/Stout	The Internet Complete Reference	$29.95
			Number of Books:	2
			Average List Price:	$28.95
Prentice Hall				
	0-13-754235-6	Grauer/Barber	Exploring PowerPoint 97	$30.95
	0-13-065541-4	Grauer/Barber	Exploring Windows 3.1	$24.95

Saturday, January 11, 1997   Page 1 of 2

FIGURE 3.12   Screen for Practice Exercise 4

Super Bowl

http://www.nfl.com

Year	AFC Team	AFC Score	NFC Team	NFC Score
1997	New England	21	Green Bay	35
1996	Pittsburgh	17	Dallas	27
1995	San Diego	26	San Francisco	49
1994	Buffalo	13	Dallas	30
1993	Buffalo	17	Dallas	52
1992	Buffalo	24	Washington	37
1991	Buffalo	19	Giants	20
1990	Denver	10	San Francisco	55
1989	Cincinnati	16	San Francisco	20
1988	Denver	10	Washington	42
1987	Denver	20	Giants	39
1986	New England	10	Chicago	46
1985	Miami	16	San Francisco	38
1984	Los Angeles	38	Washington	9
1983	Miami	17	Washington	27
1982	Cincinnati	21	San Francisco	26
1981	Oakland	27	Philadelphia	10
1980	Pittsburgh	31	Los Angeles	19
1979	Pittsburgh	35	Dallas	31
1978	Denver	10	Dallas	27
1977	Oakland	32	Minnesota	14
1976	Pittsburgh	21	Dallas	17
1975	Pittsburgh	16	Minnesota	6
1974	Miami	24	Minnesota	7
1973	Miami	14	Washington	7
1972	Miami	3	Dallas	24
1971	Baltimore	16	Dallas	13

Saturday, January 11, 1997

Page 1 of 2

FIGURE 3.13   Screen for Practice Exercise 5

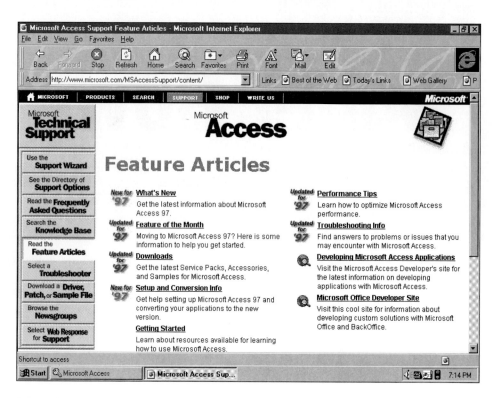

FIGURE 3.14   Screen for Practice Exercise 6

INTRODUCTION TO POWERPOINT: PRESENTATIONS MADE EASY

OBJECTIVES

After reading this chapter you will be able to:

1. Describe the common user interface; give several examples of how PowerPoint follows the same conventions as other Microsoft applications.
2. Start PowerPoint; open, modify, and view an existing presentation.
3. Describe the various ways to print a presentation.
4. List the five views in PowerPoint; describe the unique features of each view.
5. Use the Outline view to add slides to, and/or delete slides from, an existing presentation and/or to modify the text on an existing slide.
6. Add clip art to an existing slide.

OVERVIEW

This chapter introduces you to PowerPoint, one of the four major applications in the Professional version of Microsoft Office (Microsoft Word, Microsoft Excel, and Microsoft Access are the other three). In essence, PowerPoint helps you to create a professional presentation without relying on others. It enables you to deliver a presentation on the computer (or via 35-mm slides or overhead transparencies) and to print that presentation in a variety of formats.

PowerPoint is easy to learn because it is a Windows application and follows all of the conventions associated with the common user interface. Thus, if you already use one Windows application, it is that much easier to learn PowerPoint because you can apply much of what you already know. It's even easier if you use Microsoft Word, Excel, or Access, since there are over 100 commands that are common to Microsoft Office.

The chapter begins by showing you an actual PowerPoint presentation so that you can better appreciate what you will be able to do. We describe the five PowerPoint views and the unique capabilities of each view. We show you how to add slides to, and delete slides from, an existing presentation, how to modify the text of a presentation; and how to add clip art. (We will show you how to create your own presentation in Chapter 2.) We also provide two hands-on exercises, in which you apply the conceptual material at the computer. The exercises are essential to the learn-by-doing philosophy we follow throughout the text, and it is through the exercises that you will truly master the material.

One final point, before we begin, is that while PowerPoint can help you create attractive presentations, the content and delivery are up to you. It is important that you express yourself clearly and that you deliver the presentation effectively. Look at the audience as you speak to open communication and gain credibility. Don't read from a prepared script. Speak clearly and try to vary your delivery. Pause to emphasize key points and be sure the person in the last row can hear you.

PRACTICE MAKES PERFECT

You have worked hard to gain the opportunity to present your ideas. Be prepared! You cannot bluff your way through a presentation. Practice aloud several times, preferably under the same conditions as the actual presentation. The more you practice, the more confident you will be.

A POWERPOINT PRESENTATION

A PowerPoint presentation consists of a series of slides such as those shown in Figure 1.1. Each slide contains different elements, including text, clip art, photographs and/or a chart. Nevertheless, the presentation has a consistent look from slide to slide with respect to its overall design and color scheme.

You might think that creating a presentation such as Figure 1.1 is difficult, but it isn't. It is remarkably easy, and that is the beauty of PowerPoint. In essence, PowerPoint allows you to concentrate on the *content* of a presentation without worrying about its *appearance*. You supply the text and supporting elements and leave the formatting to PowerPoint.

In addition to helping you create the presentation, PowerPoint provides a variety of ways to deliver it. You can show the presentation on a computer using animated transition effects as you move from one slide to the next. You can include sound in the presentation, provided your system has a sound card and speakers. You can also automate the presentation and distribute it on a disk for display at a convention booth or kiosk. If you cannot show the presentation on a computer, you can convert it to 35-mm slides or overhead transparencies.

PowerPoint gives you the ability to print the presentation in various ways to distribute to your audience. You can print one slide per page, or you can print miniature versions of each slide and can choose between two, three, or six slides per page. You can prepare speaker notes for yourself, consisting of a picture of each slide together with notes for its delivery. You can also print the entire presentation in outline form. Giving the audience a copy of the presentation (in any format) enables them to follow it more closely, and to take it home when the session is over.

(a) Title Slide

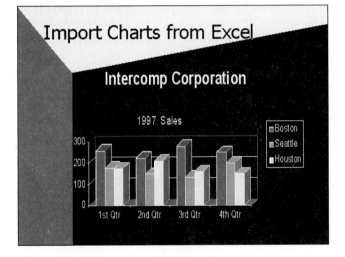

(c) Charts

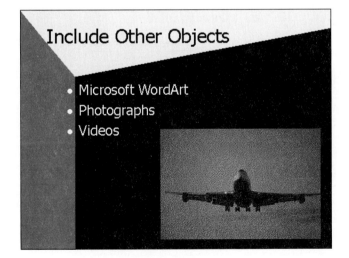

(e) Photographs

(b) Bullet Slide

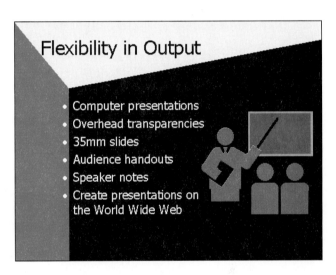

(d) Clip Art

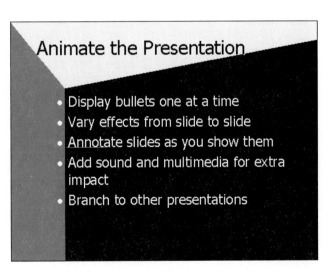

(f) Animation

FIGURE 1.1   A PowerPoint Presentation

The desktop in Figure 1.2 should look somewhat familiar, even if you have never used PowerPoint, because PowerPoint shares the common user interface that is present in every Windows application. You should recognize, therefore, the two open windows in Figure 1.2—the application window for PowerPoint and the document window for the current presentation.

Each window has its own Minimize, Maximize (or Restore), and Close buttons. Both windows have been maximized, and thus the title bars have been merged into a single title bar that appears at the top of the application window. The title bar indicates the application (Microsoft PowerPoint) as well as the name of the presentation (Introduction to PowerPoint) on which you are working.

A *menu bar* appears immediately below the title bar. The Standard and Formatting toolbars appear below the menu bar. S*croll bars* appears at the right and bottom of the document window. The Windows 95 taskbar appears at the bottom of the screen and shows the open applications—Microsoft PowerPoint, Word, and Excel. The taskbar enables you to switch from one application to the next by clicking the appropriate button.

The *status bar* at the bottom of the application window displays information about what you are seeing and doing as you work on a presentation. It indicates the slide you are working on (e.g., Slide 1 in Figure 1.2), or it provides information about a command you have selected.

The *view buttons* are located to the left of the horizontal scroll bar, immediately above the Drawing toolbar, and are used to switch between the five different views of a presentation. (The Slide view is displayed in Figure 1.2.) Each view offers a different way of looking at a presentation and has unique capabilities. PowerPoint views are discussed later in the chapter.

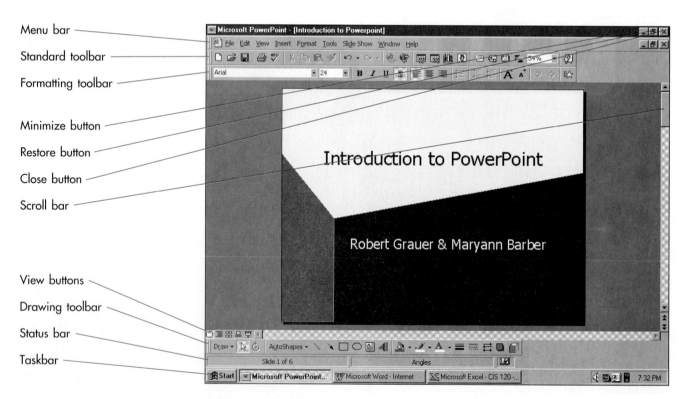

FIGURE 1.2 The PowerPoint Window

Toolbars

The Standard and Formatting toolbars are similar to those in Word and Excel, and you may recognize several buttons from those applications. The **Standard toolbar** appears immediately below the menu bar and contains buttons for the most basic commands in PowerPoint—for example, opening, saving, and printing a presentation. The **Formatting toolbar,** under the Standard toolbar, provides access to formatting operations such as boldface, italics, and underlining. The **Drawing toolbar** appears at the bottom of the window and contains various tools with which to modify the slide.

As with all other Microsoft applications, you can point to any button on any toolbar and PowerPoint will display the name of the button, which indicates its function. You can also gain an overall appreciation for the toolbars by considering the buttons in groups, as shown in Figure 1.3.

Remember, too, that while PowerPoint is designed for a mouse, it provides keyboard equivalents for almost every command. You may at first wonder why there are so many different ways to do the same thing, but you will come to recognize the many options as part of PowerPoint's charm. The most appropriate technique depends on personal preference, as well as the specific situation.

If, for example, your hands are already on the keyboard, it is faster to use the keyboard equivalent. Other times, your hand will be on the mouse and that will be the fastest way. It is not necessary to memorize anything, nor should you even try; just be flexible and willing to experiment. The more you do, the easier it will be!

The File Menu

The **File menu** is a critically important menu in virtually every Windows application. It contains the **Save command** to save a presentation to disk and the **Open command** to retrieve (open) the presentation at a later time. The File menu also contains the **Print command** to print a presentation, the **Close command** to close the current presentation but continue working in PowerPoint, and the **Exit command** to quit PowerPoint altogether.

The Save command copies the presentation that is currently being edited (i.e., the presentation in memory) to disk. The Save dialog box appears the first time a presentation is saved so that you can specify the file name and other required information. All subsequent executions of the Save command save the presentation under the assigned name, replacing the previously saved version with the new version.

The file name (e.g., *My First Presentation* in Figure 1.4a) can be up to 255 characters in length and may contain both spaces and commas. The Save dialog box also requires the drive (and folder) in which the file is to be saved, as well as the file type, which determines the application the file is associated with. (Long-time DOS users will remember the three-character extension at the end of a file name, such as PPT to indicate a PowerPoint presentation. The extension is generally hidden in Windows 95, according to options set through the View menu in My Computer or the Windows Explorer.

The Open command brings a copy of a previously saved presentation into memory, enabling you to show, edit, and/or print the presentation. The Open command displays the Open dialog box in which you specify the file to retrieve. You indicate the drive (and the folder) that contains the file, as well as the type of file you want to retrieve. PowerPoint will then list all files of that type on the designated drive (and folder), enabling you to open the file you want.

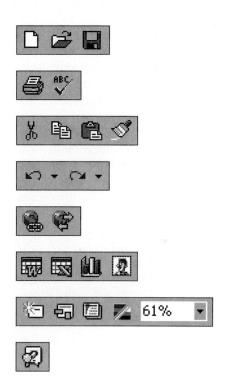

Starts a new document, opens an existing document, or saves the document to disk

Prints the document or checks the spelling in the document

Cuts or copies the selection to the clipboard; pastes the clipboard contents; copies the format of the selected text

Undoes or redoes a previously executed command

Inserts a hyperlink or displays the Web toolbar

Inserts a Microsoft Word table, a Microsoft Excel worksheet, a graph, or a clip art image

Inserts a new slide, applies a new slide layout, applies a design template, changes the display to black and white, or changes the zoom percentage

Starts the Office Assistant

(a) Standard Toolbar

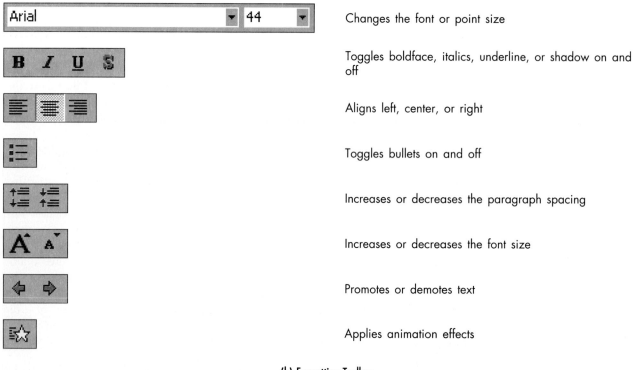

Changes the font or point size

Toggles boldface, italics, underline, or shadow on and off

Aligns left, center, or right

Toggles bullets on and off

Increases or decreases the paragraph spacing

Increases or decreases the font size

Promotes or demotes text

Applies animation effects

(b) Formatting Toolbar

FIGURE 1.3 Toolbars

The Save and Open commands work in conjunction with one another. The Save dialog box in Figure 1.4a, for example, saves the file *My First Presentation* onto the disk in the Exploring PowerPoint folder. The Open dialog box in Figure 1.4b brings that file back into memory so that you can work with the file, after which you can save the revised file for use at a later time.

The **Save As** command saves a presentation under a different name, and is useful when you want to retain a copy of the original presentation prior to making changes. The original presentation is kept on disk under its original name. A copy of the presentation is saved under a new name and remains in memory. All subsequent editing is done on the new presentation.

Drive (and folder) in which file is to be saved

Name of file to be saved

File type

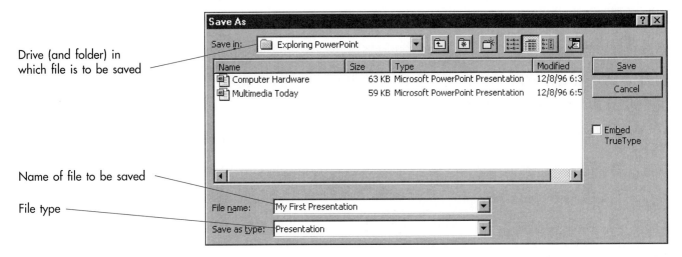

(a) File Save Dialog Box

Drive (and folder) that contains file to be opened

File to be opened

Type of file to be opened

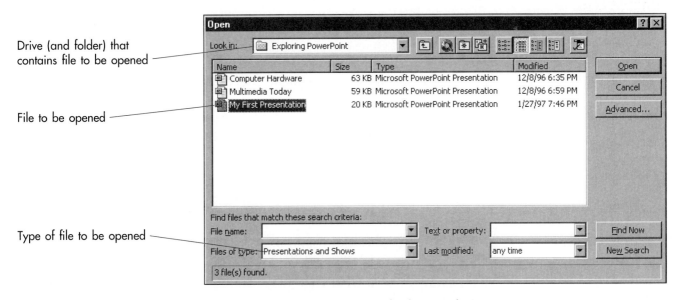

(b) File Open Dialog Box

FIGURE 1.4   The Save and Open Commands

We believe strongly in learning by doing, and thus there comes a point where you must sit down at the computer if the discussion is to have real meaning. The exercise introduces you to the practice files or data disk that is available from your instructor and/or our Web site. The data disk contains the presentations referenced in the hands-on exercises throughout the text and enables you to build on the presentations we supply.

The following exercise has you open the presentation that was shown earlier in Figure 1.1. The exercise has you change the title slide to include your name, then directs you to view the presentation on the computer and to print the corresponding audience handouts. It's fun, it's easy, and it will give you a better appreciation for PowerPoint.

HANDS-ON EXERCISE 1

Introduction to PowerPoint

Objective: To start PowerPoint, open an existing presentation, and modify the text on an existing slide. To show an existing presentation and print handouts of its slides. Use Figure 1.5 as a guide in the exercise.

STEP 1: Welcome to Windows

➤ Turn on the computer and all of its peripherals. The floppy drive should be empty prior to starting your machine. This ensures that the system starts by reading from the hard disk, which contains the Windows files, as opposed to a floppy disk, which does not.

➤ Your system will take a minute or so to get started, after which you should see the desktop in Figure 1.5a. Do not be concerned if the appearance of your desktop is different from ours.

➤ You may see additional objects on the desktop in Windows 95 and/or the active desktop content in Windows 97. It doesn't matter which operating system you are using because Office 97 runs equally well under both Windows 95 and Windows 97 (as well as Windows NT).

➤ You may see a Welcome to Windows 95/Windows 97 dialog box with command buttons to take a tour of the operating system. If so, click the appropriate button(s) or close the dialog box.

TAKE THE WINDOWS 95 TOUR

Windows 95 may greet you with a Welcome window that contains a command button to take you on a 10-minute tour. Click the command button and enjoy the show. If you do not see the Welcome window when you start Windows 95, click the Start button, click Run, type WELCOME in the Open text box, and press enter. Windows 97 was not available when we went to press, but we expect it to have a similar option.

Click the Start button

(a) Welcome to Windows 95 (step 1)

FIGURE 1.5   Hands-on Exercise 1

STEP 2: Obtain the Practice Files

➤ We have created a series of practice files for you to use throughout the text. Your instructor will make these files available to you in a variety of ways:

• You can download the files from our Web site if you have access to the Internet and World Wide Web (see boxed tip).

• The files may be on a network drive, in which case you use the Windows Explorer to copy the files from the network to a floppy disk.

• There may be an actual "data disk" that you are to check out from the lab in order to use the Copy Disk command to duplicate the disk

➤ Check with your instructor for additional information.

DOWNLOAD THE PRACTICE FILES

You can download the practice files for any book in the *Exploring Windows* series from Bob Grauer's home page (www.bus.miami.edu/~rgrauer). Use any Web browser to get to Bob's page, then click the link to the *Exploring Windows* series where you choose the appropriate book and download the file. Be sure to read the associated "read me" file, which provides additional information about downloading the file.

STEP 3: Start PowerPoint

➤ Click the **Start button** to display the Start menu. Slide the mouse pointer over the various menu options and notice that each time you point to a submenu, its items are displayed; i.e., you can point rather than click a submenu.

➤ Point to (or click) the **Programs menu,** then click **Microsoft PowerPoint** to start the program and display the screen in Figure 1.2b. Close the Office Assistant if it appears.

➤ Click the **option button** to **Open an Existing Presentation,** the click **OK.** (If you do not see the PowerPoint dialog box, pull down the **File menu** and click **Open,** or click the **Open button** on the Standard toolbar.)

Click to open an existing presentation

Close the Office Assistant

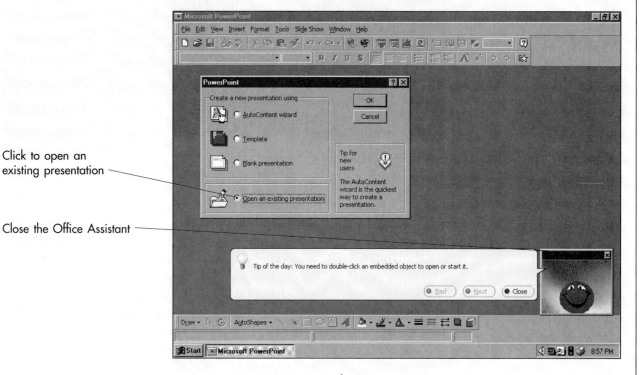

(b) Start PowerPoint (step 3)

FIGURE 1.5   Hands-on Exercise 1 (continued)

CHOOSE YOUR OWN ASSISTANT

You can choose your own personal assistant from one of several available images. Click the Office Assistant button on the Standard toolbar to display the Assistant, click the options button to display the Office Assistant dialog box, click the Gallery tab, then click the Next button repeatedly to cycle through the available images. Click OK to select the image and close the dialog box.

STEP 4: Open a Presentation

➤ You should see an Open dialog box similar to the one in Figure 1.5c. Click the **Details button** to change to the Details view. If necessary, click and drag the vertical border between columns to increase (or decrease) the size of a column.

➤ Click the **drop-down arrow** on the Look In list box. Click the appropriate drive, drive C or drive A, depending on the location of your data. Double click the **Exploring PowerPoint folder** to make it the active folder (the folder from which you will retrieve and into which you will save the presentation).

➤ Click **Introduction to PowerPoint** to select the presentation. Click the **Open button** to open the presentation and begin the exercise.

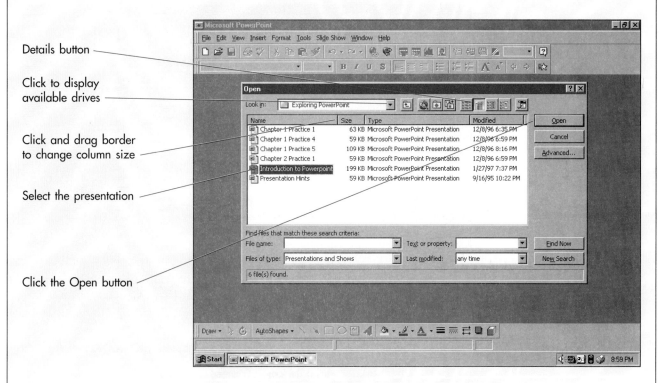

Details button

Click to display available drives

Click and drag border to change column size

Select the presentation

Click the Open button

(c) Open an Existing Presentation (step 4)

FIGURE 1.5 Hands-on Exercise 1 (continued)

A VERY USEFUL TOOLBAR

The Open and Save dialog boxes display similar toolbars with several common buttons. Click the Details button to switch to the Details view and see the date and time the file was last modified, as well as its size. Click the List button to display an icon for each file, enabling you to see many more files at the same time than in the Details view. The Properties button displays information about the presentation, including the author's name and number of revisions.

STEP 5: The Save As Command

➤ If necessary, click the **Maximize button** in the application window so that PowerPoint takes the entire desktop. Click the **Maximize button** in the document window (if necessary) so that the document window is as large as possible.

➤ Pull down the **File menu.** Click **Save As** to display the dialog box shown in Figure 1.5d. Enter **Finished Introduction** as the name of the new presentation. (A file name may contain up to 255 characters; blanks are permitted.)

➤ Click the **Save button.** Press the **Esc key** or click the **Close button** if you see a Properties dialog box.

Click Save button ——

Enter file name ——

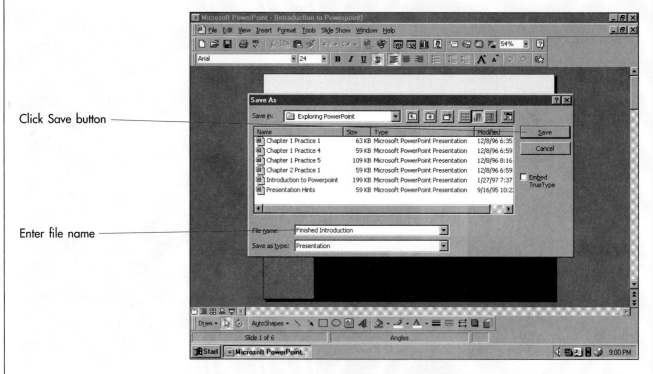

(d) The Save As Command (step 5)

FIGURE 1.5   Hands-on Exercise 1 (continued)

DIFFERENT FILE TYPES

The file format for PowerPoint 97 is incompatible with the format for PowerPoint 95. The newer release (PowerPoint 97) can open a presentation created in its predecessor (PowerPoint 95), but the reverse is not possible; that is, you cannot open a presentation created in PowerPoint 97 in PowerPoint 95. You can, however, use the Save As command in PowerPoint 97 to specify the PowerPoint 95 file type, enabling you to create a presentation in the new release and read it in the old (although you will lose any formatting unique to PowerPoint 97).

➤ There are now two identical copies of the file on disk: "Introduction to PowerPoint," which is the original presentation that we supplied, and "Finished Introduction," which you just created. The title bar shows the latter name, as it is the presentation currently in memory.

STEP 6: Modify a Slide

➤ Press and hold the left mouse button as you drag the mouse over the presenters' names (Robert Grauer and Maryann Barber). Release the mouse.

➤ The names should be highlighted (selected) as shown in Figure 1.5e. The selected text is the text that will be affected by the next command.

➤ Type your name, which automatically replaces the selected text. Click outside the placeholder to deselect it.

Save button

Click and drag over presenters' names, then type your name

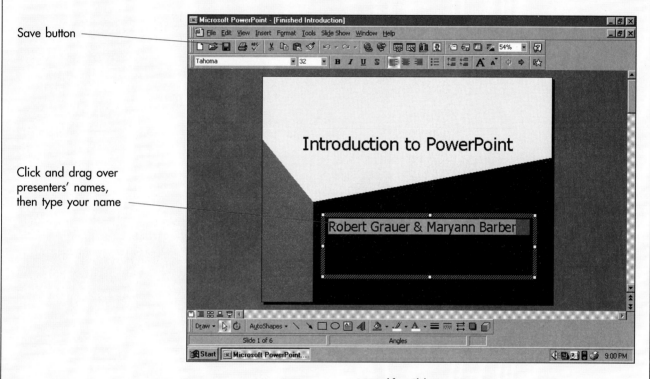

(e) Modify a Slide (step 6)

FIGURE 1.5   Hands-on Exercise 1 (continued)

THE AUTOMATIC SPELL CHECK

A red wavy line under a word indicates that the word is misspelled, or in the case of a proper name, that the word is spelled correctly but is not in the dictionary. In either event, point to the underlined word and click the right mouse button to display a shortcut menu. Select the appropriate spelling from the list of suggestions, ignore it, or add the word to the supplementary dictionary. To enable (disable) the automatic spell check, pull down the Tools menu, click the Options command, click the Spelling tab, then check (clear) the option to check spelling as you type.

STEP 7: The Office Assistant

➤ Click the **Office Assistant button** on the Standard toolbar to display the Office Assistant. (You may see a different character than the one we have selected.)

➤ Enter your question—for example, **How do I show a presentation?**—as shown in Figure 1.5f, then click the **Search button** to look for the answer.

➤ The size of the balloon expands as the Assistant suggests several topics that may be appropriate to answer your question.

➤ Select the topic, **Start a slide show**, which in turn displays a help screen with detailed information. Read the help screen, then close the Help Window.

➤ Close the Office Assistant.

Click the Office Assistant button

Click desired topic to display a help screen

Enter your question

Click the Search button

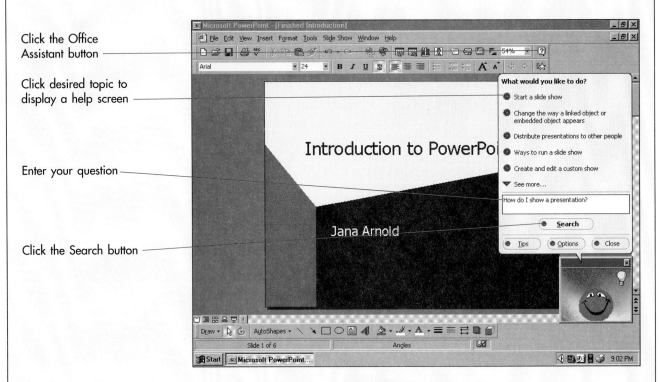

(f) The Office Assistant (step 7)

FIGURE 1.5   Hands-on Exercise 1 (continued)

TIP OF THE DAY

You can set the Office Assistant to greet you with a "Tip of the Day" whenever you start PowerPoint. If the Office Assistant is not visible, click the Office Assistant button on the Standard toolbar to start the Assistant, then click the Options button to display the Office Assistant dialog box. Click the Options tab, check the Show the Tip of the Day at startup box, then click OK. The next time you start PowerPoint, you will be greeted by the Assistant who will offer you a tip of the day.

STEP 8: Show the Presentation

➤ Pull down the **View menu** and click **Slide Show.**

➤ The presentation will begin with the first slide as shown in Figure 1.5g. You should see your name on the slide because of the modification you made in the previous step.

➤ Click the mouse to move to the second slide, which comes into the presentation from the left side of your monitor. (This is one of several transition effects available to add interest to a presentation.) Click the mouse again to move to the next (third) slide, which also comes in from the top of the screen.

➤ Continue to view the show until you come to the end of the presentation:

  • You can press the **Esc key** at any time to cancel the show and return to the PowerPoint window.

  • The last slide (Animate the Presentation) utilizes a build effect, which requires you to continue to click the mouse as you display each bullet.

➤ Click the left mouse button a final time to return to the regular PowerPoint window.

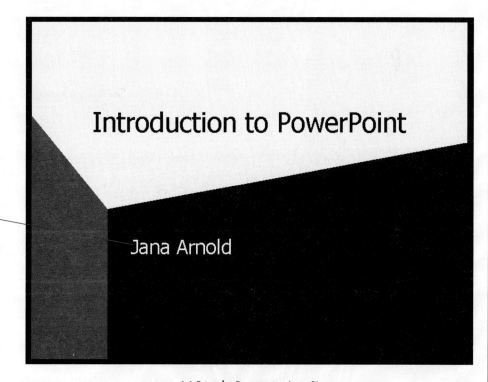

Your name should be displayed on the slide

(g) Print the Presentation (step 8)

FIGURE 1.5   Hands-on Exercise 1 (continued)

STEP 9: Print the Presentation

➤ Pull down the **File menu.** Click **Print** to display the Print dialog box in Figure 1.5h.

  • Click the **down arrow** in the **Print What** drop-down list box.

- Scroll to, then click **Handouts (6 slides per page)** as shown in Figure 1.5h.
- Check the box to **Frame Slides.**
- Check that the **All option button** is selected under Print range.

➤ Click the **OK command button** to print the handouts for the presentation.

Select All

Click here to
choose Handouts

Select Frame Slides

Click OK

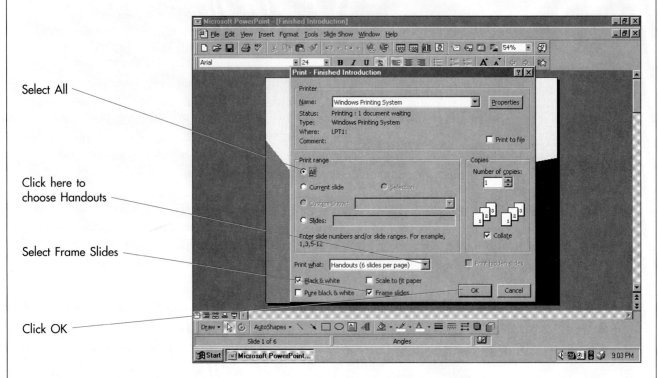

(h) Print the Presentation (step 9)

FIGURE 1.5   Hands-on Exercise 1 (continued)

THE COMMON USER INTERFACE

One of the most significant benefits of the Windows environment is the common user interface, which provides a sense of familiarity when you begin to learn a new application. In other words, once you know one Windows application, it will be that much easier for you to learn PowerPoint, because all applications work basically the same way. The benefits are magnified if you use other applications in Microsoft Office. Indeed, if you use either Word or Excel, you already know more than 100 commands in PowerPoint.

STEP 10: Exit PowerPoint

➤ Pull down the **File menu.** Click **Close** to close the presentation but remain in PowerPoint. Click **Yes** if asked whether to save the changes.

➤ Pull down the **File menu.** Click **Exit** to exit PowerPoint if you do not want to continue with the next exercise at this time.

PowerPoint offers five different views in which to create, modify, and show a presentation. Figure 1.6 shows the five views for the introductory presentation from the first exercise. Each view represents a different way of looking at the presentation, and each view has unique capabilities. Some views display only a single slide, whereas others show multiple slides, making it easy to organize the presentation. You can switch back and forth between the views by clicking the appropriate view button at the bottom of the presentation window.

The **Slide view** in Figure 1.6a displays one slide at a time and enables all operations for that slide. You can enter, delete, or format text. You can draw or add objects such as a graph, clip art, or an organization chart. The **Drawing Toolbar** is displayed by default in this view.

The **Slide Sorter view** in Figure 1.6b displays multiple slides on the screen (each slide is in miniature) and lets you see the overall flow of the presentation. You can change the order of a presentation by clicking and dragging a slide from one position to another. You can delete a slide by clicking the slide and pressing the Del key. You can also set transition and/or animation effects on each slide to add interest to the presentation. The Slide Sorter view has its own toolbar, which is discussed in Chapter 2 in conjunction with creating animation effects.

The **Outline view** in Figure 1.6c shows the presentation in outline form. You can see all of the text on every slide, but you cannot see the graphic elements that may be present on the individual slides. You can, however, open a **slide miniature** to see the current slide within the Outline view.) The Outline view is the fastest way to enter or edit text, in that you type directly into the outline. You can copy and/or move text from one slide to another. You can also rearrange the order of the slides within the presentation. The Outline view has its own toolbar and is discussed more fully in Chapter 2.

The **Notes Page view** in Figure 1.6d lets you create speaker's notes for some or all of the slides in a presentation. These notes do not appear when you show the presentation, but can be printed prior to the presentation to help you remember what you want to say about each slide.

The **Slide Show view** displays the slides one at a time as an electronic presentation on the computer. The show may be presented manually, where you click the mouse to move from one slide to the next. The presentation can also be shown automatically, where each slide stays on the screen for a predetermined amount of time, after which the next slide appears automatically. Either way, the slide show may contain transition effects from one slide to the next as was demonstrated in the first hands-on exercise.

The easiest way to switch from one view to another is by clicking the appropriate view button. The buttons are displayed in the lower-left part of the screen (above the status bar) in all views except the Slide Show view.

POWERPOINT VIEWS

PowerPoint has five different views of a presentation, each with unique capabilities. Anything you do in one view is automatically reflected in the other views. If, for example, you rearrange the slides in the Slide Sorter view, the new arrangement is reflected in the Outline view. In similar fashion, if you add or format text in the Outline view, the changes are also made in the Slide view.

Drawing toolbar

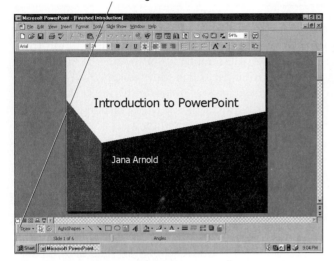

(a) Slide View

Slide Sorter toolbar

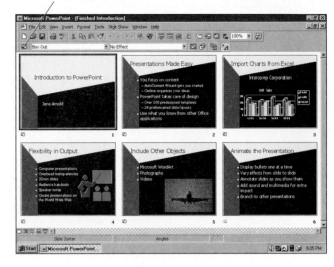

(b) Slide Sorter View

Outline toolbar

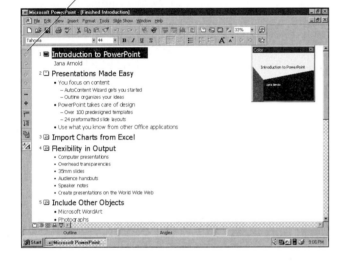

(c) Outline View

Enter notes for speaker

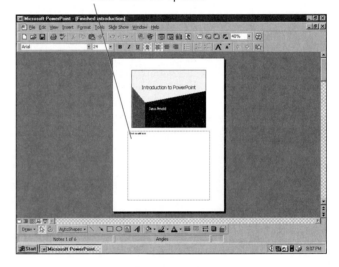

(d) Notes Page View

(e) Slide Show View

FIGURE 1.6   PowerPoint Views

ADDING AND DELETING SLIDES

Slides are added to a presentation by using one of 24 predefined slide formats known as **AutoLayouts.** Pull down the Insert menu and click the **New Slide command** to display the dialog box in Figure 1.7a, then choose the type of slide you want. (The slide will be added to the presentation immediately after the current slide.)

Figure 1.7a depicts the addition of a bulleted slide with **clip art.** The user chooses the desired layout, then clicks the OK command button to switch to the slide view in Figure 1.7b. The AutoLayout contains **placeholders** for the various

Name of selected layout

Selected layout

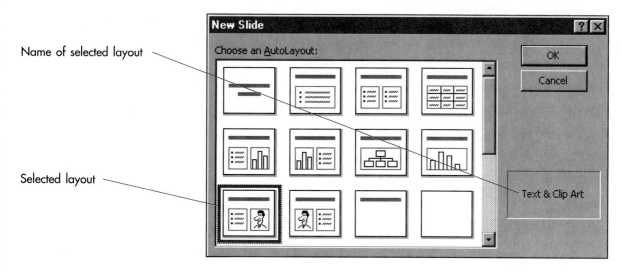

(a) AutoLayout

Placeholder for title

Placeholder for bulleted text

Placeholder for clip art

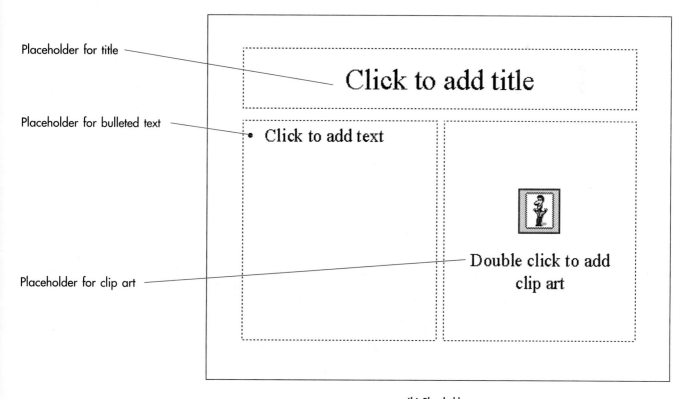

(b) Placeholders

FIGURE 1.7   Adding a Slide

objects on the slide to position them properly. There are three placeholders in Figure 1.7b—one for the title, one for the bulleted text, and one for the clip art. Just follow the directions on the slide by clicking the appropriate placeholder to add the title or text, or double clicking to add the clip art. It's that easy, as you will see in the exercise that follows shortly.

You can delete a slide from any view except the Slide Show view. To delete a slide from the Slide or Notes Page view, select the slide by making it the current slide, pull down the Edit menu, and choose the Delete Slide command. To delete a slide from the Slide Sorter or Outline view, select the slide, then press the Del key.

HANDS-ON EXERCISE 2

PowerPoint Views

Objective: To switch between the different views while modifying a presentation; to use the Microsoft Clip Gallery and add clip art to a slide; to add a slide to an existing presentation. Use Figure 1.8 as a guide in the exercise.

STEP 1: Add a New Slide
➤ Start PowerPoint. Follow the instructions from step 4 in the previous exercise to open the **Finished Introduction** presentation.
➤ Pull down the **Insert menu** and click **New slide** (or click the **New Slide button** on the Standard toolbar). You will see the New Slide dialog box in Figure 1.8a.

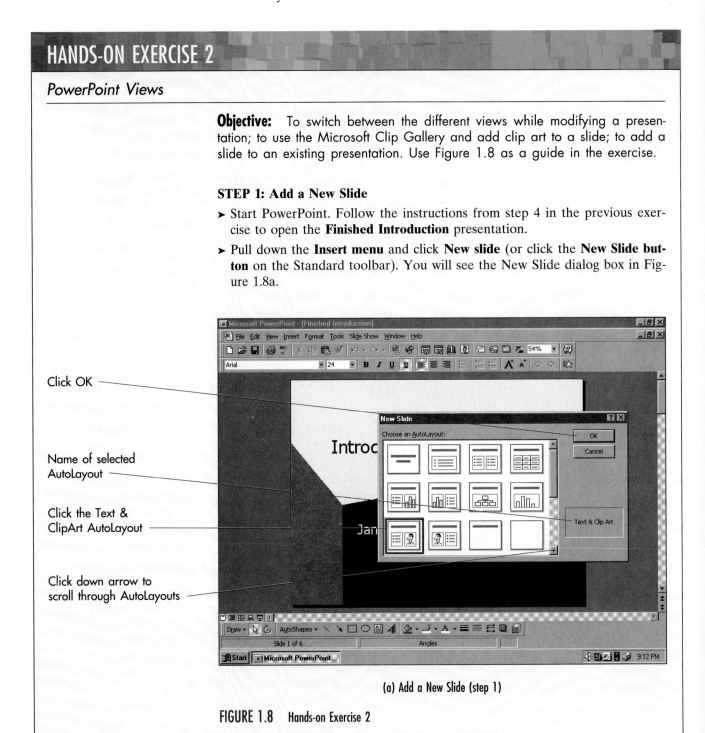

Click OK

Name of selected AutoLayout

Click the Text & ClipArt AutoLayout

Click down arrow to scroll through AutoLayouts

(a) Add a New Slide (step 1)

FIGURE 1.8   Hands-on Exercise 2

➤ Click the **down arrow** on the vertical scroll bar to scroll through AutoLayouts within PowerPoint.

➤ Select (click) the **Text & Clip Art layout** as shown in the figure. (The name of the selected layout appears in the lower-right corner of the dialog box.) Click the **OK command button.**

THE MOST RECENTLY OPENED FILE LIST

The easiest way to open a recently used presentation is to select the presentation directly from the File menu. Pull down the File menu, but instead of clicking the Open command, check to see if the presentation appears on the list of the most recently opened presentations located at the bottom of the menu. If so, you can click the presentation name rather than having to make the appropriate selections through the Open dialog box.

STEP 2: Click Here

➤ Click the **placeholder** where it says **Click to add title** in Figure 1.8b. Type **The Microsoft Clip Gallery** as the title of the slide.

➤ Click the **placeholder** where it indicates **Click to add text.** Type **Choose from many different categories** as the first bullet. Press **enter** to move to the next bullet.

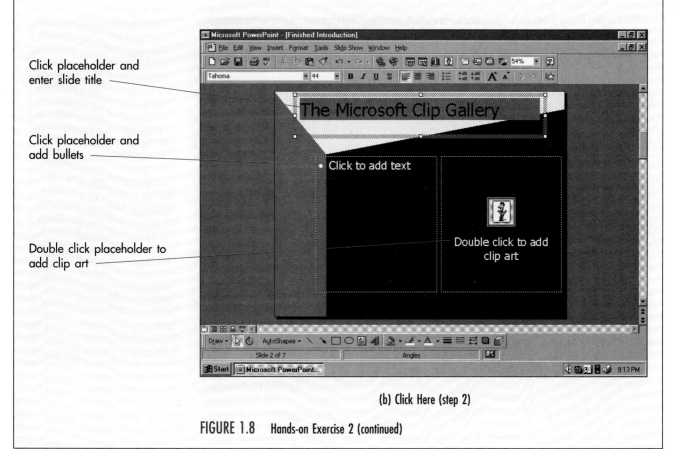

Click placeholder and enter slide title

Click placeholder and add bullets

Double click placeholder to add clip art

(b) Click Here (step 2)

FIGURE 1.8   Hands-on Exercise 2 (continued)

- Press **Tab** to indent the next bullet one level. Type **Cartoons.** Press **enter** to move to the next bullet.
- You do *not* have to press the Tab key because PowerPoint automatically aligns each succeeding bullet under the previous bullet. Type **Maps.** Press **enter** to move to the next bullet.
- Type **People.** Press **enter** to move to the next bullet.
➤ Press **Shift+Tab** to move the new bullet one level to the left. Enter **ValuPack on CD contains more than 3,000 images** as the final bullet. Do *not* press the enter key or else you will create another bullet.

BULLETS AND THE TAB (SHIFT+TAB) KEY

Bullets are entered one after another simply by typing the text of a bullet and pressing the enter key. A new bullet appears automatically under the previous bullet. Press the Tab key to indent the new bullet or press Shift+Tab to move the bullet back one level to the left.

STEP 3: Add Clip Art
➤ Double click the **placeholder** for the **clip art.** You will see the Clip Gallery dialog box shown in Figure 1.8c (although you may not see all of the categories listed in the figure).

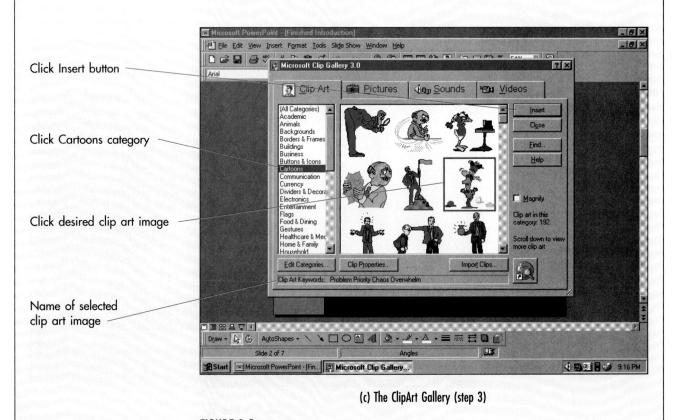

Click Insert button

Click Cartoons category

Click desired clip art image

Name of selected
clip art image

(c) The ClipArt Gallery (step 3)

FIGURE 1.8   Hands-on Exercise 2 (continued)

➤ Click the **ClickArt tab.** Click the **Cartoons** ategory. If necessary, click the **down arrow** on the scroll bar to scroll through the available cartoons until you see the image you want.

➤ Select (click) the **Problem Priority** cartoon as shown in Figure 1.8c. Click the **Insert button** to insert the clip art onto the slide.

ADDITIONAL CLIP ART

The Microsoft Clip Gallery contains over 100MB of data consisting of more than 3,000 clip art images, 144 photographs, 28 sounds, and 20 video clips. Only a fraction of these are installed with Microsoft Office, but you can access the additional objects from the Office CD at any time. You can also install some or all of the objects on your hard disk, provided you have sufficient space. Start the Windows Explorer, then open the ClipArt folder on the Office CD. Double click the Setup icon to start the Setup Wizard, then follow the on-screen instructions to install the additional components you want.

STEP 4: Select-Then-Do

➤ You should see the completed slide in Figure 1.8d. Click and drag to select the number 3,000.

• Click the **Bold button** on the Formatting toolbar to boldface the selected text.

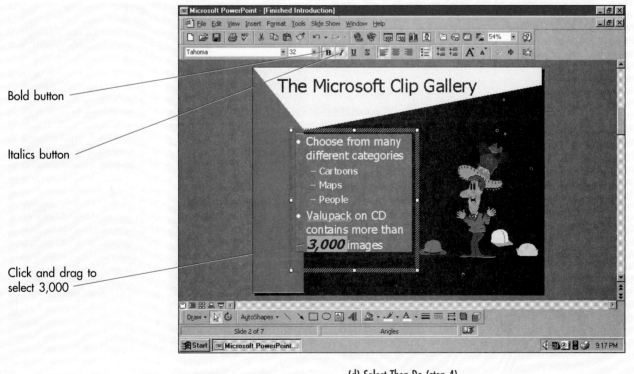

(d) Select-Then-Do (step 4)

FIGURE 1.8   Hands-on Exercise 2 (continued)

- Click the **Italic button** on the Formatting toolbar to italicize the selected text.
- Click the **Increase font size button** on the Formatting toolbar to increase the size of the selected text.

➤ Click outside the text area to deselect the text to see the results. Save the presentation.

SELECT-THEN-DO

All editing and formatting operations take place within the context of select-then-do; that is, you select a block of text, then you execute the command to operate on that text. Selected text is affected by any subsequent operation; for example, clicking the Boldface or Italic button changes the selected text to boldface or italics, respectively. In similar fashion, pressing the Del key deletes the selected text. And finally, the fastest way to replace existing text is to select the text, then type a new entry while the text is still selected. Selected text remains highlighted until you click elsewhere on the slide.

STEP 5: The Slide Sorter View

➤ Pull down the **View menu** and click **Slide Sorter** (or click the **Slide Sorter View button** on the status bar). This changes to the Slide Sorter view in Figure 1.8e.

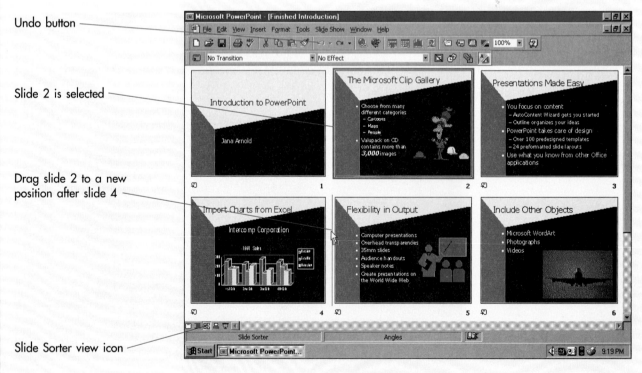

Undo button

Slide 2 is selected

Drag slide 2 to a new position after slide 4

Slide Sorter view icon

(e) Slide Sorter View (step 5)

FIGURE 1.8   Hands-on Exercise 2 (continued)

➤ Slide 2 (the slide you just created) is already selected as indicated by the heavy border around the slide.

➤ Click and drag slide 2 and move it after slide 4. (A vertical line appears in the presentation as you drag the slide to indicate where it will be placed.)

➤ Release the mouse. The existing slides are automatically renumbered to reflect the new sequence.

➤ Pull down the **Edit menu** and click **Undo Drag and Drop** (or click the **Undo button** on the Standard toolbar). The slide containing the clip art goes back to its original position.

➤ Click and drag slide 2 and move it after slide 4.

➤ Save the presentation.

MULTIPLE-LEVEL UNDO

The Undo command reverses (undoes) the most recent command. The command is executed from the Edit menu or more easily by clicking the Undo button on the Standard toolbar. Each click of the Undo button reverses one command; that is, click the Undo button and you reverse the last command. Click the Undo button a second time and you reverse the previous command. The Redo command works in reverse and undoes the most recent Undo command (i.e., it redoes the command you just undid). The maximum number of Undo commands (the default is 20) is set through the Tools menu. Pull down the Tools menu, click Options, click the Edit tab, then enter the desired number.

STEP 6: The Outline View

➤ Click the **Outline View button** on the status bar to change to the Outline view in Figure 1.8f. Press **Ctrl+End** to move to the end of the outline. Press **enter.** Press **Shift+Tab** to begin a new slide:

• Type **Five Different Views** (the title of the slide). Press **enter.**

• Press the **Tab key** to indent one level. Type **Slide view** as shown in Figure 1.8f. Press **enter** to move to the next bullet.

• Type **Outline view.** Press **enter.**

• Type **Slide Sorter view.** Press **enter.**

SLIDE MINIATURES

The Outline view displays the text of the presentation, but not the graphic elements. You can, however, open a slide miniature window to display these elements from within the Outline view. The slide miniature is shown by default but can be toggled on and off by pulling down the View menu and checking (clearing) the Slide Miniature command.

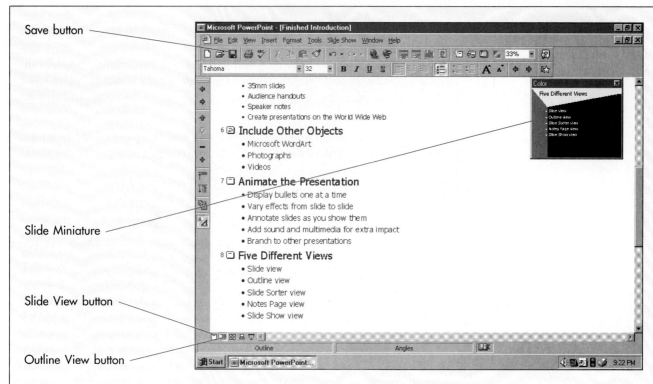

Save button

Slide Miniature

Slide View button

Outline View button

(f) Outline View (step 6)

FIGURE 1.8   Hands-on Exercise 2 (continued)

- Type **Notes Page view.** Press **enter.**
- Type **Slide Show view.**

➤ The slide is complete. Click the **Save button** on the Standard toolbar to save the presentation.

STEP 7: The Slide View

➤ Click the **Slide View button** to change to the Slide view as shown in Figure 1.8g. You should see the Slide view of the slide created in the previous step.

➤ Click the **Previous Slide button** on the vertical scroll bar (or press the **PgUp key**) to move to the previous slide (slide 7) in the presentation.

➤ Click the **Next Slide button** on the vertical scroll bar (or press the **PgDn key**) to move to the next slide (slide 8).

THE SLIDE ELEVATOR

PowerPoint uses the scroll box (common to all Windows applications) in the vertical scroll bar as an elevator to move up and down within the presentation. Click and drag the elevator to go to a specific slide; as you drag, you will see a ScreenTip indicating the slide you are about to display. Release the mouse when you see the number (title) of the slide you want.

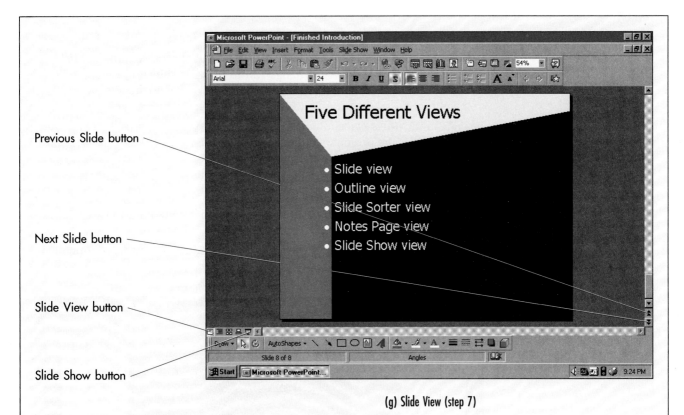

Previous Slide button

Next Slide button

Slide View button

Slide Show button

(g) Slide View (step 7)

FIGURE 1.8 Hands-on Exercise 2 (continued)

STEP 8: The Slide Show View

➤ Press **Ctrl+Home** to move to the beginning of the presentation. Click the **Slide Show button** to view the presentation as follows:

- Click the **left mouse button** (or press the **PgDn key**) to move forward in the presentation. Continue to click the left mouse button to move from one slide to the next.

- Click the **right mouse button** and click **Previous** from the shortcut menu (or press the **PgUp key**) to move backward in the presentation.

- Press the **Esc key** at any time to quit the presentation and return to the Slide view.

TRANSITIONS AND ANIMATIONS

Transitions add interest and variety to a presentation by changing the way in which you progress from one slide to the next. Slides may move onto the screen from the left or right, be uncovered by horizontal or vertical blinds, fade, dissolve, etc. Animations may also be applied to individual bullets to display the bullets one at a time with a variety of special effects (e.g., a letter at a time accompanied by the sound of a typewriter.) Transitions and animations are further described in Chapter 2.

STEP 9: The Notes Page View

➤ Press **Ctrl+Home** to move to the beginning of the presentation. Click the **Notes Page View button** to change to this view, as shown in Figure 1.8h. (If necessary, click the **down arrow** on the Zoom Control box to change to **100%** magnification so that you will be able to see what you are typing.)

➤ Click in the **notes placeholder,** then enter the text in Figure 1.8h. (The information is for the presenter rather than the audience.) Click outside the placeholder to deselect it. Save the presentation.

➤ Pull down the **File menu.** Click **Print** to display the Print dialog box.

➤ Click the **down arrow** in the **Print What** drop-down list box. Scroll so that you can click **Notes Page.** Click the **Current Slide option button** to print just this slide. Click **OK.**

➤ Close the presentation. Exit PowerPoint if you do not want to continue with the next exercise.

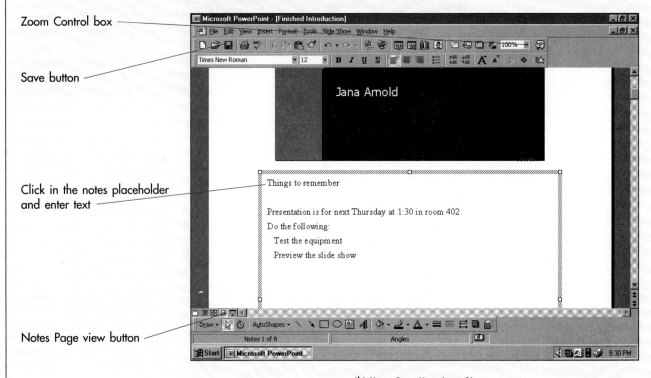

(h) Notes Page View (step 9)

FIGURE 1.8   Hands-on Exercise 2 (continued)

ADD SPEAKER NOTES IN ANY VIEW

You do not have to be in the Notes Page view in order to add notes to a slide. Go to any view (other than Notes Page), pull down the View menu, click Speaker Notes to display the Speaker Notes dialog box, add your note, then close the dialog box. Change to the Notes Page view and your note will appear. The advantage of the Speaker Notes dialog box is that you can continue to develop your presentation without having to leave a slide to add a note.

A PowerPoint presentation consists of a series of slides with a consistent design and color scheme. A PowerPoint presentation may be delivered on a computer, via overhead transparencies or 35-mm slides, and/or printed in a variety of formats.

The PowerPoint window contains the basic elements of any Windows application. The benefits of the common user interface are magnified further if you are familiar with other applications in the Microsoft Office such as Word or Excel. PowerPoint is designed for a mouse, but it provides keyboard equivalents for almost every command. Toolbars provide still another way to execute the most frequent operations.

PowerPoint has five different views, each with unique capabilities. The Slide view displays one slide at a time and enables all operations on that slide. The Slide Sorter view displays multiple slides on one screen (each slide is in miniature) and lets you see the overall flow of the presentation. The Outline view shows the presentation text in outline form and is the fastest way to enter or edit text. The Notes Page view enables you to create speaker's notes for use in giving the presentation. The Slide Show view displays the slides one at a time with transition and animation effects for added interest.

Slides are added to a presentation using one of 24 predefined slide formats known as AutoLayouts. Each AutoLayout contains placeholders for the different objects on the slide. A slide may be deleted from a presentation in any view except the Slide Show view.

KEY WORDS AND CONCEPTS

Animation effects	New Slide command	Slide Show view
AutoLayout	Notes Page view	Slide Sorter view
Clip art	Open command	Slide view
Close command	Outline view	Standard toolbar
Drawing toolbar	Placeholders	Status bar
Elevator	Print Command	Transition effects
Exit command	Redo command	Undo command
File menu	Save command	View buttons
Formatting toolbar	ScreenTip	
Menu bar	Slide miniature	

PRACTICE WITH POWERPOINT 97

1. Figure 1.9 displays the Outline view of a presentation that was created by one of our students in a successful job search.

   a. Open the *Chapter 1 Pratice 1* presentation in the set of practice files (it is found in the Exploring PowerPoint folder), then modify the presentation to reflect your personal data.

   b. Print the title slide as a cover page for your assignment.

   c. Print the revised audience handouts (six per page) and submit them to your instructor.

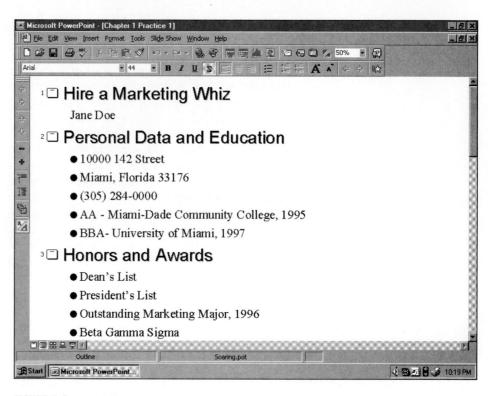

FIGURE 1.9   Screen for Practice Exercise 1

2. Ready-made presentations: The most difficult part of a presentation is getting started. PowerPoint anticipates the problem and provides general outlines on a variety of topics as shown in Figure 1.10.

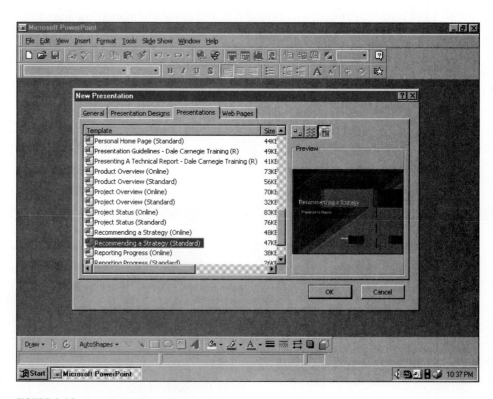

FIGURE 1.10   Screen for Practice Exercise 2

a. Pull down the File menu, click New, click the Presentations tab (if necessary), then click the Details button so that your screen matches Figure 1.10.

b. Select Recommending a Strategy (Standard) as shown in Figure 1.10. Click OK to open the presentation.

c. Change to the Outline view so that you can see the text of the overall presentation, which is general in nature and intended for any type of strategy. Modify the presentation to develop a strategy for doing well in this class.

d. Add your name to the title page.

e. Print the presentation in miniature and submit it to your instructor.

3. The Send To command enables you to import a presentation into a Word document as shown in Figure 1.11. The command combines audience handouts with speaker notes to display several slides on one page with notes for each. It also gives you the option to link the slides to the Word document, so that if a slide changes, the Word document is updated automatically. (The document is not, however, updated to reflect the insertion or deletion of slides.)

a. Do Hands-on Exercises 1 and 2 as described in the hands-on exercises in the chapter, then retrieve the Finished Introduction presentation as the basis of this problem.

b. Click the Black and White view button on the Standard toolbar. Pull down the File menu, click the Send To command, then click Microsoft Word.

c. Click the option button for the type of document you want (e.g., Notes Next to Slide so that you will create Figure 1.11 at the end of this exercise).

d. Click the option button to Paste Link the slides to a Word document, then click OK. PowerPoint will create a document similar to the one in Figure 1.11. Be patient, for this step takes time, especially on a non-Pentium machine.

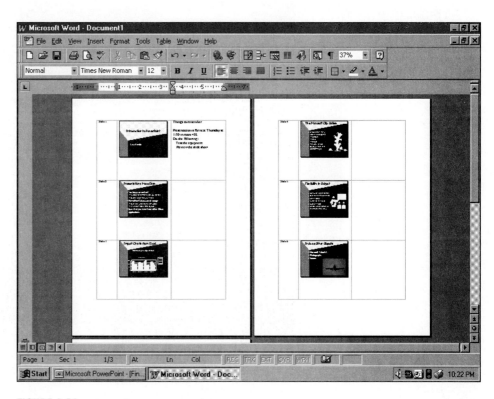

FIGURE 1.11 Screen for Practice Exercise 3

e. Change to the Page Layout view in Word and zoom to Two Pages. Click in the cell next to each slide (the Word document is a table) and enter an appropriate comment.

f. Save and print the document just as you would any other document in Microsoft Word.

g. Submit the finished document to your instructor as proof that you did this exercise.

4. A partially completed version of the presentation in Figure 1.12 can be found in the file *Chapter 1 Practice 4*. Open the presentation, then make the following changes:

a. Add your name and e-mail address on the title page.

b. Boldface and italicize the terms, *server, client,* and *browser* on slide 4. Boldface and italicize the acronyms, *HTTP, HTTPS, HTML,* and *TCP/IP* on slide 5.

c. Use Internet Explorer to go to your favorite Web page. Press the Print Screen key to capture the screen image of that page and copy it to the clipboard, then use the Windows 95 taskbar to switch to PowerPoint. Select the seventh slide, then click the Paste button on the Standard toolbar to paste the screen into the PowerPoint presentation. Size the image as appropriate.

d. Double click the WordArt image on the last slide to open the WordArt application. Change the words *Thank You* to *The End.* Change the style of the WordArt in any other way you see fit.

e. Print the slide miniatures six per page and submit them to your instructor as proof you did this exercise.

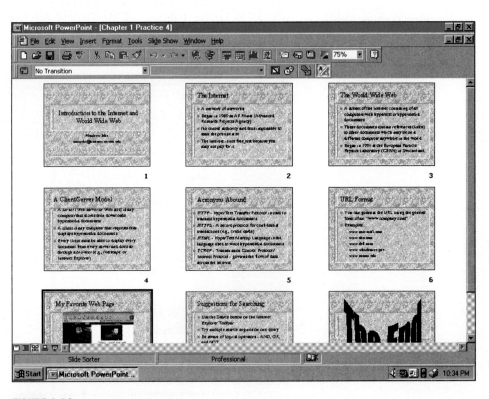

FIGURE 1.12   Screen for Practice Exercise 4

5. This problem is more difficult than the previous exercises as it asks you to create a presentation similar to the one in Figure 1.13. We have started the presentation for you in and have created the file *Chapter 1 Practice 5*. This presentation consists of three slides—a title slide and two slides containing an object and text.

   a. Go to the White House Web site (www.whitehouse.com). Click the link to White House History & Tours, then click the link to the Presidents of the USA and select your favorite president(s). Point to the picture of the president, click the right mouse button to display a shortcut menu, then save the picture on your PC.

   b. Use the Windows 95 taskbar to switch to PowerPoint, then double click the placeholder on slide two to add an object. Indicate that you are inserting the object from a file, click the Browse button, then select the file containing the president's picture.

   c. Return to the White House Web site, and click the link to a familiar quotation from your president, then copy that quotation to the appropriate slide in your presentation.

   d. Create an appropriate title for this slide consisting of the president's name and years in office. Be sure to cite the source of the picture on this slide.

   e. Repeat these steps for a second president.

   f. Create a title slide for the presentation with your name somewhere on the slide. Print all three slides and submit them to your instructor as proof you did this exercise.

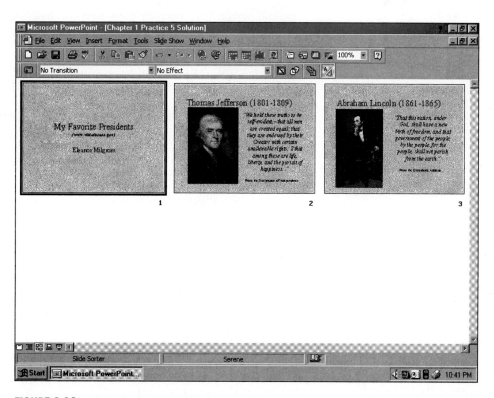

FIGURE 1.13   Screen for Practice Exercise 5

6. This exercise builds on the previous problem as it has you download pictures from the Internet for use in a presentation. Search the Web to select three landmarks, download the picture of each, then create a short presentation consisting of a title slide plus three additional slides similar to the one in Figure 1.14. This chapter did not tell you how to create a new presentation, but it's very straightforward as described below.

a. Start PowerPoint. If necessary, select the option button to create a blank presentation, then click OK to display the New Slide dialog box.

b. Choose the Title layout for your first slide. Enter the title of the presentation, *Landmarks Around the World,* and your name.

c. Click the new slide button to add a slide containing text and an object, then follow the instructions from the previous exercise.

d. Be sure to include an appropriate reference to the Web page where you obtained each picture.

e. Print the completed presentation for your instructor as proof you did this exercise.

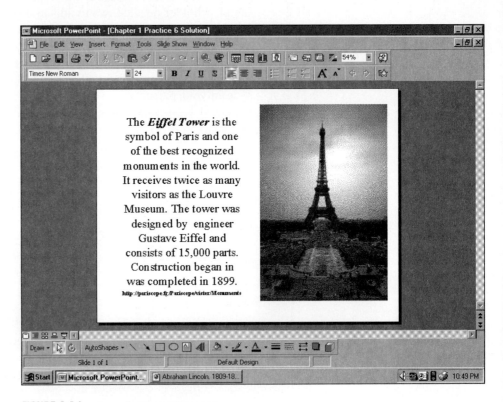

FIGURE 1.14   Screen for Practice Exercise 6

CREATING A PRESENTATION: CONTENT, FORMATTING, AND ANIMATION

2

OBJECTIVES

After reading this chapter you will be able to:

1. Use the Outline view to create and edit a presentation; display and hide text within the Outline view.
2. Check the spelling in a presentation.
3. Apply a design template to a new presentation; change the template in an existing presentation.
4. Add transition effects to the slides in a presentation.
5. Apply animation effects to the bullets and graphical objects in a specific slide.

OVERVIEW

There are two independent steps to creating a PowerPoint presentation. You must develop the content, and you must format the presentation. PowerPoint lets you do the steps in either order, but we suggest you start with the content. Both steps are iterative in nature, and you are likely to go back and forth many times before you are finished.

We begin the chapter by showing you how to enter the text of a presentation in the Outline view. We show you how to move and copy text within a slide (or from one slide to another) and how to rearrange the order of the slides within the presentation. We also illustrate the use of the Spell Check and AutoCorrect features that are common to all Office applications.

The chapter also shows you how to format a presentation using one of many professionally designed templates that are supplied with PowerPoint. The templates control every aspect of a presentation, from the formatting of the text to the color scheme of the slides. We describe how to change the template in a presentation. We also show you how to add transition and animation effects to individual slides to enhance a presentation as it is given on a computer.

The text of a presentation can be developed in the Slide view or the Outline view or a combination of the two. You can begin in the Outline view, switch to the Slide view to see how a particular slide will look, return to the Outline view to enter the text for additional slides, and so on. We prefer the Outline view because it displays the text for many slides at once. It also enables you to change the order of slides and to move and copy text from one slide to another.

CRYSTALLIZE YOUR MESSAGE

Every presentation exists to deliver a message, whether it's to sell a product, present an idea, or provide instruction. Decide on the message you want to deliver, then write the text for the presentation. Edit the text to be sure it is consistent with your objective. Then, and only then, should you think about formatting, but always keep the message foremost in your mind.

The Outline View

Figure 2.1 displays the outline of the presentation we will develop in this chapter. The outline shows the title of each slide, followed by the text on that slide. (Graphic elements such as clip art and charts are not visible in the Outline.) Each slide is numbered, and the numbers adjust automatically for the insertion or deletion of slides as you edit the presentation.

A *slide icon* appears between the number and title of the slide. The icon is subtly different, depending on the slide layout. In Figure 2.1, for example, the same icon appears next to slides 1 through 6 and indicates the slides contain only text. A different icon appears next to slide 7 and indicates the presence of a graphic element, such as clip art.

Each slide begins with a title, followed by bulleted items, which are indented one to five levels corresponding to the importance of the item. The main points appear on level one. Subsidiary items are indented below the main point to which they apply. Any item can be *promoted* to a higher level or *demoted* to a lower level, either before or after the text is entered.

Consider, for example, slide 4 in Figure 2.1a. The title of the slide, *Develop the Content*, appears immediately after the slide number and icon. The first bullet, *Use the Outline view,* is indented one level under the title, and it in turn has two subsidiary bullets. The next main bullet, *Review the flow of ideas,* is moved back to level one, and it, too, has two subsidiary bullets.

The outline is (to us) the ideal way to create and edit the presentation. The *insertion point* marks the place where new text is entered; this is established by clicking anywhere in the outline. (The insertion point is automatically placed at the title of the first slide in a new presentation.) To enter text, click in the outline to establish the insertion point, then start typing. Press enter after typing the title of a slide or after entering the text of a bulleted item, which starts a new slide or bullet, respectively. The new item may then be promoted (by pressing **Shift+Tab**) or demoted (by pressing **Tab**) as necessary.

Editing is accomplished through the same techniques used in other Windows applications. For example, you can use the Cut, Copy, and Paste commands in the Edit menu (or the corresponding buttons on the Standard toolbar) to move and copy selected text, or you can simply drag and drop text from one place to another.

(a) The Expanded Outline

1. **A Guide to Successful Presentations**
   Robert Grauer and Maryann Barber

2. **Define the Audience**
   - Who is in the audience
     - Managers
     - Coworkers
     - Clients
   - What are their expectations

3. **Create the Presentation**
   - Develop the content
   - Format the presentation
   - Animate the slide show

4. **Develop the Content**
   - Use the Outline view
     - Demote items (Tab)
     - Promote items (Shift+Tab)
   - Review the flow of ideas
     - Cut, copy, and paste text
     - Drag and drop

5. **Format the Presentation**
   - Choose a design template
   - Customize the design
     - Change the color scheme
     - Change background shading
   - Modify slide masters

6. **Animate the Slide Show**
   - Transitions
   - Builds
   - Hidden slides

7. **Tips for Delivery**
   - Rehearse Timings
   - Arrive early
   - Maintain eye contact
   - Know your audience

(a) The Expanded Outline

(b) The Collapsed Outline

1. A Guide to Successful Presentations
2. Define the Audience
3. Create the Presentation
4. Develop the Content
5. Format the Presentation
6. Animate the Slide Show
7. Tips for Delivery

(b) The Collapsed Outline

FIGURE 2.1 The Outline View

Figure 2.1b displays a collapsed view of the outline, which displays only the title of each slide. The advantage to this view is that you can see more slides on the screen at the same time, making it easier to move slides within the presentation. The slides are expanded or collapsed by using the appropriate tool on the Outline toolbar as described in a hands-on exercise. (The *Outline toolbar* appears automatically when you switch to the Outline view. As with the Standard and Formatting toolbars in Chapter 1, a ScreenTip will appear when you point to a button to describe its function.)

Text is formatted by using the select-then-do approach common to Word and Excel; that is, you select the text, then you execute the appropriate command or click the appropriate button. The selected text remains highlighted and is affected by all subsequent commands until you click elsewhere in the outline.

PowerPoint enables you to concentrate on the content of a presentation without concern for its appearance. You focus on what you are going to say, and trust in PowerPoint to format the presentation attractively. The formatting is implemented automatically by selecting one of the many templates that are supplied with Power-Point.

A *template* is a design specification that controls every element in a presentation. It specifies the color scheme for the slides and the arrangement of the different elements (placeholders) on each slide. It determines the formatting of the text, the fonts that are used, and the size and placement of the bulleted text.

Figure 2.2 displays the title slide of a presentation in four different templates. Just choose the template you like, and PowerPoint formats the entire presentation according to that template. And don't be afraid to change your mind. You can use the Format menu at any time to select a different template and change the look of your presentation.

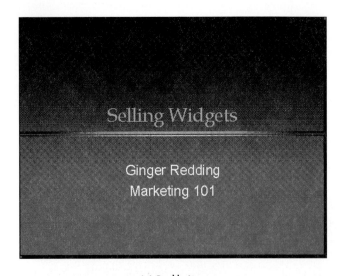

(a) Double Lines

(b) Sparkle

(c) Coins

(d) Bevel

FIGURE 2.2   Templates

Creating a Presentation

Objective: To create a presentation by entering text in the Outline view; to check a presentation for spelling errors; and to apply a design template to a presentation. Use Figure 2.3 as a guide in the exercise.

STEP 1: Create a New Presentation

➤ Start PowerPoint. Close the Office Assistant if it appears. (You can reopen the Assistant at any time by clicking its button on the Standard toolbar.)

➤ Click the **option button** to create a new presentation using a **Blank Presentation**. Click **OK**.

➤ You should see the **New Slide** dialog box in Figure 2.3a with the AutoLayout for the title slide already selected. Click **OK** to create a title slide and simultaneously close the New Slide dialog box.

➤ If necessary, click the **Maximize buttons** in both the application and document windows so that PowerPoint takes the entire desktop and the current presentation is as large as possible. Both Maximize buttons will be replaced with Restore buttons as shown in Figure 2.3a.

Click OK

Title slide is selected

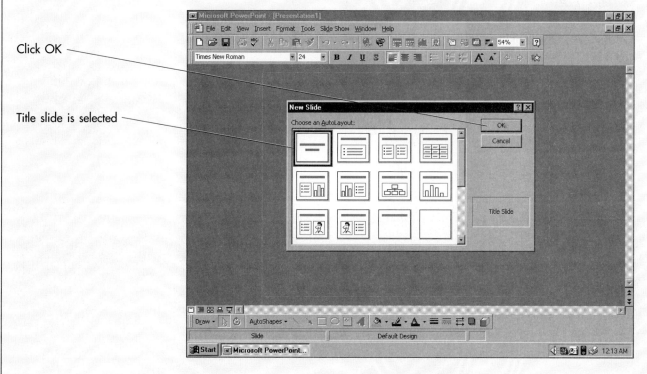

(a) Start PowerPoint (step 1)

FIGURE 2.3   Hands-on Exercise 1

CONTENT, CONTENT, AND CONTENT

It is much more important to focus on the content of the presentation than to worry about how it will look. Start with the AutoContent Wizard (described later in the chapter) or with a blank presentation in the Outline view. Save the formatting for last. Otherwise you will spend too much time changing templates and too little time developing the text.

STEP 2: Create the Title Slide

➤ Click anywhere in the box containing **Click to add title**, then type the title, **A Guide to Successful Presentations** as shown in Figure 2.3b. The title will automatically wrap to a second line.

➤ Click anywhere in the box containing **Click to add sub-title** and enter your name. Click outside the sub-title placeholder when you have entered your name.

Save button

Click in placeholder and enter title

Click in placeholder and enter name

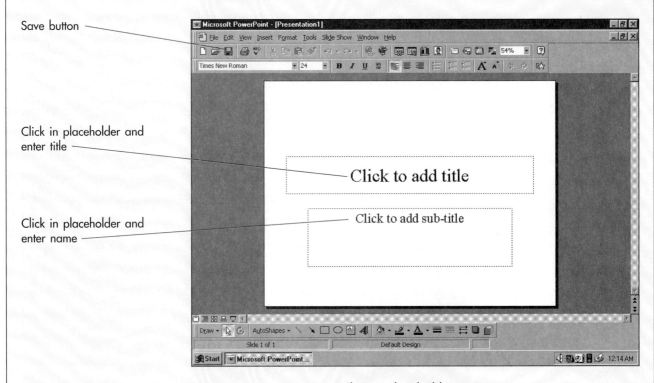

(b) Create the Title Slide (step 2)

FIGURE 2.3   Hands-on Exercise 1 (continued)

THE DEFAULT PRESENTATION

PowerPoint supplies a default presentation containing the specifications for color (a plain white background with black text), formatting, and AutoLayouts. The default presentation is selected automatically when you work on a blank presentation, and it remains in effect until you choose a different template.

STEP 3: Save the Presentation

➤ Pull down the **File menu** and click **Save** (or click the **Save button** on the Standard toolbar). You should see the Save dialog box in Figure 2.3c. If necessary, click the **Details button**.

➤ To save the file:

- Click the **drop-down arrow** on the Save In list box.
- Click the appropriate drive, drive C or drive A, depending on whether or not you installed the data disk on your hard drive.
- Double click the **Exploring PowerPoint folder,** to make it the active folder (the folder in which you will save the document).
- Enter **My First Presentation** as the name of the presentation.
- Click **Save** or press the **enter key.** Click **Cancel** or press the **Esc key** if you see the Properties dialog box. The title bar changes to reflect the name of the presentation.

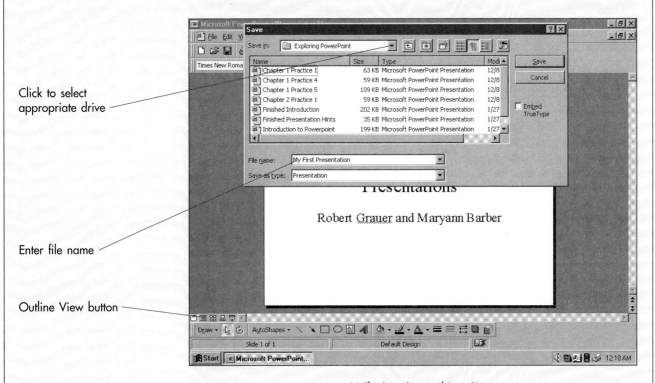

Click to select appropriate drive

Enter file name

Outline View button

(c) The Save Command (step 3)

FIGURE 2.3   Hands-on Exercise 1 (continued)

STEP 4: Create the Presentation

➤ Click the **Outline view button** above the status bar to change to the Outline view. Your presentation at this point contains only the title slide.

➤ Pull down the **View menu** and (if necessary) toggle **Slide miniature** on.

➤ Click the **New Slide button** on the **Standard toolbar**. Select the **Bulleted List** AutoLayout. Click OK. The icon for slide 2 will appear in the outline. Type **Define the Audience** as the title of the slide and press **enter.**

➤ Press the **Tab key** (or click the **Demote button** on the Outline toolbar) to enter the first bullet. Type **Who is in the audience** and press **enter.**

➤ Press the **Tab key** (or click the **Demote button** on the Outline toolbar) to enter the second-level bullets.

• Type **Managers.** Press **enter.**

• Type **Coworkers.** Press **enter.**

• Type **Clients.** Press **enter.**

➤ Press **Shift+Tab** (or click the **Promote button** on the Outline toolbar) to return to the first-level bullets.

• Type **What are their expectations.** Press **enter.**

➤ Press **Shift+Tab** to enter the title of the third slide. Type **Tips for Delivery.** Add the remaining text for this slide and for slide 4 as shown in Figure 2.3d.

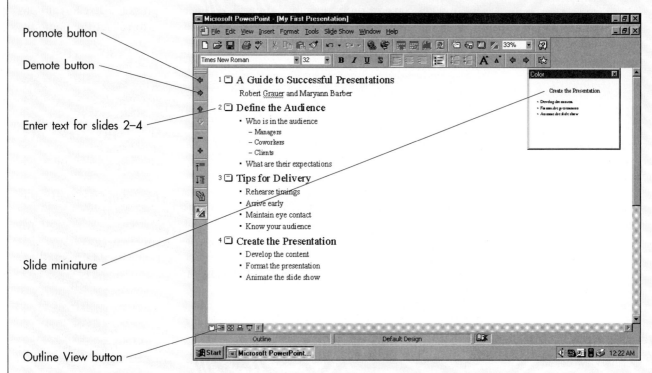

Promote button

Demote button

Enter text for slides 2–4

Slide miniature

Outline View button

(d) Create the Presentation (step 4)

FIGURE 2.3   Hands-on Exercise 1 (continued)

JUST KEEP TYPING

The easiest way to enter the text for a presentation is in the Outline view. Just type an item, then press enter to move to the next item. You will be automatically positioned at the next item on the same level, where you can type the next entry. Continue to enter text in this manner. Press the Tab key as necessary to demote an item (move it to the next lower level). Press Shift+Tab to promote an item (move it to the next higher level).

STEP 5: The Spell Check

➤ Enter the title of the fifth slide as **Develop teh Content** (deliberately misspelling the word "the"). Try to look at the monitor as you type to see the AutoCorrect feature (common to all Office applications) in action. PowerPoint will correct the misspelling and change *teh* to *the*.

➤ If you did not see the correction being made, click the arrow next to the Undo button on the Standard toolbar and undo the last several actions. Click the arrow next to the Redo button and redo the corrections in order to see the error and subsequent auto correction.

➤ Enter the text of the remaining slides as shown in Figure 2.3e. Do *not* press enter after entering the last bullet on the last slide or else you will add a blank bullet.

➤ Click the **Spelling button** on the Standard toolbar to check the presentation for spelling:

  • The result of the Spell Check will depend on how accurately you entered the text of the presentation. We deliberately misspelled the word "Transitions" in the last slide.

  • Continue to check the document for spelling errors. Click **OK** when PowerPoint indicates it has checked the entire presentation.

➤ Click the **Save button** on the Standard toolbar to save the presentation.

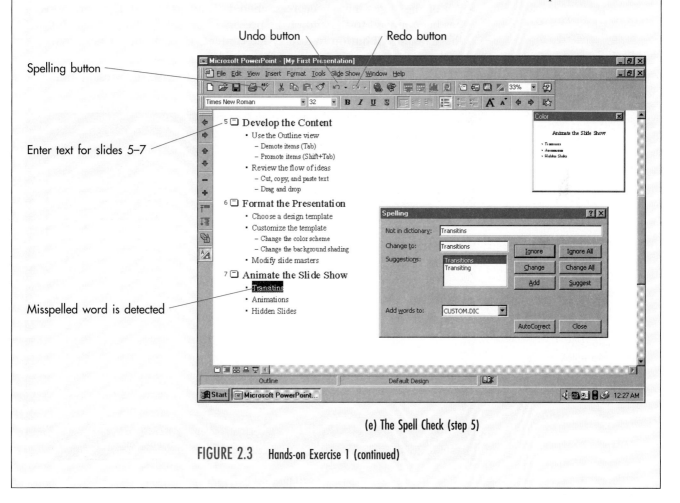

(e) The Spell Check (step 5)

FIGURE 2.3   Hands-on Exercise 1 (continued)

CREATE YOUR OWN SHORTHAND

Use the AutoCorrect feature, which is common to all Office applications, to expand abbreviations such as "usa" for United States of America. Pull down the Tools menu, click AutoCorrect, then type the abbreviation in the Replace text box and the expanded entry in the With text box. Click the Add command button, then click OK to exit the dialog box and return to the document. The next time you type usa in a presentation, it will automatically be expanded to United States of America.

STEP 6: Drag and Drop

➤ Press **Ctrl+Home** to move to the beginning of the presentation. Click the **Collapse All button** on the Outline toolbar to collapse the outline as shown in Figure 2.3f.

➤ Click the **icon** for **slide 3** (Tips for Delivery). The slide is selected and its title is highlighted. Point to the **slide icon** (the mouse pointer changes to a four-headed arrow), then click and drag to move the slide to the end of the presentation. Release the mouse.

➤ All of the slides have been renumbered. The slide titled Tips for Delivery has been moved to the end of the presentation and appears as slide 7. Click the **Expand All button** to display the contents of each slide. Click anywhere in the presentation to deselect the last slide.

➤ Click the **Save button** on the Standard toolbar to save the presentation.

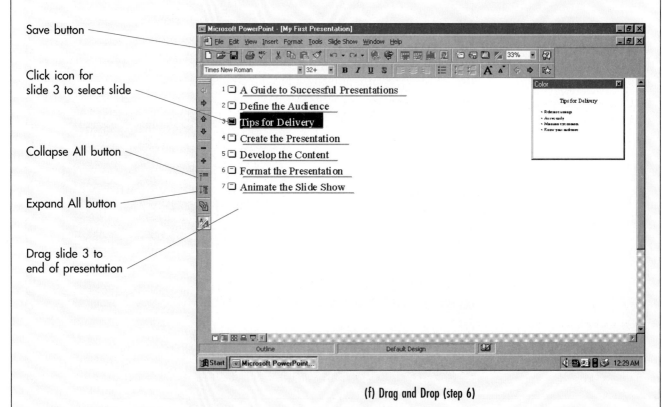

(f) Drag and Drop (step 6)

FIGURE 2.3 Hands-on Exercise 1 (continued)

SELECTING SLIDES IN THE OUTLINE VIEW

Click the slide icon or the slide number next to the slide title to select the slide. PowerPoint will select the entire slide (including its title, text, and any other objects that are not visible in the Outline view). Click the first slide, then press and hold the Shift key as you click the ending slide to select a group of sequential slides. Press Ctrl+A to select the entire outline. You can use these techniques to select multiple slides regardless of whether the outline is collapsed or expanded. The selected slides can be copied, moved, or deleted as a unit.

STEP 7: Choose a Design Template

➤ Pull down the **Format menu** and click **Apply Design** (or click the **Apply Design button** on the Standard toolbar) to display the dialog box in Figure 2.3g:

- The **Presentation Designs folder** should appear automatically in the List box. If it doesn't, change to this folder, which is contained within the Templates folder within the Microsoft Office Folder, which in turn is in the Programs Folder on drive c.

- **Presentation Templates** should be selected in the Files of Type list box. If it isn't, click the **drop-down arrow** to change to this file type.

- The **Preview view** should be selected. If it isn't, click the **Preview button** so that you can preview the selected template.

- Scroll through the available designs to select (click) the **Fireball template** as shown in Figure 2.3g. Click **Apply** to close the dialog box.

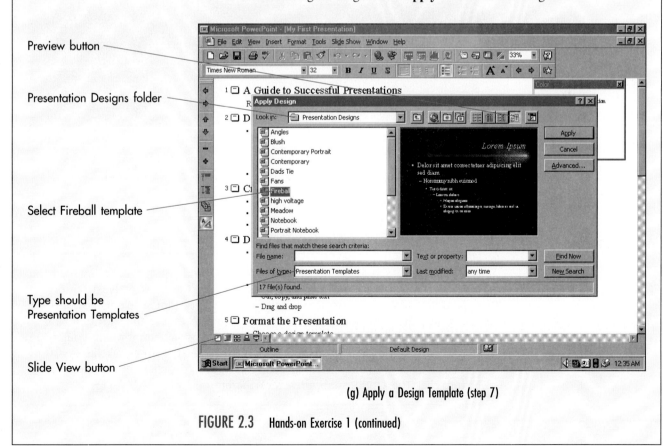

(g) Apply a Design Template (step 7)

FIGURE 2.3   Hands-on Exercise 1 (continued)

➤ You are still in the Outline view. The slide miniature, if open, will show the selected template. You can also click the **Slide View button** to change to the Slide view to see that the template has been applied. Save the presentation.

STEP 8: View the Presentation

➤ Press **Ctrl+Home** to move to the beginning of the presentation. Click the **Slide Show button** on the status bar to view the presentation as shown in Figure 2.3h.

- To move to the next slide: Click the **left mouse button,** type the letter **N,** or press the **PgDn key.**
- To move to the previous slide: Type the letter **P,** or press the **PgUp key.**

➤ Continue to move from one slide to the next until you come to the end of the presentation and are returned to the Slide view.

➤ Exit PowerPoint if you do not want to continue with the next exercise.

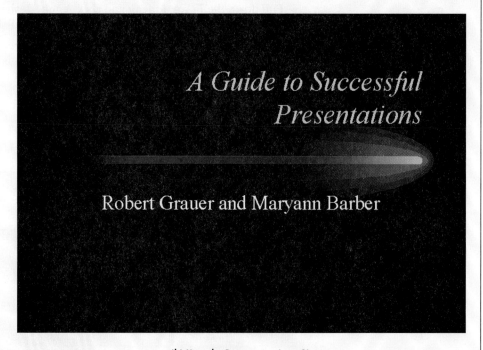

A Guide to Successful Presentations

Robert Grauer and Maryann Barber

(h) View the Presentation (step 8)

FIGURE 2.3   Hands-on Exercise 1 (continued)

TIPS FROM THE OFFICE ASSISTANT

The Office Assistant indicates it has a suggestion by displaying a lightbulb. Click the lightbulb to display the tip, then click the Back or Next buttons as appropriate to view additional tips. The Assistant will not, however, repeat a tip from an earlier session unless you reset it at the start of a new session. This is especially important in a laboratory situation where you are sharing a computer with many students. To reset the tips, click the Assistant to display a balloon asking what you want to do, click the Options button, click the Options tab, then click the button to Reset My Tips.

CREATING A SLIDE SHOW

You develop the content of a presentation, then you format it attractively using a PowerPoint template. The most important step is yet to come—the delivery of the presentation to an audience, which is best accomplished through a computerized slide show (as opposed to using overhead transparencies or 35-mm slides). The computer becomes the equivalent of a slide projector, and the presentation is called a slide show.

PowerPoint can help you add interest to the slide show in two ways, transitions and animation effects. **_Transitions_** control the way in which one slide moves off the screen and the next slide appears. **_Animation effects_** vary the way in which objects on a slide appear during the presentation.

Transitions are created through the Slide Transition command in the Slide Show menu, which displays the dialog box in Figure 2.4a. The drop-down list box enables you to choose the transition effect. Slides may move on to the screen from the left or right, be uncovered by horizontal or vertical blinds, fade, dissolve, and so on. The dialog box also enables you to set the speed of the transition and/or to preview the effect.

Animation enables the bulleted items to appear one at a time with each successive mouse click. The effect is created through the Custom Animation command in the Slide Show menu, which displays the dialog box of Figure 2.4b. Each bullet can appear with its own transition effect. You can make the bullets appear one word or one letter at a time. You can specify that the bullets appear in reverse order (i.e., the bottom bullet first), and you can dim each bullet as the next one appears. You can even add sound and make the bullets appear in conjunction with a round of applause.

Transitions and animation effects can also be created from the Slide Sorter toolbar as shown in Figure 2.4c. As with the other toolbars, a ScreenTip is displayed when you point to a button on the toolbar.

ANIMATE THE OTHER OBJECTS

An animation effect can be applied to any object on a slide although it is used most frequently with bulleted text. You can create a special effect by animating another object, such as a piece of clip art or a chart. Point to the object, click the right mouse button to display a shortcut menu, then click the Custom Animations command to display a dialog box in which you choose the desired effect(s).

AUTOLAYOUTS

Every slide in a presentation is created according to one of 24 predefined slide formats known as AutoLayouts. The AutoLayout determines the objects that will appear on a slide (e.g., text, clip art, a chart, or other object) and specifies the placement for those objects. (Any text entered through the Outline view is automatically formatted according to the Bulleted List AutoLayout.)

What if, however, you want to add a graphic element, such as clip art (or a chart) to a bulleted slide that was created initially from the Outline view? The easiest way to do this is to change to the Slide view, then change the AutoLayout of the slide from a Bulleted List to one containing text and clip art (or text and a chart). This procedure is illustrated in steps 1 and 2 of the next hands-on exercise.

Preview transition effect

Click to see list of
available transition effects

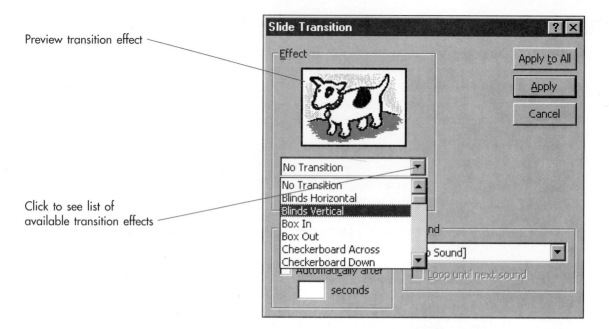

(a) Transitions

Bullet transition effect

Sound options

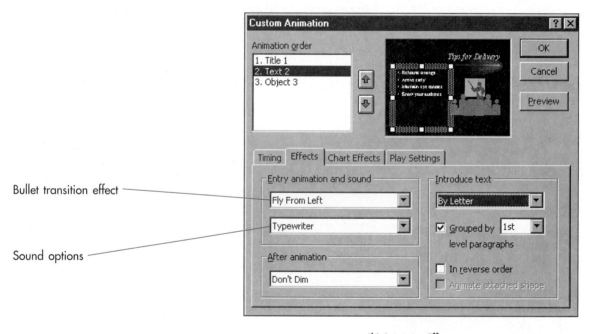

(b) Animation Effects

Rehearse Timings

Slide Transition Effects   Text Preset Animation

Summary Slide

Hide Slide

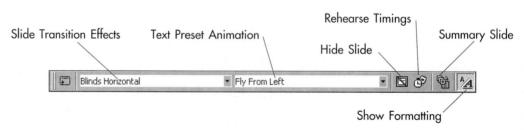

Show Formatting

(c) Slide Sorter Toolbar

FIGURE 2.4   Transitions and Animation Effects

Animating the Presentation

Objective: To change the layout of an existing slide; to establish transition and animation effects. Use Figure 2.5 as a guide in the exercise.

STEP 1: Change the AutoLayout

➤ Start PowerPoint and open **My First Presentation** from the previous exercise. If necessary, switch to the **Slide view.** Press **Ctrl+End** to move to the last slide as shown in Figure 2.5a, which is currently a bulleted list.

➤ Pull down the **Format menu** and click **Slide Layout** (or click the **Slide Layout button** on the Standard toolbar).

➤ Choose the **Text and Clip Art layout** as shown in Figure 2.5a. Click the **Apply command button** to change the slide layout.

Click Apply

Click Text &
Clip Art AutoLayout

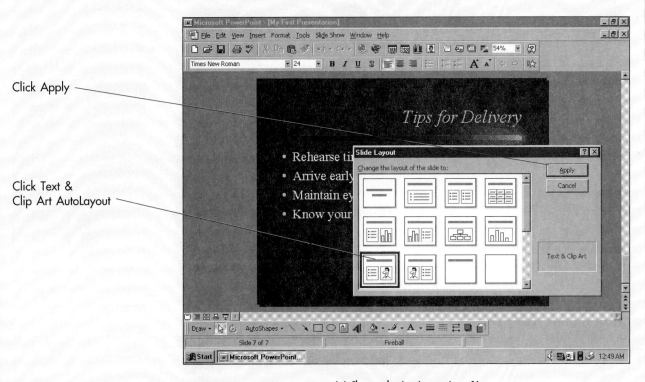

(a) Change the AutoLayout (step 1)

FIGURE 2.5   Hands-on Exercise 2

THE DOCUMENTS SUBMENU

One of the fastest ways to get to a recently used document, regardless of the application, is through the Windows 95 Start menu, which includes a Documents submenu containing the last 15 documents that were opened. Click the Start button, click (or point to) the Documents submenu, then click the document you wish to open (e.g., My First Presentation) if it appears on the submenu.

STEP 2: Add the Clip Art

➤ Double click the **placeholder** on the slide to add clip art. You will see the Microsoft Clip Gallery dialog box as shown in Figure 2.5b (although you may not see all of the categories listed in the figure).

➤ Click the **Clip Art tab.** Select the **Academic category**. Click the **down arrow** to scroll through the available images until you can select the image in Figure 2.5b. Click **Insert** to add the clip art to the slide.

➤ Save the presentation.

Click Clip Art tab

Click Academic category

Click clip art image

Keywords for selected clip art image

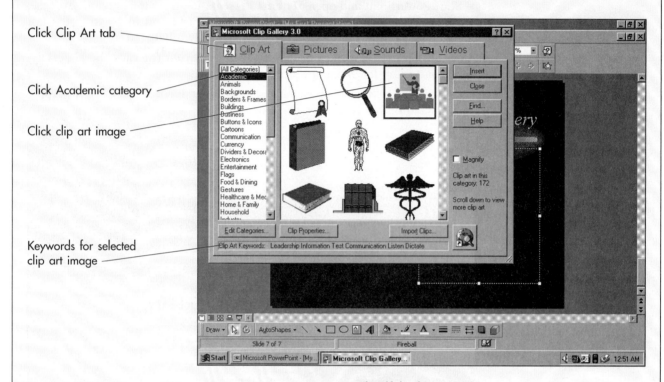

(b) Add the Clip Art (step 2)

FIGURE 2.5   Hands-on Exercise 2 (continued)

FIND THE RIGHT CLIP ART

The Find button within the Clip Gallery enables you to search for specific images. Open the Clip Gallery, then click the Find button to display the Find Clip dialog box. Click in the Keyword text box, then enter a key word (e.g., communication) that describes the clip art you want. Click the Find Now button, and the Clip Gallery will search for images that match the description. Be sure to have the Office CD-ROM available, or install the additional clip art to your hard drive.

STEP 3: Add Transition Effects

➤ Click the **Slide Sorter View button** to change to the Slide Sorter view as shown in Figure 2.5c. The number of slides you see at one time depends on the resolution of your monitor and the zoom percentage.

➤ Press **Ctrl+Home** to select the first slide. Pull down the **Slide Show menu,** then click **Slide Transition** to display the dialog box in Figure 2.5c. Click the **down arrow** on the Effect list box, then click the **Blinds Vertical** effect. You will see the effect displayed on the sample slide (dog) in the effect preview area. If you miss the effect, click the **dog** (or the **key**) to repeat the effect.

➤ Click **Apply** to accept the transition and close the dialog box. A slide icon appears under slide 1, indicating a transition effect.

➤ Point to slide 2, click the **right mouse button** to display a shortcut menu, then click the **Slide Transition command.** Choose **Checkerboard Across.** Click the **Slow option button.** Click **Apply** to close the dialog box.

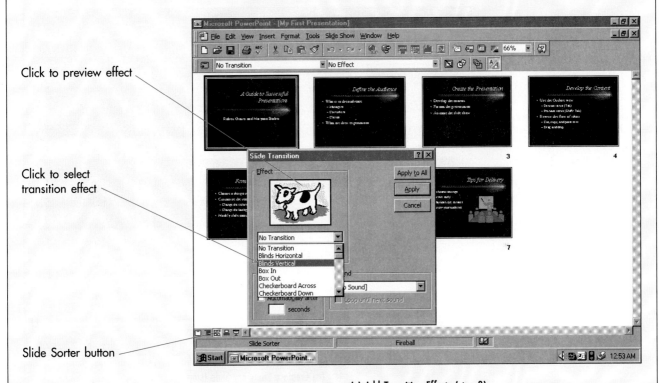

Click to preview effect

Click to select transition effect

Slide Sorter button

(c) Add Transition Effects (step 3)

FIGURE 2.5   Hands-on Exercise 2 (continued)

CHANGE THE MAGNIFICATION

Click the down arrow on the Zoom Control box to change the display magnification, which in turn controls the size of individual slides. The higher the magnification, the easier it is to read the text of an individual slide, but the fewer slides you see at one time. Conversely, changing to a smaller magnification decreases the size of the individual slides, but enables you to see more of the presentation.

STEP 4: Create a Summary Slide

➤ Pull down the **Edit menu** and press **Select All** to select every slide in the presentation. (Alternatively, you can also press and hold the **Shift key** as you click each slide in succession.)

➤ Click the **Summary Slide button** on the Slide Sorter toolbar to create a summary slide containing a bullet with the title of each selected slide. The new slide appears at the beginning of the presentation as shown in Figure 2.5d.

➤ Click and drag the **Summary slide** to the end of the presentation. (As you drag the slide, the mouse pointer changes to include the outline of a miniature slide and a vertical line appears to indicate the new position of the slide.)

➤ Release the mouse. The Summary slide has been moved to the end of the presentation and the slides are renumbered automatically.

➤ Save the presentation.

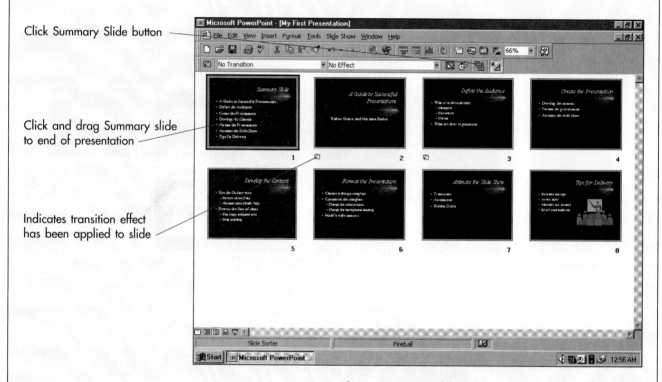

(d) Create a Summary Slide (step 4)

FIGURE 2.5 Hands-on Exercise 2 (continued)

SELECTING MULTIPLE SLIDES

You can apply the same transition or animation effect to multiple slides with a single command. Change to the Slide Sorter view, then select the slides by pressing and holding the Shift key as you click the slides. Use the Slide Show menu or the Slide Sorter toolbar to choose the desired transition or animation effect when all the slides have been selected. Click anywhere in the Slide Sorter view to deselect the slides and continue working.

STEP 5: Create the Animation Effects

➤ Double click the Summary slide to select the slide and simultaneously change to the Slide view. Click anywhere within the title to select the title.

➤ Pull down the **Slide Show menu**, click **Preset Animation** to display a cascade menu, then click **Typewriter** to display the title with this effect during the slide show.

➤ Click anywhere within the bulleted text to select the bulleted text (and deselect the title). Pull down the **Slide Show menu** and select **Custom Animation** to display the dialog box in Figure 2.5e.

➤ Click the **Effects tab.** Click the first **drop-down arrow** under Entry animation and sound to display the entry transitions. Click **Fly From Left**.

➤ Click the **drop-down arrow** to show the Introduce Text effects and select **All at Once.** Click the **drop-down arrow** for sound effects, then scroll until you can select **Screeching Brakes**.

➤ Check that the title appears first within the animation order. If not, select the title, then click the up arrow to move it ahead of the text. Click **OK** to close the dialog box. Click outside the placeholder to deselect it.

➤ Pull down the **Slide Show menu** a second time. Click **Animation Preview** to display the slide miniature window to see (and hear) the animation effect. Close the miniature window. Save the presentation.

Title appears first in the animation order

Bulleted text is the selected object

Animation effects

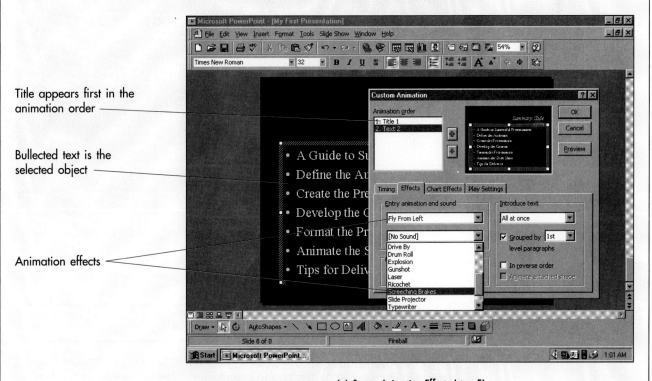

(e) Create Animation Effects (step 5)

FIGURE 2.5   Hands-on Exercise 2 (continued)

STEP 6: Show the Presentation

➤ Press **Ctrl+Home** to return to the first slide, then click the **Slide Show button** to view the presentation. You should see the opening slide in Figure 2.5f.

➤ Click the **left mouse button** to move to the next slide (or to the next bullet on the current slide when animation is in effect).

➤ Click the **right mouse button** to display the shortcut menu and return to the previous slide (or to the previous bullet on the current slide when a build is in effect).

➤ Continue to view the presentation until you come to the end. Click the left mouse button a final time to return to the regular PowerPoint window.

➤ Exit PowerPoint if you do not want to continue with the next exercise.

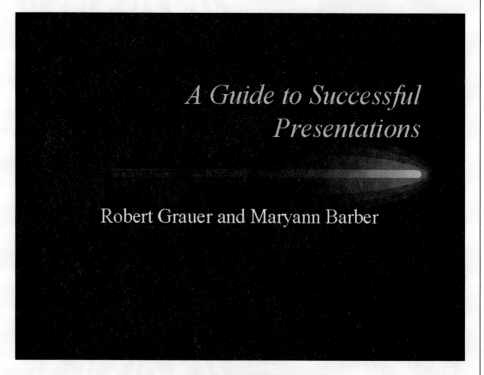

(f) Show the Presentation

FIGURE 2.5   Hands-on Exercise 2 (continued)

THE MEETING MINDER

The Meeting Minder enables you to keep track of action items as they occur during a presentation and to summarize them at the end of the presentation. Click the right mouse button at any time to display a shortcut menu, click Meeting Minder, then click the Action Items tab in the Meeting Minder dialog box. Enter the description assigned to Due Date for each item, click OK to close the dialog box, then continue through the slide show. An Action Items slide will appear at the end of the presentation with the items you added during the show.

There are in essence two independent steps to creating a PowerPoint presentation. You must develop the content, and you must format the presentation. Both steps are iterative in nature, and you are likely to go back and forth many times before you are finished.

The text of a presentation can be developed from the Slide view or the Outline view or a combination of the two. The Outline view is easier because it displays the contents of many slides at once, enabling you to see the overall flow of your ideas. You can change the order of the slides and/or move text from one slide to another as necessary. Text can be entered continually in the outline, then promoted or demoted so that it appears on the proper level in the slide.

A template is a design specification that controls every aspect of a presentation. It specifies the formatting of the text, the fonts and colors that are used, and the design, size, and placement of the bullets.

Transitions and animation effects can be added to a presentation for additional interest. Transitions control the way in which one slide moves off the screen and the next slide appears. Animation effects are used to display the individual elements on a single slide.

The AutoContent Wizard facilitates the creation of a new presentation. The Wizard asks a series of questions, then it uses your answers to suggest a presentation based on one of several general presentations included within PowerPoint. The end result of the Wizard is an outline based on the topic you selected. The outline is very general, as it must be, but it provides the essential topics to include in your presentation. It is the best way we know to jump-start the creation process and get you started immediately.

KEY WORDS AND CONCEPTS

Animation effect	Outline toolbar	Slide Sorter toolbar
AutoCorrect	Promote	Summary slide
Demote	Slide icon	Template
Insertion point	Slide master	Transition

PRACTICE WITH POWERPOINT 97

1. Figure 2.6 displays the title slide of a presentation that can be found in the Exploring PowerPoint folder on the data disk. Much of the presentation has been created for you, but there are several finishing touches that need to be made:

    a. Open the existing presentation titled *Chapter 2 Practice 1,* then save it as *Chapter 2 Practice 1 Solution* so that you can return to the original presentation if necessary.

    b. Replace our name with your name on the title slide.

    c. Move the slide on Modems after the one on Multimedia Requirements.

    d. Delete the slide on The PC, Then and Now.

e. Add a slide at the end of the presentation on software that should be considered in addition to Windows 95 and the Microsoft Office.

f. Change the layout of slide 7 to a Two-column Text slide. Modify the text as necessary for the new layout.

g. Select a different design template.

h. Print the completed presentation in both outline and handout form. Submit both to your instructor.

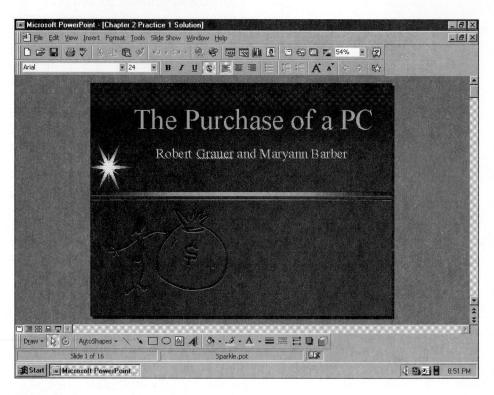

FIGURE 2.6   Screen for Practice Exercise 1

2. Figure 2.7 displays a very general outline for a presentation. The outline can be accessed through the AutoContent Wizard or directly through the File New command.

a. Pull down the File menu, click New to display the New Presentation dialog box, click the Presentations tab, then double click the Generic (standard) presentation.

b. Change to the Outline view to display the presentation in Figure 2.7. (Some slides have been collapsed in our outline as can be seen by the underlined slide titles.)

c. Choose any topic you like, then prepare a presentation on that topic using the outline provided. You need not follow the outline exactly, but it should provide a good beginning. The completed presentation should contain from six to ten slides.

d. Apply a new (different) design template to the completed presentation.

e. Print the completed presentation in both outline and miniature slide form. Submit both handouts to your instructor.

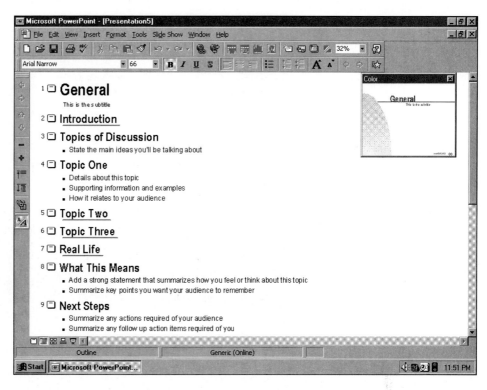

FIGURE 2.7   Screen for Practice Exercise 2

3. Figure 2.8 displays the Slide Sorter view of a presentation to sell an idea or product. The template is available in the ValuPack folder on the CD-ROM. (The complete path is ValuPack\Template\Present. Change the file type to Presentation Templates, then select the Sell_S template.) Assume that you have been appointed the Director of Marketing for a national corporation, then modify the presentation as follows:

   a. Change the title slide to reflect the product you wish to sell.

   b. Modify the remaining slides to reflect your sales strategy. You can change the slide layout and content.

   c. Use the Header and Footer command in the View menu to print today's date on every slide except the title slide.

   d. Modify the Slide master to include uniform clip art in the lower right corner of each slide (except the title slide).

   e. View the slide show of the completed presentation. Slide transitions are built into the presentation as can be seen by viewing the transition icon under each slide.

   f. Print the completed presentation in slide miniature form.

4. The potential uses of PowerPoint are limited only by your imagination. Figure 2.9, for example, displays an award certificate that was created using the drawing tools within Microsoft Office. The template is found in the Certificate Online presentation in the ValuPack folder on the CD-ROM.

   a. Modify the template to award yourself for your efforts in this class.

   b. Use the existing slide as the basis for three additional awards for real people in any category. Experiment with the various animation effects. It's best if you have a sound card so you can hear the sound of applause as the certificate is displayed.

   c. Print the completed presentation and submit it to your instructor.

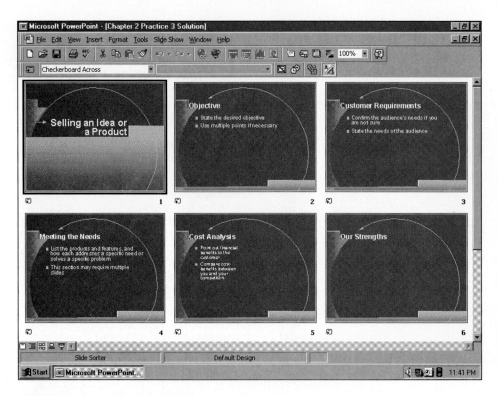

FIGURE 2.8   Screen for Practice Exercise 3

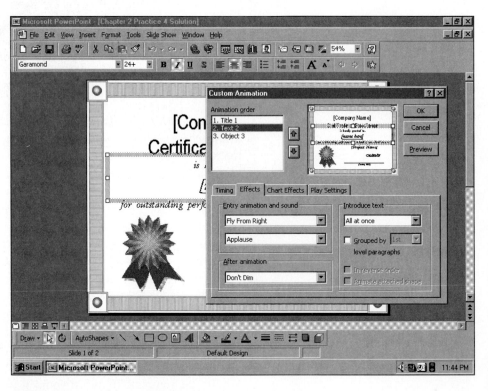

FIGURE 2.9   Screen for Practice Exercise 4

5. The presentation in Figure 2.10 is one of several provided by Dale Carnegie & Associates. Use the AutoContent Wizard to select the Presentation Guidelines presentation. (Alternatively, you can pull down the File menu, click New to display the New Presentation dialog box, click the Presentations tab, then double click Presentation Guidelines from the list of available presentations.)

   a. Go to the first slide in the presentation, then switch to the Slide Show view and view the entire presentation.

   b. Print the presentation in Outline view or Slide Miniatures (six slides per page) and keep it as a guide. This is a valuable reference, which you can use the next time you have to deliver a presentation.

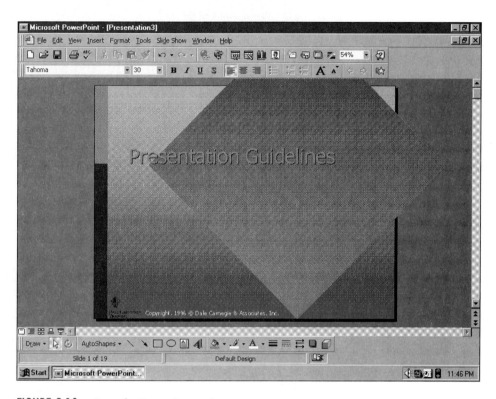

FIGURE 2.10   Screen for Practice Exercise 5

6. Figure 2.11 displays the Outline view of a presentation for a Creativity Session. (The template is available in the ValuPack folder on the CD-ROM. The complete path is ValuPack\Template\Present. Change the file type to Presentation Templates, then select the Brain_S template.) Ask your instructor to divide the class into groups of three or four students each. Each group is given the assignment of creating a presentation to attract publicity for a political issue of interest to you and your classmates. Your group has a meeting scheduled for next Monday, at which point you are to decide on the issue and an associated strategy. Modify the text of the Creativity Session to facilitate the upcoming meeting.

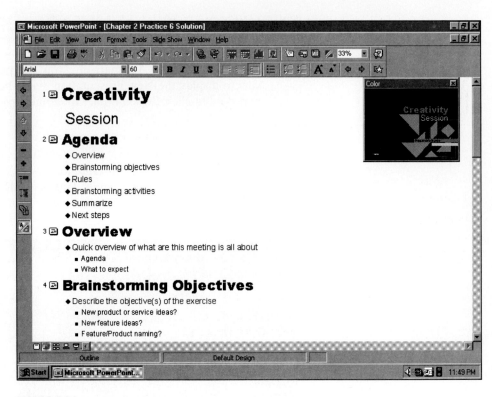

FIGURE 2.11   Screen for Practice Exercise 6

Index

A = Access
E = Excel
P = PowerPoint
W = Word

Formula, E5
Formula bar, E7
Fraction format, E51
Function, E5, A87

G

General format, E50–E51
GIGO (garbage in, garbage out),
    A14
Go To command, W50–W51
Grammar check, W30–W31,
    W37–W38
Group footer, A80, A105, A113
Group header, A80, A104
Grouping records, A103–A116

H

Hanging indent, W76
Hard page break, W68
Hard return, W2
    display of, W21
Help, E9, W24
Horizontal alignment, E52–E53
Horizontal ruler, W6
Hyperlink, W53, W110
    formatting in Word, W118
Hyperlink field, A35
Hypermedia, W109
Hypertext, W109

I

Incompatibilities, in file type, E24
Indents, W76, W78, W86
Indexed property, A37
Information, versus data, A78
Inheritance, A64, A83
Input mask property, A37, A43
Input Mask Wizard, A43
Ins key, W13
Insert command, E19–E20, E26–E29
Insert Comment command, E62
Insert Footnote command, W111,
    W115
Insert mode, W4
Insert Picture command, W99, W116
Insert Symbol command, W100,
    W107
Insertion point, A5, P36, W2
Internet, description of, W109

L

Landscape orientation, E21, E63, W68
Leader character, W79
Left indent, W76
Legend, E82
Line chart, E110–E111
Line spacing, W80
Linked object, E99
Lookup Wizard, A62–A63

M

Macro, A4
Margins, W73
    versus indents, W76
Max function, A105
Meeting Minder, P54
Memo field, A35
Menu bar, P4
Microsoft Access
    introduction to, A3–A4
    starting of, A7
    version of, A11
Microsoft Clip Gallery, W99,
    W102–W103
Microsoft Excel
    incompatibilities in, E24
    starting of, E13
Microsoft PowerPoint
    starting of, P10
Microsoft Word
    file types in, W35
    starting of, W11
    version of, W16
Microsoft WordArt, W101,
    W105–W106
Min function, A105
Mixed reference, E40
Module, A4
Monospaced typeface, W63–W64
Move operation, E41–E42
Moving text, W49
Multiple data series, E89–E99
Multitasking, E100, W116
    Alt+Tab shortcut, E104

N

Name box, E7, E15
New Slide command, P19, P20–P21
Noncontiguous range, E58, E60

S

Sans serif typeface, W62–W63
Save command, E9–E10, P5, P7, W8–W9, W13–W14, W32
Save As command, E24, P7, P12, W32, W35
Scientific format, E51
ScreenTip, E15, W5, W21
Scroll bar, P4
Scrolling, W51–W53
  with the keyboard, W58
  with a mouse, W57
Select query, A91–A92, A96–A103
Selection area, in a form, A70
Selection bar, W69
Selective replacement, W51
Select-then-do, E50, P23–P24, W48
Serif typeface, W62–W63
Shortcut menu, displaying of, W48
Show row, A91–A92
Show/Hide ¶ button, W18, W21
Shrink to Fit command, W61–W62
Simple Query Wizard, A96
Sizing handle, E76, W100, W103
Slide elevator, P26
Slide miniature, P17, P25
Slide Show view, P17–P18, P27
Slide Sorter toolbar, P48
Slide Sorter view, P17–P18, P24–P25
Slide view, P17–P18, P26–P27
Social security number, formatting of, E61
Soft page break, W68
Soft return, W2
Sort row, A91–A92
  with multiple fields, A106
Sorting and Grouping command, A88
Source range, E39
Special format, E52
Special indent, W76
Spell check, P43, W26–W28, W36–W37
Spreadsheet, introduction to, E2–E5
SQL view, A92
Stacked columns, E89, E90, E98
Standard toolbar, E7–E8, P5–P6, W5, W7
Status bar, E7, P4, W6
Sum function, A105
Summary slide, P52
Symbols font, W100

T

Tab order, A68
Table, A2, A4–A5
  creation of, A38–A47
  design of, A32–A37
  modification of, A62
  moving in, A8–A9
  opening of, A8
Table Wizard, A35, A39–A41
Tabs, W79–W80
Tabular report, A78–A79
Taskbar, E102
Template, P38, P45, W119
Text field, A35
Text format, E52
Thesaurus, W29–W30, W38–W39
Time format, E51
Times New Roman, W62–W63
Tip of the Day, A24, E17, P14, W15
Toggle switch, W3
Toolbar, E7–E8, P5–P6, W5, W7
  customization of, W85
  hiding or displaying, W20
  missing, A88
Top Values property, A109
Transition, P47–P48
Triangle, as record selector symbol, A5
Type size, W64–W65
Type style, W64
Typeface, W62–W63
Typography, W62–W66

U

Unbound control, A47, A82
  adding to a report, A88
Undo command, A19, A55, E26, P25, W23, W49, W60

V

Validation rule property, A37, A44–A45
Validation text property, A37, A44–A45
Vertical alignment, E52–E53
Vertical ruler, W6
View menu, W20, W54–W55